THE BEST PLAYS OF 1952–1953

Illustrated with photographs, and with

Drawings by HIRSCHFELD

from
"Me and Juliet"

BURNS MANTLE YEARBOOK

THE BEST PLAYS
OF 1952–1953

EDITED BY LOUIS KRONENBERGER

DODD, MEAD AND COMPANY

NEW YORK　　　　　　　TORONTO

1953

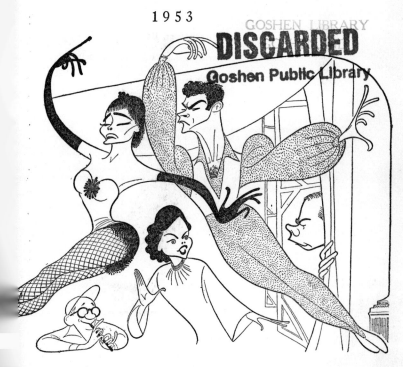

822

COPYRIGHT, 1953,
BY DODD, MEAD & COMPANY, INC.
Library of Congress Catalog Card Number: 20-21432

PRINTED IN THE UNITED STATES OF AMERICA

EDITOR'S NOTE

IN editing this, the thirty-sixth volume in the *Best Plays* series, I am under a number of pleasant obligations. Much the greatest is to my wife, Emmy Plaut, whose assistance amounts to nothing less than collaboration. Thanks are due for editorial help to Dorothea Oppenheimer; and for permission to reprint its report on Hits and Flops, to *Variety* and Mr. Abel Green. For their summaries of the season, I am indebted to Miss Cassidy, Mr. Tynan, M. Josset, Mr. Sherwood and Mr. Schallert; and for generously granting the use of original drawings, to Mr. Ayres, Mr. Bay, Mr. Mielziner, Mrs. Motley, Mr. Oenslager, Miss Sharaff and Mr. White.

And I cannot begin this new enterprise without stating my great satisfaction at being joined in it by Mr. Hirschfeld.

LOUIS KRONENBERGER

CONTENTS

PHOTOGRAPHS

Following page 182

THE BEST PLAYS OF 1952–1953

THE BEST PLAYS OF 1952–1953

THE SEASON IN NEW YORK

PRAISE, of a kind, can assuredly be bestowed on the 1952-53 season. I think no one would question that it got more interesting as it went along, that in fact toward the end it got vividly controversial. Whether there was ever much to acclaim, there came to be more and more to argue about; and since the arguments involved some of the biggest names in the theatre, they possessed real news value and endowed the season with at least an outward sense of vitality. Hence, for those who love the theatre with a fierce, indiscriminate, purblind passion, there again was happy proof of its undying lure: only to that smaller group who seek real justifications for rapture would all the fuss over, say, Bette Davis suggest that Broadway might be a little starved for substance.

But Broadway had more than its skirmishes. It had its special, its even rather varied, blessings. They were not, however, very numerous; nor for the most part new; nor to a large extent native. They stemmed, at intervals, from the America of the moment; but they stemmed more often from England or Europe, from the fifth century B.C. or the 1600's or 1910 or 1934; they were rattled off in French, they were even chanted in Greek. Usually, where they were fresh-minted in the image of Broadway, there was decidedly more alloy than silver, or they ranked among the smaller coins. It was not a year when Broadway's own workers did her proud. But thanks to what Broadway imported, and further to what Broadway revived, the season was about as safe from lasting notoriety as it was far from undying fame. In terms of new work, I think almost everyone would agree that it provided a very pleasing mystery play and a very pleasing musical. Beyond that, tastes were unaccountable and tempers might run high. Beyond that, any listing of the Best Ten merely certified that certain plays seemed definitely better than others, rather than that all of them, or most of them, or conceivably any of them, were especially good.

The season began with a single production in June, and was then put in escrow till September. But the single production was properly solitary, for its career was to be almost anointedly special. The

3

show, "Wish You Were Here" (music and lyrics by Harold Rome; book by Arthur Kober and Joshua Logan) had been adapted from Mr. Kober's long-ago success, "Having Wonderful Time." On opening night, its origin was perhaps not violently evident: plot, people, background did seem passably familiar; but Mr. Kober's tremulous chronicle of life at an adult Jewish Summer camp; of vacationers panting after pleasure, clutching at romance, yearning for gentility; had all but vanished. In its place had sprung up something as glaring and emphatic as a Broadway sky sign. Touching gaffes had be-

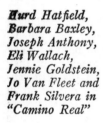

Hurd Hatfield, Barbara Baxley, Joseph Anthony, Eli Wallach, Jennie Goldstein, Jo Van Fleet and Frank Silvera in "Camino Real"

come brassy gags; a wistful comedy of manners was now a sequence of monkeyshines: in the bold *avant-garde* manner of David Belasco, the show displayed a real swimming pool, real hot dogs, and what looked like real rain. It appeared to be Mr. Logan's evening: Broadway's most successful man of the theatre had lopped off all outmoded excrescences, including the idea of human beings.

But Mr. Logan was to prove very quickly why he was Broadway's most successful man of the theatre. The show, for the most part, was panned, and the substitution of slickness for the old Kober

warmth was particularly deplored.   But never did adapters prove
more adaptable.   A few days later, a theatre column reported that
Mr. Kober and Mr. Logan were at work trying to instil warmth into
the libretto they had just denuded of it.   And thanks to the new
injections—and perhaps the huge advance sale, and the lack of other
new shows, and the support of Walter Winchell—"Wish You Were
Here" inched and then hopped and then broadjumped its way into
becoming a smash hit.   It astounded the defeatists with its dauntless
Pickett's Charge; it perhaps even brought sunshine to the reviewers,
whom Mr. Logan thanked for their helpful critiques; and it gave
Broadway plenty to talk about through the long, uneventful,
warmth-rich Summer days.

In September the season got going for good with "Mr. Pickwick,"
Stanley Young's agreeable *montage* of comic scenes and situations
from "The Pickwick Papers"—a treatment that dieted the book of
tediousness but also drained it of blood.   If comedy could just about
hold its head up during the season, it was by virtue of not displaying
a very American face.   For much of its laughter during 1952-53,
Broadway had English and Continental writers to thank: indeed,
only once did a new American light comedy rise above formula, reach
beyond factory methods, to freshen farce with imaginativeness, or
prefer humor to gags; and this once, as it happened, came almost at
the start.   Mary Chase's "Bernadine" had a family resemblance to
her "Harvey"—a touch of his madness, a trace of his magnetism,
and all of his invisibility.   Chronicling those greatest of daydream-
ers, teen-age boys, Mrs. Chase could indulge her fine talent for
escapism: put a wand in her hand, or a wishbone, and she is almost
always amusing.   Here, moreover, she was as rewarding for the lingo
favored by Buford's set as for their reveries and longings.   With
Mrs. Chase, the gods exactly reversed their procedure with Antaeus;
Mrs. Chase is imbued with vitality so long as her feet are *not* on
the ground, are wildly in the air: here, as before, she quite fails,
even at satire, with her sane, her sensible, her middle-aged, her mid-
dle-class citizenry; and "Bernadine," delightful where uninhibited,
turns limp as soon as it turns life-sized.

Only very late in the season, and on very different terms, did
American comedy even try again to go beyond formula; but though
Andrew Rosenthal's "Horses in Midstream" sought the level of ur-
bane problem comedy, it quite lacked the leverage.   For the rest,
American comedy writers emerged as various types of skilled and
unskilled labor, punching their stencils, operating their machines.
Popular comedy is, of course, the chief product of every Broadway
season, the commodity that enlists the least talent, displays the least

taste, attracts the most backers and collects the worst reviews. In the main, this species of playwriting seems to me the easiest to account for and the simplest to dispose of. It is frankly purveyed as entertainment; it is unabashedly commercial; it is said to make multitudes happy; it has been known—at least once or twice—to make almost everyone laugh; and though it plainly does Broadway no credit, without it Broadway could not survive. Among its wares, last season, could be cited "A Date with April," "Whistler's Grandmother," "The Pink Elephant" and several more. There weren't so many as there used to be: perhaps standards haven't risen, but costs have. One such work, "The Fifth Season," managed to find just the right star: to a playwright's collation of stale buns and assorted leftovers, the Yiddish Theatre's Menasha Skulnik brought his own lunch, as it were; and his steadily resourceful, richly accented performance should carry "The Fifth Season" into its own second one.

Only once during the season was the operator so well trained, did the machine run so smoothly, as to raise the question how far mere proficiency is a virtue. The question, in the case of Mr. George Axelrod's "The Seven Year Itch," was perhaps the more interesting because the setup—compared with the run of popular comedy—was a little more sophisticated. The play, dealing with one of those New York husbands who lead Summer-bachelor lives and have been just long enough married to be in the gravest danger when on the loose, highlighted one of the most frequent and fetching of upper-middle-class dilemmas. Mr. Axelrod posed and solved the problem briskly, and his play should run on Broadway for two years. The only question is whether or not the members of the audience like to do their own comic mental arithmetic. There are those who do not enjoy having jokes exclamation-pointed, or double meanings painted bright red; who feel that the essence of sophistication consists in leaving things unstated, and that knowingness can be more hostile to urbanity than naïveté. Mr. Axelrod honed and stropped his wit in public; kept sex on twenty-four-hour duty; and by giving his hero's dilemma a gaudy emphasis, robbed it of all its guilty charm. Yet it seems fair to say, and quite without irony, that beyond knowing his business Mr. Axelrod very likely offered his best: for a play like "The Seven Year Itch" is not just an incident of our stage; it is a product of our whole culture.

From overseas there was Shaw's long overdue "The Millionairess," which has a considerable octogenarian sprightliness, but a rather skimpy Shavian skill, and in which Katharine Hepburn banged about with fiendishly unflagging gusto. Beyond the Shaw, there were two foreign comedies with authentic if intermittent wit and gaiety. Peter

Tom Ewell and Vanessa Brown in "The Seven Year Itch"

Ustinov's "Love of Four Colonels" was spectacularly uneven; but it could scarcely not be. To spoof, first—in a series of dialogues—four different nations, and then—in a series of playlets—four different national dramas, is a formidable job requiring not only a great many separate jokes, but such as don't easily form a unified whole. "Four Colonels" is more fairly judged as a series of *jeux d'esprit* or charades, some of them very good, some enjoyably spotty, and two or three quite dismal. But where it comes off, the play has real wit, and sometimes—even where it doesn't—real gaiety: at least on two or three occasions during the evening, one had a sense of fountains playing, rather than of faucets being turned on; the sense of a genuine comic temperament, rather than—with the "Seven Year Itches"—of a mere technique.

"My 3 Angels" gained greatly on Broadway from Walter Slezak's performance as angel-in-chief; he gave it what it needed in English—something not only funny but foreign. For from the Spe-

wacks' American version of this impudent and escapist morality
play, something Gallic had itself escaped. No doubt, too, the story
is a little thin, and, in making merry with murder, skates, here and
there, on thin ice. But beyond what is piquant in the theme, enough
remains in the telling for an enjoyable evening. Treating of three
friendly scoundrels possessed of every criminal art and penal grace,
it makes a nice practical French "Christmas Carol" in which it
seems simpler to bump Scrooge off than to convert him.

   The season's more serious side could just barely hold its head up
for a different reason—that it might be something to make a target
of as well as to pat. It was indeed for its drama that the season,
as it advanced, became increasingly contentious. Ripe tomatoes
rather lack the testimonial value of laurel wreaths, but any season's
drama must arouse interest that, while being crowned by the one,
is a mooshy crimson from the other. In addition, the drama contributed a very newsworthy cluster of names. Such veteran playwrights as John van Druten and Moss Hart had new plays; so had
our two most famous American playwrights since the thirties, Tennessee Williams and Arthur Miller; so had what are perhaps our
two most promising, William Inge and Arthur Laurents; while from
abroad there were plays by, among others, Terence Rattigan and
George Tabori. And what several of them wrote came to be im-
moderately written about. Mr. Inge's "Picnic" made news in the
most complimentary sense, by winning both the Critics Circle and
Pulitzer awards; but again in the most controversial sense, by being
both applauded and denounced for its staging. Mr. Miller's "The
Crucible" was bound to be controversial because, in 1952-53, no
play's subject matter could easily have been more so. Mr. Williams'
"Camino Real" created the most heated wrangle of all, by provoking
—more than any new play in years—passionate disagreement, being
booed and bravo'd with equal fervor.
   Since, however, "The Crucible" didn't open till January, "Picnic"
till February and "Camino Real" till March, the season was more
than half over before the fur began to fly. October, theoretically
Broadway's month of heaviest traffic, brought only Mr. Laurents'
"Time of the Cuckoo" and Ugo Betti's "The Gambler." The Betti
play had the rare trait, for Broadway, of being almost ostentatiously
uncommercial, and the never contemptible virtue of trying to get
something said. But this metaphysical inquiry into murder spoke—
or worse yet, babbled—in too many borrowed accents; suggested,
most palpably, a Pirandello deprived of his wit; and most curiously,
a nineteenth-century German romanticism disinterred in its grave-

clothes. Mr. Laurents' "Cuckoo" proved a simpler and more successful undertaking. Treating of Americans in a Venetian *pensione,*
it dramatized the complexities and difficulties of international romance: forthrightly, with a young painter who, though well content
with his wife, sins with his landlady; more exploratively, with a
lonely American spinster whose amour with a merchant of Venice,
about as stony as Shakespeare's, first brightens but ultimately sad-
dens her existence. Mr. Laurents, employing the classic scene and
subject matter of Henry James and E. M. Forster, of innocents
abroad, of love in a *warm* climate, brought a good deal of honest
perception to his theme. This for me is Mr. Laurents' best play,
better indeed than his facile "Home of the Brave"; one with shrewd
comments and effective scenes; one where, in terms of love, there
is much to be said on both sides; or where—in line with Hebbel's
requirement for sound drama—*all* the people seem in the right.
(The Hebbel theory might profitably replace, for a time, Broadway's
vulgar current dramatic yardstick, that there has to be "someone to
root for.") If the play yet falls short, it is because Mr. Laurents
cannot curb his talent for stating the obvious; and cannot, or will
not, show a proper respect for tone. By rights a rueful comedy,
"Cuckoo" lapsed into sentimental drama, only in the midst of its
drama to start playing for laughs.

Mr. Terence Rattigan's "The Deep Blue Sea" could almost be
condemned on the single ground that any playwright who would
twice rescue a character, at the very last moment, from suicide, lacks
all sense of the dignity of his material. The material itself was
neither good nor bad: that is to say, it was trite, but no more trite
than most things that succeed in becoming tragic. But Mr. Rattigan
was in no mood for the tragic: his abandoned lost lady must in the
nick of time be saved and, worse yet, glibly indoctrinated with a
will to live; there was a strong sense about it all of the wiped tear
and the Wednesday matinee. Mr. Rattigan is a sufficiently gifted
playwright for one to have a kind of contemptuous admiration for
almost everything he writes: he is one of the theatre's most perfectly
trained servants, who has never yet shown himself its rebellious, or
even quietly resolute, master. It must in fairness be confessed, however, that on Broadway "The Deep Blue Sea" was much harmed
by miscasting; for Margaret Sullavan never conveyed the desperate,
Older-Woman emotions of the heroine; nor very well could she,
looking so attractively young.

"Climate of Eden" seems to me the most interesting enterprise of
Moss Hart's career. The Edgar Mittelhölzer book from which Mr.
Hart adapted it posed much the difficulty that Paul Osborn must

have encountered with "The Innocent Voyage." For, in essence, its virtues—indeed, its whole story vein—are rather literary than dramatic; while, as it happens, the book reveals an irony, a way of turning in upon itself, that Mr. Mittelhölzer handled with ease and Mr. Hart either failed to grasp or was foiled, in the theatre, from achieving. Yet he transplanted well enough for certain things in the book to grow in alien, at times even in hostile, soil. And his very scene and situation offered much that was agreeably unorthodox and exotic; so that beyond what was good about the play, there was an appeal of sorts in what was merely different.

In early December—Mr. van Druten's "I've Got Sixpence" having ineffectually argued the need for faith, and Mr. N. Richard Nash's "See the Jaguar" having provided a sententious morality play in the form of a Western—the curtain descended on new drama, to rise again late in January on "The Crucible." Mr. Miller's story of the Salem witchcraft trials, so impossible not to associate with the uproar over witch-hunts today, was necessarily born controversial. This was a matter not of subject alone, but of Mr. Miller's approach to his subject; for Mr. Miller seemed much less interested in the facts that created Salem's belief in witches than in the technique of its witch-hunts. He did not plumb the fierce Calvinist repressions that made Salem's a very special sickness and its inhabitants peculiarly pathological cases: scanting precise motives and causes, he stressed general manifestations and effects, so that Salem came to seem no more strictly emblematic than convincingly flesh and blood. Mr. Miller's juggling of historical facts was unimportant compared to his foreshortening of perspective and his reducing human beings to mouth-pieces. He threw over history a baleful glare rather than a revealing light; he became too much absorbed with parallels— despite the axiom that parallel lines never meet. Even on its own strict terms, the play lacks broad sociological relevancy, since it pivots, not on the evils of self-righteous fanaticism, but on a slut's quite personally motivated lie.

As drama, furthermore—from being compelled to treat of a whole community and to handle a whole sequence of clamorous acts and misdeeds—the play could only, as an evening-long experience, seem a little wearing. But however much dented as art or realism, "The Crucible" had yet its dramatic, and certainly its melodramatic, virtues. Some of its scenes were powerful theatre, others had a grim and sober force.

Where "The Crucible" was concerned with witch-hunts, "The Emperor's Clothes," with a somewhat comparable sense of social protest, eyed the police state. But Mr. Tabori's play was as polythematic as Mr. Miller's was single-minded, his treatment as rich in bric-a-brac as Mr. Miller's was unadorned. Writing of a small boy's lurid, fiction-fed and completely fictional fancies which, when aired, bring in the police to investigate his blacklisted-schoolmaster father, Mr. Tabori had a wonderful chance for a sardonic satire on the flimsy foundations and brutal procedures of police-state activity. And indeed he did write, in the scene where two goons grill the father, a terrifying *reductio ad absurdum* of such methods: one of the most effective scenes in the contemporary theatre. Unhappily, Mr. Tabori's gift for writing good scenes is coupled with his inability to write an honestly unified play. Knowing the sentimental value of family relationships when under stress, Mr. Tabori let social satire spill over into domestic drama; human life into home life. Worse, knowing the value of big final curtains, he sacrificed humanity to heroics. Much as in "Flight into Egypt" the season before, he choked "The Emperor's Clothes" with too many themes, enlivened—but in the long run drugged—it with too much theatre. "Faire de l'effet sans effet"—to achieve effects without calling attention to them: Paul Valéry's desideratum may be too much to ask for in the theatre, though it is perhaps what Chekhov strove after. But to sacrifice the general effect to the passing one, the whole play to single scenes: Mr. Tabori is one of a number of talented playwrights who thus sin against the first canons of playwriting, and make good "theatre" seem less the partner of drama than the confederate of trash.

Though under fire as a production, "Picnic" was the most generally well-received of the more serious plays, even those with the strongest reservations not denying it its virtues. Mr. Inge's naturalistic round dance of frustrated, unfulfilled, life-hungry women catches something of the mischance and misbegottenness of life itself; imparts some of the pity born, in a writer, of helplessness before the facts. In this story of a stallionlike youth's sudden entrance into such a world of women, sex has to do with personal possession as much as with passion; involves the loneliness, the deeper-than-physical longing, of all—and particularly of all anonymous—humanity. That Mr. Inge in the artistic sense, like his characters in the human, can at times only approximate, only paraphrase an emotion; that he gives us a familiar moan or whimper rather than the *cri juste*, reduces the freshness and sharpness of his story. But he has a real feeling for character, a good sense of homely detail. "Picnic" is essentially a modest play, which is why the matter of its staging was so vital. It brings up the whole question of sensitive minor writing in a country that makes a fetish of size, and in a medium that can't resist the sensational.

With "Camino Real," I would mention first a real concern for excluding it from the Ten Best. Mr. Williams deserves the particular respect due a writer who is both gifted and established; the play itself had fiery advocates; and was plainly born of agitated emotions. But in fairness to the ten I chose, undistinguished as I think some of them are, I had to reject it: for by my lights "Camino Real" is a serious failure. It seems to me not just the failure of a method, or even of a vision, but the most self-indulgent misuse of a talent.

"Camino Real" is a play in which time and place aren't specified; but they are obviously modern and Latin-American, with the scene a public square strident with such symbols as a luxury hotel and a flophouse, a pawnshop and a bordello. The action runs to sixteen episodes, or "blocks," along the Camino Real. The cast is large, miscellaneous and blatantly meaningful. Among the set figures are a cynical hotel proprietor who spits on common humanity; Storm-Trooperish police who cudgel it; street cleaners who cart its bodies off to the city dump. In contrast, as a Candide-like protagonist, is a young American prize fighter with a bad heart, about whom file and flow all manner of beings—madams and loan sharks, cooch-dancers and homosexuals, a down-at-heel Casanova, a Camille who must herself buy love, a Byron who escapes to die for an ideal in Greece, a Don Quixote who escapes into a world of his own illusions.

Mr. Williams' is a streaming phantasmagoria of trapped and tormented people in a corrupt and treacherous world: for what he pictures there seems no cure, from it no realistic release, only romantic anodynes or heroic self-abnegation. It is all palpable enough, but as something one is pelted with rather than made a vital part of. The play becomes more and more explosive just because it never really explodes; it provides the whip without the whip hand; exhibits that feverish excess that is the foe of true intensity. Even more disastrously, it trades in the very luridness, lushness, decadence that—in the world itself—the author is presumably at war with. This is far more damaging than Mr. Williams' use of surrealist rather than realistic technique: there is no necessary clash between his being appalled as a man by reality and his fleeing as a writer from realism. He is plainly at liberty to contrive a playwright's Hell, conjure up a poet's, or even fabricate a madman's. But Mr. Williams, in my view, has no better harnessed his imagination than he has channeled his feelings; the play emerges a patchwork of every stage manner from Lorca to "Hellzapoppin." It is as mor-

bidly picaresque, as uncontrolled as a nightmare, and as unco-ordi-
nated as a scrapbook. Nor does the play's wealth of décor make
up for its weakness of design; there can be no appeal here from the
dramatist to the poet—not only is the writing more insistently
purple than the mood is black, but much of it is as nerveless and
flaccid as it is gaudy. Elia Kazan staged the play very vividly as
theatre; it doubtless defied being anything more.

The season was most to be congratulated, I think, for its revivals.
Maugham's "The Sacred Flame" was a real mishap, and both "Room
Service" and "The Bat" suffered from age and mediocre acting.
But there was a "Children's Hour" that, despite production flaws,
remained vivid and powerful after eighteen years; there was the most
full-bodied "Porgy and Bess" that Broadway had seen; and an "On
Borrowed Time" that, thanks to a magical performance by Victor
Moore, seemed more appealing than when first produced (and, to
my mind, overrated) in 1938. But it was at the City Center, with
Albert Marre in charge, that revival in English had its headquarters.
There, though Mr. Marre failed to bring off a "Merchant of Venice"
with Luther Adler as Shylock, he made a gay picture book of "Love's
Labour's Lost." In doing so, a good deal, to be sure, besides love's
labor was lost: offering Shakespeare's poetic but poky Renaissance
comedy as an elegant Edwardian Oxonian frolic (automobiles and
croquet games), the City Center stressed the props and blurred the
poetry; but so prettily, that an audience that might have yawned
at musical speech was diverted by anachronistic toys.

It was with its final production, a "Misalliance" directed by Cyril
Ritchard, that the Center—and indeed the season—achieved its
gayest evening. The success of the enterprise was all the more
gratifying for being so wildly unforeseen, the theory being that in
"Misalliance" Shaw had written something quite unplayable. The
truth seemed rather to be that for thirty-five years no one had seen
it played; or, very possibly, that no one had *ever* seen it played
right. Mr. Ritchard played it, with unfrightened insistence, for
farce—aware that, more soberly treated, it can mean so many things
as at length to mean nothing at all. The play's particular quarry,
of course, is parents and children, a subject for which Shaw had
quite perfect Shavian qualifications: he was never a parent and
quite possibly never a child. But "Misalliance" professes to probe
all aspects of family life—though the family, for Mr. Ritchard,
seemed far less to call for study as an institution than to deserve
being confined in one. So treated, "Misalliance" became a hilarious
extravaganza in which grown men claw the carpet in temper fits,

planes fall out of the sky, pistols are cocked, china smashed and women pursued like escaping convicts.

If Mr. Ritchard gave us our gayest evening, the National Theatre of Greece provided our grandest. Offering an "Electra" and an "Oedipus" in modern Greek, it triumphed in the less notable of the two. Its "Oedipus," despite a vocally splendid men's chorus, fell generally short: Alexis Menotis' Oedipus, in particular, dropping so far below the required grand style as to seem like a tradesman. But Katina Paxinou's Electra, if not inspired, was generally impressive; while that frequent stumbling block for Greek drama today, the management of the chorus, was something to marvel at. The women's grave movement, their resonant chanting, above all their swift, sudden, intensely dramatic confrontation of the audience, held one breathless. Here, if nowhere else, the season touched at greatness.

But what shed a wider luster on the season was the visit, with their troupe, of Madeleine Renaud and Jean-Louis Barrault. They were rewarding whether one wanted to hear good French, watch brilliant acting, see famous plays, study repertory method or encounter a variousness that brought authority to Marivaux and Molière, daring to Kafka and Shakespeare, disciplined abandon to farce and expressiveness to pantomime. There were no doubt many things—indeed, entire productions—to argue over; though there, of course, the troupe's foreignness might enter in, or one's own shaky French. But, however much might seem injudicious very little was boring; and to enjoy the productions, a knowledge of French often seemed less vital than an instinct for style. Certainly Kafka's "The Trial" was open to controversy. But if it seemed far from ideal for Americans to get Kafka by way of Gide, a novel in terms of the stage and the stage in the trappings of German expressionism, at the least it was enjoyably misguided and exhilaratingly wrong. The "Hamlet," I daresay, couldn't help seeming "wrong": "Hamlet" in French, even in Gide's, can be as weird as "One, two, buckle my shoe" in German. But if "Hamlet," when deprived of its poetry, must seem to fall short as art, it can yet—it can in a sense all the more—fascinate as playgoing. There were actually some amazing moments—in her awful obsceneness when mad, for example, the Ophelia was true, not traitorous, to Shakespeare. But what was perhaps most valuable, one saw the whole play in a quite new, because alien, light; and thus one saw, and saw into, things obliquely but sharply, the way one might gain new insight into a girl through meeting her mother.

But one's greatest thanks and tribute—beyond specific instances of performance and production—went to such wholly French classics, put on with so French an air of style, as "Les Fausses Confidences" of Marivaux and the "Amphitryon" of Molière.

It was not a season rich in fights or fashions. A battle over drama critics raged in Hartford and Chicago, but did not play Broadway. Wherever waged, such feuds are doubtless a good form of bloodletting, and just about as efficacious as bloodletting for curing the disease. What rumbled on Broadway, without ever quite exploding, was the matter of the director's role in relation to the playwright's. In the case of "Picnic," there was considerable dissent over Joshua Logan's staging—over, as it were, its neon-lighting the sex, and making everything too sharp and emphatic; and there were murmurs of changes in the script itself, with the publishers planning, at one stage, to include the original ending. There were backstage rumblings, again, in the case of "The Crucible," of collisions between Mr. Miller and Jed Harris; and "The Crucible" was later staged, with an added scene, by Mr. Miller himself. In the degree that all this involves personalities and inspires gossip, it is no more than a natural part of the profession, or of any profession; but in the degree that it affects the creative life of the theatre, it raises fundamental issues. Obviously, as a collaborative enterprise, the theatre must often provoke conflict among its collaborators: and this is ten times truer of a commercial theatre, where the aim is not just a "right" production but also a remunerative one. But Broadway, today, would seem increasingly a director's theatre; Rodgers and Hammerstein aside (and they write musical comedy), no writing names bulk productionwise so large as Mr. Logan's or Mr. Kazan's or Mr. Ferrer's, with other directors not very far behind them. These men have made an enormous contribution to the success of plays at the box office; an impressive one to their success on the stage. All the same, any theatre where a set of directors overshadow and outrank a set of playwrights is either badly lacking in creative talent, or is functioning without a proper respect for what talent there is. Despite the fact that certain of these directors may—and, indeed, do—show that respect, one kind of directorial aim must, in such a theatre, give way to another kind. Bold but always valid interpretation must succumb to effectiveness as a thing in itself; Toscanini's way with Beethoven lose out to Stokowski's way with Bach.

As for fads and fashions, there were again—following 1951-52—readings, there again were one-man shows. And Emlyn Williams again combined the two: turned up, in whiskers and white tie, to impersonate Dickens—this time impersonating thirty-six Dickens characters as well in a one-man version of "Bleak House." If the result was scarcely "Bleak House," it was often pleasant; and as a one-man show, it revealed a showman and vocal quick-change artist of astonishing skill.

Flushed by the brilliant success of "reading" Shaw's "Don Juan in Hell," Paul Gregory launched a prompt successor: "John Brown's Body." The Benét poem had, often, its own kind of eloquence and, story-wise, much popular appeal; but these proved things that could cut two ways. They encouraged—as "Don Juan" quite forbade—popular treatment: vocal gadgetry and choral effects that smacked of the radio; styles of acting that smote one another down. Where Tyrone Power seemed genuinely and vigorously American, Raymond Massey intoned, in spots, with graveyard solemnity, and Judith Anderson was a touch too fond of the grand style. "John Brown's Body" was not altogether without rewards, but it quite lacked artistic distinction.

Two great comic personalities appeared as shows in themselves. "An Evening with Beatrice Lillie" was the season's most glamour-drenched title, a sort of dream-about-to-come-true. For many people, the dream did; the "Evening," for me, proved a letdown, partly because of its specific contents, partly because of its general form. Beatrice Lillie is the funniest comedienne alive, but not along night club lines, not doing uneven solo numbers. To triumph fully, she has to play against something—has to upset full-stage apple-carts, stand vast production numbers on their ear; and she herself must suddenly punctuate elegance with epilepsy, exchange the drawing room for the booby-hatch. Here, rather than playing against something else, she had to play against her own best genius.

On the other hand, Danny Kaye, heading a vaudeville show at the Palace, combined, for a solid hour and a half, the comedian, the showman and the virtuoso into an entertainment that seemed one of the wonders of show business.

There was another remarkable performance—this time in "Midsummer," a sentimental period comedy that made every stop along the matinee route. But in Geraldine Page it brought to Broadway the unquestioned new actress of the year. Already hailed for her off-Broadway performance in "Summer and Smoke," Miss Page, this time in a role that was at moments more hindrance than help, played with an extraordinary blend of charm and skill.

One further thing that made virtually everyone happy was Frederick Knott's "Dial 'M' for Murder." An English thriller that proffers murder without mystery, it was as urbane in tone as it was sound in workmanship: an excellent host, Mr. Knott—in terms of suspense—always refilled the audience's glass before it was empty.

Musicals—the thing Broadway does best—had rather an off year. They sported the most persuasive names; they spared no possible expense; they brought leading ladies from Hollywood and Britain and France; but only once was there any shouting in the streets, only once did things click, jell, hit the jackpot—in that varied assortment and tasteful arrangement of talents, "Wonderful Town." There is, to be sure, nothing spectacularly original or brilliant about it. But that it comes off so well notwithstanding is proof of how pleasantly balanced and sustained, how unfailingly professional, it is. The libretto is amusing, the lyrics are gay, the score is fresh; and the whole thing fits Rosalind Russell like a gantlet—as loosely, that is, as a bouncy, freewheeling musical should. In her first musical-comedy role, Hollywood's Miss Russell triumphs in a broad, basic, all-round-performer way. Thus, where she might fall short on sheer acting, she rides high doing antics; and where she could only flop as a singer, she does fine as a kind of sore throat.

Hollywood had earlier visited Broadway in the person of Miss Bette Davis; and *her* much less lustrous fate in "Two's Company" was perhaps owing to almost opposite methods: she seemed to approach musical comedy with a kind of quaking gallantry, as though it were some Eleusinian mystery or Masonic rite. Her performance was a perfectly respectable one, but in a medium where to perform respectably is to fail. There was, for the audience, too much the sense of watching someone merely stay on a horse rather than excel as a rider: and as Miss Davis went, so went the show. Only Hiram Sherman, as commentator, outflanked his material.

For the rest, the season proceeded from the abysmal at the beginning to the uninspired at the end. "Buttrio Square," which opened the ball, was a monster of tedium; while "My Darlin' Aida" had Aida flourish during the Civil War, and at moments seem the cause of it.

Three "name" shows festooned the second half of the season. "Hazel Flagg" was a cheerful, stertorous yarn of a Vermont girl who pretends to be dying of radium poisoning and who—yearning for bright lights at the end—is brought to New York for a final fling at the public expense. As a kaleidoscopic Big City binge, it had life and variety; and so had Helen Gallagher as Hazel. But Jule Styne's music was predominantly noisy, and Ben Hecht's satire pretty primitive. Once again musical comedy, in the very act of satirizing something else, ended by satirizing itself—all its own excesses of blare, size, manpower and length.

"Can-Can" turned out a disappointment. No one, as Arnold Bennett once said of Noel Coward, can bring together a finer collection of automobiles on opening night than Cole Porter. But this time Mr. Porter had nothing in the way of lyrics or music to match them; and Abe Burrows, in his libretto, far oftener favored Broadway at its brassiest than Burrows at his best. Fortunately, "Can-Can" had real virtues, too: Jo Mielziner's charming sets, Michael Kidd's superlative dances, and, in red-headed Gwen Verdon, the musical-comedy sensation of the season.

As it began, so 1952-53 ended—with a musical, and with one that might induce a dash of moralizing. In "Me and Juliet," Rodgers and Hammerstein provided an onstage, offstage, backstage tribute to show business. There was a pleasant score, there was pleasant dancing, there were likeable Joan McCracken antics, there were miraculously expert Jo Mielziner sets. Yet the show, for all that, seemed tame and even a little flat. Its satire was weak-kneed, its sentimentalism ready-made; and Rodgers and Hammerstein had gone at show business less as spoofers or sentimentalists, really, than as salesmen glibly whooping it up. With their dazzling record, they would be more than entitled to a failure—and "Me and Juliet" is by no means a failure. But it does, I think, fall decidedly short in the one way that something shouldn't fall short—not from unsuccessful experimenting, not from unbridled excitement, not from overstretched talent or even from a pretentiousness that bespeaks aspiration: "Me and Juliet" falls short from a quite unmistakable absence of daring.

THE SEASON IN CHICAGO

By Claudia Cassidy

Drama Critic, Chicago *Tribune*

CANDID observers on the local scene have been suspecting for seasons that not even geese will lay golden box-office eggs forever in return for the theatrical kind. Perhaps the goose has turned, and not just to television. For while the season of 1952-53 responded in part to Chicago's wistful plea for more good shows—there were more shows—business got so bad by Spring that when an amiable sadist reassured an anguished company manager, saying, "Never mind, business in Chicago always picks up by Labor Day," he wailed, "But it's Decoration Day I'm worried about."

Undeniably, the bookers stirred themselves. We had 33 shows, 13 more than last season, on which the customers made their own comment by attending for a total of 200 weeks, or about six weeks a show. A few, notably "The Fourposter" with Jessica Tandy and Hume Cronyn, and "Point of No Return" with Henry Fonda, ended self-limited engagements with sold-out houses and slowpokes gnashing their teeth in exterior darkness. "Gigi," Gilbert Miller's first in our midst since "Harriet," came timidly, and twice extended its stay. But the longest run of the new season's crop was 18 weeks for "Stalag 17," launched with Labor Day, and the runner-up was 16 weeks for "Dial 'M' for Murder," expertly duplicated for January opening with Richard Greene as the star. Considering that two other expert duplications, "The Moon Is Blue" and "Guys and Dolls," had held over from the previous season for totals of 61 and 36 weeks, respectively, there was something wrong with the golden egg market, and the situation demanded a whipping boy.

So it was open season on critics, belabored in most cases not for what they are, which is vulnerable, but for what they are not. J. J. Shubert, for instance, seemed to think them salesmen falling down on the job. Theatre, he said, is a business like a department store, and no newspaper sends critics into a department store to disparage the merchandise. Ideally, he would dispense with critics. As a practical substitute, because shows "on the road" are plainly not ready to be seen opening night (a quaint term surviving in the lexicon), he had instructed his theatres to send critics' seats for second nights.

Jerome Robbins, Vernon Duke, Ogden Nash and Charles Sherman in rehearsal for "Two's Company"

Not much came of it. The newspapers bought first night seats until producers began sending them, and as locations remained unchanged the gesture smacked of box-office collusion. The public, fascinated by the department store analogy, said it would happily embrace Mr. Shubert's point of view, providing it could examine his wares and, if it decided to buy, pay on the way out.

As for Mr. Shubert's contention that because Chicago is the theatrical kiss of death, producers bring their shows here last, if at all, it was plainly a misfortune that his smoldering indignation was detonated by the demise in one week of the touring "Paint Your Wagon." This unhappy caravan, toting the amiable Burl Ives, just about clinched the growing local conviction that Chicago is the theatrical equivalent of the place old elephants go to die.

Speaking of piteous pachyderms, another to turn up its toes here was a peculiar version of "A Tree Grows in Brooklyn," with Joan Blondell unfortunately cast as Aunt Cissy. This ran three weeks for an altogether interesting reason, which may have set the Theatre Guild back so far only a new set of Lunts can reclaim it. At the behest of the Council of Living Theatre, Guild subscription offered

its patrons eight instead of six plays. The withered "Tree" was one
of them. "Point of No Return," enticing bait in the prospectus,
was not.

Among other musicals, "Porgy and Bess" looked in early in the
season, Europe-bound, and "Call Me Madam" had the misfortune
to open the night of the Eisenhower inauguration, so that the chatty
calls to "Harry" gave even Republicans a twinge. "Top Banana"
did not flourish as long as Phil Silvers' admirers thought it should,
but at season's end the town had taken "New Faces" to heart, and
"Pal Joey" had just swaggered in with designs on the Summer.

A faithful star, Katharine Cornell, came in "The Constant Wife,"
a long absent one, Helen Hayes, in "Mrs. McThing," and a new
one, Julie Harris, in "I Am a Camera." Some of the other plays
had touches of curiosa to rival the witch of the Blue, Blue Mountains.
"Josephine," the Sally Benson treatment of F. Scott Fitzgerald stories, with Betsy Von Furstenberg as its Lake Forest belle, closed
in a week, not without indignation. Critics who had mildly observed
that no one act seemed to know what the others were doing were
haughtily informed that it could scarcely be otherwise, as only a
part of the rewritten material had gone in. "Why be so cranky
about it?" inquired co-producer Luther Greene.

"The Country Girl" also had an unusual opening. Robert Young
was reported ill, so Paul Kelly flew in from the coast and spent the
day rehearsing the way he had played it. But Mr. Young quickly
recovered, and Mr. Kelly was content with a curtain speech, if a
confused audience was not. And puzzlement as to why "The
Shrike," which once struck like a coiled rattlesnake, took an inter-
minable time to start each scene, was explained eventually by Van
Heflen, its baffled star. The author, Joseph Kramm, had staged it,
although the playbill did not say so. Having worked on the London
production, he wanted a brief lag at the start of each scene, the
way they did it in London to quiet the clatter of lap trays.

So it goes. For one good show worth its playgoing salt, too many
funeral bak'd meats did coldly furnish forth the marriage tables.
If bookers say "The Deep Blue Sea" with Uta Hagen lasted a week
and such moronic trash as "Maid in the Ozarks" kept running,
that is true. The mangy "Maid'" got the choicer theatre, flooded
the town with cut rates, and lured those who aren't content with
rock bottom in taste, but like digging a hole. "The Deep Blue Sea"
drew many Chicagoans to Milwaukee the previous week when Margaret Sullavan was still in the show. It opened here on a Friday,
when reviews are a weekend problem. By Monday it had decided

to close, though the playgoing part of the town had not had a chance to decide what to do about it.

Plainly our theatrical climate is not ideal, but Chicago does not furnish that climate, merely the reaction to it.

Here is the record for the 1952-53 season, compiled as of May 30:

Shubert Theatre: 41 weeks—"Guys and Dolls," 23 weeks this season, 36½ in all; Gilbert and Sullivan, 1½; "Call Me Madam," 13; Betty Hutton show, 2; "Pal Joey," 1½ to date.

Harris Theatre: 38½ weeks—"The Moon Is Blue," 4 weeks this season, 61 in all; "I Am a Camera," 7; "Gigi," 11½; "Dial 'M' for Murder," 16.

Blackstone Theatre: 32⅓ weeks—"Bagels and Yox," 5 weeks this season, 8 in all; "The Fourposter," 10; "The Country Girl," 6; "Paint Your Wagon," 1; "Paris '90," 3; "The Male Animal," 6; "The Deep Blue Sea," 1⅓.

Erlanger Theatre: 32 weeks—"Stalag 17," 18; "Point of No Return," 4; "The Shrike," 4; "Mrs. McThing," 6.

Selwyn Theatre, 28⅓ weeks—"Bell, Book and Candle," 11 weeks this season, 25 in all; "The Fig Leaf," 1½; "The Constant Wife," 4⅓; "Josephine," 1; "Farfel Follies," 4; "Affairs of State," 2½; "Maid in the Ozarks," 4 so far.

Great Northern Theatre: 24½ weeks—"Bagels and Yox," 2; "A Tree Grows in Brooklyn," 3; "Top Banana," 14; Emlyn Williams, 1; "New Faces," 4½ so far.

Civic Opera House: 4 weeks—"Porgy and Bess," 4; "Don Juan in Hell," 2 performances.

THE SEASON IN SOUTHERN CALIFORNIA

By EDWIN SCHALLERT

Drama Editor, *Los Angeles Times*

ONE way and another Southern California achieved a better theatrical season than usual during 1952-53. It was a period of fits and starts, most of which got nowhere on a permanent basis, though they were hopeful auguries. Prevalent problems were principally familiar ones. However, matching debits against credits for a 12-month time, one can truthfully say that this often arid dramatic oasis is conforming with the fabulous invalid format by somehow surviving.

It was Henry Duffy, an old maestro of the show business in Los Angeles, who gave a brief spell of extra life to the footlight scene in its middle portion. Prior to that the area dominated by the City of the Angels was relying for anything like creative endeavor on La Jolla, which successfully brought forth a native production of "The Moon Is Blue" and sent "The Lady's Not for Burning" up to San Francisco.

At the close of the season glowing forecasts were being recited concerning what the Council of the Living Theatre, in association with the New York Theatre Guild (American Society of the Theatre) might be offering. Forerunner on this program, which arrived in May, was "Point of No Return" with Henry Fonda and a New York company, practically intact, which met with high approval.

Another heralding that went on as the season approached its close was the Equity Theatre Project, first effort of this kind on the West Coast, which had ambitious aims and purposes, and also financial aid from the eastern headquarters. Pre-eminently this was designed to help awaken the western stage from its slumbers, to give the acting fraternity and sorority in the Hollywood district something to keep them busy and stimulated during slack seasons, and incidentally to yield a little revenue for those taking part. How well the Project was destined to fulfill the advance charting was still a matter of conjecture as the 1952-53 fiscal year ended about June 1st. But those who were devoting themselves to the enterprise, had their hearts in it.

Tyrone Power, Judith Anderson and Raymond Massey in "John Brown's Body"

The initial pilot play was "Ned McCobb's Daughter," with Julie Mitchum, elder sister of Robert Mitchum, known on television and in night clubs, as the title character. This was to be followed by Bernard Shaw's "Major Barbara" and two other presentations.

The idea of such a project was particularly timely, considering how chaotic conditions became in the film industry, with contracts for talent being written off right and left in the studios, owing to the big change-over from two-dimension to three-dimension films, wide screen and various other processes. What is more, many players, viewing the success of some of their confreres in the television medium, have been swinging toward that more and more. The screen seems to be harder hit than the stage by this exodus.

Hence, it was felt that the Equity Theatre Project was launched at an auspicious time, and it was hoped through pilot shows given for invited audiences to attract both bookers and backers for the individual attractions. The undertaking, while it compares with the Equity Library and Equity Community Theatre presentations in New York, is also decidedly different.

When one retrospects on the 1952-53 season, one finds on the credit side in Southern California a very good assortment of touring attractions. These began with "Stalag 17" in June, 1952, as presented by a cast headed by George Tobias and John Ericson. This was a welcome event because it followed a long hiatus for such productions at the Biltmore Theatre.

The high spots during the season were notably the two-week visit, all too short, of Jessica Tandy and Hume Cronyn in "The Fourposter"; the advent of Julie Harris in John Van Druten's "I Am a Camera," with Charles Cooper in the William Prince part; Audrey Hepburn's blithely entertaining appearance in "Gigi," with Margaret Bannerman, Michael Evans, Josephine Brown, Doris Patston and Bertha Belmore forming a pretty fair supporting company. Neither Miss Harris nor Miss Hepburn had previously starred in Los Angeles on the stage.

Though Miss Harris was seen during the year in "Member of the Wedding" on the screen, she had not appeared with the company that brought that attraction, as well as Ethel Waters, to the Coast the previous season. Miss Harris' visit was the occasion of a real box-office hit, during an engagement that ended too soon.

Other touring events were the visit of Katharine Cornell in the revival of "The Constant Wife" with Robert Flemyng and John Emery as her supporting male leads; "The Country Girl," of Coast origin, with Robert Young, Nancy Kelly and Dane Clark; "Bell, Book and Candle" with Joan Bennett and Zachary Scott; the First Drama Quartette in "Don Juan in Hell"; "Call Me Madam," as part of the Los Angeles Civic Light Opera season, with Elaine Stritch in the Ethel Merman role and Kent Smith. Add to these "The Moon Is Blue," with David Niven, Diana Lynn and Scott Brady, which emerged from La Jolla, and the one-man, one-woman shows proffered by Emlyn Williams, with his Charles Dickens readings, and Cornelia Otis Skinner in her "Paris '90."

Interesting about the First Drama Quartette was its return to the point of its beginning in "Don Juan in Hell," with a matured quality quite evident in the readings, and the further fact that Vincent Price substituted once or twice during the engagement for Charles Laughton as the Devil. Laughton was occupied with rehearsals for "John Brown's Body" at the time. Price provided a very interesting interpretation in conjunction with Charles Boyer, Sir Cedric Hardwicke and Agnes Moorehead.

"John Brown's Body," sponsored by Paul Gregory, impresario of the Drama Quartette and Charles Laughton readings, was seen in performances on the outskirts of Los Angeles, including Beverly Hills, just before this unique attraction with Tyrone Power, Raymond Massey and Judith Anderson took off for Broadway. The so-called platform play seemed to have other devotees, it might be noted, though so far Gregory has been the most successful in the management of these events.

Duffy's brave try at restoring a permanent theatre in Los Angeles met success in his presentation of "Affairs of State," with Marsha Hunt, Otto Kruger, Taylor Holmes, Donald Woods and Ann Doran and Joan Blair as alternates, which he held for seventeen weeks at the Carthay Circle Theatre, erstwhile home of big film premieres. Following this he reinstated Billie Burke on the stage in a luxuriously designed production of "Life with Mother," in which Carl Benton Reid appeared as Father, but while this lasted for eight weeks the Duffy enterprise faded with its closing.

The theater seemed to have a wonderful location, and certainly "Affairs of State," as cast, pleased the majority of its audiences. Miss Burke, too, is a winning personality, it was conceded by all, even though "Life with Mother" was less approved. However, Duffy was evidently not in a position to apply those stimuli which are peculiarly necessary to stir the public anew to the allurements of the stage in a city where theatre has been in a run-down condition for so long as Los Angeles.

The problem of getting new and provocative Broadway hits undeniably faced this producer, whose courage has often been proved exceptional. Even as Harold J. Kennedy failed in the long run in theatres of smaller capacity, so Duffy finally met his Waterloo unhappily in a larger showhouse. And it is a matter for real regret.

In the face of this rather tragical outcome, Edwin Lester, as the guiding genius of the Los Angeles Civic Light Opera repertoire, still maintains a serene position of prestige. "Call Me Madam," which followed "Song of Norway," and the curtain-raising vaudeville entertainment of Judy Garland, reported on as part of the 1951-52 season, gave way to a re-run of "South Pacific," which again had Janet Blair as the feminine star. The late Irene Bordoni made her final appearance in this show as Bloody Mary. Webb Tilton and David Burns were the others.

"Jollyanna" was the year's experiment. The cast was headed by Bobby Clark, doing his routines of comedy, and Mitzi Gaynor, former light opera find, before she signed for 20th Century-Fox films. Bill Baird's Marionettes, John Beal, Marthe Errolle, Beverly Tyler, Biff McGuire and Gus Schilling all took part in this E. Y. Harburg and Fred Saidy show, with music by Sammy Fain and "added music" by William Friml, which fell short of being a hoped-for sensation.

A genuinely noteworthy production of "Carousel" inaugurated the 1953 Civic Light Opera season in May. Directed by Rouben Mamoulian, the revived work had as its principals Jan Clayton in her original role; William Johnson, Murvyn Vye and Betta St. John.

A touring "Oklahoma!", not part of the Light Opera Association season, also made a three-week stop at the Biltmore Theatre. For the rest, musical shows were mostly confined to central staging situations, with the Greek Theatre failing to yield any entrants, such as prevailed there during the immediate post-war years.

Central staging, which had practically kept show business going the prior season, lost some ground during 1952-53. The Gallery Stage, which had augmented the Circle and the Ring, ceased operations in the Spring months, after some rather interesting work. Contrastingly the arena effort at the outlying desert resort of Palm Springs, which had been proceeding quietly for several winters, attained new stature when Ann Harding starred in "The Corn Is Green" at the Palm Springs Playhouse, her first venture into central staging. She had previously done this play with regular staging at La Jolla Playhouse. She also appeared in it during the 1952-53 season at the Sombrero Playhouse at Phoenix, Ariz., operated by Ann Lee and Richard Charlton.

Of theatres in the round, Circle continued its policy of presenting new plays, while the Ring kept up a constant succession of shows, with some new ones included. Most noteworthy of the Circle's new offerings was "Montmartre" by Pierre La Mure, also known as "Moulin Rouge," and dealing with Toulouse-Lautrec. Gene Reynolds appeared as the artist, with Constance Dowling as Marie Charlet and Don Elson as Van Gogh. The Circle also presented "A Streetcar Named Desire," with Shelley Winters, and "A Saint of Little Consequence," Irish play by John Crilley, while Lion Feuchtwanger's "The Devil in Boston" ended an 18 weeks' run during the season with Cathy O'Donnell and Norma Eberhardt alternating opposite William Schallert.

The Ring had sixteen weeks with "Look, Ma, I'm Dancin'," presented "The Laugh Maker" as a new event by Jerome Lawrence and Robert E. Lee; "The Milky Way," "Ethan Frome," with Kathleen Freeman seen to special advantage, and "The Play's the Thing." The Gallery Stage made a specialty of lighter affairs, including the musical, "Great to Be Alive," and the rather clever "The Maid and the Martian" (new) by Joseph Barbera.

The Pasadena Playhouse augmented its importance as a theatrical stronghold during the season by emphasis on professional appearances. Alex Nicol, who understudied Henry Fonda in "Mister Roberts," was given the opportunity to play the title role in a very popular production. K. T. Stevens and Hugh Marlowe, who once toured in John Van Druten's "Voice of the Turtle," undertook the same author's "Bell, Book and Candle." Harpo Marx was the prop man in "Yellow Jacket" on another occasion, while Raymond Burr acted in "Twentieth Century," Onslow Stevens in "The Happy Time," Wilton Graff in "The Country Girl," and Douglass Montgomery, late in the season, in a double bill composed of "The Showing Up of Blanco Posnet" by George Bernard Shaw and "Magic" by G. K. Chesterton.

"Billy Budd," "Ring Around the Moon," "Stalag 17," "The Mikado," Victor Herbert's "The Fortune Teller," "A Christmas Carol" were also in the Pasadena repertoire. "Nightshade" by Ken Englund and Sidney Field had its world premiere, but though interesting in idea, needed revision.

The 1952 Midsummer Drama Festival, dealing with "Great Americans" received the Freedoms Foundations Award. It was recited that the Pasadena Playhouse was the only theatrical institution to be given the 1952 award. The plays included "Valley Forge" by Maxwell Anderson, "Ben Franklin" by Louis Evans Shipman, "The Patriots" by Sidney Kingsley, "Harriet" by Florence Ryerson and Colin Clements, "Abe Lincoln in Illinois" by Robert Sherwood, and "Robert E. Lee" by John Drinkwater.

La Jolla Playhouse again proved the consistency of its program, and succeeded in staging the premiere of "Strike a Match" by Robert Smith, which had as leading players Pat O'Brien, Eva Gabor, Richard Egan and Tom Brown. This went on a tour through the Southwest, to St. Louis and elsewhere, though it wasn't deemed material for Broadway.

"The Lady's Not for Burning" had Vincent Price, Marsha Hunt and Beulah Bondi in leading roles, while Miss Hunt also appeared with Tom Powers in "Affairs of State." Miss Harding was in "The Corn Is Green" with Diana Barrymore and Douglas Dick. Fay

Wray and Onslow Stevens were among those present in "The Happy Time," while Monica Lewis and Carleton Carpenter were recruited from the films for "Remains to Be Seen," and Nancy Kelly and Howard Duff headed the cast of "Season in the Sun." Groucho Marx, with Mary Philips assisting, had a field day in "Time for Elizabeth."

It was "The Moon Is Blue," later offered in Los Angeles with the same cast and Otto Preminger identified as director, that touched off the season.

The Laguna Beach Playhouse supplemented the La Jolla endeavor, with Selena Royle appearing in "Black Chiffon" and "Yes, My Darling Daughter." "Second Threshold," "The Letter," "The Willow Whistle," a new play that didn't click, "While the Sun Shines" were presented with casts including Marjorie Steele, Susan Cabot, Peter Adams, Don Randolph, John Bryan, David John Stollery, Betty Paul and others.

The Tustin Playbox, which had a previous history, was reactivated, with a repertoire comprising "The Imaginary Invalid," "See How They Run," "Candida" and "Light Up the Sky," this being a Summer, though not a seaside, operation. The Alhecama Theatre in Santa Barbara proffered such plays as "State of the Union," "The Circle," "Berkeley Square," "Dark of the Moon," and "Ah, Wilderness!" through the regular theatrical season.

Besides "The Corn Is Green" with Ann Harding, the Palm Springs Playhouse had Edward Arnold in "Apple of His Eye," Marsha Hunt in "Private Lives," Victor Jory in "For Love or Money" and Teddy Hart in "Three Men on a Horse." Also appealing to the Winter tourist trade, the Sombrero Playhouse in Phoenix staged "Life with Mother," starring Billie Burke, before it came into Los Angeles; Somerset Maugham's "Theatre," with Kay Francis; "Jason," with Franchot Tone; "Bell, Book and Candle," with Teresa Wright and Victor Jory; "Hay Fever," with Miriam Hopkins, as well as "The Corn Is Green," with Miss Harding.

Occasional events during the year included, among others, "The Web and the Rock" from Thomas Wolfe, with Eugenie Leontovich, who had Earl Colbert as her male lead, and "Farfel Follies," with a notable singer in Bas Sheva, Myron Cohen and others, presented by Mickey Katz and Hal Zeiger.

Best of these independent enterprises was that of Maurice Schwartz at the Civic Playhouse, formerly the Century Theatre. He opened "Take Now Thy Son," which was not too successful, but had a long run with his traditional play, "Hard to Be a Jew."

"Out of the Frying Pan," "Danger, Men Working," with Jeff

Corey; "Flame-Out," war play by Alan Mowbray, the actor, which had promise; "Burning Bright" by John Steinbeck, and "The Philadelphia Story" were among plays fleetingly offered. Preston Sturges sponsored a very interesting rendition of "The Road to Rome," with Carolyn Jones in the Jane Cowl role, and Robin Hughes, Richard Hale, Margaret Brewster and Nico Lek among those in the cast. Miss Jones may be recognized as the victim of murder in "The House of Wax," three-dimensional film which aroused so much interest and protest. "Road to Rome" had a lengthy run at Sturges' theatre-restaurant, The Players.

"The Drunkard" in its 20th year; the Turnabout, Padua Hills Theatre with its Latinesque divertissements; the pageant outdoor play, "Ramona" all continued their careers. The dramatic offering during the Ojai Festivals was "This Way to the Tomb" by the British Ronald Duncan, which takes the form of a Masque and a satirical anti-Masque—a take-off on a television show. Dallas Boyd, Al Hurwitz, previously seen in "The Laugh Maker" at the Ring Theatre; Vivian Marshall, Richard Allan, Stanley S. Newcomb and others appeared. Still active were numerous smaller theatres like the Call Board, Geller Workshop, Sartu, Carousel, etc., in the Los Angeles area.

In conclusion it may be remarked that new compasses could very well give a more definite purpose to theatrical efforts in Southern California. The ground seems to be somewhat more fertile than heretofore.

THE SEASON IN LONDON

By Kenneth Tynan

Drama Critic, London *Evening Standard*

The New Plays

IT is eight years now since the war ended. To compare our dramatic harvest with that of the eight years following the first world war is a melancholy exercise. Then, a London playgoer had his choice of O'Casey, Coward, Galsworthy, Drinkwater, Maugham, Shaw, O'Neill, Cocteau, Toller, Kaiser, Pirandello, and Jean-Jacques Bernard, all of whom were turning out new plays. Where a flood once roared, a trickle now drips. I would place four living dramatists in the first rank: Tennessee Williams, Arthur Miller, Jean Anouilh and Jean-Paul Sartre. The English group belongs in the second rank, which is reserved for those who have not yet produced an indisputably great play: T. S. Eliot, Christopher Fry, Terence Rattigan and—putatively—Roger MacDougall. MacDougall, the author of "Macadam and Eve," "The Gentle Gunman" and "To Dorothy a Son," is the only member of the quartet to have had a new play produced during the 1952-3 season. This was "Escapade," which cost only $8000 to stage, and repaid its production costs within the first fortnight of its London run.

"Escapade" is far from a great play, but it is certainly the finest comedy to have been written in England since the war. Tragedies about pacifism are two a penny: this is that courageous rarity, a comedy on the same theme. MacDougall's fable concerns a blustering middle-aged peace-monger whose three sons, having run away from school and winged a teacher in the leg with a home-made blunderbuss, steal an aeroplane and fly off, bearing an anti-war manifesto, in the general direction of Venice, where a U.N.O. congress is in session. At his best, MacDougall is capable of rhetorical prose as witty and cogent as anything in James Bridie; but scratch him, and (as with Bridie) an ink-stained schoolboy bursts out, shouting debating-society slogans at the top of his voice. Whenever this brat looms up, the play becomes light comedy instead of the serious comedy it was meant to be. Yet the play performs a public service by encapsulating a public mood. It touches a chord, peace, to which we all respond in the same way; it argues a case in

Cyril Ritchard, Katharine Hepburn and Robert Helpmann in "The Millionairess"

which we are all plaintiffs. And towards the end it develops, magnificently, into heroic comedy: the boys' lunatic flight over the Alps takes you soaring into the region of pure epic, where farce and valor co-exist, and a man's whole business is (in a phrase of Maurice Bowra's) "the pursuit of honour through risk." Hereabouts MacDougall does justice to himself, and his play grows as large as its theme.

Two other straight plays have kept many a cocktail party from flagging—Charles Morgan's "The River Line" and Graham Greene's "The Living Room," of which the former ran for six months and the latter seems likely to run forever. Morgan's theme is austere: responsibility. Three wartime companions—a young American, an English naval commander, and the Englishman's French wife— meet and dine two years after the war is over. They share a common guilt: their lives first converged on "The River Line," an escape route through France for allied prisoners-of-war, one of whom—a tall, poetic major nicknamed "Heron"—they killed on suspicion of treachery. Act II flashes us melodramatically back to the circumstances of his death; and in the last act we learn that he was, in fact, innocent. Can the savage and peremptory rules of war ever find, in peace, forgiveness? That is the play's poser.

Morgan solves it in his own remote way, spreading across it the heavy, exquisitely folded grave-clothes of his Sunday-best prose. He discusses abstract problems as if they were dead friends on whom he was conducting a loving post-mortem. And if you catch an oppressive smell in the air, a whiff of antiseptic, that is all part of the Morgan method; it is the price we pay for hearing him speak, a groping prophet, about "interior grace" and that "creative pause" without which, he insists, life is no more than a bloodstained rush of expedience. Morgan carries a portable cathedral around with him, which he cannot shed even when his characters are talking about dinner or the weather. If he were only less of a master, "The River Line" would have been more of a masterpiece. It was acted well by Pamela Brown, as the Frenchwoman, and superbly by Paul Scofield, who projected, through the part of the American, his own unique and highly eccentric personality, on which I dote.

"The Living Room" is Graham Greene's first play, and arguably the best first play by an Englishman since Ronald Mackenzie's "Musical Chairs" in 1932. Its subject-matter can be compressed into two texts. One from Shaw: "You can't make a man a Christian unless you first make him believe he is a sinner"; and one from a nameless producer: "The triangle may not be eternal, but I'm taking bookings until Christmas." Greene has tried to weld these two propositions, one cosmic and one commercial, into a dramatic entity.

In "The Notorious Mrs. Ebbsmith," Pinero scandalized a Victorian audience by making his heroine throw a Bible into the fire; and comforted them immediately afterwards by having her pull it out again. Greene's heroine, so to speak, chucks it in and leaves it there. She is a young orphan, overwhelmingly in love with a middle-aged lecturer in psychology, who is saddled with a hysterical wife. That is the textbook triangle: Greene now sets about projecting it to infinity. For the girl is Catholic. She has come to live with a pair of ancient aunts and a crippled uncle who is a "useless priest": they inhabit a glum suburban house in which strange rituals persist, among them a refusal on the part of the female inmates to admit that they ever go to the bathroom except to take a bath. Greene, in addition to being a Papist, is a born rebel, and I take this sepulchral mansion to symbolize the more obscurantist aspects of the Roman faith. Childishly scared of death, the aunts have sealed off every room in which anyone has died. Confronted with her adultery, the girl vacillates between her lover and her God—between, as Greene is careful to indicate, an earthly and a heavenly father-image—and finally cries out to the priest that she is one of God's "happy failures."

The climax is a disappointment. The wife, a rapacious neurotic, stages a suicide attempt, which belatedly restores to her husband a sense of duty; and the girl, doing the far, far better thing, takes poison. The whole superstructure of sin and salvation dissolves into nothingness: she behaves, in her crisis, just like a cardboard figure of Victorian melodrama. Having tied a modern Catholic knot, Greene cuts it with an old-fashioned theatrical ax. The result is fascinating as a problem picture, but incomplete as a theatrical experience. A fitting caption for it might run: "Be it ever so lustful, there's no place like Rome."

"The Living Room" has given to little Dorothy Tutin a chance which has been withheld from young English actresses for nearly thirty years: the chance of playing a long, serious part in an important new play. Her role is half of what must be one of the most fully documented love-affairs in dramatic literature: we are privy to all her secrets, sexual and spiritual alike. She responds with a blazing diamond of a performance—the very nakedness of acting.

None of the other new plays has reached this level. Noel Coward's "Quadrille" was described on the program as "a romantic comedy," which is a phrase to beware of, since it can (and in this case does) mean comedy gone flabby with sentiment, comedy which is all situation and no plot. "Quadrille" rather suggests Oscar Wilde rewritten in a rectory garden by Amanda Ros at her most verbose. The time is 1873: the Marquess of Heronden is eloping to the Riviera with the wife of an American railroad tycoon. Presently their abandoned spouses pursue them, discovering at the end of Act II that they, too, are in love with each other. And that is all. The excuse for this monstrously overloaded tea-trolley of a play is, of course, the presence in it of the Lunts, who play together, as millionaire and marchioness, like sandpaper on topaz.

My reaction to "The Happy Marriage," another comedy success, was that it should be instantly annulled on grounds of mental cruelty. Like "Quadrille," it demonstrates the English public's incorrigible loyalty to anything which is twenty years out of date and performed by a popular married couple. The partners here are John Clements and Kay Hammond, whose union (in the script) is jeopardized by a quack psychiatrist who holds that marital fidelity is a disease which only adultery can cure. The dialogue, adapted by Mr. Clements from the French of Jean-Bernard Luc, is bountiful, to say the least, and composed in a chilling vein of roadhouse breeziness. Mr. Clements also directed the play, and, with the jolly pomp of a corseted Guards officer, stars in it: few men can ever have shouted "Mea culpa!" more loudly in public. His wife lurches swooning in his wake, deserving better things.

"Dear Charles," another prosperous adaptation, was taken by Alan Melville from a Parisian farce whose plot was filched from a Broadway flop called "Slightly Scandalous." Melville's version is an adroit bid for such critical clichés as "inimitable Gallic wit" and "a difficult subject delicately handled." It is simple, symmetrical and unsubtle: in short, a hit, or—to be more inimitable—a success mad. A middle-aged Frenchwoman discloses to her three children that their dead papa, whom they have always regarded as a demigod, never really existed at all. He is just a picture over the chimney-piece, and they are all illegitimate. Determined to acquire a husband, Mama invites the three fathers to spend a week under her roof, at the end of which time she will choose between them.

The play is an iron-clad vehicle for mother; and mother is the plump Anglo-French comedienne Yvonne Arnaud, who blossomed on to the stage on opening night, nodded her acknowledgment of our applause, and conducted the entertainment as if it had been a soirée to which she, the theatre's universal aunt, had personally bidden us. Her *réclame*, however, was shamelessly stolen by Charles Goldner, as her third lover, a ribald and exhibitionistic Polish musician. Goldner's performance, in a flimsily written part, would delight any lover of creative acting. He can make bricks out of straw; Mme. Arnaud can make only bric-à-brac. Histrionically, she is a gifted interior decorator; but he is an architect.

R. C. Sherriff evoked some congratulations on having written, in "The White Carnation," a part which Ralph Richardson found actable. Over the last few years, the connection between Richardson's demeanor on stage and that of a human being in life has been getting progressively more tenuous. He has taken to ambling across the boards in a spectral, shell-shocked manner, choosing the most

Kenneth Walton, Miss Lillie and Reginald Gardiner in "An Evening with Beatrice Lillie"

unexpected moments to leap and frisk, like a man through whom an electric current was being intermittently passed. Sherriff tried to exploit these eccentricities in an earlier play, "Home at Seven," in which Richardson played a man who had been stunned into a state of amnesia. Now he has gone the whole hog: before the curtain rises on "The White Carnation," Richardson has been blown to pieces by a flying-bomb. He is a ghost returned to haunt the house in which, seven years before, he was killed. The author has been unable to decide whether he wanted to write a J. B. Priestleyish play with overtones of Ouspensky or a straight Ealing comedy about the place of a spook in a bureacracy; and the writing is too weak to disguise this basic uncertainty. But as the central zombie, Richardson is entirely at home. He may not be very effective competing with other actors on the flat, but across the Styx he is wonderful.

American legitimate imports have had a shaky time. "Remains to Be Seen" and "Stalag 17" were quickly on and off; Mel Dinelli's thriller, "The Man," expired after two months; and "Second Threshold," Philip Barry's variation on the theme of "Death with Father," had a short run in the Autumn, chiefly distinguished by reason of Clive Brook's sulky, patrician richness as the would-be suicide. Of modern American drama in its favorite mood, rebellion against victimization, we saw two examples: Joseph Kramm's "The Shrike" and George Bellak's "The Trouble-makers," neither of which caught on with the public. The José Ferrer part in Kramm's play was performed by Sam Wanamaker, a burning, bright, tigerish actor with a great talent for martyrdom but none at all for pathos. Bellak's piece, a melodrama about witch-hunting in a small-town university, was another theatrical hand raised in protest. Four tipsy thugs beat up and accidentally murder a campus colleague who has been expressing pinkish sympathies in the college magazine: they do this in the presence of the boy's room-mate, whose conscience is the theme of what follows. Should he keep mum or squeal? Bellak's message is that those who wink at persecution are as contemptible as those who persecute; and it is expressed with a blistering, black-and-white heat which generates enormous theatrical excitement.

"The Seven Year Itch," restaged in London with a predominantly English cast (including Rosemary Harris, who made her Broadway debut in Moss Hart's "Climate of Eden"), is an importation which has thrived; and so, against all prophecy, is "Affairs of State," which opened in August 1952 at an out-of-the-way theatre, and ran through Winter and Spring.

The Revivals

Olivier, during 1952-3, was theatrically inactive; Michael Redgrave and Peggy Ashcroft retired to Stratford-on-Avon, where they magnoperated in "The Merchant of Venice," "Antony and Cleopatra" and "King Lear"; and Alec Guinness went trekking off to Stratford-on-Avon, Ontario, to play two sick Shakespearean kings— "Richard III" with a bent back, and the King of France with a fistula in "All's Well That Ends Well." London, in its coronation year, had to make do with the Old Vic, and John Gielgud's repertory at the Lyric, Hammersmith.

Claire Bloom's display in the Vic's "Romeo and Juilet" was something of a revelation: eschewing blushes and simpers, she played the part as a mettlesome adult, finding in it moments of a desolating harshness. This production of Hugh Hunt's was more lively than its successor, "The Merchant of Venice": Paul Rogers, a relentlessly somber Shylock, spoiled the fancy-dress party of the play by coming as a leper. "Julius Caesar," which followed, would have been greatly improved by a little laryngitis: it was a rowdy romp, and insult was added to injury when Mark Antony requested the loan of ears whose drums he had already perforated. Everything was sacrificed on the altar of voice production, a recurrent fault in the English classical theatre. "Murder in the Cathedral" was impressively revived under Robert Helpmann's balletic direction, with Robert Donat returning to the stage in the part of Eliot's slaughtered saint. What singles this actor out from all his contemporaries (save perhaps the late Godfrey Tearle) is his possession of the gift of courtesy. He sweetens even pride with civility; and he can suggest pain more tellingly by smiling than most actors can by wincing. The Vic's season, financially more successful than any since the Olivier-Richardson days of 1945-46, ended with an orgiastic production by Tyrone Guthrie of "Henry VIII."

John Gielgud's sojourn in suburban Hammersmith opened lamely with "Richard II," directed by the master as a sort of essay in mass ventriloquism; a triumph of elocutionary style over humanity. It was a Pyrrhic victory, involving the martyrdom of some first-rate actors; among them Paul Scofield, whose drably metrical Richard was a shadow of the performance we had expected. I long, some day, to see a Richard whose "rash, fierce blaze of riot" is not just a flickering taper of whim. Next came a much more enjoyable "Way of the World," which set sail with Gielgud, a benign Mirabell, at the helm, a crowd of agile character actors manning the rigging, and Eileen Herlie smuggled aboard as ballast. The galleon's figurehead was Margaret Rutherford as the man-hungry Lady Wishfort— an inordinate performance, filled with a monstrous vitality. One of Miss Rutherford's rarest skills is that of acting with her chin alone. I recall with especial pleasure the chin in doubt, the chin commanding, and the chin at bay. The only weakness in the production was Pamela Brown's oddly apologetic Millamant, from whose mouth the great speeches did not flow, but leaked, feebly, in dribs and drabs. The last of Gielgud's three offerings was Thomas Otway's "Venice Preserv'd," written in 1681, and conceivably the best verse play in English since the death of Shakespeare. Under Peter Brook's direction, the torchlit melodrama of conspiracy leapt into life, grinning and scowling as on the day of its birth.

Within half a mile of Gielgud's company, another classical repertory was functioning: that led by Donald Wolfit, at the King's Theatre. Wolfit is a peripatetic barnstormer whose visits to London are usually of short duration: this time he has settled down, with a remarkably lymphatic supporting cast, to perform a repertoire including "Lear," "Macbeth," "Twelfth Night," "As You Like It," "The Wandering Jew" and a double bill of Sophocles' "Oedipus Rex" and "Oedipus Coloneus." A burly tragedian of considerable power, Wolfit is egregious in the strict etymological sense of the word: he stands well apart from the herd. And normally well up-stage of them.

At the Savoy Theatre, a dressy company of sixteen, headed by Clive Brook and Isobel Jeans, marked time in an opulent revival of Wilde's "A Woman of No Importance." And Noel Coward came to town (some said, to grief) in the involved locutions of King Magnus in Shaw's "The Apple Cart."

The Musicals

The transatlantics flourished most: "Porgy and Bess," "Guys and Dolls" and "Paint Your Wagon." The last-named was in many ways an improvement on the Broadway version, although its cast was headed by an English father-and-daughter team, Bobby and Sally Ann Howes. The first-night audience went in trepidation, prepared to murmur "A plague on both your Howeses!"; but it need not have worried. The Howeses triumphed. Something similar happened to the newcomer Jean Carson, on the opening night of "Love from Judy," Hugh Martin's lively musical adaptation of Jean Webster's "Daddy Long-Legs": with red hair falling down her neck and cream face smiling, Miss Carson set foot in the charmed cloisters of those whom, for all their flaws, we recognize as stars.

The most characteristic musical play of the season was "The Glorious Days." Its star was Anna Neagle, a staunch little actress—is she known in America?—whose films have established her in the English mind as the embodiment of all that is noblest in her sex—or perhaps, in this context, gender would be a more respectful word. "The Glorious Days" was her coronation tribute: Anna Neagle rolled into one. It is as hard to explain her to America as it used to be to explain Aimee Semple MacPherson to England; but the effort must be made. First, she acts in a manner so sparing of personality as to be almost incognito; second, she sings, shaking her voice at the audience like a tiny fist; and third, she dances in that non-committal, twirling style once known as "skirt-dancing," which was originally invented to account for the presence on the stage of young women who could neither sing nor act. In the course of "The Glorious Days" she appeared as Nell Gwynn, Queen Victoria, a war-time ambulance-driver, and the ambulance-driver's mother. More than two dozen people collaborated on the words, music, settings, choreography and direction: and send not to know for whom the bell tolls, because it tolls for all of them. The prevailing tone of the show—one not uncommon in West End musicals—was a mixture of cynicism ("They'll lap it up") and joviality ("God bless them!"). "The Glorious Days" served to demonstrate, for its generation, an ancient theatrical truth: that the gap between knowing what the public wants and having the skill to provide it is infinitely wider than most producers ever dream.

THE SEASON IN PARIS

By André Josset

Playwright; and Secretary-General of the International Theatre Institute, UNESCO

THERE are forty-five theatres in Paris which run to 23,000 seats. From the greatest to the smallest, they house in theory forty-five shows a year, though in practice many more, for the guillotine beheads many new plays on their first night, and of the survivors, about half are riddled with shot and we see the course of the wild duck as it plunges into the marsh of low financial returns, and slowly drowns.

From the middle of September, 1952, to April, 1953, about 140 plays, including revivals, were presented in Paris. Of course, I do not include in this figure the plays presented in the National Theatres (Comédie Française and Salle Luxembourg). These theatres are obliged to produce, alternately, plays from the classical and modern repertories, whatever the box-office returns may be. This ruling is enforced by law and its essential aim is to revive daily some great work from the past or from modern times. In the case, however, of a play that is a great success, the rule of alternating is relaxed. When this is the case, the fullest possible number of performances is given. I shall speak shortly of some of the successful plays that were presented this Winter and Spring at these finest French theatres.

Naturally, I have not seen all 140 productions. Moreover, the aim of this article is to give a lively picture of the 1952-53 Paris season, citing the plays which seem to me most worthy of note, rather than drawing up theatre statistics.

In Paris, in September, the majority of theatres are still closed. The season opens generally between October 1st and 15th.

We hail first an old master: Sacha Guitry, who opened the season on October 1st at the Théâtre des Variétés, a theatre which is even more illustrious than Sacha and infinitely older, for it dates from the eighteenth century; but it is still luxurious and velvet-lined, sumptuous as a dark rose and probably eternal. How can I convey the impression the play made on me without being unkind? The play was entitled *"N'Ecoutez pas Mesdames"* (Don't Listen,

Ladies). Does this imply that there was gossip about them? In any case, the gossip was not ill-natured. Was this thin old gentleman with his long wristbands, this wooden silhouette moving beneath the lights, with a faraway look and an air of ironic disillusion —was this the man who held Parisian theatregoers spellbound for so many years? All the same, this strange person who seemed to step straight out of 1913, a witness of worm-eaten days, has retained admirable vitality. He makes films, writes comedies, produces them and plays in them. The only thing he no longer tries to do is marry again. One feels respect for a writer who has been the flower of an excellent, artificial, slightly intoxicating theatrical genre, today bitter and outworn.

On the next day, October 2nd, Marcel Achard showed us what he can do for our entertainment at the Théâtre Antoine by conducting us with *"Les Compagnons de la Marjolaine"* (The Companions of Marjolaine) into the world of gendarmes in 1890. Gendarmes, in France, form a sort of military police whose duty it is to keep watch over the civilian population. In those days, they wore enormous cocked hats with silver braiding, large boots and swords. Corporal Lecoq, very much in love with his wife Cora, lives in a sleepy village which promises little chance of his being promoted. The murder of the squire seems to Lecoq to be the chance of a lifetime, particularly as he suspects the squire's wife. But the investigation he makes with awkward zeal brings Cora's gallant past to light in an unexpected way and there is more to follow. In spite of a few good satirical and poetic scenes, the resulting rustic, comic, sentimental police imbroglio did not arouse much enthusiasm. The tedious ending made one suspect that the author no longer had faith in policemen's hats as a source of inspiration. Splendidly played by two leading actors, Mme. Arletty and M. Bernard Blier, Marcel Achard's comedy held the stage for three and a half months.

On October 3rd, the Théâtre Saint-Georges presented *"La Dame de Trèfle"* (The Queen of Clubs) by Gabriel Arout, a daring play, the theme of which was the resemblance between a much-loved woman and a prostitute encountered in a bordello. Is the prostitute the woman the hero loves? Is he the victim of a frightful deception or a chance resemblance? The truth continually escapes him and he finally strangles the prostitute, only to learn on returning home that the woman he loves has left on a voyage. He will never hear anything more about her. This play appealed to me. It ran for four or five months.

There was a day's respite and then Marguerite Jamois presented Robinson Jeffers' tragedy "Medea." After Pitoeff, death carried off

in a short space of time Charles Dullin, Louis Jouvet and Gaston
Baty, so that of the four great artists of the Cartel, none remains.
Marguerite Jamois, discovered by Baty, was always his star and
later succeeded him in the management of the Théâtre Montparnasse. Will this fine theatre, sober, mysterious, tinged with melancholy, remain what it has been, the palace of great works, of striking
décor and enchanted lighting? We live in an age when it is difficult
to present classical tragedy without a large official subsidy. Although
the French government does all it can in this field, it cannot compel
the theatre-going public to rush to hear the recital of legendary
crimes they know by heart. Robinson Jeffers has written a flawless
text, full of wild clear poetry that one feels, even through the translation. Like Judith Anderson, Marguerite Jamois was equal to the
play. The lovely Asiatic viper kills with the ferocity, and in a way,
with the innocence of a wild beast caught in the trap of men. A
critic said of the actress that her interpretation was not modern
enough. Should she have played the part of the Fury as if she were
indulging in small talk at the hairdresser's? Robinson Jeffers' play
closed at the end of six weeks.

October 18th, Edouard Bourdet's play *"Hyménée"* was revived at
the Théâtre de la Michodière. I wonder how a translator would
find the exact equivalent for this word. It suggests a society wedding in a smart church with expensive flowers and a certain snobbery. In this setting, we see the last romantic love of a man of forty-
five stifling beneath nuptial flowers that will silence its voice forever. He is in love with the bride to be, and their rendezvous in the
hall on the night preceding her wedding is described with great tact.
In her innocence, the young girl promises her suitor the consolation
of an unconsummated marriage. Of course she does not keep her
promise, for it sometimes happens that girls betray their lovers
through their husbands. Pierre Fresnay plays the part of the lover
and Yvonne Printemps the role of an invalid in love with him, who,
though smiling and gentle, does her utmost to hurt the man she
loves by her hypocrisy. The play leaves a strange impression of a
world already lost in time, already fossilized, as if seen through the
glass of an aquarium. In the green water of the prewar period the
characters seem to be incrusted with madrepores; they are ladies
and gentlemen leading a life which is much too easy, with servants
who are too well-trained. What gives the play its present old-fashioned air is that it is too well-written, too smart and too natural;
for this effect of naturalness so admirably imitated without a single
false note for two and a half hours, with scenes brilliantly handled
by a master who is highly critical of his work and says only what

need be said, this naturalness became gradually embarrassing and ended by giving the play an admirably polished but imperceptibly chilling character. *"Hyménée,"* a masterpiece of period theatre, and disciplined theatre, had a fine career: a full house for six months.

We move into the completely different world of the Mediterranean coast with *"Madame Filoumé,"* a Neapolitan play by an Italian author presented by the Théâtre de la Renaissance on October 28th. Blue sky, blazing sunshine, a balcony garden, a rococo drawing room. In the bright light and the warm shadow of this room an unusual adventure takes place. M. Filoumé's mistress, who has been ill for some time, pretends she is about to die. Distracted, M. Filoumé consents to marry her as the last sacrament. However, the dying woman is suddenly cured after this marriage *in extremis* and plans to take a long-meditated revenge on her husband. M. Filoumé took her in from the street and she has three children of whom she alone knows the fathers. What can a selfish old man do against a shrew who has won all legal rights for herself? The only solution left to him is to soften his heart and discover a vocation for fatherhood. Mme. Filoumé will never tell him which child or children are his. He will be obliged to leave them all he possesses, the more so as he loves all three of them equally. Extravagant presumption. Valentine Tessier was a picturesque and triumphant Madame Filoumé. The author did his best to persuade us that Madame Filoumé was always right; she remains nevertheless a frightening old woman. She got three months.

At the Comédie Française on November 5th, there was a new presentation of Molière's "Don Juan." This play, which is hardly ever staged, had tempted Louis Jouvet. I remember one of the wonderful settings composed of arcades built one upon the other in the style of a *"plaza de toros,"* and the final scene representing Don Juan's ultra-rococo Spanish tomb with his servant claiming his wages. The distant, icy courtesy of the hero suggested a hell lurking in the background and seeming to emanate from him. What mattered now Don Juan's effrontery and final gestures? One felt that he would sink into the abyss at any minute, like the poisoned wretches who still smiled and tried to attract the attention of pretty girls while death was devouring them. Some of the most beautiful and elegant women in Paris were in at the kill with an air of cold politeness. They were all sitting in the first row, their wax faces wearing fixed smiles, their diamonds sparkling cruelly in the darkness; and on gazing at these pretty heads stretched out towards the oldest misunderstanding in the world, one wondered who was the true executioner, they or Don Juan.

Alexis Minotis and Katina Paxinou

from "The Greek National Theatre"

On November 11th, a paraphrase of "Robinson Crusoe" by Jules Supervielle was put on at the Théâtre de l'Œuvre. Perhaps this charming play in three acts, the second of which was a great success, met an unjust fate. Or should one conclude that theatre is an art which demands powerful conflicts in comedy no less than in drama? And yet "Medea's" career has already ended after one month. Here we are again at the Théâtre Montparnasse on November 19th, this time to see *"La Puce à l'Oreille,"* a vaudeville piece by George Feydeau which met a happier fate than its predecessor. It should be observed, moreover, that "Medea" by Jean Anouilh at the Théâtre de l'Atelier met with the same sad fate as at Montparnasse. In this play there was no dramatic conflict whatsoever; apart from verbal violence, there was no action. The style was beautiful but dramatic construction seemed to have been neglected. The theatre took its revenge, and will indeed continue to ill-treat authors and producers until they understand that they must, first and foremost, lead their public by the hand without ever letting it go, must keep the play and audience moving together if their public isn't to rebel—protesting that it did not buy tickets to see a novel. This was the procedure of our masters, the classical writers; and it was for this reason, doubtless, that I visited the Comédie Française, among a crowd of familiar faces, to see the revival of "Mithridates" by Racine, a monument which has weathered the storms of three hundred years and still stands erect, showing no sign of wear. In this theatre, France's leading actors display their talents to the full and spectators are oblivious of time, despite the versification, the sometimes heavy phrases, the long rejoinders. "Mithridates" was a great success with Jean Yonnel, Jean Marais and Annie Ducaux in the leading roles.

On December 11th, the Théâtre de la Madeleine put on *"Hélène, ou La Joie de Vivre"* by André Roussin and Madeleine Gray, adapted from John Erskine's "Private Life of Helen of Troy." The famous legend, completely altered, is presented as seen through the eyes of the palace doorkeeper. Menelaus, returned from the ruins and carnage of Troy with his reconquered wife, is wholly in love with her again and allows her to follow her temperament of seductress without seeing what is going on beneath his eyes. The last scene, in which the doorkeeper recounts the end of the tale while the actors are silent and mime the action as he speaks, is hilarious and forms a highly comic innovation. The whole play has a rhythm and is written in a fine style. It was the success it deserved to be and is still playing as I write. Pierre Dux, Sophie Desmarets and Louis Ducreux play *"La Joie de Vivre"* in a sprightly fashion which is a true reflection of the title.

A new theatrical undertaking which has attracted much attention, is the Théâtre National Populaire directed by Jean Vilar. This theatre, which receives a state subsidy, seeks to present great theatrical works to popular audiences in the working-class suburbs of Paris and the larger provincial towns. This is an excellent principle, for the theatre needs closer contacts with the cinema-going public. But it is a principle which raises program problems, as *"Le Prince de Hombourg," "Le Cid"* and *"Mère Courage,"* Jean Vilar's choice of repertory has not always been judged a happy one. Certain critics have even been so hostile that Vilar's position as director was several times menaced. What was the idea behind the presentation of *"La Nouvelle Mandragore,"* a play by a new author who presumed to rewrite and rejuvenate Machiavelli's famous *Mandragora?* The action of the play, totally lacking in substance, unfolded in a mist of boredom. One may ask oneself, too, what lay behind the choice of *"Nuclea."* It also fell down on opening night and was never able to pick itself up again. People were surprised too that the director of the Popular Theatre did not present any plays by the famous contemporary French authors. All this has led to sarcastic quips that apparently nothing existed in the theatre until the day Jean Vilar and his disciples came onto the scene. This is not my suspicion, but it has been repeated by many people, and I merely mention it as germane to one of the season's important endeavors. Since the presentation of *"La Mandragore"* the Popular Theatre has put on two plays of a wholly different order of which I will speak later.

On January 13, 1953, one of the most famous comedies of Jules Romains was put on at the Salle Luxembourg (the second theatre of the Comédie Française). The play was called *"Monsieur Trouhadec saisi par la débauche."* It was a great success. It is the satirical story of an illustrious professor of geography at the Sorbonne, weighed down with years and honors, an old fossil who is cynical yet ingenuous, and still capable of passion. During a stay at Monte Carlo, circumstances lead him to become the friend of a retired burglar who takes him for a colleague; later, the conqueror of a ravishing actress; and by extraordinary luck, the winner of enormous sums at gambling. This farce, which at certain moments recalled Molière, delighted the public. In modern production one rarely comes across an author who creates realistic, striking characters. More importance is given nowadays to situations than to character-drawing, no doubt because it is easier to exploit an idea by technical means than to portray real characters. Jules Romains is the descendant of great theatre writers who have left their mark by creating characters who are not forgotten. His "Knock" and *"Le Trouhadec"* will remain in theatre repertory, I believe, because these two plays contain the essence of the theatre—well-delineated characters full of life and vigor.

The time has come to speak of a very great success—*"L'Heure Eblouissante,"* presented at the Théâtre Antoine on January 16th. Not that the play itself is as dazzling as the hour it recalls. Written by an Italian lady, adapted by a French author with mordant, quizzical humor, the play, in spite of its qualities of construction, might have received an honorable welcome and no more. But a heaven-sent stroke of luck came to its aid. Two actresses revealed great talent in this play—Jeanne Moreau and Suzanne Flon. Then a sudden attack of influenza forced Suzanne Flon to withdraw for a few days. Jeanne Moreau immediately proposed to play Suzanne Flon's part as well as her own. Though I in no way wish to suggest that a spirit of jealous rivalry existed between the two women, who are both charming, it seems natural to suppose that they were keen competitors. The whole circumstance passed off with perfect understanding on both sides; the one actress playing both roles, attracting great curiosity and receiving great applause, the other lying in bed and receiving consolatory bouquets. Shortly afterwards, Suzanne Flon was able to resume her part and the two actresses, both very much pleased, moved together down the highroad to success.

On February 24th, *"Pasiphaé,"* a poem by Henry de Montherlant, received its première at the Comédie Française and Marivaux's *"Le Jeu de l'Amour et du Hasard,"* was revived. The impressive blood-red décor and the remarkable interpretation of *"Pasiphaé"* were not enough to save the poem, but Marivaux's delightful comedy charmed the audience as it has done for two hundred years. Hélène Perdrière, a famous comedy actress and a new *"pensionnaire"* of the Comédie Française made her official début at this theatre, and was "borne to the heights" as we say in France.

I feel embarrassed at having to speak of *"Lorenzaccio,"* presented on February 28th by Jean Vilar, after the failure of *"La Mandragore."* For my own part, I cannot bear this play where the usually light and gracious Musset tried to compete with Shakespeare; moreover, it is difficult to accept a Florentine background in which everything looks dismal. The enormous black curtains, with a glimpse of cold blue sky, were in my opinion the opposite of anything Florence calls to mind. The play was well received, however, by the press.

On March 6th, at the Théâtre de l'Athénée was given the première of *"Sud,"* a play by the Franco-American writer Julien Green. The conclusions to be drawn from the opening night should serve as a lesson to all authors. Whatever the subject treated, it should be looked at squarely and dealt with clearly. Should the author, for one reason or another, not dare to present the subject with clearness enough for it to be understood, why write the play at all? The subject of *"Sud"* is striking and tragic: a Pole, who is a naturalized American and a Union officer at the outbreak of the Civil War, discovers that he is capable only of abnormal relationships. The young man in whom he is interested is wholly chaste; he is not even aware of the atrocious passion he begets. I use the word "atrocious," for the configuration of inborn vice and innate purity creates for the hero of the story a harsh dilemma. He challenges the pure young man to a duel and allows himself to be killed. Had this subject which opens the doors of a mental hell, had this tragedy of a soul been fully treated in all honesty, the audience would doubtless have been moved. As it was, Julien Green's exceptional discretion led him to such secrecy that the audience did not understand what the play was about—particularly as the true subject lay hidden behind two girls who for no apparent reason occupied the foreground. It was only after the opening night that the author agreed to clarify his intentions. This excess of prudence was almost fatal to him, but the play was able to continue because of the curiosity it aroused.

The time has now come to devote a special paragraph to the fate of American plays produced in Paris. After the presentation of "A Streetcar Named Desire" the other works of Tennessee Williams were awaited with interest. "The Rose Tattoo" was received very favorably, though it was presented in a much smaller theatre and by a cast with fewer big names. As I write, the play is continuing a satisfactory run, though its box-office success cannot be compared with that of "Streetcar." "The Heiress," again, was very well received and had a very long run. "The Fourposter" has just been put on in an adaptation by Colette. This skillful play also pleased the public, perhaps on account of the acting. An interesting experiment served to raise the question of doing American plays in English in Paris. One cannot say "The Glass Menagerie," presented by Mr. Arthur Klein at the Théâtre de Rochefort was a financial success, but the critics who understand English all went to see the play, and on the whole, the press reports were good. Earlier attempts of the same kind had had to be abandoned, chiefly because the English-speaking public in Paris is either not big enough or not interested enough in seeing plays in their own language. But "The Glass

Menagerie" ran for a fortnight.   Mr. Klein, moreover, has decided
to organize a tour in Switzerland, Belgium, Luxembourg and Germany and to give performances for university audiences in these
countries.   In the future, other companies may be able to pay their
way if Paris is regarded as a first stop.   I am speaking only of
plays; for with such musical comedies as "Porgy and Bess" and the
ballet productions of the American National Ballet Theatre, there
are no such difficulties.   Theatres fill to overflowing for these performances, exactly as they would for French productions.

On April 16th, the première of André Obey's play *"Une Fille pour
du Vent"* took place at the Comédie Française.   It is difficult to
imagine what evil genius persuaded the author to try to rewrite the
story of the sacrifice of Iphigenia offered up to death by her own
father in order that the Greek ships may move against Troy.   The
subject of this new play seems to be the blind stupidity and credulity
of men face to face with slogans advocating war and destruction.
But the play is nothing more than a heap of shoddy and trivial writing, the aim of which was doubtless to "be modern" in the most
outmoded fashion.   The play was booed and failed almost immediately.

There followed a delightful evening, thanks to Jean Vilar and his
Théâtre National Populaire—*"La Mort de Danton,"* by the nineteenth century German author, Buchner.   A magnificent fresco depicting the French Revolution and the Reign of Terror, with passages
full of anguished melancholy, human voices rising from the depths of
the abyss, wild songs and laughter, mighty shouts of fallen fighters,
voices broken by the sorrow of the world.   Buchner has been criti-
cized for having replaced the prodigious, authentic words of Danton,
Robespierre and Saint-Just with speeches of his own.   It is indeed
difficult to express the thoughts of these great men better than they
did themselves; but one must try to put oneself in the place of the
author swept away by the torrent of his subject, and himself inspired.   Moreover, if the author had put faithful quotations into his
text, would they not have been at variance with his own style?   I
feel that Buchner was right to sacrifice sublime and all-too-well-
known phrases and to keep only a few of great power which were
truly apropos, such as Saint-Just's speech to the Convention.   Does
this fascinating epic wish to bring out the idea that, in the last resort,
the sacrifices men make in the name of their ideals have always
been in vain?   Not at all.   The final scene of the play, the steps
of the scaffold which Danton climbs after all his friends, do not lead
to nothingness.   They lead to other steps, towards other achievements, in the direction of other goals.   I do not know if the author

meant to suggest this with his beautiful conclusion, but this was the feeling it evoked in me as I gazed, at the end, at the guillotine standing erect on the deserted stage.

A fine enough theatre season in Paris, as you may see. We know that there must be a variety of dishes to please all the guests; but one should try to understand that from a financial point of view it is no greater gamble to offer powerful works that sweep the public along than plays that pander to what vulgar people imagine is the public's liking for vulgarity.

THE TIME OF THE CUCKOO *

A Comedy in Two Acts

By Arthur Laurents

[Arthur Laurents, *born in New York in 1918, received his B.A. from Cornell University. His professional career began with the writing of radio scripts, work which he continued to do even after joining the Army. "Home of the Brave," his first play, brought him a $1000-grant from the American Academy of Arts and Letters. Aside from this year's popular "The Time of the Cuckoo" he also wrote "The Bird Cage," produced in 1950.*]

(BOTH acts of the play take place in Venice, in summertime, in the garden of the Pensione Fioria.)

The garden of the Pensione Fioria is a green oasis of quiet (near the center of Venice) bordering on a small canal. A tree rises from the flagstone floor; a dining section is under a vine-covered arbor; a high stone wall is also trellised with leaves. This wall borders on one side a small Venetian canal, then turns to continue along the back of the garden. On the canal side the wall allows of a small door and three steps leading down to a gondola landing. Just above and beyond the corner of the wall is visible part of a small foot-bridge over the canal.

There is an entrance to the garden from the gondola landing, another from a little street beyond the garden wall, a third from the Pensione itself.

Signora Fioria and two of her American guests are sitting in the garden during the late afternoon. From the canal are heard cries of "Gondola! Gondola!" Nearer, the Pensione's maid sings in her happy strident voice.

The American couple impress one as being typically handsome, and typically American. The Yaegers, June and Eddie, try very much to conform to accepted ideals, but it is not always easy.

There are difficult moments caused by June's romantic love for her husband, that grants no lapses on his part. There are such lapses, some of them caused by her own insensitive reactions to his painting career; and some by his not conforming as much as he would like to the behavior expected of him.

Quite otherwise is Signora Fioria. An intelligent, perceptive, and sardonic woman in her forties. She has a thoroughly uncomplicated and unworried approach to sex. Her physical attractiveness is more in her body than in her face, and most of all in her manner.

Eddie is trying to drink his Cinzano lukewarm, and the Signora quietly smokes and sips her coffee. June does her nails, as she tries to learn all about Renaissance painting from a large book on the table in front of her. Suddenly, Signora bellows her maid's name, Giovanna, at just the moment that Eddie realizes he can learn to do without many things, but not without ice, while June discovers Tiziano is really Titian. The cry of the gondolier prompts June to remark to Eddie that he is not very ambitious.

EDDIE—You're talking to the wind. No one gets a rise out of me this evening.

JUNE—I meant the gondolier, honey.

FIORIA (*after a moment*)—Why don't you think he is ambitious?

JUNE—There's nothing but pensiones around here. Why doesn't he park or whatever they call it, over there by the big hotels like the Danieli or the Europa?

FIORIA—He likes it here.

JUNE—Not very ambitious.

EDDIE (*to* FIORIA)—You can't win.

FIORIA—I think that gondolier does quite well here anyway. Don't you, Mr. Eddie?

EDDIE (*glances at her, then gets up, stretching*)—Oh, there's always an American who can be hooked.

Giovanna, the sloppy but nice-looking maid, finally shuffles down the steps of the house, with two bowls in her outstretched hands. As she presents them to Eddie, she carefully explains in her own kind of English what they are. "LEM-MON," she says of the ice. "Ice!" she manages for the lemon. Corrected, she knows enough to say "To hell wit' English," and her carpet slippers flopping, she goes back into the house and resumes her singing.

The Yaegers busy themselves with their drinks and watch a woman cross the footbridge. She is well in her thirties, blondish, plump and pleasantly attractive. She carries a large shoulder bag,

a guidebook, a dictionary and one or two packages. Her name is
Leona Samish. As she calls out a greeting, Signora Fioria rises and
returns it. Leona announces with a laugh that she fell into a canal:
then she comes through the garden gate, laughs ruefully at herself,
and puts her parcels down. After introductions to Eddie are over,
he says, "You know my wife." Leona says sure she knows "cookie"
and goes on: "And you're the husband. Is there anyone on this
continent who isn't spoken for? It's like Noah's Ark: everybody
in twos and I'm Noah." Fioria then begs to know how in the
world she fell into a canal, and Leona explains: "Well—you may
not be aware of it, but you are looking at Leona Samish, Girl Tourist. I have to take a picture of everything. Even those bloody
pigeons in front of San Marco. And that was a narrow escape, too.
Anyway, this afternoon, I bought a goblet. Eighteenth-century
Venetian glass, fellas. The wildest dark rose. And the only one
left, damn it. I got it in a cute little shop—Di Rossi's." Signora
Fioria tells Leona that she should know Signor di Rossi, and apparently, Leona already does. The silver-gray hair has caught her
eye. At Eddie's insistence, Leona gets on with her tale of picture
taking:

LEONA—I wanted to get a picture of the shop where I bought the
goblet, but a plain simple picture wouldn't do. I never even owned
a Brownie before this trip, but I have to have composition in the
lousy picture. An authentic old Venetian church on one side and
an authentic old Venetian lady on the other. So—(*Acting it out
now.*)—I start backing up. I back up and up and right in back of
me was an authentic old Venetian canal. (*They laugh sadly; come
back to table.*) I felt so foolish.
FIORIA—But it happens.
EDDIE—Who fished you out?
LEONA—I have an admirer. A little monster has been following
me. The only male who has, I might add, and he's possibly a hot
ten if he's a day. The minute I got to that gondola landing yesterday, there he was: "Lire, Signorina, lire."

They all know Mauro, who wears enormous blue jeans, sings *Home
on the Range*, and has an unusually precocious business sense.

When June says that they must let Leona change into dry things,
Leona agrees, but would like to make sure they will be there when
she comes back. She'll only be a minute, she assures them, hurrying into the Pensione as another American couple come down the
steps. The McIlhennys are elderly tourists, and when June asks

them if they like Venice, Mr. McIlhenny tells Fioria "No disrespect intended, ma'am, but to me, it's just Luna Park on water." Mrs. McIlhenny tries to make up for this by explaining that they've really seen practically everything, and by tomorrow, they'll pick up the ends. When June suggests the large art exhibit at the Public Gardens, poor Mr. McIlhenny makes known his feelings on art— "If I have to look at one more painting, I'll yip." And made to feel he should apologize to Mrs. Yaeger, whose husband is an artist, he says that he's got bad feet for standing. For the last few months, the McIlhennys have been just about everywhere in Europe. Perhaps, Mrs. McIlhenny adds, they may have crowded things a bit, but her husband is firm in thinking his travel agency has done a crackerjack job in planning every single step of the way. To prove this, he shows their day's itinerary to Eddie, who reads: "Eight A.M.—breakfast; nine—Doge's Palace and Bridge of Sighs; 10 A.M.— San Marco Cathedral; 10:30-12:30—I. A." The I. A. stands for the two hours of "Independent Activity" that the travel bureau has allotted them. The whole trip, Mrs. McIlhenny says rather wistfully, has been lovely—not exactly what they had expected, perhaps—but, well, lovely.

Leona returns freshly turned out and eager that they all have a drink with her. But the McIlhennys are on their way to the restaurant assigned them for the evening. Mrs. McIlhenny remembers, however, to tell Leona about a jewelry shop that she is sure has garnets. "Garnets are my one passion," says Leona. "Well, garnets and people. And Venice and the Pensione Fioria and an evening like this." Mr. McIlhenny remarks that he can't drink because Wop food has ruined his digestion, and departs with his wife, leaving the others to apologize to their Italian hostess. Only Signora Fioria will have time for a drink, because the Yaegers are already late, and must go and dress. They'll take a rain check, Eddie says, as they go in.

Leona had rather thought that everyone ate in, at a pensione. But no—even Fioria is dining out with an old friend, one Signor Faustino who has been sophisticated enough to stay in the Italian government for the past fifteen years. But why did Leona ask if she were going out with Di Rossi? Leona says that she saw him in the piazza last night, and of course you couldn't miss that silvergray hair. Fioria, instead of leaving, sits a little while with Leona, who tries her best to show how truly independent she is. Occasionally, though, the loneliness creeps in as she describes her friends at home, and the young couple that reminded her of them on the boat, and then in her description of Paris: "Everything everybody

*José Perez,
Shirley Booth,
Dino DiLuca
and Lydia St.
Clair in "The
Time of the
Cuckoo"*

ever said, wrote, or sang about Paris is true. Except you shouldn't be allowed there unless you're in love. Paris is just laid out for it." Fioria says, "So is Venice." Leona agrees that that's true anywhere. But, she continues, she really doesn't know what she expected. Another American girl of indefinite age, that she met on a train, was waiting for something, too. Some "wonderful mystical magical miracle." "The bargains that some people expect on a hot six-week vacation." But she won't accept Fioria's kind invitation to dine with her and Signor Faustino.

FIORIA—When in Italy, you should meet Italians.
LEONA—Two's company.
FIORIA—Oh, Miss Samish! Signor Faustino and I are, oh, for several years now, we have been—ahh—(*Waves her hand, as though to pluck the word from the air.*)—unexcited.

Leona decides either to go to the concert, like last night, or perhaps to take a gondola. But Fioria advises against taking one alone. Tells her to wait. And she mustn't let Giovanna hurry her through dinner.

LEONA—Giovanna?
FIORIA—After sunset, she rushes around like an American. She has a friend: Alfredo. All day long, she is only recuperating from the night before.
LEONA—I should be so sick.

When Leona is left in the garden, she seems a little lost. When Giovanna comes, Leona jokes with her, then wanders to the table and sits down. She sips her drink, rummages around in her large bag for cigarettes, pulls out a pen and postcard. She starts to write to a married couple at home of the glories of Venice, and then she adds that if they were here, they would be a quartet: "Mio amico has silver-gray hair. . . ."

June interrupts this postcard-writing till Eddie joins her. They bid Leona good night as they go off to Harry's Bar. On impulse, Leona calls to them, "Say! Why don't I get it over with and give Harry his big break tonight?" The Yaegers are embarrassed and hesitate, and Leona catches on that she would be unwelcome. She quickly covers up, and gaily says good-by to them in Italian:

LEONA—Buona sera. Or do you say—what is it?—Ciao.
EDDIE—Well, you really say "ciao" to family and very close friends, otherwise, buona sera. Or—arrivederci.
LEONA—Oh. Arrivederci, Signor. Arrivederci, Signora."

And as they pass over the bridge, she picks up her glass, and salutes herself, with the intimate "Ciao." After Giovanna leaves her dinner tray, and departs, Leona is alone in the quiet garden. From the canal comes the soft cry, "Gondola! Gondola!"

Scene II

The heat of the afternoon sun has closed all shops and shutters in Venice, and the Yaegers are lying stretched out on canvas chairs in the Pensione's garden. Eddie has a hangover with resulting frayed temper and nerves, and his worries over not getting down to work make him, if possible, even more touchy. June's obtuseness is not helping matters. Has his art deteriorated from Museum quality to Christmas-card prettiness? June merely sighs with relief that this is what's bothering him. "Isn't that silly? I thought the trouble was all because of me." Eddie makes a muttered reply that sometimes he thinks "language is a means of excommunication." This is what goes on frequently between them. And June continues to make matters worse with "Eddie, I love you. It doesn't matter a hoot to me if you can't paint like you used to. I don't care if you paint at all. All I want is for you to be happy and to love me."

Leona finds them baking in the sun, eyes shut, and, apparently, peaceful. They hear her tiptoe past them, and at once try to make amends for their behavior the night before. Leona tries to brush off the apology, but as Eddie continues to explain, Mauro comes in from the gondola landing on the prowl for more lire from Leona. Instead Leona berates him for not taking her on a scheduled tour of the Academia. Mauro importantly dismisses this. Business kept him: "I work for my friend, de Gondolier. Every customer I bring, he pay me." This time, "the one shop in Venice that doesn't close in the afternoon" finds it almost impossible to sell anything to the lady; but Mauro does manage to snag a cigarette off her before he's chased away. Eddie then goes into the house, telling a hesitant June to follow. Before she does, she finishes her explanation of last night's lack of cordiality: "Those friends we were with— Well— she's a very rich American who collects art. The husband is a kind of Italian count. Eddie's here on a fellowship. The Contessa buys us drinks and dinner, and maybe when Eddie does a painting, she'll buy it. Oh, she's very nice. But she kind of doesn't like unattached women around." All of this embarrasses June, and she asks to see what Leona has in her box. Leona shows another eighteenth-century goblet from Di Rossi's. After admiring it, June starts to go in, and Leona, once more comfortable with the girl, asks if she might go swimming with them later. June tactfully says that if they decide to go they will certainly let her know.

Meanwhile Renato di Rossi has come over the bridge and gone into the calle behind the wall. Now, as Leona is re-packing her purchase from his shop, he enters the garden. Forty-odd, he is so charming that it wouldn't occur to anyone that he does not always tell the truth.

Leona is very much surprised and somewhat nervous to find he has come to see her. "Oh. (*Sits.*) Oh! You found some more of those glasses."

Di Rossi—Unfortunately, no. But perhaps there is something else I might find for you?

Leona—You don't happen to know a good black market in money?

Di Rossi—The best. And very legitimate. (Leona *laughs.*) But that's easy. Give me something difficult.

Leona—Why?

Di Rossi—So I can do it for you.

Then Leona explains that she has been trying to find some garnets. She has some difficulty in explaining what "garnets" are. When at last he understands, he says that there aren't many left in Venice. In reply to Leona's saying he mustn't go to any trouble, he answers, "For you, it is not trouble."

Leona—Signor di Rossi, why did you come to see me?

Di Rossi—It is only natural. After all, you are not going to keep buying glasses every day.

Leona—No.

Di Rossi—So—I came.

Leona—But why?

Di Rossi—Why? You knew I would.

Leona—I did not!

Di Rossi—Maybe it's my English.

Leona—Maybe it's mine. (*Turns away.*)

Di Rossi—Listen. Two nights ago, I am in Piazza San Marco. You are in Piazza San Marco. We look. Next day, you are in my shop. We talk about glasses, we talk about Venice. You like Venice? I like Venice.

Leona—Molto bella.

Di Rossi—Si, molto bella. I understand your jokes. Ecco. We talk about Venice, glasses, but we are not speaking about them, are we? No. So, last night, I am in Piazza San Marco again, you are in Piazza San Marco again.

And although Leona insists that half of Venice is in the piazza each night, Di Rossi answers that they are not, however, in his shop next morning. And if the only reason for Leona's coming there was for glass, how did it happen that she had not searched elsewhere in Venice? Leona is quite shaken by his directness and speed in getting to the point. He finds her simpatica, and wishes her to have coffee with him. But she wants to be sure that he doesn't take her for a rich American, and tries to explain this as clearly as possible. It is not too easy, but Di Rossi on the whole understands even if he misses a word here and there: "You say you are not rich, and if that is why I am here, I am making an error. You do not know me very well yet, Signorina, so you are not insulting me. But yourself you know . . . then why do you insult yourself?" Leona still can't believe what is happening; Di Rossi makes it doubly clear by telling her that she attracts him.

The package-laden McIlhennys arrive just at this moment, and after introductions are made, and Mrs. McIlhenny chirps her "come sta?" at Di Rossi—(thus exhausting her Italian)—she must show off some of her loot. They have been at a glass blowing place near San Marco, and she unwraps just one package. This contains a goblet identical with Leona's, and it cost Mrs. McIlhenny 2100 lire.

The McIlhennys go into the house, leaving behind an angry and suspicious Leona.

DI ROSSI—I did not run out and have that glass made for you.
LEONA—Of course not. It's eighteenth century, cookie!
DI ROSSI—Do not call me "cookie"!
LEONA—It's politer than some other names that come to mind.

Di Rossi has some difficulty in convincing Leona that he is not trying to sell her anything, that he only wants to be with her, and to know her better. Because "what happens after that, happens— or does not happen." She melts a little, gives in, and accepts his invitation for that evening.

After Di Rossi crosses the footbridge, Fioria, the usual cigarette dangling, comes out of the Pensione, and watches Leona wrap her goblet. Signora admires it politely, and when Leona begs to know if it's eighteenth century, Fioria takes it in her hand for a closer look. "Yes, it is. (*Shrugs as she hands it back.*) But it is so lovely, what is the difference?"

Scene III

In the twilit garden a young man smokes and listens to far-off music, as he waits for Leona. When she comes out of the Pensione, she is surprised to see the young salesman from Di Rossi's shop, who has come not with more glasses but with a message from Di Rossi that he will be late. Leona makes conversation with the young man over an American cigarette, which he thinks is "marvelous," like everything American, including Americans: they all have money. She asks the young man questions about Di Rossi, who, she learns, is very fond of her, and can only be late for his date because he is such a devoted father. He is an excellent father to a large number of children, the youngest of whom he took to the Doctor, the oldest of whom, Vito, is now speaking to Leona. Leona then learns that there is also a wife who is in splendid shape. This is more than she had bargained for, and she angrily tells Vito that his father must not come. The boy says that Di Rossi will be very disappointed; but Mama, Leona says, will be very glad. Vito is perplexed by this, and Leona blurts out: "I just don't understand anything, not a thing!" Vito is sure that his father could explain it all, but Leona wants none of that, and repeats that Di Rossi must not come.

The boy leaves; Giovanna comes into the garden to clear tables, and tells Leona that there has been some trouble upstairs. The Yaegers, apparently, have had a row. June enters just in time to hear the maid's version of it, in which her tears and his anger are featured. She tries to brush it off as exaggerated; but she admits that this marriage seems to be going the same way as her previous one to a saxophone player. "It was just as lovely in the beginning with Skipper. I must do something because all of a sudden with him, too, everything went crazy. If he wasn't playing cards all night, he was drinking. So I cleared out."

LEONA—Why?

JUNE—A man does things like that he doesn't love you enough. I have to be everything to someone I love.

Leona is highly irritated over this and advises June that she asks too much and should not push her luck too far. But she softens towards the girl, and asks her to have a drink with her, to get her husband, and they'll all go to Harry's Bar. But it seems that when the Yaegers have fights, each goes his own way for a while. June always picks a movie, any movie, and that's where she is going now. Leona doesn't promise to go with her, but says she will walk along and see what's playing.

Fioria, always managing to be on hand after one of the Yaegers' fights, sees the two go out the garden entrance, and settles herself at a table to wait for Eddie. When he comes he spars with her briefly, then makes the accusation: "You think after a fight, I'll be available." Fioria blandly replies, "I think after a fight you may be available. You were once before"—and that time had been very pleasant for them both. Eddie agrees, but still insists that she should know he doesn't love her. This is of no concern to Fioria, who laughs that Americans worry about the most idiotic things; all she is asking is for him to run the risk of some trouble with his wife, not to feel guilty, and to enjoy himself so that she may enjoy herself. Mauro is hailed, and comes from the gondola-landing to ask whether they wish a gondola once again. He then holds the gate open for them, and Eddie and Fioria step through together.

They are observed by a shocked Leona who has returned to the garden, and by Di Rossi as he comes over the footbridge. Leona savagely attacks a grinning Mauro as he comes back into the garden counting his share of the gondolier's take. Mauro is only saved from Leona's wrath by Di Rossi's prompt interference and soothing "Va bene—va bene." But he doesn't understand why his friend should so suddenly turn on him. Finally, Leona accepts his "I work, I get pay—" and tells him she's sorry, and wins him over with a Chesterfield. But as he leaves, she admits that she can't accept what happens to Venice at night.

Di Rossi—Are you going to be angry at Venice now? Your friend Eddie would do the same thing in Kansas City.

Leona—Not in a gondola.

Di Rossi—That is an advantage of Venice. Miss Samish, you were shocked.

She won't admit to being shocked, she says that it's the dishonesty that she doesn't like. Dishonesty of any kind, including Di Rossi's lying about his son. And she won't accept vanity as an excuse, either. It wasn't that the son was grown-up, it was the bald fact of Di Rossi's being married that put her off, and he knew it would. And she adds, indicating the canal, that it's not surprising that he approves of that "Albany night boat."

Then, as with Fioria and Eddie, the difference between the American and Italian attitude emerges. Says Di Rossi: "It is what we do but not what you do. It is neither right nor wrong. Right and wrong do not exist in the air, Miss Samish!" An angry Leona answers: "Pretending anything is fine and dandy just because you want to do it." That allows Di Rossi to retort: "It is fine to *do* as long as you feel bad about doing it. You Americans go so on and on about the sex."

LEONA—We don't take it lightly.
DI ROSSI—Take it, don't talk it!

However, he bridles when Leona suggests that then his own wife might behave like Fioria? Of course not! She is a mother! So Leona momentarily has made a point. But Di Rossi tells Leona that she will never find romance by being romantic about it. He well knows what she dreams of in Venice: a rich, handsome young nobleman, who is unmarried.

DI ROSSI—Well, I am a shopkeeper. Not handsome. Not rich, not young, not witty, not brilliant. No title—no gondola. And not unmarried. But, Miss Samish, I am a man, and I want you. But you? "It's wrong, it's wicked, it's this, it's that." You are a hungry child to whom someone brings ravioli. "But I don't want ravioli, I want beefsteak!" You are hungry, Miss Samish. Eat the ravioli!

Leona confesses that it isn't at all the way she thought it would be, and the world that she comes from is so very different. But if only she could be sure that he really wants her, for she wants someone so badly. Di Rossi tells her, "And I, too." He pulls her into his arms and kisses her hard, then he gently releases her with: "For a lady from a different world you do that very well."

Since it is now too late for coffee, and almost too late for the concert on the piazza, Leona suggests that they go to Harry's Bar, that she has enough money for both of them. Di Rossi objects, because he does not want her to think that he is interested only in her money, but Leona says that she's "given up thinking for Lent" and hands Di Rossi enough lire to take care of a fairly gay evening. He compliments her on her trying hard to be her idea of a Venetian. Leona agrees: "Yes, I'm trying. Mama used to say: 'Enjoy yourself, it's too late already.'" And with his assurance that she is not ravioli—though he likes ravioli—Leona takes Di Rossi's arm and they set forth.

ACT II

It is late afternoon, but the garden still glows with sunlight, as Leona and Fioria have drinks at a table near the canal wall.

Leona is saying how pleased she is with Di Rossi's legitimate black-market man, who gave her an unusually good rate of exchange. In fact, she is so pleased with life in general that she hasn't bothered to do any sightseeing all day. But some of the problems of an American in Italy still trouble her, such as Fioria's advice not to make things hard for herself: "It'd be great if you could come here from America with nothing but a suitcase. But—you don't come over that way." And to Fioria's saying that if Leona saw Di Rossi last night, and will again tonight, this must be her "miracle magical," she answers: "Not quite, I used to think when I fell in love, I'd hear a waltz. No waltz, Signora—" Merely because he is not what she hoped for? Fioria is impatient with such a view and declares that since everything is imperfect, is one to have nothing? "Stop looking at the moon. Look at *here*. See the things as they are and make from them the best you can."

LEONA—Yes, the *best*.
FIORIA—Indeed the best; only a squanderer takes anything.

The Yaegers, who come into the garden, a happy arm-in-arm pair, point up this discussion with one of their own, when they are left to themselves. June thinks that it might be better if Leona's date didn't show up; but Eddie wants her to live up her vacation. And with Di Rossi as a starting point, they air their ideas on infidelity. June insists that Di Rossi can't love his wife if he is so willing to hurt her by chasing Leona; Eddie, on the other hand, finds proof that what a wife doesn't know doesn't hurt her.

EDDIE—Did you know I was unfaithful last night?
JUNE—Sure.
EDDIE—You did not.

And they have their joke about the many signorinas that Eddie was out with "last night," then Eddie suddenly tells June that he loves her.

JUNE—Then tell me what you really did last night. What's so funny?

EDDIE—You. If I say I don't love you, you say I'm in a bad mood. If I say I do love you, you say: What did you do last night?

and June, half jokingly, insists on knowing exactly what he was up to. Eddie truthfully tells her that he picked up a very intelligent brunette, and was unfaithful to June, even though he loves her. June doesn't believe the story.

EDDIE—What would you do if I were unfaithful?
JUNE—Kill you. No. Kill her and maybe you. . . . Die, I guess.
EDDIE—It wouldn't mean I didn't love you.
JUNE—It'd mean you didn't love me enough.
EDDIE—Then I guess I don't love you enough.

This is no longer fun for June, and she asks Eddie to stop his kidding. Then, she lies back in the canvas chair, untouched, unworried, and content. And when Leona comes out to call Eddie to the telephone saying the Contessa wishes to speak to him, June purrs to Leona about her day with Eddie, about every day and night with him. To Leona, who has heard nothing from Di Rossi, all this is a further source of irritation. After the Yaegers leave to avoid the importunate Contessa, Leona calls for Giovanna, and when the girl doesn't appear because she is again answering the phone, Leona becomes quite angry and calls loudly for her. When at last she appears, Leona's tone becomes pleading. Has there been no message for her? Giovanna appears not to understand. Leona in desperation acts out a charade for Giovanna. She imitates the ring of the telephone, and Giovanna leaving her cleaning to answer. Then she imitates herself, singing and soaping away in the bath; and Giovanna's charging up the stairs, knocking at Leona's door, and getting no answer. So, down she lunges to the phone to tell Di Rossi, "No, no Signorina Samish." The performance receives delighted applause from Giovanna, but there has been no message. Says Leona: "For me no Signor di Rossi. For me no signor. . . . Well, what's so special about Venice? But he should've called, and he should've come. It's not fair, Giovanna. Everybody's got someone, it's not fair! Why can't I? Why can't it be? It doesn't have to be perfect, just a little, just a little is all I—" and she stops dead, for Di Rossi is actually coming into the garden. Giovanna with affectionate happiness watches Di Rossi apologize for being so late, and kiss Leona's hand. Then she quietly goes into the Pensione.
Di Rossi explains that never has he had to bargain so hard or so

long, as he takes a parcel from his pocket. And, to a stunned Leona, he describes the trouble he has had with Signor Papini over this garnet necklace. "But it was worth it, yes? (*He holds up the necklace;* LEONA *stares at it.*) It is *granate*, Leona. Garnets. Don't you like it? (*She has been trembling and now she bursts into tears and runs into his arms.*) Oh, Leona . . . Carissima! (*He kisses her hair, caresses her back, as she cries.*) What did you say? I can't hear you. . . . What? (*He smiles tenderly and holds her close.*) Ah, mia cara. I am happy, too!"

SCENE II

Leona is giving a cocktail party at the Pensione. The garden, decorated with lanterns and lights, is very festive and the guests are very festive, too. Everyone thinks everyone else is charming and gay, as they watch a reluctant Mauro push a drunken Giovanna about in imitation of a dance. Everyone is drinking martinis, except Mauro, who is working on the antipasto, instead. Leona comes out of the house with another large tray of hors d'œuvres; she is dressed to the nines, sporting her new necklace and a fine edge. To each of the guests, she says, "You're charming" and shows off her necklace, then, "Now you really are charming. Did I tell you who gave it to me?"

EDDIE *and* JUNE—Uh-huh.
LEONA (*to* DI ROSSI)—Did I thank you for it?
DI ROSSI—Not in the last ten minutes.
LEONA—Scusami.
DI ROSSI—English! English!
FIORIA—Your own rules.
LEONA—Pardon, pardon. (*Going to* DI ROSSI.) I'll thank you. (*Kisses him.*) Thank you. You know I'm easily the most charming person here.

Leona wants Mauro and Giovanna to give an encore, but Giovanna gets up with much difficulty from a prone position on the ground, and loops into the house calling for her "Alfredo." Then when Mauro proves too shy to dance with Leona, the hostess dances over to Di Rossi, holding out her arms. "Cookie wants to dance. Signor? I mean Monsieur?" Di Rossi takes her in his arms and they dance closely. Leona wants to go riding in a gondola later on. June calls out, "Oh, yes! Can we come?"

LEONA—No. (*They dance.*)

JUNE—What a hostess! (*To* EDDIE *and* FIORIA.) The hell with them. Let us get our own gondola. (FIORIA *breaks into laughter.*) What's so funny?

June elegantly snubs the two of them, and discovers Vito standing at the garden gate. Although Leona is much embarrassed at having Di Rossi's son at her party, she goes the rounds with him, wise-cracking that he's big for his age. But Di Rossi is disturbed for other reasons. Vito tells his father that Signor Papini is waiting right outside the gate, and he won't wait until tomorrow for his money. He's either to have it tonight, or he'll have his garnets back. Di Rossi tries to brush this off but cannot. After a considerable pause, Leona, wretchedly humiliated, tells him, "You're too charming," and gets her purse.

LEONA—This is the first time I've felt at home in Venice. Cookie, it happens every day in America. We invented it: the installment plan and the installment man—

and she asks how much is needed.

DI ROSSI—Most, I have paid.

LEONA—How much more?

Di Rossi tells her there is still a balance of ten thousand, and Leona snaps that it's worth it at half the price, and gives Vito the necessary bank notes. Di Rossi tries to thank Leona, and says he will repay her tomorrow, but as he takes her hand, she can't look at him. And when shortly after, Vito returns, Leona gulps down another martini, feeling that there is more nastiness to come. And she is right, for Signor Papini won't accept her lire. It's not good money. Leona cries out: "All that lovely legitimate money you got for me?" and draws away from everyone. Di Rossi frantically looks at each bill, but except for the first two, they are all counterfeit. Several times he tries to muster up enough English to speak to Leona, but he can't, and furthermore she won't let him.

Leona is ready to have her say. She first yells to Eddie to turn the damn music off, and when Di Rossi says that he'll see the black-market man tomorrow, Leona lets loose with: "Why not tonight? Why don't you talk to him now? Why don't you turn your charm on him? *Why don't you go?*" and over Di Rossi's shocked protests,

Leona says that she's had all the ravioli talk that she's going to.
"Why weren't you smarter? Why couldn't you have managed it so
I wouldn't know? Why didn't you ask? Why didn't you steal?
Why didn't you let me alone? Why did you tell me lies you knew
I wanted to hear?"

DI ROSSI—Not lies! Era vero, era vero! Tutto quello che ho
detta.
LEONA—English! English!
DI ROSSI—I cannot in English!
LEONA—No. You couldn't in Italian!
DI ROSSI—If I only want money, there is many tourist richer
than you!
LEONA—Maybe you had to take what you could get, like the
rest of us!
DI ROSSI—What are you doing to us? This is ugly and stupid!
I . . .

He asks to be forgiven, and since Leona won't listen he leaves. But
Leona still shouts after him, and then retreats once more and sits
by herself, until the hurt and the drink make her burst out again.
This time she turns on her guests: why don't they laugh at her instead of being so tactful? "I think I'm hilarious. First I coy
around like a sixteen-year-old: 'Look at the necklace cookie got
for a present.' Then I have to buy the present myself. Then it
turns out my money is phony. That's highly comical. *Why don't
you laugh?*" And when June says she doesn't think it's funny,
Eddie says exactly the wrong thing to Leona: "I don't think it's
tragic either." She lets fly with: "Considering your voyage the
other night, I don't think we'd agree on what's funny or tragic."
Leona's last pleasant gesture is telling Mauro to run along and
take a platter of hors d'œuvres with him. From that moment on
she's out to make trouble: she dots any i's that need dotting in
Eddie and Fioria's affair, and causes June to cry out despairingly
and run into the house. Eddie can do nothing but follow. Only
then does she realize how much damage she has done, and she tries
to excuse herself and apologize, but Fioria won't let her get away
with this: "You were hurt? By yourself! You threw out Di Rossi!
He only wants money? You think so because you think so much
of money and so little of yourself. I am older; I have half as much
money; but I have twice as much men! They do not think of
money because I do not think of money. And if in a few years they

do, I will not throw them out. Oh, that is crude, vulgar, immoral, anh? You know why you threw out Di Rossi? Because he is not your dream of perfection. That dream, that ideal, does not exist, Miss Samish. It never did, it never will! And never this way!" and she leaves Leona with the comment, that since she was the hostess, she should clean up the mess.

Leona is angry, drunken, self-pitying; and she tells herself many maudlin things, and finally bursts into tears: "Oh, why couldn't you love me, Renato? Why couldn't you even just say you loved me?"

Scene III

It is the morning after and Eddie, Fioria and Di Rossi are having a breakfast post-mortem in the garden. Di Rossi tactfully leaves for the house, as the other two edgily discuss the end of their affair.

Though Fioria tells Eddie that she refuses to mourn in silence, she will not join the chorus of "Love-me-want-me-give-me" even though it means ending up with her Signor Faustino. Eddie tries to defend his actions by arguing, "If you really love, how can you be unfaithful?" To which Fioria realistically replies: "I think perhaps your way is to shut your eyes and pretend you are living the ideal." Whereas she accepts the here and now, and makes it a little sweeter.

A very neat and tidy June comes quietly into the garden, but hesitates on the steps when she sees the two together. Di Rossi follows from the house, and thus eases things. June not only has had her coffee upstairs, but she has packed the Yaeger clothes for a move to the Contessa's. Eddie not being about, she had accepted an invitation from the lady that morning. Her reasons were that they would be saving money, that Eddie would have a fine studio, and if it didn't work out, they needn't stay. Eddie is startled, and thinks that June is trying to get even with him; but after a minute he agrees that it is a sensible thing to do.

Leona, scared to death to meet the others, has to be urged to come out of the house. Everyone makes it as easy as they can for her. She just feels terrible, without a hangover. And when Eddie goes in to pack the final carton, and she finds out that the Yaegers are moving away, she again becomes aware of what she did the night before. June consoles her in a new grown-up way. "It wasn't you or anyone else . . . If he weren't upset about his work, there wouldn't have been a thing . . ."

Leona is grateful, but turns to Fioria: "I can clear a house quicker than mumps—I'm great for business." Fioria doesn't console her, merely states that Leona only made it happen one day sooner. Other guests are to arrive that afternoon and the following day; and bellowing for Giovanna, she enters the Pensione.

An embarrassed Leona has finally to face Di Rossi alone. He first of all reports that the black-market man will make good. Then, in reply to the feelers that Leona puts out, he shows that he now is only a "friend." Leona won't let go: "Because of seventeen dollars —because I was so stupid to let it matter, you mustn't." But he must. He feels much too old and tired for this kind of thing, and she is too complicated for him. "We do not live very long but all this arguments, this explaining, this convincing, Leona, make life even shorter." It is truly too much for Di Rossi.

Leona tries to joke in her usual way, but when Di Rossi says that it would be wise to return the necklace to Papini, she despairingly insists on keeping it, even if she must pay for it. "I've got to take something home from Europe!" And this makes Di Rossi lash back, "And of course, it must be something you can touch. That is so important! Do you know, my dear, the one time, the only one time when you were not suspicious of me? When I gave you that necklace!" Leona pleads with him, she doesn't blame him for being insulted, and she won't be complicated any more. Di Rossi is sorry, but in spite of all the love Leona offers, he can't respond. "The feeling" has gone for him. So what can he do? "Niete, cookie. Niete, at all." And Mauro, returning Fioria's platter, finds them stonily standing there.

Mauro goes into the house, and they say the good-bys that are left to them. Leona begs to know whether Di Rossi ever really wanted her, and he gently assures her, "I am a man who cannot find a pleasure without affection. For you, I shall always have affection." He kisses her hand and says his "Addio." Leona watches him leave; raises the hand he kissed to her cheek; weeps softly.

Mauro runs out of the house and seeing her, doesn't know what to do. When he suggests showing her the Accademia, she doesn't think she wants to do anything but return home. When the boy hears that she is going back to America, he fishes out a Parker 51, and Leona as automatically refuses to take it.

MAURO—But this no cost you nothing. Is from me. Present.
LEONA—Why?
MAURO—Ah, Lady . . .

Leona hugs Mauro to her, and tells him: "Maybe some day I'll just say thank you. O.K., we go to Accademia."

MAURO—Accademia molta bella!
LEONA—Si. In Italy, everything molta bella.

And she tries to smile again.

BERNADINE *

A Comedy in Two Acts

By Mary Chase

[Mary Coyle Chase, *whose "Bernadine" delighted audiences this season, began her career in her native Denver as a special writer for the* Rocky Mountain News, *of which her husband is city editor. Her first play, "Now You've Done It," produced in New York in 1937, made no particular impression, but when "Harvey" came along in 1944 it fully established Miss Chase on Broadway. "Harvey" won the Pulitzer prize and ran for 1775 performances. Her "Mrs. McThing" (which was one of the Ten Best in last year's* Best Plays) *is still serving as a touring vehicle for Helen Hayes.*]

IN a short prologue, a young man in airforce uniform, Arthur Beaumont, tells about his old high school gang, and the 3.2 beer joint they used to frequent. Grown-ups went to the Shamrock, too, but could never really enter the world the boys had created for themselves in its back room.

ACT I

On a Spring afternoon, when the gang is shoving off for the Shamrock Bar, a couple of sixteen-year-olds are dying to tag along with T-shirted, H-lettered members Carney and Olson. Doing their best to sound big, the youngsters brag of knowing the head of the gang, Beaumont (Mac says he even speaks to him), and of how much money they have (Gibbs says he has three dollars), and how Mac's father is going to have a secondhand Plymouth (real soon). Carney tries to show Gibbs that his blowing is all off-key, in contrast to Mac's behavior which is comme il faut.

CARNEY—Never slap it down like that. If you see a chance to slide it in, slide it in. But otherwise—

When the four boys arrive at the door of the Shamrock, Carney is still trying to show Gibbs the error of his ways. The boys are seen by Wormy Weldy's mother, Ruth, and Jean Cantrick's mother, Selma. Ruth delivers a critical, albeit sentimental pronouncement on youth, at the same time that Carney paints for Gibbs a discouraging future if he continues the way he's heading. And Olson adds his analysis of the whole thing: "In this world, Gibbs, there's big wheels and there's twinks. . . . There's ugh me fixes . . . take your pick."

Jean Cantrick, known to the boys as the sharpest babe in town, arrives, shirttails flying out of her blue jeans, full of orders for her mother to hurry up. Selma dutifully goes off with Jean, after accepting a cocktail invitation from Ruth to meet her old friend, Enid Lacey.

At this point, Buford Weldy, out to meet the boys, meets his mother instead, and is marched off on a shopping trip.

Scene II

In the back room of the Shamrock, Tub, Fudge, and Beau are lolling around listening to a juke-box version of *Memphis Blues*, and arguing the merits of Migsy Spanier, when Carney and Olson enter, tailed by the eager younger boys. Beaumont greets the younger boys languidly, and allows them to remain on probation, which is immediately violated by Gibbs. He can't be hushed up or snubbed.

Gibbs (*to* Beaumont)—My dad says your dad is the best engineer in the whole state.

Beaumont—Well!

Gibbs—He says not another man could have built that Mt. Secrist tunnel with nature against him.

Beaumont—I barely—know the man.

But Gibbs goes on and on, to each member in turn. When he addresses Fudge as Friedelhauser, Beaumont tells him: "His name is Bidnut—Fofo Bidnut. He is the traveling man—hard candies. How is business, Mr. Bidnut—little slow, eh—little slow!"

When Beaumont lets them know what he did the night before, in his stylish and off-hand way, Gibbs subsides. A friend of Beau's was in town, arrived from Idaho in her fifty-two Cadillac convertible, and she simply wouldn't keep her hands off him. All Gibbs can manage now is "Wow." But he revives enough to ask who she is.

Bernadine Crud, the boys explain. Mac then wants to know where she goes to school. "School!" Beaumont replies. "She's through school. She's lived. She's a little older—little beat up looking but not too much—misty and dreamy. Her hair is blond about so long. You couldn't miss her. When she walks down the street, her eyes flash a message—live on, boy, dream on—I'm waiting for you. But as for actual conversation she knows only one word— The word is—yes."

MAC—Yes?

TUB—That's a good word.

GIBBS—Jeepers, where does this babe live?

BEAUMONT—Now that is an interesting question. She lives in a little town in the mountains of Idaho. On the banks of the Itching River, a place called Sneaky Falls— It's way up in the mountains. Terrible roads . . . buses not running. Of course, you could make it in a super jet. You've heard of it, of course.

GIBBS—Oh, sure, sure.

MAC—I never did.

Gibbs is now shown the door because the gang has found out that he's the type of character that gives their school a bad name; but Mac is allowed to remain, being an all-right guy. He is promptly admitted to the gang with all the proper formalities.

BEAU—You can hang around, McElroy. . . . Now tell us the story of your life in two words.

MAC—Two words . . . gosh.

The boys then show him. Fudge says: "I slug"; Carney says: "I scheme"; Olson says: "I Bull"; and Tub being careful of his language, says: "I conquer." Beau says his is "I laugh," and all of them accept Mac's: "I . . . I wonder."

When the gang realizes they're missing member Weldy, Mac is shocked that a wild man, who has been expelled from schools, and is the scourge of theirs, is their friend. He is reassured with the information that Wormy has switched from violence to dames. Then Mac, wanting to be tactful, allows as how Wormy isn't afraid of anything, but he's told that isn't so. Wormy is afraid of his mother.

As Beau shows out the new member with the farewell: "It was tender—it was real—" Tub suddenly recollects something, tells the boys that as Wormy was dragged off by his mother, he managed to get the word through that he was desperate for a date that night.

Scene III

In Mrs. Weldy's living room, the atmosphere becomes icy as Wormy's mother answers a telephone call from Beaumont. She makes it very clear to Buford that he can't bring home a 35 in Algebra and expect to career around all week-end long. Wormy piously tells Beau off as his mother listens, but as soon as she goes to answer the door, he fiercely urges Beau to: "Start calling some numbers for me. I'll get out. I don't care how, but I've got to. It's a crisis." And it is, because Ruth has brought in good boy Vernon Kinswood. This fellow, at the drop of a hat, will describe every symptom his mother has ever had: he highly disapproves of the gang, and just loves to talk to older women, and then race home to repeat their gossip to his mother.

Selma Cantrick arrives from her shopping, and would like to be rid of the boys. Kinswood bores her. And as he gives his chronological listing of his mother's illnesses, Wormy despairs of ever getting away, and even Ruth thinks it would be nice if the boys would take Buford's new dog for a walk. Wormy can't wait to start, as Ruth, in an aside to Vernon, tells him to keep her son away from *those boys*.

Scene IV

A half-hour later, Wormy has ditched Vernon, and made the Shamrock back room. His coat is off and his hair is rumpled; and everyone else is in a similar state of exhaustion trying to get him a date. One boy is still futilely thumbing through the directory, while another looks through his little black book. It's got so bad that they've decided to try to palm off Wormy on someone as a blind date; once his name is heard, the girls won't have him.

CARNEY—You don't want a date. You want a wrestling match. Why are we knocking ourselves out . . . I wonder. Wormy, you're deceiving yourself. You don't know what a louse you really are.

WORMY—Listen—you guys are supposed to be my friends.

FUDGE—You threw Louise Hostetter in a creek.

BEAUMONT—Why did you throw that woman in a creek, Wormy? That's a lousy technique.

Wormy hates to answer all this but, pinned down, explains: "My old lady told me to be home by ten and it was eight-thirty before I got there, so I began to worry. I figured if I was going to make any time with the babe—I'd better begin. My old lady never closes

an eye until I get in. So—I reached over and put my arm around
her. Right away she got heavy with me, and so I said: 'Look,
Babe, don't take this personally. I make these passes at everybody,' and she throws me in the creek. Well, the whole thing annoyed me and I climbed out and threw her in. She wasn't hurt any.
There wasn't more than two inches of water in it. I tell you the
woman means absolutely nothing to me—nothing."

Tub is highly annoyed that he was allowed to call the creek girl,
and criticizes Wormy's technique no end. Wormy tries to justify
himself: "What time do I have for technique?" Beau, for one, is
in complete agreement, and tells him: "Up at Sneaky Falls everything is different. Up there the mothers have to come to the sons
for spending money and permission to leave the house." The boys
then start to dream about wonderful Sneaky Falls, but another
nasty phone report on Wormy brings them right back to where they
were. Apparently, Wormy has covered the south side of town as
well. Carney bursts out: "Wormy, your name among the women
in this town and surrounding suburbs is about as gladsome as Jack
the Ripper's."

Vernon catches up with Wormy at this wrong moment, and wants
Wormy to come home with him and the dog, and to stay away from
these awful boys. The gang chases him away, while Wormy sounds
off on his old lady. Beau once more consoles him: "Up at Sneaky
Falls, the mothers and the boys aren't even members of the same
family. It works perfect." Wormy tries to explain what's wrong:
"She's always half a mile behind me. When I wanted a car, she
bought me a tool chest. When I want a girl, she buys me a dog."
And there was even more to humiliate him: Tonight his mother had
a date, and he hadn't. Beau reveals to him that those old characters don't have dates, "they have seating arrangements."

But Wormy still insists on a date for himself, although he is smart
enough to pass up a jailbait sister that is offered him. Suddenly he
jumps up, having worked out the whole thing. And he's not going
after Cantrick, either; that's one girl he turns down first. No, he's
after a really hep older woman: "What I'm after is the slinky stuff
with the come-on look and the warm, warm glance." He won't be
warned off, because "somewhere in this town there's a woman who'll
relax in my arms—when I enfold her, she'll stay folded, a woman,
well, if she feels like pushing me away, she'll have character enough
not to do it . . . so Bernadine, be there, be there . . ."

SCENE V

In the living room of her house, Ruth Weldy is pouring coffee for Selma, and their glamorous friend, blonde Enid Lacey. Enid, a youngish divorcee, has just been telling the girls about being accosted—and propositioned—in the Barclay Hotel lobby.

Enid is smiling about it, but Ruth and Selma are already blaming the young man's parents. But (they are reminded): "This Bidnut boy said he was an orphan, who was about to be shipped off to South America for seven years"—so, the mothers then get their licks in at the U. S. Navy and Washington.

Enid found the boy very appealing. Ruth and Selma then begin to feel sorry for him, and Ruth goes so far as to suggest that they give a farewell party for him, but the realist, Selma, straightens her out: the boy is after a very different kind of entertainment.

Enid leaves the others for a moment to take a call from her current beau, giving them just enough time to discuss her hair and her sex life. When she returns, they all resume talking about the young man. By this time, Ruth feels so much sympathy for the boy that she knows why he acted this way: young girls are always dated so far in advance that it is a hopeless matter to get a date with one of them. She's seen her son stand at the phone for hours on end; and as for Selma's daughter, Jean, she is thoroughly heartless when it comes to dates.

Then Ruth announces the little test she always makes whenever something comes up about a boy: "I always say, 'What if it were Buford?' Then I get the right answer. Of course, Buford is such a baby I couldn't imagine his ever thinking of anything like this." But in such a case, if Ruth were dead, she would hope that some lovely, maternal creature would take her son in hand for *that experience.* Kinswood breaks in on the ladies, and while he is speaking to Ruth alone, Enid tells Selma that she doesn't think she'll be seeing all of them at the club tonight, after all.

SCENE VI

In the Barclay Hotel lobby, among the pillars and potted palms, with the hotel orchestra playing somewhere off in the distance, Wormy is chasing after a pretty blonde.

The vanguard of his gang see him leave. Carney, as he peers after Wormy, gives the score on Wormy to the late arrivals. Beau, entering hastily, shudders with the others at this sorry performance. After some derogatory remarks on Wormy's methods, Beau shows what true smoothness is, by buttering up a suspicious hotel manager who approaches the gang.

Wormy returns to the center lobby, and begs the gang to leave him alone; they oblige. But then Jean Cantrick finds Wormy sitting on an ottoman waiting for a new fast woman to work on. In spite of Wormy's insisting that the place is swarming with them, the girl won't believe that there are any such things around. Jean is annoyed by this, but a little worried that she might be taken for one of the ladies herself. Wormy hoots at the idea.

WORMY—There is about these creatures—an air of mystery and allure—I said allure.

Jean, when Wormy points out a floozy to her, thinks she is terrible-looking, and wants to know who could "fall in love with anyone who looked like that?"

WORMY—Who said anything about love? This is life.

Cantrick feels she could walk just like that woman. "Anybody could do that. Think I can't?"

WORMY—Cantrick, I wouldn't make myself ridiculous in public if I were you. You are not equipped by nature for that kind of a role. . . .

Jean quickly takes up this challenge, and prances off stage in an unintentional burlesque of the blonde. When she promptly and proudly returns, she is followed by a lecherous-looking 45-year-old man. Her glow of conquest quickly fades as the man tries to make off with her. When Wormy sees the lecher using force on Jean, he glimpses his own tactics with horror, and hauls off. The man lets go of Jean's arm, and just as a fight is in the making, the gang whizzes in, then quickly whooshes off dragging the lecher with them. The manager and bellhop arrive on the scene and demand an explanation of Beaumont, who furnishes one: "We caught that character over there cutting little pieces out of the upholstery with a jack-knife—about so big—imagine!" The manager is grateful that the boys caught the psychopath, and the manager and Beau leave Jean and Wormy together to patch things up, which they do briefly, then start to scrap over Jean's date for the evening, whom Wormy characterizes as a dead fish. And Wormy waxes indignant—Jean has known him always, yet been willing "to sell me out to a dead fish you've only known about six months—that was low!"

JEAN—You brought it on yourself, Buford.
WORMY—From now on you're just Langley's goofy girl friend—and, kid, he is certainly welcome to you.

Jean then taunts Wormy with her approaching date with Langley and Wormy snarls that she shouldn't keep him waiting. As Jean angrily flounces off, Wormy sneaks a look after her, then sits down on the ottoman very angry with himself. The gang rushes back to tell Wormy about the queer character they roughed up, and what he said about the young girl, accusing her of luring him on. Wormy promptly forgets his anger with Jean, immediately defends her and denies the man's accusation. Carney interrupts: "Wormy—here comes your old lady!" Wormy thinks he's lost, but Beau devises and directs a successful maneuver—a human wall of boys to hide Wormy. Ruth Weldy—accompanied by Vernon—approaches the stiff row of boys. For a while there is a bit of vaudeville, with the boys talking to Vernon and Ruth while making asides to Wormy. Ruth preens herself that they have no idea why she is at the Barclay, all the while her son pops his head out between boys' legs, and is being shushed by Beau. Ruth thinks aloud that those awful, hard-faced boys were probably down here to sneak into the bar; and though she finds their stance and behavior peculiar, she finally goes off with Vernon to look elsewhere for her son. Beau, Tub and Olson then think it's time that Wormy take some sensible advice and come away from the hotel, but Wormy says he's going to wait for the woman he saw earlier, even if she brushes him off again. And he therefore goes away. The boys, in a final bit of horseplay, take the phone from a bellhop who is paging "Mr. Kratke." Fudge plays Mr. Kratke, with splendid assists from the gang: the girl "Mr. Kratke" is talking to has a pretty rough time of it.

As the boys find this beginning to pall, they suddenly see Enid, dressed in evening clothes, cross behind the pillars. The boys streak after her, and Beau hails her as "Bernadine," and asks if she has ever been to Idaho. Enid suspiciously inquires after his parents: he tells her that they're dead, and is rather noble about it all—except he's now off for seven years in the U. S. Navy and could they go somewhere and talk? Enid gives him a cold and decisive "No!"

The boys leave, and Enid asks the bellhop to call her beau at the Athletic Club to say that she will meet him at the country club. The bellhop goes out, and Wormy comes in—to greet Enid joyfully. And with no pulling of punches, he says he wants to spend the evening with her . . . "But listen, sugar, you and I are not going to spend the evening in conversation . . . or canasta." Nor, he continues, does he intend to look at pressed flowers in books. He has money and can borrow a '46 Nash—"We can go out to the Rancho . . . that's a spot about five miles out. Shall we dig it?"

ENID (*who has made up her mind*)—Yes. I will have to go by my apartment. And I have my own car . . . that is, if you don't mind riding with the top down. It's a convertible.

WORMY—I can stand it. What kind of a car do you drive, doll face?

ENID—A Cadillac . . . I got it last week. Shall we go?

WORMY—A '53 Cad convertible! Shall we go? Oh, Bernadine. . . . At last!

ACT II

A few minutes later, Enid enters her apartment and calls to a wary Wormy to follow. He does, and becomes increasingly jumpy —and less the man of the world—as Enid goes out to lock the door, and then disappears behind a screen. Wormy, between furious pulls at a cigarette, wants to know if she lives here alone. Yes, Enid tells him, as she comes to the ottoman, and places a wine decanter and two small glasses on a table next to it. Wormy is still tense and worried that there may be people somewhere in the apartment. Told to relax, he blusters that he's plenty relaxed—but downs his wine in one gulp. Enid barely touches hers. As she kneels on the ottoman by his side, Wormy tells her: "You seem a lot taller in here than you did when we were down there, and this afternoon, too. You seemed like a little bit of a woman then, Bernadine." Enid wants to know why he keeps calling her Bernadine. Is it the name of his girl? Wormy explains that it's a kind of day-dream his crowd has—his crowd that's composed of smooth operators and big wheels.

ENID—Big wheels?

WORMY—Make time with women—know how to hold their liquor—and something else too . . . a kind of know-how . . . savvy . . . sharp . . . hep . . .

Enid continues to question the boy on why he came to see her, and slowly gets him to tell her what he feels about himself, and about girls of his own age, and eventually, about the one girl he used to like—the only one who never bored him. He'd seen her this afternoon; but she had turned out to be an awful jerk, and that had really surprised him: he had thought there was more to her. He tries to explain what happened the last time he took her out:

WORMY—And of course on the way home, I'd park. And then I'd put my arm around her, like this. (*Puts his arm around* ENID.) There was something I wanted to say to her. But she'd go . . . (*Here he pushes* ENID *violently over to the other side of the ottoman. His face is fierce with memory.*) And then I'd get so darned burned up with her . . . I'd go— (*Makes another lunge—grabs* ENID *to him.*) And she'd go— (*Flings her violently back again to the other side of the ottoman.*)

This behavior is so strenuous that Enid cries out, and Wormy says that's just the yak his girl used to make. By now not only frazzled but frightened, Enid is about to withdraw to a safer spot, out of Wormy's reach, when the boy—staring ahead of him—starts to describe in loving terms how his girl used to look as she sat beside him in the parked car, with the street light falling on her face; how truly sweet she was—but why did she have to put on so?

Enid, knowing now how to console him, says that one day all the antagonism in the man-woman relationship disappears and all one wants is to teach the other person selflessly. Wormy can't quite believe this, and says it sounds one-sided and kind of soft in the head. But he takes Enid's hand, which isn't withdrawn, and he is allowed to touch her arm, and he joyously realizes "Bernadine!" Enid returns the caress, which throws Wormy off completely, because no one has ever been so nice to him. He feels that in return he should straighten Enid out—she shouldn't go around falling for guys' lines and bringing them to her apartment. Why, most guys are just wolves and he's just like all the others! Enid, however, pooh-poohs this, forcing Wormy to show her how gullible she was with him. He wasn't from Idaho, and he had never been in an orphanage—"even on visiting day." Enid takes all this in her stride: Wormy isn't the first man, she says laughing, who invented a story to tell a woman, and she continues to smile as each new revelation is forced on her. Wormy finds her wonderful and kisses her hand; and Enid finds him very attractive until he tells his real name, Buford Weldy. At this she drinks her wine in one gulp, and breaks in on Weldy: she must tell him something she hadn't told before. Just as he warned her not to believe the stories of strange men, so

he, she tells him, must not approach older women. Enid continues:
"She could learn to adore you . . . no matter what your name
might be." To Wormy that sounds fine—but Enid goes on: "And
she could steal away your youth so quickly . . . make it pass like
a dream." Says Wormy: "That's what all guys want!" That's
what he wants, and pleads to be allowed to stay. But Enid has
mustered all her determination and says no. But as Wormy unhappily goes off, she runs after him; then recollects herself and
advises him to find the right girl. And to keep on looking, because:
"Believe me, some day you'll find one who won't push you away."
. . . And as he leaves, she collapses on the ottoman, sighing with
nervous relief.

Scene II

On the street, the gang is gathering. To warm up for Saturday-
night action, they amuse themselves by waylaying a stranger.
When this routine is over, Beau gives the barest outline of their
evening. "In the kitchen of the Palms Restaurant there is upon the
wall to the left of the door . . . a cold air blower. *Now* . . ."

Boys—Yeah. . . . Yeah?
Olson—The chef is always in that kitchen. He stands there
right under that blower.
Beau—That poor fellow! Oh, well, has he always played the
game fair?
Boys—Naw!
(*They resume singing "Bernadine" and drift off right, disappear-
ing on the chord "A-men."*)

Scene III

Kinswood is sitting alone with his books as Ruth Weldy quickly
comes in after looking in vain for her son. There was nobody at
home at the Griners', but Leonard Carey and the Olson boys were
both home for dinner. Has Buford called home?

Kinswood—Nobody called but the Climax laundry wanting to
know if they could send a couple of men out to pick up the sheets.
Ruth—Pick up the sheets! At this time of night! The Climax
people know better than that.
Kinswood—I thought it was rather strange. He asked for you,
but before that he asked for Wormy.

Ruth realized this was a trick of the Olson boy to get hold of Buford. Obviously, then, the gang had no idea where he was either. Was there anything that she should know about her son? Kinswood tells her: "Why, no, Mrs. Weldy, I don't think so. Except of course you know he's girl crazy." This is one thing Mrs. Weldy doesn't know, and won't believe, of her son. But if by any chance he has that reputation, it comes from the company he keeps. She decides to go to a roadhouse where she thinks she still might find her son, and leaves Kinswood behind to take any messages that might come in about Buford, as well as one for herself. The telephone rings the minute she leaves—a call for Buford. Kinswood does his best to track down who it is, but fails, and can only end up saying, "Well, listen, if this should turn out to be Dink Olson, you haven't fooled me a bit." And jams down the receiver—just as Wormy appears.

Kinswood informs him that his mother is just about out of her mind from worry over him, and grills him as to where he has been. Wormy merely answers that he's been around. After more of Kinswood's virtuous anger, Wormy admits that it was wrong of him. And he won't let Kinswood attack members of his gang: "Listen, Kinswood. I know Beaumont better than you do. The one person in the world he's got plenty of feeling for is his old man. It's the one thing he never cracks wise about." Kinswood then takes a swipe at Griner for being a wolf and a bum. "Listen, Griner is a wolf. And he's not a lazy bum. He worked all last Summer in a garage to buy his clothes this Winter. His old man had to give up his law practice on account of a brain operation." Kinswood feels sorry for saying what he did: "Well, I didn't know that about Griner. I sympathize with anybody's got *illness* in the family."

Kinswood sympathizes, while Wormy begins to think of all the good times he had with all those guys, who, Kinswood adds, "won't amount to a damn." "They never planned to," Wormy answers. Still, Kinswood had the right idea: stay on the beam, be good to your parents and never worry about dames. Kinswood yelps: "Me . . . never give a thought to dames! You crazy? I give 'em plenty of thought." And he has it all figured out, too. He's going to copy a 35-year-old man-about-town—R. L. Pomfrey, the owner of a yellow Jaguar, that's constantly filled with gorgeous young things.

KINSWOOD—When Pomfrey was in school, I hear, he didn't date at all. He didn't have a car. Didn't have any dough. But he kept sluggin' till he got out of school and got this Jaguar. He's got a place in the mountains for week-ends and an apartment in town. He can have anybody he wants . . . now. (KINSWOOD *leans*

back.) I'll paint my Jaguar maroon color. These snoot-faced girls
. . . like Hobbs and Johnson and Cantrick who wouldn't look at me
now . . . they'll be glad to look at me then. But I won't look at
them. Because by that time they'll be old and washed up and I'll
drive by with a carload of beauties—

Wormy (*he has caught only one line*)—Cantrick . . . old?
You're yakin', just yakin'—Kinswood. (*He now looks at* Kinswood *with sudden disgust*.)

Kinswood—Where are you going, Weldy?

But Wormy is gone.

Scene IV

In the back room of the Shamrock, the gang is listening to a juke-
box rendition of Tchaikowsky with their usual argument over
whether it sends them or not. Wormy joins them and is greeted by
Carney: "Hey, Weldy, you should have been with us. We went by
the Palms Restaurant. Beau kept the chef talking and we reversed
the exhaust fan . . . a 40 mile gale blew through that dining room
. . . blew hats, napkins, food, butter, soup, spaghetti . . ." Wormy
squelches him with "Kid stuff! Why don't you guys grow up?"
The boys are horrified by Wormy's sudden superiority, and cover
up as best they can with a discussion of last night's dates at the
Rancho and Beehive. They deliberately ignore Wormy when he
tries to impress them with a description of his own date. They
merely exchange glances, and carry on their own conversation.
Beau eventually takes pity on Wormy, and allows him to tell about
his big evening.

In the midst of Wormy's bluff about staying at Enid's apartment,
Enid herself appears in the back room. This causes an uproar.
First, the gang sings *Bernadine*, then launches into first-aid routines: two boys rush around holding another by his hands and feet.
In all this excitement, they almost knock Enid over. Wormy yells
at them that if they don't lay off, he'll take Enid outside. The boys
stop the wrestling that by now has started, and retreat to a table
away from Enid and Wormy, but they hang on, conspicuously, to
their every word.

Actually, Enid has come to ask Wormy to say nothing at home
about his being to her apartment, because, it develops, the Weldys
and Enid are old, old friends.

This is a ghastly blow to Wormy. And when Enid lets him know
how much she's been thinking about him, he makes things even

worse for himself by telling her: "Look, doll, you don't have to con me just because you're a friend of the family's. Attractive to you! . . . I didn't notice you had any trouble kicking me out. . . ." The gang hear not only this, but also Enid's reply: "By the way, where did you go tonight? I called your house all evening." Wormy now is so sunk that when Enid gets the boys all het up by blowing them a farewell kiss, Wormy warns them off with: "Wait. . . . That's not Bernadine. . . . That . . . is a friend of my old lady's."

After the lady has left, Wormy breaks down completely; there's no more gumption or sass left. He tells his friends that he was put out of Enid's apartment. He refuses to be consoled by their telling him such things happen to everyone—and after all, she was a friend of his mother's. But a humble Wormy won't accept this. "I didn't have to tell her my real name, but I did that— Why? Because I haven't got wolf teeth, that's all. And if you haven't got them, you never get them. I'm a chicken . . . that's all . . . a natural-born chicken. And if you want to do anything about that . . . come on . . . I'll slug the first guy that tries to tell me I'm not chicken. (*He waits*.) Well, I guess I can always be a companion to my old lady. . . . She's the only woman who yearns for me. So long, you guys, and good luck . . . and I mean good luck." Just then, however, his mother storms in, full of what she thinks about the gang, and intends to do about its members. As a last resort, she intends to go to Beau's father and tell him a few of the things that have been going on. With that Ruth starts to leave, and peremptorily orders her son to come with her. He is so angry at her that he as abruptly refuses. As Ruth gets more excited Wormy becomes more stubborn. He refuses ever to come home, and flashing his draft card under his mother's nose, threatens to join the navy. Ruth is helpless, her Wormy has turned. Now her only ally, Ruth suddenly finds out, is her son's gang. They tell him he'll be in service soon enough, and he'd better calm down: but he dashes out. Then, Ruth acts up in a way that embarrasses every boy in the bar. She spills over with mother love, and with the feeling that nothing in this world is good enough for these young men. When she finally leaves, the relief is overwhelming. Tub lets loose with: "The look on her face when he said he was joining the navy! That was perfect."

BEAU—It was good but not perfect. Now up in Sneaky Falls, Idaho, it is the mothers who join the navy . . . and the boys run around like crazy, mailing them boxes of raisin cookies.

After all this, Beau needs beer, and Olson is sent to get Helen. When she brings in her tray of glasses, she also brings a message for Wormy from, it turns out, Miss Jean Cantrick. She has been calling all evening.

The boys then start a search party for Wormy: they're to look for him at every hangout in town. But Carney brings in Wormy before they have a chance to get out of the door. An unbelieving Wormy calls the number Cantrick left for him: his voice, as he tells her not to cry over being stranded by that Peter Langley, is understanding and very adult: "Everybody gets a bum deal once in a while . . . That's life . . . youngster . . ." He borrows Tub's car, and departs to a chorus of "The wheel . . . the Winnah! the King!" (*Blackout*.)

EPILOGUE

Beau comes out in his airforce uniform to tell about Wormy's triumphant ride to Cantrick's side, and of his wise decision to tell her of nothing but his love for her.

DIAL "M" FOR MURDER *

A Play in Three Acts

BY FREDERICK KNOTT

[FREDERICK KNOTT—*born in 1919—hit the bull's-eye with his first play, "Dial 'M' for Murder," but after finishing the script, had to wait three years to see it in production. This came after a BBC presentation on TV. Like his main character in "Dial 'M' for Murder," Knott is a former tennis champion. He was a member of the tennis team at Cambridge and came to the United States with the Oxford-Cambridge team to play against Harvard and Yale in 1937.*]

IN an attractive London flat, facing Charrington Gardens, Tony Wendice lives with his wife Margot.

The apartment, though not large, is a comfortable one of bedroom, living room, and kitchen. The pleasant living room has French windows leading to a terrace, thence to a garden exit. The kitchen is off the hall, which is up two steps from the living room. The entrance to the bedroom is opposite the heavily curtained windows, near the fireplace.

The furnishings of the apartment consist of a sofa close to the fireplace, a coffee table in front of it, and a large table directly behind. There is a writing table in front of the windows: its chair has its back to them. In the entrance hall, there is a chair on one side of the door, and a coat rack on the other.

When the hall door is open, a narrow passage shows outside, with stairs leading up to the apartments above. The stairs pass the hall doorway at about the fifth step.

The principal decorative features of the living room are the silver cups in the bookcases and the group of photographs near by—reminders of Tony Wendice's tennis championship days. The only feminine touch is the wicker mending basket, filled with stockings, scissors, etc., on a small table.

* Copyright, 1952, as an unpublished work, by Frederick Knott; copyright, 1953, by Frederick Knott. Published by Random House, Inc.

ACT I

Scene I

Max Halliday, a mystery writer recently returned from America, is having a drink with Margot before the fire. They are making strained and tentative conversation. Margot only half-listens to Max's description of his weekly television chores: how he has to dig up fifty-two ways of murdering people, and fifty-two original solutions to the murders. She is also listening for her husband's footsteps. Suddenly, she says to Max that she has been unable to tell Tony about him: she could only refer to Max as a radio writer—a mere casual acquaintance—she met while Tony was in America. Max hopes: "Things are o.k. now between you and Tony?"

MARGOT—They couldn't be better. (*Rather intensely*.) And I want to keep them that way.

MAX—I'm very glad—at least I guess I will be when I get used to the idea.

MARGOT—Thank you, Max.

MAX—I couldn't do this for anyone else, you know.

Margot confesses that there is something else she has to tell him. She had kept one of the letters Max wrote to her, while burning the others. He would know the one. Max admits that he probably should never have written it.

MARGOT—I know. But I loved it just the same. I used to carry it round wherever I went. Then one day Tony and I were going to spend the week end with some friends in the country. While we were waiting on the platform I noticed my handbag was missing . . . and the letter was inside.

MAX—I see. . . . Where was this?

MARGOT—Victoria Station. I thought I must have left it in the restaurant but when I went to look for it, it had gone.

MAX—You never found it?

MARGOT—I recovered the handbag about two weeks later from the lost and found. But the letter wasn't there. (*Pause.*) Then a week after I received a note. It told me what I had to do to get the letter back.

She describes the blackmailer's threat to deliver the letter to her husband unless she followed his instructions. Margot said she mailed the bank notes to the store address she was given, but when she didn't receive her letter, she went to the store and found that the blackmailer hadn't picked up his money. And she hadn't dared tell Tony about her relations with Max or the letter; she knows Tony, and Max doesn't.

MAX—You don't have to tell me. Just the thought of meeting him makes me, shall we say, uncomfortable.

MARGOT—Oh, you'll get on fine. He's changed a lot this last year. . . . Now, he's a model husband. (*Slowly and thoughtfully.*) In fact, it was exactly a year ago that it happened.

MAX—What happened?

MARGOT—Tony suddenly grew up. He seemed to change overnight from a rather selfish little person into a perfectly reasonable grownup. You remember that night—I came to say good-by?

Max remembers only too well. Tony had gone off to play in a tennis tournament, and Margot had come to tell Max they must not see each other again. After their miserable farewells (Margot now tells him), she had returned home and cried herself to sleep on the sofa. When she woke up, she found Tony standing there. It was then that he told her he had given up tennis for good. And the next morning, to prove to Margot that he meant to settle down, he had got himself a regular job.

"What," Margot wistfully asks, "were we doing—exactly a year ago?"

MAX—I was putting the mushrooms into the spaghetti. I nearly turned around and said, "I can't go through with this. Let's find Tony and have it out with him."

MARGOT—I felt that way, too. I wanted so much to say something—and all I could do was to stand there—quite uselessly—with a drip on the end of my nose. . . ."

After a while, Margot proposes a toast: "Max, let's drink to—the way things turned out." As they raise their glasses, they hear Tony's key in the lock.

Tony Wendice meets Max with his usual easy charm, showing none of Max's awkwardness. He inquires about Max's trip: "Is this your first visit to London?"

MAX—Uh—no—I was here a year ago for a vacation.

TONY—Oh, yes, that's right. Margot told me. You write for the radio, don't you?

Tony offers all sorts of sociable suggestions for Max's trip this year, until Margot reminds him they are late for dinner, and must be getting their coats on.

TONY—Oh, darling. Slight alteration in plans.

MARGOT—Now don't say you can't go.

TONY (*with a shrug*)—I'm afraid so. Old man Burgess is flying to Brussels on Sunday and we all have to get our monthly reports in by tomorrow.

Margot urges him to finish quickly so he can join them after the theatre.

TONY—Give me a ring in the intermission. If I'm inspired I might make it. . . .

As Margot is getting her things on, Tony, in fine good humor, asks Max if he will go with him to a stag party the following night—a sort of farewell dinner to some American tennis players that he and some friends are giving near by. Tony refuses to be put off when Max protests he's no tennis player, and that, anyway, his dinner jacket has not arrived. After Max agrees to go with him, he bids Margot and Max good-by, and watches them go off.

As soon as the couple is out of the door, Tony turns off the main lights of the room, pulls the curtains to, and makes a strange telephone call.

He speaks to a Captain Lesgate about a car he heard the gentleman had to sell. Giving his own name as "Fisher," and a twisted knee as his excuse for not being able to come to Lesgate's place, Tony persuades the Captain to come to Charrington Gardens in about an hour's time to make the sale.

TONY—About an hour? That's extremely good of you. (*Anxiously.*) By the way, will you be bringing the car?

LESGATE—I'm afraid I can't tonight because it's . . .

TONY (*relieved*)—That doesn't matter. I had a good look at it. Perhaps you would bring the registration book and any necessary papers.

And so it is set.

Scene II

An hour later, in the softly lit room, Tony has prepared for Lesgate's arrival. He has put a pair of white gloves on the arm of the sofa, and placed an old leather suitcase against the wall near the desk. When the bell finally rings, Tony assumes a painful limp as he admits his visitor.

Lesgate finds Tony's face familiar, and wonders whether they have met before. Tony answers that the minute he saw him, he recognized him for a former Cambridge man, named Swann. And, on the strength of their having been together at the University, Tony says to Lesgate, who sits down on the sofa, that he's going to serve his very best brandy.

Lesgate—You know, I think I must have seen you since we left Cambridge.

Tony—Ever been to Wimbledon?

Lesgate—That's it—Wendice—Tony Wendice— (*Bewildered.*) Then what's all this about Fisher?

Tony—What's all this about Lesgate?

Having embarrassed his visitor, he plays cat and mouse with him. He calls Lesgate's attention to Cambridge by showing him a picture of an old reunion dinner they had both attended. He then recalls the time that Lesgate was treasurer of the College Ball, when some of the proceeds were stolen. Then he asks what Lesgate is doing now. Lesgate says he deals in property, and quickly changes the subject. Tony, however, is very talky, and lets Lesgate know all about his own life.

Tony—I sell sports equipment. Not very lucrative but it gives me plenty of spare time.

Lesgate—Well, I'm here to tell you you manage to run a very comfortable place.

Tony (*modestly*)—My wife has some money of her own. Otherwise I should hardly feel like blowing a thousand pounds on your car.

Lesgate—Eleven hundred. Yes, people with capital don't realize how lucky they are. I'm already resigned to living on what I can earn.

Tony (*pause*)—Of course you can still marry for money.

Lesgate—Yes, I suppose some people make a business of that.

Tony (*quietly*)—I know I did.

LESGATE (*with a laugh*)—You mean the girl you fell in love with happened to have some money of her own.

TONY (*pause*)—No. I always intended to marry for money. I had to. Whilst I was in first-class tennis I met wealthy people all over the world—I was somebody—while my wind lasted! I decided to snap up the first chance I got. I nearly married a tubby Boston deb with five million dollars; it got as far as pictures in the papers and then she threw me over for an heir to a chain of grocery stores. Funny how they stick together. I finally settled for a good deal less —a lot more easily. My wife had been a fan of mine for some time.

Lesgate is startled by his bluntness, but rather admires it. Tony explains: "To know what you want to pay for—that's the thing." But why did his wife marry him, Lesgate asks?

TONY—I was a tennis star. She would never have married a commercial salesman.

LESGATE—But you've given up tennis. She hasn't left you.

TONY—She nearly did.

Over some more brandy (LESGATE *saves* TONY *from using his game leg by bringing the bottle to the coffee table*)—Tony reveals the intimate details of his marriage with Margot. He tells Lesgate that Margot quickly tired of trailing in Tony's wake from tournament to tournament, so he had gone off to play in America without her. When he returned he found his wife was no longer in love with him, and from her secretive manner, he realized she had found someone else in his absence. One day, when he was supposed to be playing tennis, he followed her to a studio in Chelsea. "I could see them through the studio window as he cooked spaghetti over a gas ring. They didn't say much. They looked very natural together. Funny how you can tell when people are in love. Then I started to walk. I began to wonder what would happen if she left me. I'd have to find some way of earning a living to begin with. Suddenly, I realized how much I'd grown to depend on her. All these expensive tastes I'd acquired while I was at the top—and now big tennis had finished with me—and so, apparently, had my wife. I can't ever remember being so scared. I dropped into a pub and had a few drinks. As I sat in the corner I thought of all sorts of things . . . I thought of three different ways of killing him. I even thought of killing her. That seemed a far more sensible idea—and just as I was working out how I could do it—I suddenly saw something which completely changed my mind. (*Pause.*) I didn't go to that tournament after all. When I got back she was sitting just where you are now. I told her I had decided to give up tennis and look after her instead."

And, he continues, he had no need for immediate violence, because Margot's friend had been called back to America. But then she began to receive weekly letters from America, all of which she burnt —except for one. She made such a point of always keeping it with her, that Tony had to know what was in it, so he stole it. Then, hoping to make his wife confess to him, he sent her blackmail notes. But she never came to him, so he held on to the letter—which he now takes from his wallet and lets drop on the sofa. Lesgate picks it up, looks at it curiously, and returns it to Tony who puts it back in his wallet.

And what is more, it was the sight of Lesgate in the pub that night that changed Tony's murder plan. By an odd coincidence, a little while back, some Cambridge men were talking of Swann's war-time court-martial, and his years in prison. This brings Lesgate to his feet with: "I take it you won't be wanting that car after all?"

TONY—Don't you want me to tell you why I brought you here?
LESGATE—Yes, I think you'd better tell me.

So Tony drops his fake limp and moves around the room wiping ash trays, glasses and table edge with his handkerchief. He wipes the brandy bottle and even takes Lesgate's glass from him to wipe it free of fingerprints. And all this time he tells Lesgate what became so clear to him that night. . . . "Only a few months before, Margot and I had made our wills—quite short affairs leaving everything we had to each other in case of accidents. Hers worked out at just over ninety thousand pounds. Investments, mostly—all too easy to get at. And that was dangerous as they'd be bound to suspect me. I'd need an alibi—a very good one—and then I saw you— And he had been following Lesgate ever since. He had made it his business to find out everything about him, with the end in view of getting something on him—and using it to "influence him."

Tony found out about his dog-racing days, his name-changing from Swann to "Adams"—his frequenting a place in Soho that the police closed down, because it was a hangout for drug addicts. He checked with Lesgate's landlady, and found out he had skipped owing considerable rent, as well as money to fellow lodgers. He followed him when he changed his name once more, to "Wilson," and observed his steady dates with a Miss Wallace. "She certainly was in love with you, wasn't she? . . . Poor Miss Wallace."—And his final switch from "Wilson" to Captain Lesgate; to a new mustache; to a fancy apartment; and to its owner—a wealthy widow named Van Dorn.

When Lesgate hears the end of Tony's recital—he was selling Mrs. Van Dorn's car for three hundred pounds more than she was asking—he casually asks: "Where's the nearest police station?" And proposes to tell the police how Tony is trying to blackmail him into murdering his wife. Tony laughs at this.

LESGATE—Suppose I tell them how you followed her to that studio in Chelsea—how you watched them cooking spaghetti and all that rubbish. Wouldn't that ring a bell?

TONY—It certainly would. They'd assume you followed her there yourself.

LESGATE—Me? Why should I?

TONY—Why should you steal her handbag? Why should you write her all those blackmail notes? Can you prove that you didn't? You certainly can't prove that I did. It will be a straight case of your word against mine.

LESGATE (*amused*)—Huh, that ought to puzzle them. What could you say?

TONY—I shall say that you came here tonight—half drunk—and tried to borrow money on the strength that we were at college together. When I refused you said something about a letter belonging to my wife. As far as I could make out you were offering to sell me the letter. It has your fingerprints on it. Remember? (*Takes wallet out of pocket and shows it to him.*) Then you said if I went to the police you'd tell some crazy story about my wanting you to murder my wife. But before we go any further, old boy—do consider the inconvenience. You see, I'm quite well known . . . and there would be pictures of you as well. Sooner or later a deputation of lodgers and landladies would come forward to testify to your character. And someone is almost certain to have seen you with Miss Wallace. (*Pause.*) You were always careful not to be seen around with her—I noticed. . . .

Tony tells Lesgate that he knows he's going to agree, "for the same reason that a donkey with a stick behind him and a carrot in front goes forwards and not backwards." And he tells Lesgate that the "carrot" will be one thousand pounds in cash.

LESGATE—For a murder?

TONY—For a few minutes' work. That's all it is. And no risk.

I guarantee. That ought to appeal to you. You've been skating on very thin ice.

LESGATE (*with a great effort to appear amused*)—I don't know what you're talking about.

Tony was talking about poor Miss Wallace's death (reported in all the newspapers) from an overdose of cocaine . . . "no one knows where she got it. . . . But we know—don't we? . . ."

Lesgate then wants to know about the thousand pounds, which Tony says is in a check room somewhere in London. Tony opens a drawer in the desk and, using his handkerchief, takes out a bundle of one-pound notes. He throws this across the room so it lands on the sofa—and says, "You can take this hundred pounds on account." Lesgate says that "the police would only have to trace one of those notes back to you and they'd hang us from the same rope." But Tony has been cashing extra money every week—"Always in fivers. I then change them for these at my leisure"—and he takes his bank statement out of the desk to show Lesgate, but warns him not to touch it. The thousand pound drop in his bank balance Tony can always attribute to losses at the race track.

Tony says that Lesgate will have to do the job the following night, which is much too soon for Lesgate, but Tony tells him, "It's got to be tomorrow. I've arranged things that way." And he′s planned to have it done exactly where a startled Lesgate is now standing, with his back to the window.

TONY—Tomorrow evening, Halliday—that's the American boy friend—and I will go out to a stag party just down the road. She will stay here. She'll go to bed early and listen to Saturday Night Theatre on the radio. She always does when I'm out. At exactly twenty-three minutes to eleven you will enter the house by the street door. (*Moving to hall.*) You'll find the key of this door under the stair carpet—there.

(TONY *opens the hall door and leaves it wide open. He looks around to see that no one is watching and then points to one of the stairs which is clearly visible through the open door. He then comes in and closes the hall door.*)

LESGATE—The fifth step.

TONY—That's the one. Go straight to the window and hide behind the curtains. (*Pause.*) At exactly twenty minutes to eleven, I shall go to the telephone in the hotel to call my boss. I shall dial the wrong number—this number. That's all I shall do. (*Pause.*)

When the phone rings you'll see the lights go on under the bedroom door. When she opens it the light will stream across the room, so don't move until she answers the phone. (*Pause.*) There must be as little noise as possible. (*Pause.*) When you've finished, pick up the phone and give me a soft whistle. Then hang up. Don't speak, whatever you do. I shan't say a word. When I hear your whistle I shall hang up and redial—*the correct number* this time—I shall then speak to my boss as if nothing has happened and return to the party.

Lesgate gets further instructions to empty the leather suitcase, which Tony had put near the desk, and to fill it with some of the silver trophies, to suggest that the killer had to leave suddenly without his loot. He must be sure the garden windows are open and that the latchkey has been put back under the stair carpet. Thus it will appear that the intruder had entered from the garden, had been surprised by Margot and—to prevent her from screaming—had attacked her, run for his life when he discovered he had taken hers.

Lesgate tries to find flaws in the plans but Tony can give him a satisfying answer each time. He is sure he has forgotten one thing though: how will Tony be able to get in without Halliday's seeing him retrieve his key from its hiding place on the step?

TONY—No, it won't be my key under the carpet. It will be hers. I shall take it from her handbag and hide it out there just before I leave the flat. She won't be going out so she won't miss it. When I return with Halliday I'll use my own key to let us in. Then, while he's searching the garden or something, I'll take her key from under the stair carpet and return it to her handbag before the police arrive.

Lesgate has one more question: "How many keys are there to that door?" "Just hers and mine," Tony assures him.

The telephone rings; and as Tony talks pleasantly to Margot on the phone, he watches Lesgate test his plan to murder her. First Lesgate puts on the white gloves, then he goes through all the motions that Margot would make when the phone call rouses her from bed. Next he checks the curtain as a hiding place, and the windows for possible creaking. When he has thoroughly considered what is asked of him, he goes to the sofa and regards the money lying there.

Tony, during the rehearsal, tells his wife he unhappily can't meet her and Max—he is still working on the report. But of course they must go on to dance somewhere after the theatre. He says to Margot: "All right. 'By, sweet—enjoy yourself"—and looks at Lesgate. "Well?" Lesgate quietly accepts: "It's a deal."

ACT II

Scene I

It is the next evening: Tony and Max, dinner-jacketed for their party, have a drink with Margot before leaving. Margot entertains Max with Tony's clipping books, pointing out pictures of the fancy folk he used to play tennis with. Max amiably tells Tony there's a book in all this, and Margot suggests that the two men collaborate on a detective story with a tennis background. How, Tony wants to know, does Max go about writing a detective story?

Max—Forget the detection and concentrate on crime. The crime's the thing. Imagine you're going to steal something, or murder somebody.

Tony—Is that what you do? Hmm! Interesting.

Max—I always put myself in the criminal's shoes and keep saying: "Well, what do I do next?"

And he will only concede a perfect murder on paper, "because in stories things turn out as the author plans them to—in real life they don't—always. (*He catches* Margot's *eye and they give each other a little smile.*)

Tony urges them to drink up; then saying he can't find his latchkey anywhere, he asks Margot for hers. While Margot is in the bedroom, and Max is putting on his overcoat in the hall, Tony has a chance to open the French windows without being noticed. Margot returns with her bag: she is most reluctant about lending her key to Tony, not wishing to stay home that evening. She might want to go to the movies; she doesn't care to listen to Saturday night radio thrillers when she is alone.

When Max says, "You can always leave your key under the proverbial doormat," Tony quickly discovers that he has had his key all the time. But he harps on the problem of getting into movies on Saturday night, and mentions all the many things Margot could and should be doing at home. For instance, she could fix his clipping books. To put an end to Tony's sulks, Margot agrees to stay in and paste up his books. Tony, once more pleasant, gets her the scissors from her mending box, and when they discover there's no paste, Max helpfully offers to make some, and Margot follows him to the kitchen.

Tony grasps this opportunity to open Margot's bag, remove her key, and put the bag back where it was on the coffee table before the two reappear with a cup of flour paste.

As Tony puts on his raincoat, he suggests a nightcap with Margot, but she says she doesn't care to be awakened. When the men have gone, she begins obediently to cut and paste the clippings and to listen to the radio program that she doesn't like.

SCENE II

Later that night, Margot has finished pasting up the book, left it and the scissors on the desk, and gone to bed.

Later yet, the light of the fire shows a hatless Lesgate silently entering the front door, and as silently closing it. He crosses to the curtains and while doing so, removes his tan silk scarf with gloved hands, and ties knots in it at either end. As the phone rings, he hides behind the curtains. Margot, awakened by the ringing, snaps on her light and comes across the living room to the desk phone, putting on her dressing gown as she comes. To pick up the receiver, she goes around to the far side of the desk, standing with her back to the windows—and to Lesgate, who emerges scarf in hand. He starts to strangle her; and though she struggles desperately, clawing at the scarf, his hold tightens on her throat. She gradually swivels towards him, and is forced back against the desk, then bent back, and down, along the desk-top, her head hanging over its ledge with Lesgate almost on top of her. Margot's right hand gropes wildly for the scissors, finds them with the album, and rams the points into Lesgate's back. He slumps over her, then very slowly rolls off the desk to land supine on the floor.

Margot manages to gasp to the person on the phone: "Get the police—quickly—police!" When Tony calls out her name, she realizes who is at the other end, and implores him to come home at once. In utter panic, she is at first unable to tell him what has happened, then calms down enough to say: "A man attacked me— tried to strangle me. . . ."

TONY—Has he gone?
MARGOT—No—he's dead—dead.

After a sizeable pause, Tony tells Margot that she must be sure not to touch anything, or speak to anyone—until he returns. She promises and hangs up. The panic returns, and she starts to sob. She tries to get some air, and pushes open the garden windows and goes out. The scarf falls off her shoulders in the garden.

When she comes back into the room the sight of the body so shakes her that she scarcely can reach her room. Once there, she locks the door behind her.

Tony's hurried steps are heard, he lets himself into the apartment, switches on the lights, and as he takes his key out of the lock and puts it in his raincoat pocket, he sees everything at once—the body on the floor—the handbag on the table. He quickly crosses to the body, turns it over, and starts to search for the key in Lesgate's raincoat pocket. When he hears Margot unlock her door, he quickly rises. She runs into his arms, and as he holds her, he asks about the bruises on her throat. She tells Tony the man put something around her neck—like a stocking. But she asks him to cover up the corpse instead of calling the doctor.

Tony goes to the bedroom and Margot, feeling faint, goes for her handbag. As she fishes around in it, Tony comes back with a blanket. He stops with horror, but Margot only brings some aspirin from the bag's depths and asks a relieved Tony to furnish the water.

After the body is covered, Margot feels a little better and asks Tony to shut the windows. He reminds her: "No—we mustn't touch anything until the police arrive— (*Looking at open window.*) He must have broken in— (*Looking around room.*) I wonder what he was after? (*Looking at bookcase.*) Those cups, I expect."

MARGOT—When will the police get here?

TONY (*startled*)—Have you called them already?

MARGOT—No. You told me not to speak to anyone— Hadn't you better call them now?

Tony agrees to in a minute, but objects to Margot's getting dressed for the police.

TONY—They're not going to see you—

MARGOT—But they'll have to ask me questions—

TONY—They can wait until tomorrow. I'll tell them all they want to know—

and he continuously searches for something, looking about all the time he is talking to Margot.

Margot turns as she gets to the bedroom door and suddenly asks Tony why he phoned her. But he changes the subject: she said the man used a stocking to choke her? A stocking, or a scarf, Margot answers. Tony expects the police will find it, and urges her to go to bed. He will call the police.

When he is alone, he goes through Lesgate's pockets, and this time triumphantly comes up with the key—which he puts back in Margot's bag. Then, and only then, does he call the Maida Vale Police Station. Warning him not to touch a thing, they say they'll be over in two minutes.

Tony makes good use of his time. He finds Lesgate's scarf outside the window, takes it to Margot's workbox, compares it with a stocking in the box—pockets the scarf, and drops the stocking where it will be seen. Then, taking Max's letter from his wallet, he kneels over Lesgate and puts it into the dead man's pocket.

Scene III

Sunday morning finds Margot still in a nervous state—she has downed some breakfast, but has left the dishes on the coffee table. When she mentions Max, Tony says he will be right over, and where had she met him? Margot reminds him that they had met at Peggy's once—"and then I met him again just before he went back to New York."

Margot tries to remember something she wanted to ask Tony, but it slips her mind as he tells her he closed the bedroom shutters. "People have started to go out for their Sunday papers. We now have a collection of refined snoopers." This appalls Margot, as does the reporter's phone call that follows. Margot supposes "we shall get a lot of that." Tony tells her: "Not for long—as soon as the inquest's over they'll forget all about it—so will you."

Margot has no such optimistic view of things; she now wonders why the police stayed so long last night. She came in to ask them when they "all stopped what they were doing and looked at me. I felt such a fool. (*Slowly*.) And on the desk—were a pair of shoes. . . . His, I suppose. (*Putting hand to head*.) It was horrible!"

TONY—Darling—before I forget—the sergeant wanted to know why you didn't phone the police immediately.

MARGOT—But how could I? You were on the phone.

TONY—I know, but . . .

MARGOT (*agitated*)—You distinctly told me not to speak to anyone until you got here.

TONY—I know, darling. But I told him a slightly different story.

MARGOT—Why?

Tony—I said that you didn't call the police because you naturally assumed that I would phone them from the hotel.

Margot—Why did you say that?

Tony—Because—it was the perfectly logical explanation—and he accepted it. You see, if they got the idea that we had delayed reporting it—even for a few minutes—they might get nosy and start asking a lot of questions and . . .

Margot—So you want me to say the same thing?

Tony—I think so. (*Doorbell rings.*) Just in case it comes up again. I expect that's Max. Let him in, will you, darling? I'll just get rid of these.

As Tony goes into the kitchen, Margot answers the door and lets in a gentleman who politely introduces himself as police officer Chief Inspector Hubbard. When Tony returns, he again says who he is. Tony says all the information was given to his sergeant; but, apparently, Hubbard wishes more. He would, if permitted, like to look around the apartment. Tony appoints himself guide, and leads Hubbard out, leaving Margot alone with the blanket marking the spot where Lesgate's body had been.

The men come back, having found that Lesgate couldn't have entered either through the bathroom or the barred kitchen window. Tony suggests that he entered through the garden. Hubbard is noncommittal, inquires of Tony where he was when this all happened.

Tony—I was at a dinner party at the Grendon Hotel.

Hubbard—Just down the road?

Tony—Yes. By a curious coincidence I was actually phoning my wife when she was attacked.

Hubbard knew all about that, and merely would like to know what time was the phone call. Neither of them can say. Hubbard helps out: "You phoned the police at three minutes to eleven, sir." Tony then figures: "Let me see—in that case it must have been—about a quarter to eleven. By the way—won't you sit down, Inspector?" And Tony waves the Inspector to the sofa, and sits upon a stool at his feet.

Margot finds out that the police think they know the identity of her assailant, although they haven't settled on which of the many names he assumed is his real one.

As the Inspector goes on with his questioning Margot's nervousness does not help her. Tony, however, is very co-operative, and even seems to remember the dead man's face from the photographs

Hubbard passes to them. Not Lesgate, though, or Wilson—but Swann rings the bell for him. And he takes down his Cambridge reunion picture for Hubbard's inspection. Furthermore, he's sure he saw Swann, sans mustache, at Waterloo Station about six months ago.

Hubbard has Margot act out the happenings of the previous night and queries her on why she went all around the desk to answer the phone. Margot has some difficulty in explaining to Hubbard that this is her habit, so that she can write down any message with her free right hand. Then she gets on to the next step: the man must have come from behind the curtains to strangle her—with something like a stocking. "He pushed me over the desk. I remember distinctly feeling for the scissors. . . ."

HUBBARD—Where were those scissors usually kept?

MARGOT (*pointing*)—In that mending basket—I'd forgotten to put them away.

Why, Hubbard inquires, did she think he came from behind the curtains? Margot is utterly bewildered. Had she drawn the curtains herself?

TONY (*a little weary of all this*)—I drew them, Inspector—before I went out.

HUBBARD—Did you lock the window at the same time?

TONY—Yes.

HUBBARD—Are you quite sure of that, sir?

TONY—Perfectly sure. I always lock up when I draw the curtains.

How, Hubbard wants to know, do they think the man got in the room when no one had broken in.

Tony insists he must have come through the garden window, because it was wide open on his return. "At least . . . Margot, are you sure you didn't go out into the garden last night and forget to lock up afterwards?"

MARGOT—I did go out for a moment. After—after he attacked me. I wanted to get some air. I pushed the window open and stood on the terrace outside.

Hubbard would like to know if she then called for help, but Margot answers simply that she had just spoken to Tony. When she can't remember whether the window was already open, Hubbard gets back

Richard Derr, John Williams,

Gusti Huber and Maurice Evans in "Dial 'M' for Murder"

to the old subject of why she hadn't immediately notified the police.

Margot, with Tony's eyes on her, tells as best she can what he had instructed her to tell the police. Why hadn't she called a doctor? The man was obviously dead—"one look at those staring eyes—" When Hubbard counters then she had seen his face before, Margot loses control. Tony, ostensibly putting in a helpful word, asks how could the man have entered the apartment if it wasn't through the garden?

The Inspector coolly states that they're sure he entered through the front door, because the man's shoes had no garden mud on them, but door mat fibers were stuck to the soles.

Suddenly, Tony brightly comes forth with the tale of Margot's handbag being stolen at Victoria Station with her key inside of it. Hubbard shows interest when she says nothing was stolen but money, and the bag was returned to her two weeks later.

HUBBARD (*with sudden emphasis*)—Are you quite sure about that?

Margot will only answer "Yes."

HUBBARD—He could have had your key copied and he could have used it to open this door—but of course, he didn't.

TONY—Why not?

HUBBARD—Because if he had—the key would still have been on him when he died. But no key was found when we went through his pockets.

Hubbard, with Tony's help, now connects the man Tony saw at the station with the loss of the handbag. So Inspector Hubbard suggests that they now come to the station and make official statements.

Max joins them at this juncture, and after introductions are made, he is able to help the Inspector place the time of Tony's phone call at twenty to eleven—"When Mr. Wendice got up from the table, I thought for a moment we were leaving the party, so I looked at my watch."

HUBBARD—Thank you, sir. You see, it was when Mrs. Wendice came in here to answer his call that she was attacked.

MAX (*to* TONY)—You mean you were phoning Margot?

MAX—But I don't get this. I asked you if we were leaving and you said you were just going out to phone . . . your boss.

MARGOT—Tony, I know what I was going to ask you. Why did you phone me last night?

Hubbard would like to straighten this all out, and asks: how long was Tony on the phone with his boss?

TONY (*smugly*)—As a matter of fact I never did speak to him— I couldn't remember his number—so I rang my wife to ask her to look it up in the address book on the desk.

The boss' home number is an unlisted one: but, naturally, when Tony heard what had happened, he never called his boss.

Hubbard listens to all this, and when Margot goes for her coat, he asks Max for his address and phone number, in case the police wish to get in touch with him. He hands him his own notebook to write them in. "Ever been over here before, sir?" Max unknowingly satisfies Hubbard: "Yes, about a year ago."

While Tony makes sure the garden exit isn't blocked by curious crowds, Hubbard confronts Max with the fact that his letter was found on the dead man.

Margot comes back and finally admits to having lost the letter from her handbag, and Max shows the Inspector the two blackmail notes Margot had received. But Margot still says she never saw the blackmailer. Hubbard warns her that when she is making her statement, she must not withhold evidence, on pain of being put in a very serious position.

Then the Inspector sums up for Margot in the presence of both men: "She killed the man—in self-defense—she said. But there are no witnesses. . . . You suggest he came in by the window—and we know he came in by the door."

A frantic Margot takes out her key and wildly waves it at Hubbard, but he concludes: "You could have let him in." When she asks: "Don't you even believe I was attacked?" he answers that she could have done that to herself—with the silk stocking they found, which oddly enough was darned with thread from her own work basket, and whose mate was discovered at the bottom of her waste basket. Margot, now thoroughly frightened, cries: "Tony, there was a pair of stockings in here." Tony, with a great show of indignation, accuses Hubbard and his men of framing his wife. He calls his lawyer on the phone and tells of the killing. "The police are here now. And don't laugh—but they're suggesting that Margot killed him intentionally. . . ."

HUBBARD (*interrupting*)—I wouldn't say that if I were you.

After Tony rings off, Hubbard tells him: "Mr. Wendice, I should advise you . . ." "Our lawyer," Tony answers, "will give us all the advice we need, thank you."

Max helps a dazed Margot through the French doors; as Hubbard is about to follow, he turns around.

HUBBARD—Are you coming, sir?

TONY—But of course, Inspector.

HUBBARD—Mmmm—I see— Yes— I just wondered—(*and goes out leaving* TONY—*in complete command of the situation—to follow*).

ACT III

SCENE I

After a few months during which people have kept staring into his apartment, Tony has moved a bed into the living room, and with the garden windows shuttered, has managed some privacy for himself.

The place is a mess: a waste-paper basket is filled to overflowing; next to it is a paper carrier full of groceries; the bed hasn't been made in days, and a whiskey bottle and glass have been left on the desk. On the floor is Tony's suitcase, half-packed.

The shuttered room is dark as Tony lets himself in with his key and turns on the lights. He puts the key in his raincoat pocket and leaves the coat on the chair. He deposits his blue attaché case on the bed, switches on the radio, then returns to the case to unlock it. He takes out a pack of bills and pockets them, then locks up again. A marketing report comes over the air, then the news item: "The Home Secretary has written to the lawyers of Mrs. Margot Wendice to say that he has decided that there are not sufficient grounds to justify his recommending a reprieve. At the Old Bailey last November, Mrs. Wendice was found guilty of the murder of Charles Alexander Swann and was sentenced to death." . . . When the weather forecast takes over, Tony snaps off the radio and makes a phone call. It is a business call involving considerable amounts of money for the publication rights to Margot's letters. When the man at the other end objects to his terms, Tony gives him more time to think it over—"Only I'm going away the day after tomorrow." (*The door buzzes.* TONY *glances anxiously at the door. Quietly.*) Excuse me, I shall have to ring you back." He lets in Max, who isn't too sure he's wanted. Tony assures him it's all right.

At the same time he catches sight of his blue case on the bed and quickly covers it with some clothes.

Tony shows Max, who is extremely upset, a communication he had just received from the Home Secretary, and tells him there is nothing more to be done. Max is sure there is, if Tony is willing to risk everything, even imprisonment. For several weeks Max has worked on a story that Tony must go with to the police. It starts off with a familiar ring: "You'll have to tell the police that you hired Swann to murder her."

TONY (*rises*)—What are you talking about?

And he is told that this is Max's business, he's been doing it for years—he knows what he's doing. The prosecution's case rests on three things alone: "My letter, her stocking, and the idea that because no key was found on Swann, she must have let him in herself. (*Pause.*) Now Swann is dead. You can tell any story you like about him. You can say that you did know him. That you'd met him and worked out the whole thing together. Now the blackmail. Swann was only suspected of blackmail for two reasons. Because my letter was found in his pocket and because you saw him the day Margot's bag was stolen." Step by step, Max has worked out the whole case as Tony planned it and as it had happened.

Tony charily plays for time and suggests Max go with him to the police.

MAX—No. I couldn't do that. They know the sort of stuff I write. If they suspected we'd talked this out they wouldn't even listen. They mustn't know I've been here.

Tony now protests it's all too ridiculous, even the stock motive of his being Margot's main beneficiary.

MAX—Well, it's worth a try. They can't hang you for planning a murder that never came off. Face it. The most you'd get would be a few years in prison.

Tony jeers at him: "That's fine coming from you, Max." And politely blames the turn the trial took on Max's part in the case, and the consequent loss of sympathy. If, however, the story were thoroughly convincing, Tony fishes, how could he have forced Swann to murder? In reply to Max's "For money"—Tony asks, how could he have got Margot's money when it would be tied up for months?

No, there's a flaw. Max says he'll solve it in the short time left.

The door bell rings, and at the sound of footsteps in the hall, Max hides in the kitchen.

Tony lets in the diffident Inspector Hubbard, who has come—not on Margot's case—but on an entirely different one. It concerns stolen money. Hubbard's men have been on the look-out for anyone paying large amounts in pound notes, and came upon Tony's paying a £60 garage bill in cash. Tony's bank was of no help to Hubbard, so Tony must be.

TONY—Do you really think I've been receiving stolen money?

HUBBARD—Until you tell me where you got it—I shan't know what to think—shall I? (HUBBARD *feels around in his pockets and then goes to hall and takes a tobacco pouch from one of the pockets of his raincoat.*) You see, if you got that money from someone else you didn't know—well, that might be the very person we're looking for. Hullo! (*He stoops down and appears to pick up something from the carpet just beneath his raincoat.*) Is this yours, sir? (*He holds up a latchkey.*)

TONY—What is it?

HUBBARD—Somebody's latchkey. It was lying on the floor—just here. (TONY *crosses to hall and feels in the pockets of his raincoat. From one of them he takes out his latchkey and holds it up.*) No. I've got mine here. (HUBBARD *opens hall door and tries to fit the other key into the lock.*)

HUBBARD—No. It's not yours. (TONY *puts his key back into his raincoat pocket.*) It may be mine, then. . . .

As Hubbard appears to discover his key had dropped through a hole in his pocket, Tony starts to explain away his paying cash to his tailor and liquor man as well as to the garage: he won a large sum of money at the dog races and had hated to admit to gambling while his wife was under sentence of death. A sympathetic Hubbard takes down his hat from the peg and is about to leave when he asks if by any chance Tony has a blue attaché case? Tony, now wary, replies that he was going to report its loss this afternoon. He thinks he left it in a taxi. Well, says Hubbard, the shop people had reported his carrying it when settling his accounts.

Unnoticed by either Tony or Hubbard, Max had opened the kitchen door and overheard the entire interview. He now comes out. "Before you go, Inspector, I think Mr. Wendice has something to tell you." Tony plays dead to this suggestion, so Max not only uncovers the attaché case on the bed, but breaks it open. He stacks six bundles of money on the desk for Hubbard's inspection and says that Tony got all this money to pay Swann with after Swann should have murdered Margot, only he was stuck with it when Swann was killed instead. Tony had been living off it ever since his wife went to prison.

Tony lightly tells Hubbard that to save Margot, Max had concocted a fantastic story for him to tell the police— "Correct me if I go wrong, Max—" and outlines it. Max prompts him about the stocking; goes into the hall to show where the key was hidden; shows, too, that Tony's phone call was the murder signal.

Tony sits down at this, but an unimpressed Hubbard comes to his aid by questioning Max on Tony's entrance to the apartment with his own key that night, which was supposedly established in court.

TONY—Come on, Max—your move.

Max takes him up, and once more goes to the hall door—opens it and says Swann could have taken the key from the ledge, unlocked the door, then put the key back in place. Hubbard tartly interrupts that he for one is only concerned with how Tony got the money. Max obliges once again by opening the desk and taking out bank statements; and though Hubbard casually says no large amount has been withdrawn, Max points out the steady weekly withdrawals of £30, £40, £45. In reply to Max's threatening "Where did you get it?"—Tony warns him he won't care for what he's going to say: the money was Margot's. "You see she was about to give it to him when she killed him instead." Max sneers: "Do you expect anyone to believe this?" But the Inspector, who is at the desk, murmurs: "Mmm? Well, it certainly seems to fit in with the verdict at the trial." Max rages at this, but seemingly the Inspector will not play along with him.

At Tony's request, Max starts to leave, but aims one parting shot and it has the desired results: "What will happen when Margot hears about all this?"

TONY—She'll deny it, of course.
MAX—And perhaps she'll change her will— You'll have done it all for nothing.

When Hubbard is alone with Tony, he becomes very gentle with him. First he tells him he's right to ask his lawyer to keep people from seeing Margot and thus saving her further upset. Then he urges Tony to put all his cash in the safekeeping of a bank. And last, while instructing him to pick up Margot's possessions (including her handbag) at the police station and while Tony's back is turned, he calmly switches raincoats, leaving his own on the hall chair. As he pleasantly takes his leave, he tells Tony that the desk sergeant will help him.

The minute the Inspector leaves, Tony's every gesture becomes hurried. He stuffs the wads of money into the paper food carrier, turns off the heater, goes to the hall chair for his raincoat, puts it over his arm, switches off the lights, and closes the apartment door behind him. The outside door closes noisily.

And Hubbard lets himself in again. He snaps on a small flashlight and goes to the phone, where he orders his men to "Start the ball rolling." As he turns the flashlight on Tony's bank statements, a harassed Max bursts in through the garden shutters.

The Inspector's one thought is to get Max out again, and when Max airs his many ideas, Hubbard says savagely: "Shut up! (*Almost frantic.*) If you want to save Mrs. Wendice, keep quiet and let me handle this." The men become motionless as the street door is heard to close and someone tries a key in the apartment door without success—and after ringing the door bell twice, goes away.

MAX—What in the hell is all of this?

HUBBARD (*letting off steam*)—They talk about flat-footed policemen! May the saints protect us from the gifted amateur! . . .

Hubbard looks out into the garden for a few seconds, and then advises Max to prepare for a surprise: Margot comes through the garden window, followed by a policeman—a Margot dressed as in the past, and carrying the same handbag, but greatly changed by her months of hardship.

She doesn't understand why her key wouldn't fit into the lock, or what Hubbard wants to know about a blue attaché case. Hubbard, after a moment, knows she is truly puzzled, and has her sit down on the sofa. He gives her handbag to the officer to take to the station house at once.

Max wants to know why she is here, but all she knows is that she was released at the prison and brought home by a policeman. Hubbard carefully tells Margot that the police strongly suspect her husband of planning her murder. Somehow, this has no effect on Margot. Hubbard explains further about Tony's expenditure of large sums, and then about the key in her bag that didn't fit this apartment lock.

Three loud knocks on the ceiling warn them to be quiet. Steps are heard outside the door; the steps retreat and the street door slams. Hubbard goes to the hall and finds out from his guard that it was Tony, who is off now in the direction of the station house. Hubbard immediately calls the sergeant, "Now, look—give Wendice these books and the handbag and make sure he sees the key. . . . Better make him check the contents and sign for it. If he wants his own key and raincoat . . . er, tell him I've gone to Glasgow." And he tells the sergeant to ring him when Tony leaves the station house.

During this conversation Max has gone to the hall, opened the door, looked and felt along the ledge, then looked at the spot where Swann had died. Hubbard wants to know if he's figured it out, and Max hasn't. Saying it took him just a half hour to solve it, Hubbard then tells him about the key: "He didn't use it because he doesn't realize it's there. He still thinks it's in his wife's handbag. You see, you were very nearly right. (*To* MARGOT.) He told Swann that he would leave your key under the stair carpet, Mrs. Wendice, and told him to return it to the same place when he left. But as Swann was killed he naturally assumed that your key would still be in one of Swann's pockets. That was his little mistake. Because Swann had done exactly what you suggested, Mr. Halliday. (*Going through the motions.*) He unlocked the door—and then returned the key *before* he came in . . ." and it was still there.

And the key Tony put in the handbag was Swann's own key, which Hubbard only discovered after having a brain wave—when he went to Mrs. Van Dorn's where the key instantly opened her apartment door.

Margot finds out that she was brought home to see if she knew about the key on the stairs. Now she has a delayed emotional reaction: she weeps on Max's shoulder, with his arms around her.

The telephone signals that Tony is on his way back to the apartment. Hubbard instructs the officer upstairs to thump when Tony draws near, and explains to the tense couple, "Sooner or later he'll come back here. As I've pinched his key, he'll have to try the one in the handbag. When that doesn't fit he'll realize his mistake, put two and two together and look under the stair carpet." Unless he does that, there is no proof—"But once he opens that door—we shall know everything."

The thump announces Tony's return. The street door opens and

closes; a key is tried in the lock, but doesn't fit. After a longish
pause, the footsteps go away; but suddenly the street door opens
and shuts once again, and steps once again approach the door. After
a silent moment, a key is heard in the lock, the door opens, and
Tony is revealed looking first at the key, then at the step. He had
remembered indeed; and the police close in.

THE CLIMATE OF EDEN *

A Play in Two Acts

By Moss Hart

[MOSS HART, *born in New York in 1904, began his theatre career at eighteen as office boy and typist for a producer. He first attracted Broadway attention with "Once in a Lifetime," which he wrote in collaboration with George S. Kaufman. Other well-known collaborations with Kaufman were the 1935 Pulitzer prize winner "You Can't Take It with You," and "The Man Who Came to Dinner." Hart is also the author of "Lady in the Dark," "Winged Victory," "Christopher Blake" and "Light Up the Sky." He has achieved a further reputation as a director. He is married to Kitty Carlisle, singer and actress.*]

IN a clearing of the jungle in British Guiana stand the unpainted, two-story house and the faded blue church of the Reverend Gerald Harmston.† From the dark green jungle can be heard the screeching of monkeys and the trilling of birds, while a steamship's whistle announces the ship's arrival at the landing.

The Reverend Harmston, coming out on his porch, asks his youngest child if he's tracked down his sister. Running to his father at the foot of the steps, Berton reports, "Daddy, I can't find her anywhere. I've looked in all our regular hiding places, and I can't find her."

"She's still mad at me," his father replies. "Don't worry any more, my boy. Here's the steamer. Come on. She'll stay mad at me until dinnertime, now." Berton keeps calling, "Ollie!" as he follows his father.

The rest of the family—Mrs. Harmston, Mabel and Garvey—proceed to set the dining-room table. While setting it they speculate as to what their arriving guest will be like.

---

† The play on the stage lights up various parts of the house and church as they successively become the scene of action.

MABEL—He's probably very thin and very pale. He has to be, of course, because he's ill with his nerves.

MRS. HARMSTON—Not necessarily, Mabel. I've known some fat people to be ill with their nerves, my dear.

GARVEY—How long will he stay, Mother?

MRS. HARMSTON—I don't know, my dear. In his letter he said, "May I stay with you for a short while or for always. Until my spirit has healed."

They wonder at his coming at all—the Harmstons haven't seen their nephew since he was a child of seven, and his mother had severed all connections with Mrs. Harmston when she married their father. Will he fit into their kind of life, wonders Mabel, and does he know what sort of missionary her father is?

MRS. HARMSTON—I don't know, but he'll be very different from anything we've known for the past twenty-four years. Might be good for us, too. Kind of a test. A test of the lights by which we live.

GARVEY—But, Mother, we see lots of people from the outside world—Captain Raymac of the steamer, and the people who stand on the landing.

The difference, his mother explains, is that he will be a part of their lives.

Her husband and the steamer captain now arrive with the guest. Natives, hurrying from the landing, say Good Evening as they pass, while Gregory thanks Captain Raymac for being so good to him. Then he is introduced to everyone in the family, except the still-missing Olivia. She is missing, her father says, because she's annoyed at him. "She wanted to bring the harmonium out of the church and set it up by the landing place, and as you came off the steamer she wanted to play *See the Conquering Hero Comes.*"

Mabel now goes into the house to draw a tub for Gregory, and Harmston makes sure that a native, Logan, will bring Gregory's bags to the house before carrying up the provisions. When Berton indulges in some off-color humor, Harmston hits the child extremely hard. He then calmly tells Gregory: "Premeditated obscenity is against our aesthetic codes, Berton knows that." Just as calmly, the boy admits he was in the wrong.

Mrs. Harmston urges the boys to come in and get ready, and shows Gregory through the house to his upstairs room, waiting to see him settled. Olivia, who has been hiding all this while in the church, now decides to rush out, straight to Gregory's room. She bursts in upon them, and her mother introduces her. She promptly wants to know if her father had warned Gregory against her.

GREGORY—No. Berton did mention that you're queer.

OLIVIA—Berton would. He's my close friend.

GREGORY (*holds out his hand*)—I'm still waiting to shake your hand.

MRS. HARMSTON—Well, what's the matter? Aren't you going to take your cousin's hand?

OLIVIA (*still ignoring his hand, she comes close to him, tilts up her face and whispers*)—I love and pity you.

MRS. HARMSTON (*laughing*)—Oh, Olivia! Don't overdo it!

Mabel comes to announce Gregory's tub is ready, and they all start to leave their guest. Olivia wants him to know: "That's our best washstand. Do you like the marble top? We decided to give you our best one, though Daddy held out against it for quite a while. We had quite a—" Mrs. Harmston insists that they leave Gregory alone, but Olivia first manages a bit of advice: "Be careful with the tub, Gregory. It goes bong! and then plang!"

When Gregory is finally alone, he does more than show the effects of a long journey: he has a trembling fit. He closes his eyes, and when he opens them sees a large spider on the mosquito netting. This sends him to his suitcase, to find a whiskey bottle. He tries to undress, to get ready for dinner, but his privacy is immediately violated by Berton barging in. Having got rid of him and taken off his trousers, Gregory is next addressed by Olivia, from the door:

OLIVIA—How wide is the world? How broad is the bush? (*Sitting on the bed.*) Are you ashamed for people to see you naked?

GREGORY—Well, I— (*He manages to get his robe on.*)

OLIVIA—Mother said you might be, but I thought not. It looks as if she was right. That was a password—"How wide is the world, and so on." Berton and I have passwords. We've just made up our minds to share one or two with you. We had a conference over you.

Olivia then says, almost in the same breath, that dinner is ready and he ought to marry Mabel. She is next pleased to see that he hasn't killed the spider, and promises to trap it for him.

OLIVIA—If you don't betray me. I can be a tigress to people who betray me. (*She laughs.*) But I believe you're good. (*She smiles up at him.*) Doucement ils passent, les beaux, les tendres et les bons. (*He trembles violently this time, turns his face from her and reaches out a hand to the washstand to steady himself.*) Gregory! What's the matter? Are you ill?

GREGORY—No. It was the French. Your suddenly speaking French.

OLIVIA—You mean you're allergic to French?

GREGORY (*smiling faintly*)—In a way, yes. Brenda—my wife— spoke it and wrote it fluently. She once wrote a little tale in French. One evening she read it for me in our flat. Your voice reminded me—

And Olivia finds out everything she could want to know about Gregory's wife, including her "hate" for him.

GREGORY (*quietly*)—She watches me now. (*As though no longer aware of her presence.*) She watches me continuously. Everywhere I go her eyes follow me and surround me.

OLIVIA—But didn't you say she was dead?

GREGORY (*vacantly*)—Not she herself. She's imperishable. (OLIVIA *stares at him—waiting for him to go on.*) She went out of her way to destroy me. (*In a low, desperate voice.*) Maliciously! Deliberately! She— (*He breaks off, gulping.*) My God, I'm not sane! Why am I telling all this to a little girl! I must be mad.

OLIVIA—Gregory, listen to me! Are you listening to me? Maybe I'm the right one to understand it! Daddy talks to me about many things because he respects the way I see things—and he's a wonderful man! How did she die?

GREGORY (*softly*)—Drowning.

OLIVIA—Were you with her?

He explains that he followed her to the Barbados—she met with the accident before he arrived.

OLIVIA—Wasn't she a very good swimmer?

GREGORY—Very. (*Smiles.*) But it appears that she bit off more than she could chew this time. She left me all her money. There was a lot of it.

OLIVIA—You mean that even though she—you mean that she *still* left you all her money?

GREGORY—Yes. She left everything to me—"with all the deep love I've carried and will forever carry for him." Those are the exact words.

OLIVIA—And you really believe she hated you? (*He begins to tremble and look about him in panic.*)

Olivia comforts him, saying her father isn't any goody-goody missionary: he'll help, and if Gregory will trust her, she will too.

OLIVIA (*rises*)—I believe you're mad, but I'm going to try to get you better. If I try to help you, you'll co-operate? You won't suddenly go mad and try to stab me and hide my body in a trunk, will you?

GREGORY (*he smiles and rises*)—No, Olivia. I don't think I will. I don't think I'm that kind of mad.

OLIVIA—I must go, Gregory. I've got to go and help Mother in the kitchen. (*Softly.*) I still love and pity you. (*After she goes, GREGORY waits a moment, then picks up his towel and trots off to his bath. As he does this, the family begin to arrive in the dining room. Eventually GREGORY joins them, seats himself and bends his head.*)

REVEREND—We never say grace, my boy. I don't believe in overdoing religion.

OLIVIA—Daddy is a practical missionary.

Reverend Harmston considers that religion without a dash of humor can be an awful bore.

Next, Olivia lets Gregory in on the cook's hate for her. Reverend Harmston warns Gregory that he'll need all his patience with these children, and Garvey adds: "Berton and Ollie are like two ticks." Whereupon Berton snaps back: "If we're ticks, you're a louse. A louse that tickles people in kitchens. And we know who."

But the children at least promise to protect Gregory from "the local influences." The Reverend Harmston explains that the place is full of "psychic phenomena," an aftereffect of the bloody slave insurrection of 1763. "Have you noticed anything yet? Sensed anything out of the ordinary?" asks Reverend Harmston. "No," says Gregory. "You will, my boy."

Gregory has sensed nothing out of the ordinary, but he acts strangely himself when Olivia remarks of Mabel: "She'll make you a good wife." With that, Gregory drops his knife and fork, excuses himself and hastily leaves the room.

When the children all want to go after him, they are ordered by their father to stay where they are. He thinks this is a good time for a conference.

Olivia tells the wide-eyed family about her long talk with Gregory, and all he told her about his wife; she thinks some of it has to do with his drinking too much. Garvey hears about Gregory's money, and immediately thinks of innumerable things he can endow them with. Olivia enters into the spirit of this and votes for a piano. But the Reverend lectures them on hankering after the young man's money: "Half the happiness we've achieved in this wilderness is due to our not having had enough money to enjoy all the amenities of civilization." Mabel agrees with her father, and Olivia insists they misunderstood her. Anyhow, she has her own theory about Gregory—he's not looney, he's something "there's a word for it but I won't bother to mention it." Partly because "it has an indecent sound"—she finally expresses the opinion that he has a mild case of "Shittsophrenia." After the laughter has died down and her father smilingly tells her, "There's a 'Z' in it somewhere," she analyzes Gregory's condition, concluding that what they see of him now is but a "shadow."

Reverend Harmston abruptly calls a halt to the conference and, on the pretense of hearing something in the corridor, finds a moment to talk privately to his wife. She asks if he thinks Gregory dangerously ill? "I think he may very well be," he replies, "dangerous to himself and dangerous to us."

MRS. HARMSTON—Then we must send him back.

REVEREND—Is that your answer, Joan? (*She looks at him. A pause.*) I feel this young man is hovering between the will to live and the will to die. His is a voice we have not heard in many years. But if our life here means anything we should be able to answer him. (*A fractional pause.*) How do we answer him, Joan?

MRS. HARMSTON—Let him stay.

(*The lights come up in* MABEL'S *and* OLIVIA'S *room—next door to* GREGORY'S. *The girls are getting ready for bed, and* OLIVIA, *ever observant and always curious, questions her sister.*)

OLIVIA—You were smiling a minute ago while you were rubbing your stomach. I watched you. As though you were remembering something. What were you remembering, Mabel? Whenever I ask you, you just smile and say: "Nothing."

MABEL—I wasn't remembering anything, Ollie. Honestly.

OLIVIA—I don't understand you, Mabel. I know you're not lying, but—people who appear quiet and sweet and nothing more must be hiding the passions that are in them. They must be! Purposely! Why do you want to hide yours, Mabel? I've never heard you say you hate anyone—or love them, either. You never get angry and you never say spiteful things. Why? Why don't you want other people to see your fires and devils?

MABEL—Perhaps I haven't got any?

Olivia is sure she has, because all people do. She is also sure that Gregory and Mabel would make a good couple. Mabel tries to put a stop to such talk; lets Olivia take down her hair for her and collect all the hairpins.

OLIVIA—You have such nice long hair. I can imagine how he's going to enjoy running his fingers through it. Do you think he'll like the freckles on your breasts?

MABEL—Ollie, *stop* this silly talk! I'm not going to answer you! (*There is silence for a long moment. Then:*)

OLIVIA—I wonder what he'll be like when he arrives!

MABEL—Who?

OLIVIA—Gregory.

MABEL—Gregory? But he's here already!

OLIVIA—No. Only his shadow.

The lights come up in the church. The whole, scrubbed, neatly dressed native congregation is singing a hymn. All the pews are filled, and a spirit of gaiety fills the place. Lighted candles and vases full of wild flowers along the walls lend a festive note, too.

As the hymn is finishing, the Reverend Harmston takes his stand by the lectern and smiles down upon his congregation. He nods with approval at Olivia who, it would seem, has been playing the harmonium faultlessly. Pausing after the end of the hymn, the Reverend then asks all "to spend a few moments or so in pleasant reflections on past dreams and fancies." There is a general shuffle and scraping of feet among the congregation. All heads bow reflectively—some resume their seats, and some kneel.

Gregory, next to Mabel, asks if he should sit or kneel, and is told he may do as he chooses.

GREGORY—Have your past dreams and fancies been pleasant? (*She nods slightly, her face still averted.*) Have I been in any of them?

MABEL (*her voice barely audible*)—One or two.

GREGORY—You have been in many of mine. (*He puts his hand into his pocket and brings out a gold chain and locket.*) I want you to have this.

It belonged to his wife, he tells her.

There is a shrill crescendo from the harmonium, and as if it were the signal, Reverend Harmston rises, and in his deep mellow voice speaks to his congregation: "I believe—"

CONGREGATION—In what I can sense.

REVEREND—And I believe—

CONGREGATION—In the reality beyond the shadows— (*And to the soft accompaniment of the harmonium:*)

REVEREND—Verily, I believe—

CONGREGATION—In God the Father of all Myth—

REVEREND—And in Jesus Christ—

CONGREGATION—And in Jesus Christ— Born of Joseph and Mary—

REVEREND—Jesus, among men, the King of Dreamers—Creator of many beautiful parables— And I believe in the Bible— A book of lovely legends.

When the responses are over, Reverend Harmston announces that Howard, of the Drama Group, will read the passages from Chapter Three, Ecclesiastes. The native then reads beautifully, bringing out the music that lies in the words. When he has finished, there is enthusiastic applause, and even "Good boy, Howard," from Mrs. Harmston, and a loud "Bravo" from Captain Raymac. Gregory is curious if this happens every Sunday; Mabel tells him, "It's different every Sunday."

When the applause has died down, Reverend Harmston makes the week's announcements about school vacations and art classes. "Adult classes will be resumed in two weeks' time for all literate members of the community, and Mabel will hold a class for illiterates who wish to improve their speech. On Tuesday night at eight there'll be a concert in the Library Hut. Mrs. Harmston hasn't quite made up our program of records yet, but you can look out definitely for Beethoven's 'Seventh Symphony' and Rimsky-Korsakov's 'Scheherazade'—and more important, there will be a first performance of an original prelude by William of the Medical Group. (Applause.) And now for a fine piece of good news. Our finances now permit the building of several more houses in the residential area. (Applause.) As a result, I'm glad to tell you that at least ten more couples will be given permission to have babies. (Murmur of applause.) Their names will be announced shortly. (Groans.) We'll probably have a get-together, as on the last occasion, and discuss how these couples should be selected—that is, whether you prefer to draw lots or whether you prefer to let those who are first on the waiting list have the preference. (Natives—'No, sir.')"

Saying they'll decide later, Harmston now gives them a taste of the ghost story that will be read on Thursday night. When he is finished reading the teaser and they want to know what is coming next, he says: "Aha! Come to church Thursday night and find out." —and sends them home in love and friendship.

After church, the natives form little visiting groups, while Berton gallops off into the jungles with a native child, and Mabel introduces Gregory to her native friend Robert. As they talk, Gregory acts unpleasantly superior: "How very lucky you are, Robert! Religion, work, frank love and wholesome play all neatly packaged for you. All that, plus a dash of nudism and the local influences to take care of the unconscious at the same time. I'm just a barbarian by comparison, Robert."

Robert politely excuses himself. But Mabel, horrified at Gregory, decides against the walk she was to have with him and swiftly follows Robert instead.

Reverend Harmston comes out and talks to Gregory, while Olivia asks them to guess where Mabel's gone: "She's gone to have a swim in the creek with Berton and Garvey and Robert and Robert's sister." That, says the Reverend, was meant for Gregory. "She probably thinks you'll be tempted to find your way to the creek to watch Mabel and the boys besporting themselves in the water."

GREGORY—Why should I be tempted to do that?

REVEREND—Well, we all bathe naked here. I suppose she thought it would shock and titillate your civilized sensibilities to see Mabel swimming around in the nude—

After Reverend Harmston orders Logan to get back up-river to work, he goes on with his conversation. He is pleased at the way Gregory has taken to their way of life. "Speaks well for the local influences." Gregory would like someone to tell him just what these are, but all the Reverend will say is: "Psychic. Haven't you come to realize yet that the essence of our life here is evasion? The chief fault of the civilization you left behind is its obsession with conclusions. Nothing, my boy, creates greater disillusion than the arrival at a conclusion—" And he advises taking life with a pinch of salt—"that's why we can throw ourselves into it with such heartiness and extract all its richness. We—damn! Excuse me a minute—I think there's a flea in my pants!" He gets up and slaps himself vigorously. "Got him!"

Reverend Harmston admits to being quite a talker, but notices Gregory is not, and attributes that to being "resigned to the insolubility of the problem of living and seeing no point in further discussion."

GREGORY—You're very shrewd—and very fond of words.
REVEREND—Words are my weakness, my boy. I like spinning them out. If I hadn't more pressing occupations, I could spend all my days spinning out words. I can also take a hint. Go back to your book. I'll get on with the business of the day. See you at dinner.

Mabel comes back from her swim and, having decided to forgive Gregory, she sits down with him, and drinks in his compliments. He finds her much changed since his arrival: no longer diffident and aloof. Olivia comes along just in time to catch a mumbled remark. Mabel asks him if he likes the change in her, and though he says something very indistinctly, she catches it.

OLIVIA—"Indeed, indeed, repentance oft before I swore—" (*They turn their heads, startled, as she appears before them, smiling.*) You ought to have answered: "But was I sober when I swore." Don't you know your Omar Khayyam?
MABEL—What's the idea of creeping up on us, Olivia?
OLIVIA—The better to overhear you, my dears.
MABEL—I hope you liked what you overheard.
OLIVIA—"I like the smell of you."—You smell of creek water, that's what you smell of.

And she sits down between them determined to be the *enfant terrible* and embarrass her sister. She succeeds when Gregory asks if she's been swimming in the nude, too. "Yes," she replies. "And I haven't got freckles on my chest and belly, by the way." With this, she gets rid of Mabel, who dashes for the house.

Having a clear field with Gregory, she gets down to what she wants most to know:

OLIVIA—Did you murder your wife?
GREGORY (*stares at her for a moment, then rises and turns away from her. Then he casually points to a tree*)—What palms are those, Olivia? I've been meaning to ask you. They're quite beautiful.

OLIVIA—Aeta palms. The core of the wood is very good for stropping razors. Was it a razor you used to cut her throat? Or did you strangle her and throw her body into the ocean so that it could never be found?

GREGORY (*turns*)—I think you're right. Today would be a good day to see the ruins. Especially with you. Who lived in them?

Olivia enjoys her tale of rape and murder that occurred centuries ago on this spot, and she even brings forth the ghost of a ravished maiden to worry Gregory with. When he won't turn around to see if the ghost is behind him, she admires his presence of mind. But tells him, "Lord help you if you dream about Luise (the ghost) tonight, and sleepwalk and sleepact. Yield to her and your soul is lost forever." And she explains that, "Sometimes the local influences make you dream, and you sleepwalk and act out your dream and you don't remember anything afterwards."

Gregory now reveals that he was the "local influence" the other night outside the dining room. And he had been interested in her theory of his "Schizophrenia."

OLIVIA (*slowly*)—This is the first big shock you've given me. I don't know whether to hate you or not.

GREGORY—Why? I think you're an extraordinary family and I think your father is a remarkable man.

OLIVIA—Yes, remarkable! A wonderful man! He's my hero— and I'll kill you if you try to destroy my faith in him! (*And crying, she runs off into the jungle.*)

In the early dawn there is a terrific commotion. Ellen is frantically pulling at the church bell rope. She is still in her nightdress, and so is Mabel who is the first person to answer the clanging. The children then pile out of the house, ready for mischief even at this hour, and go for Ellen. The Reverend finds them all in a heap, and finds out from Ellen what the trouble is. "Me sleep in my hammock in de kitchen, Parson, when me hear a scream and batter-batter sound, like two people fighting on de kitchen steps. Me sit up and wait and then me hear man walking down de steps—" And then she got up and found: "Blood! Blood! Blood all over de steps! Murder happen, Parson! Murder!"

Olivia comes back from an inspection tour and says Ellen is right: "A murder *has* been committed." Then Mabel comes out, worried that Gregory isn't in his room or anywhere about. When the excitement mounts further, Reverend Harmston coolly tells Logan to clean up the mess on the back steps. Mrs. Harmston then appears and says it's nonsense to speak of murder: "Don't be silly! There's a chicken head lying in the bush behind the kitchen steps—" Why was Ellen ringing the bell like that? "Wait!" says Mabel. "Ssh! What's that?" "Footsteps," breathes Olivia.

And out of the jungle comes a smiling Gregory, carrying a head-less chicken. The elder Harmstons are not amused, nor is Olivia, who icily asks what he used to slash the chicken's throat with. Gregory shows them his razor and describes the neat slit it makes. And gratuitously adds: "The local influences seem to have set some-thing ticking in me." He feels perfectly wonderful this morning.

The Reverend Harmston isn't too appreciative: he now has to make an explanation to all the natives who answered the summons of the bell. His boys follow him, and Mrs. Harmston goes back into the house. But Mabel is stopped by Gregory. She is distinctly nervous being near him but becomes irritated, too. She thinks he has a perverted sense of humor and she doesn't care for his playing mad: "All you're doing is having a good laugh at us."

GREGORY—You're so *intelligent*. That is exactly what I *am* doing. But you're wrong about my mental health. I used to think differ-ently myself until—until I murdered my wife.

MABEL—You're not talking to Olivia, you know.

GREGORY—You don't believe me, then?

MABEL—I don't think you could harm a fly. (*He catches her arm and pulls her around to face him.*) If you're trying to put on another insane act, don't bother. It won't impress me. (*And she is not impressed, till as she tries to free herself, he says:*)

GREGORY—No. Oh, no. You're not going. I've waited a long time for this. I followed you to Barbados, you know.

MABEL—Barbados—!

GREGORY—Yes. To Barbados. You pretend to forget, don't you? Barbados. You tried to cheat me by getting yourself drowned. But I knew I'd catch up with you in the long run. And you'd be wear-ing the locket. (*His hand goes to her throat, and his free hand waves the razor.* MABEL *shows how frightened she is.*) You're frightened. I'm glad. If you're really afraid of me I won't harm you. I might even laugh at you. But you must undress. You were always sensitive about revealing your body—even to me, remember? Go ahead. Undress—or I'll have to rip the things off you! You're pitying me, aren't you? I can see it on your face. It always touches me when you pity me. Please don't do it. Be quick and get this over. I don't want to harm you. Go ahead. I'll have to slash you with this if you don't. Go ahead. *Please!*

Mabel, all pity, manages to take the razor from his hand and fling it into the bushes—while telling him she's not his wife. When Gregory crumples on the steps, she sits beside him, cradling his head in her arms. "It's all right, Gregory. It's all right. It's all right."

He doesn't remember what he's done, doesn't know why there's blood on his hand. Mabel tells him quietly: "You killed a chicken for dinner tonight to save Logan the trouble. Wash up and come for a walk with me, Gregory. You promised to take me for a walk yesterday. Come along. It won't take me a moment to change."

GREGORY—Strange. My mind seems to have gone blank. All right, Mabel. (*They go into the house and upstairs, each to his own room.* (GREGORY *stands in his—dazedly.* MABEL *starts to take off her gown. While they are going upstairs,* OLIVIA *appears and picks up the razor. She stands looking up at the house as the curtain falls.*)

ACT II

In the twilight, Berton worriedly listens to Olivia's passionate, jealous outburst against Mabel.

OLIVIA—I'm sorry, Berton dear, but sometimes I must frighten you. I tell you everything, so I must tell you this, too. I believe the soul of Luise has entered Mabel.

BERTON (*almost in a whisper*)—Ollie—!

OLIVIA—I do. I foresaw the whole thing last night— (*Softly.*) "Tomorrow I may be myself with yesterday's seven thousand years. . . ." I'm full of poetry tonight, Berton—that's always a sign I'm foreseeing things—

And as she's off on her poetry jag, Berton becomes so frightened that he darts into the house.

Gregory, coming along with his sketching things, not only finds her full of poetry, but given to embarrassing confidences about Mabel.

OLIVIA—Why are you doing all this sketching?

GREGORY—To prevent me from losing my temper with silly little girls.

OLIVIA (*in a real rage, furiously*)—Why will you insist on calling me *little!!* I'm not so little—I'm fourteen—and I'm quite grown up. Haven't you discovered that yet?

GREGORY—Oh, quite. I'm not attempting to cast aspersions on your youth. But you're still a little girl. A wonderful little girl, Olivia.

OLIVIA (*turns to him*)—In another year or two my chest won't be as flat as this, you know.

GREGORY—We can only trust not.

And with that he has the tigress or, more properly, Cassandra on his hands. Olivia prophesies dire happenings, and ends with: "Some day I'll give you back your razor—or," she continues, "I might kill you with it instead."

The Reverend Harmston comes into the dining room with the roast, and calls for Gregory as the family gathers for dinner.

Garvey, hearing the chug-chug of a motorboat, insists it sounds like the launch coming in. Olivia, making sure that everyone hears her, says—twice: "It's not the only thing coming."

Gregory tells of seeing a snake and asks if it might have been dangerous. Garvey volunteers a description of the "bushmaster," the only deadly snake around. "Deadly's the right word. The venom paralyzes you in less than five minutes, and a few minutes more and you're dead. It goes for you on sight and without provocation. Psst—" Mrs. Harmston tells Garvey to stop scaring Gregory: "The snakes around here are absolutely harmless. And the bushmaster's a rare visitor."

The Reverend has finished his carving now, and turns his attention to Gregory, asking if he's coming to church next Sunday? When Gregory answers that he thinks so, Reverend Harmston asks him point blank:

REVEREND—Like to sit next to Mabel again?

GREGORY—Why, yes— Yes, of course I would. Why?

REVEREND—Just thought I'd ask. If that's the only way we can get you to church, I'll insist on it. Reason I'd like you to come is that next week is Communion Sunday. No formalities, of course. We don't go in for baptism or confirmation here. But we do light special candles. Symbol of festivity and warm hearts—and of life;

the flickering ephemeral flame of life. The church really looks lovely—I'd like you to see it.

Olivia suddenly pushes back her chair and asks to be excused. She has something to attend to upstairs. Once she's left the room, Berton anxiously tells them all: "Olivia is in danger—from—from herself." But the others just wonder what mischief she's up to now. She quickly shows them, as she comes back into the room with blood running from a cut on her arm. Berton cries out. Olivia says she has cut herself—on purpose—with a razor. "It's Gregory's razor. The one he used to kill the chicken—"

MABEL (*half-rising from her chair*)—Where did you get it from? OLIVIA—
"I sometimes think that never blows so red
   The rose as where some buried Caesar bled!"
GARVEY (*groaning*)—Oh, she's quoting poetry again! We're in for one of her foreseeing spells, I guess— That's all this is! The old nonsense! She's probably going to—
OLIVIA (*snarling*)—Shut up, you filthy rutting jackass!
REVEREND—Olivia! Leave the table! (OLIVIA *makes no move.*) At once!
OLIVIA—I won't.
REVEREND (*unhurriedly rises and moves around to her chair. He grasps her by the shoulder and jerks her to her feet; the chair falls backward to the floor with a loud clatter, and the knuckles of her hand whiten as she tightens her grip on the knife on the table. The REVEREND grasps her wrist and the knife falls clinkingly to the floor. Speaking softly*)—Upstairs! (*Slowly she exits.*)

When Mabel comes up to her room, she finds it in darkness, and Olivia stretched out, brooding. Since, however, Mabel has brought some buttered bread, knowing her sister would be famished, Olivia immediately hops up to eat, telling her: "You're sweet, Mabel. And good. I like you so much—I'm sorry I have to hate you." When Mabel wants to know what this is all about and where she got Gregory's razor, Olivia enjoys telling her surprised sister: "You threw it at me. It just missed cutting my shin by an inch."

Mabel is thoroughly upset that Olivia witnessed the scene that Gregory doesn't remember. Olivia knows why he doesn't remember: "That was the end of his sickness. And you haven't told him anything, have you?—You're afraid—if he's well, he may go away —and you're happy just waiting, aren't you—you're in love with

him—!" And Olivia works herself up into quite a tizzy of jealousy, while Mabel just stands quietly by, and watches Olivia as

(*She flings out of the room. Simultaneously, the* REVEREND *and*
MRS. HARMSTON *come out of the house and stand on the steps for
a moment, looking up at the sky. Through the following scene,*
MABEL, *in her bathrobe, paces slowly up and down the bedroom,
as if thinking something through. In* GREGORY'S *room, the lamp
comes on and he sinks into a chair with a book that lies unopened
on his lap.*)

As Olivia runs blindly out of the house, her father stops her. She
announces that she is not going to the concert; she's staying home,
like Mabel, because of the heat. Reverend Harmston orders her to
get something to eat and proceed to the Hut. She refuses to obey.

REVEREND—Don't say that again.
OLIVIA—I'm not obeying.
REVEREND—Don't say that again.
OLIVIA—I'm not obeying. (*The* REVEREND *slaps her across the
face.*)
    MRS. HARMSTON—Gerald!
REVEREND—Going now?
OLIVIA—Yes.

The Reverend tells her to have a little snack and go on to the Hut,
like a good girl—and he and his wife walk off for a breath of air.
Olivia then stands utterly still. When Ellen comes out to toss some
water into the bushes, Olivia begs her to hit her, "with all the hate
you have for me." After a moment's hesitation, Ellen hits Olivia a
stinging blow. When Olivia says to do it again, Ellen hits her again.
Olivia sobs: "Now I *am* crying. Tears. For the first time." She
puts her hands to her face to feel the tears—then runs off into the
darkness.
    Mabel, meanwhile, has reached a sort of decision. She surprises
Gregory by coming into his room. He brings her a chair from the
hall and waits for her to speak, realizing she has something to tell
him. Seeing that it is hard for her to speak, he turns off the lamp
and sits with her, listening to the concert music that comes from
the Hut. Mabel finally gathers up her courage and says: "A week
ago you told me I'd changed. I didn't admit it then, Gregory, but I
know now that I *have* changed. It's you that's responsible." Gregory tries to ward off any further confessions, but Mabel tells him that

she loves him. "You think I'm drawn to you because you're the
first man I've known from another world? I'm not. I thought it
might be that myself—when you first came here I thought so. But
yesterday I felt—I never felt like that before." Gregory tells her to
let him know what really happened yesterday.

GREGORY—I must know what happened between us yesterday.
All that afternoon I felt a sense of shock—as though a lump of grit
had detached itself from some part of my mind. And afterwards
a wonderful relief spread through me—like a serum in my blood. I
must know why—it can't remain an unremembered hour, Mabel—
You must tell me.
MABEL—You held a razor over me—you thought I was your
wife—
GREGORY (*breathlessly*)—Oh, my God—
MABEL—Don't, Gregory—it's all right. I was terribly frightened
—but suddenly I knew somehow this was the end of it—and I just
wanted to help you—and love you—

She goes to Gregory and asks him to take her in his arms. She
sees that he wants to, but he moves away and whispers: "Yes, yes—
I'd like to put my arms around you—the way I put my arms around
Brenda—and the others—and the others! Do you hear that—you
innocent? What do you know about love? Would you know when
I put my arms around you that, no matter how I tried, sooner or
later I'd go on to the others—the way I did with Brenda?" He
takes her by the shoulders roughly. "Do you understand? Is it
plain? Now let me alone—get out and let me alone! Get out!—
Forgive me! I owe you more than that— Don't love me, Mabel!
I can't love the way you do. Each man loves in his own way—mine
seems to be to betray those who love me. Don't ask me why—I
don't know." He sinks into the chair.
Mabel comes lovingly to his side, saying he can't forbid her to
love him, and adds that she'll wait—and won't come to him again.
And she is very happy.
When a rock hurtles through the window, Gregory picks up the
letter that is wrapped around it and learns through the message
written in Olivia's blood that passion starts early: "My flat chest
burns for you." He also learns that she witnessed everything the
day before.

MABEL (*soothes him*)—It doesn't matter, Gregory.
GREGORY (*repeats*)—"It doesn't matter!" There's no gulf be-

tween what matters and what doesn't matter for you, is there? (*He shakes his head.*)   How wonderful you all are!   What a shining innocence there is about all of you.   What is it?   There's the *climate of Eden* about this place!   What secret do you all possess?

MABEL—We love—

In the bright sunlight, Gregory has arranged his easel on the porch, and sits painting.   Garvey joins him and watches him work.

GREGORY—Hello, Garvey!   How long is Olivia being sent away for?

GARVEY—Depends when Daddy thinks she's been punished enough.   She might have to stay up-river with the Buckinghams for a month or more.

They agree that they will miss her.   Gregory wants to know about Garvey's family—does his mother "really subscribe to all this—this way of living?"

GARVEY—What makes you think she doesn't?

GREGORY—Well, to be completely truthful, I've rather the impression that she was not quite as abnormal as the rest of the family, if you don't mind my putting it that way.   (*Painting.*)

Garvey doesn't mind, but answers that actually his mother is one of them.   He tries to make Gregory understand what his father is trying to do—"though I don't think if you stayed here for ten years you'd get to know him as he really is.   I wish I could—"   He stops suddenly and points off to the jungle.   "See the fair-skinned fellow in the first boat?   Know who he is?"   Gregory remembers, "Isn't he supposed to be a child of your father's—outside wedlock?"   But that's just it, Garvey says, he isn't.   Garvey found out about a year ago, when he accused his father of being a tyrant, that Reverend Harmston deliberately had himself framed as the father of this child so that his wife and the natives would stop thinking of him as God. So there is this boy, Osbert, "a sort of living symbol of Daddy's weakness.   That's the kind of man he is, Gregory—only even that doesn't explain anything about what he's trying to do here—"   Garvey then gives Gregory a note from Mabel and says, as Gregory reads it, "Mabel's in love with you, Gregory.   It's the real thing, I think.   I've seen her goofy over one or two of our fellows here, but it wasn't like this."

Mrs. Harmston comes out and shows her pleasure at Gregory's

going shirtless at last. "I do wish we could have done away with clothes entirely. In a hot climate like this! It's so absurd wearing clothes." When her son kids her about how for years she wore a bathing suit, she haughtily orders him off, and so is alone with Gregory. She first asks him how he's been sleeping and, when he says "perfectly," says she wants to be sure he hasn't been disturbed. Gregory asks, "Disturbed? By what? The local influences?"

"No," Mrs. Harmston replies, "I'm not talking about the local influences. I mean disturbed by dreams."

And why should he be disturbed by dreams, Gregory asks. Mrs. Harmston then stops her indirect approach:

MRS. HARMSTON—I'm afraid it will always be difficult saying anything to you. Our standards are so different. What I mean in simple language is, have you and Mabel been sleeping together? Please don't look shocked—though I can understand how you feel. I'm not trying to censure you. I'm only interested, that's all.

GREGORY—Interested!

MRS. HARMSTON—Yes, I'm her mother, after all. Don't you think it's natural I should be?

She now answers Gregory's question to Garvey—whether she was really one of these "abnormal" people. She *is* so completely, that she doesn't even mind telling Gregory that Mabel, though not at all dissolute, has had a lover since she was sixteen. She thinks Gregory has met him—Robert. "They were very fond of each other for a long time, but then something went wrong and they called off the friendship. But they had a sweet, joyous affair." Gregory can't stand listening to any more, and begs her to let him get on with his painting. But the paint brush, in his tight grip, snaps in two. When Mrs. Harmston leaves he goes up to his room, and then, still trembling, goes into Mabel's. He calls out savagely for "Brenda!!", picks up the locket from the bedside table and stares at it. Then jarred by the steamer whistle, returns to his room and frantically begins to pack.

At the same time, the Reverend Harmston is entertaining two of his native pupils in the dining room. As he is giving them books to read during their school vacation, he sees Gregory in the doorway and, aware that something is wrong, tells the children to run along.

Gregory wants to know how soon the steamer leaves, and is told not for an hour. Reverend Harmston remarks that this decision to leave is very sudden. What has happened? Gregory tells him: "I nearly killed your daughter; I held a razor over her head." He goes on to tell how he thought he had got rid of his murderous hatred for his wife, but that today it had come back. So he must leave. "Why," asks the Reverend calmly, "why? We're all capable of murder—every one of us is quite capable of killing each other or ourselves, at some point. What happened today that exploded that hate in you again, Gregory? Isn't that the important thing to know, my boy? For yourself? Can't you tell me? Is there some way I can make it easier for you?"

Gregory finally works it out, through realizing that what re-aroused him to violence was Mrs. Harmston's telling him about Mabel's affair. It wasn't, as he had always lied to himself, because his wife had a lover that he hated her—it was because he himself was unfaithful. "I saw my own failure in her eyes—her pity—in her love for me. I'm saying it out loud—to you—to myself—for the first time. For the first time!"

And so Reverend Harmston is able to ask him: "She killed herself, didn't she? Just swam out to sea? It wasn't—an accident? It was suicide, wasn't it?" Gregory nods, unable to speak. "And she loved you?"

GREGORY—Yes. She loved me deeply.

REVEREND—My daughter loves you, too, Gregory. And the decision of whether you stay is hers and yours alone. She's already given you her answer, hasn't she? (*Sighs.*) Am I fearful for her? Yes, as her father I am. But to me, Gregory, there is a penance of the soul—and that's what you've begun—that is as important as life itself—even Mabel's life. We're not afraid of death—here—life is the important thing. Mabel has made her decision. Now you must decide.

As Gregory in a dazed fashion begins to finish his packing, Olivia arrives at the door. She is bedraggled and all scratched up, and murmurs wildly: "Death!"

When finally she has Gregory listening to her, she says that Mabel was killed by a bushmaster; that Garvey couldn't save her, and he took her to cottage eleven, where she now lies. Her father and mother are there now, and sent her to inform Gregory. Gregory hears the mournful singing, and also the hammering of the nails in the coffin. But still he shakes Olivia, shouting that he won't believe her. Olivia cries out: "She's dead! She's dead! You think I'm joking? Mabel's dead! You never take anything I say seriously. But she's dead! Dead! If you don't believe me, go and see!"

And she runs out of the room. Slowly, mechanically, Gregory goes out of his room, and the house. He meets Logan, sadly eager to share the news. Gregory says he knows. But what he doesn't know is that the dead person is Ellen's mother, who died of a stroke. And it is for her the Reverend Harmston is making the coffin.

Mabel comes back out of the jungle; and crying, "My darling—my darling!", Gregory takes her in his arms.

In the deepening dusk, Reverend Harmston sits listening to Gregory, watching him pace up and down below the porch. He has been talking for some time, explaining himself and now pleading for Olivia. Gregory feels that he owes Olivia a deep debt for keeping him here. Her father, however, insists it is a matter between Olivia and himself.

The members of the family come out all spruced-up, on their way to what Mrs. Harmston calls the "chumming up" party. It is the only night in the year that the natives listen to every word the Reverend says: it is the night for reading the list of those who may have babies.

After they have all set forth, Reverend Harmston tells Gregory that he isn't going to give him permission to marry Mabel. If, after they live together for a while, the Reverend is convinced they love each other, then: "I'll marry you. And I wish you both enduring bliss. Forgive me for cutting this short, Gregory. Olivia! Olivia, where are you?"

Olivia comes out of her hiding place in the church and politely greets her father. But she must tell why she played the trick on Gregory. She was jealous of Mabel and just wanted to see Gregory's face when he heard she was dead. "The other woman," says the Reverend. "You've seen the other woman for the first time." He shakes his head. "Strange—arrival and departure. You arrive at womanhood—Gregory leaves."

Her father has to console her and explain that this isn't the life for Gregory, even if he now thinks it is. "But he'll never be without part of us and part of this place—Mabel will be with him." And he reminds his miserable young daughter: "A time to keep and a time to cast away. Remember? You're leaving your girlhood, Olivia. It's come so soon— It will be hard for you, my dear. It's the first big loss for you—the loss of your girlhood. So many of the fancies you treasure will fall away and for a while you'll be alone—only nothingness will stand behind you. But it will be hard for me, too, Olivia—perhaps even harder. Your girlhood has sustained me." And she is allowed to stay home by herself, to bid farewell to her girlhood, and good-by to her lovely fancies.

THE LOVE OF FOUR COLONELS *

A Comedy in Two Acts

BY PETER USTINOV

[PETER USTINOV—*born in London in 1921—is one of England's most discussed playwrights and has also written for the films. When his smashing hit, "The Banbury Nose," opened in London in 1944, James Agate made the assertion that he was the greatest genius currently writing for the English stage. Ustinov was born in London of Russian parents, educated at Westminster, took up acting at seventeen and is known today as a gifted actor. His first long play, "The House of Regrets" was produced in London in 1943 and was given much critical acclaim. His second (written in three days) was "Blow Your Own Trumpet," and though not a great success, it further demonstrated his talent.*]

AFTER World War II, the Allies have set up an administrative office at Herzogenberg, near a wooded section of the Hartz Mountains. Four Colonels—from France, Britain, the U. S. and Russia—represent their respective countries, and jointly govern the district.

The pin-up art of the four countries is the sole decoration of the office's bare plywood walls. A framed portrait of Stalin shares honors with a naked girl playing with a beach ball, a Utrillo reproduction, and a drawing of bulldog with young. The room is scantily furnished: trestle table, four chairs, filing cabinets.

There are doors on the left and right of the room, and through a large window at the back of the office one can see the dark forest and the turrets of a faraway castle above the tops of the trees.

A monumental silence has settled on the two Colonels in the room. The American Col. Wesley Breitenspiegel and the English Col. Desmond de S. Rinder-Sparrow have run out of conversation. Minutes pass and not a word is said. But the American doesn't give up. He tries again, declares he's not a funny man, but a romantic. The Britisher is mildly amused. Wesley doesn't fit the picture.

WESLEY—You have before you a man who only dreams of one thing—to disobey an order in the most glamorous possible way.

DESMOND (*shocked*)—Disobey an order?

WESLEY—Yes . . . I'd like to have led the Charge of the Light Brigade, against all expert advice.

DESMOND—You'd have to have been a British officer to do that.

Against such literalness, Wesley can do nothing but claim Custer's Last Stand for himself.

Nor is Desmond taken with Wesley's talk about his psychiatrist. He thanks God: "In England we can't afford them."

One can understand the French Colonel's hope—on entering the room—that he is late.

DESMOND (*smiling*)—Not looking forward to it?

AIMÉ—Enormously. Last week we all talked in French. For once I could relax and tell you all what I thought of you with no fear of contradiction.

DESMOND—It beats me why we should all have to talk French when all of you know English.

AIMÉ—It is a question of honor. English may be more convenient, but it will not be used if there is the chance of the French language being slighted.

According to Aimé, when it's Russian week, "It's then Ikonenko pushes all his legislation through, and we get into trouble."

AIMÉ—It's strange how I hate this place, and yet I know in advance I'll be sorry to leave it. Have you ever noticed how in life, hatred is as binding as love? The pathos of leaving a detested school, or a mistress who has begun to bore you?

DESMOND (*charming*)—Heavens, I always begin to bore them first.

AIMÉ (*a little disarmed*)—I must remember that. It's a perfectly charming remark.

Aimé then sums up for them: Wesley is a romantic, he himself is a realist, while Desmond is a thoroughly nice fellow, and "That's why we get on so badly." And nothing gets done. The only decision they have come to is to transfer their H.Q. to the inaccessible palace. And that has proved impossible. No sooner have the American soldiers opened a path through the underbrush, than it has closed.

Wesley, the romantic, doesn't believe his lieutenant who reports this phenomenon, and has sent him off to a psychiatrist. Aimé, the realist, is willing to accept it as the work of fairies.

The Russian Colonel, Ikonenko, enters with a briefcase. When he is informed by Wesley that he is late, he says nothing, seats himself, spreads his papers in front of him, then tells his not-yet-seated colleagues: "Now *you're* late." He pompously reminds them that next week he will be chairman and that "the official language for the seven days commencing on the 18th will be Russian." Aimé protects his country's honor: it will be his turn and that of the French language the week following. Desmond stands up for Britain's turn. Then they make an aimless parliamentary show. Wesley is questioned by Ikonenko on the American's report of clearing the forest, and the Russian announces that he received independently a report from his own Lt. Bulganov. When Wesley backs up his own man's report, Aimé needles him about sending his lieutenant to a psychiatrist.

Ikonenko, firm in setting them all an example, reads out loud his own document: "It is easy to understand that the lack of progress in the clearing of the undergrowth is due to (1) the lack of will to work shown by the American soldiers unversed in Socialist doctrine, (2) the consistent sabotage exercised by Reactionary Diversionists and Fascist Hyenas—"

Wesley wishes to get on the record his censure of the low Soviet tactics in this operation, and asks for a show of hands. Wesley and Desmond vote, but Aimé surprises everybody by getting up and going to the door. Wesley excitedly thinks this might mean "a split in the Atlantic bloc" and Ikonenko is all for wiring Moscow. Aimé reassures them: "There comes a time during the day when even the most strongly constituted of us has to leave the room. I'll be back in a minute."

On his return, Aimé announces that the Mayor of Herzogenberg is waiting to see them, and brings him in.

Courtesies disposed of, Wesley demands to know what is the matter with the jungle around the castle. The Mayor cautions them not to try to conquer it. "In these parts, we know better than to try. We leave it to others—." In recent years, he continues, a Gauleiter tried to enter and failed. An officer of the Gestapo is now in an asylum for the same reason.

Ikonenko threatens to have his troops take the castle at dawn, which causes consternation among his colleagues. The Mayor placates them and asks if they are married. Ikonenko refuses to discuss his private affairs. The Frenchman admits to both a marriage and a mistress. He even adds that his wife has a lover. Desmond has a wife and three dogs, and Wesley has a wife and a psychiatrist. "Then," says the Mayor, "if you all have something worth living for, children, forget the Castle. I appeal to you before it is too late."

The same strange things that happened while the Mayor was talking to the Gauleiter, happen now. The outside door opens as if blown open, but there is no wind. An old cracked bell rings out. A *Man*, tall, thin, and dressed like a tramp, appears. The Mayor wastes no time in grabbing his hat, and disappearing.

IKONENKO—Who are you?   Have you a permit?

The Man says he has an appointment. Ikonenko states there are never appointments during conference hours.

MAN—All you need to do is look in your appointment book, dear.

The Man comfortably settles himself in a chair, and tells Ikonenko there's no point in calling his soldiers: they're all asleep. Literal-minded Desmond has looked in the appointment book, and finds Prof. Diabolikov, written in Russian. Ikonenko denies having written it, and demands the Man's permit.

MAN (*searching in his vest coat*)—You really are most difficult to convince. Here you are. What's this? (*He pulls out scroll.*) Oh, no. This is permission from Nero to taunt the lions before their dinner of gospelers. Here we are. No. A front-row ticket for Robespierre's execution. A disappointing affair. (*Reclines on table.*) The weather was far from perfect. There's a special kind of weather which is ideal for executions, you know. You need an Autumn morning, really, to surround the scene with an aura of poetic melancholy, with just enough of an orange sun to catch the blade. For lions, on the other hand, you can't do better than your midsummer heat, in which the poor beasts are torn between an oppressive lethargy and their greed for blood. Such leonine quandaries drag out the agony of the gospelers deliciously. (*With a giggle sits up.*) But what am I doing talking about it as though it still went on today. No, alas. The taste for limited horror was dissipated. A decadence set in. Our love of quality was polluted by a love of quantity. Nowadays we do things on a majestic scale, with guns and bombs and gases, and it's surprising how the human species obeys our every whim in this direction—

Ikonenko receives the permit, and immediately pronounces it a forgery. The Man obligingly produces another signed by Stalin and suggests the Russian had better be careful about what he calls this one. Ikonenko admits: "The situation is open to review," but places the Man in protective custody, and rings and rings for the sleeping soldiers. Meanwhile, the other colonels are amused by the Man's trick of producing the special brand of tobacco that each man smokes, though nothing for the Russian, since he knew he smoked nothing. Aimé senses who the stranger is: "The devil."

MAN (*falsetto*)—Who?
AIMÉ (*charming*)—The devil.
MAN—Why, do I look like him?
AIMÉ—I don't know. I've never met him. But he's someone I've always wanted to meet. We have so much in common.
MAN—I'm glad you've never met him, dear, because I've never heard that I look like him before, even from those who know us both very well. (*Sits in chair.*) I don't want to seem catty, or say anything behind his back which could give offense, because I have the very, very highest regard for him, but I don't think looks are his strong point. Dear me, no.

Ikonenko cries sabotage when his men fail to come, and after the Man resists arrest, Ikonenko sees his duty, and shoots twice. The Man's only reaction to the slugs in his belly is to scratch the spot where they tickled him. Thoroughly frustrated, Ikonenko faints away.

It is now the Englishman's turn to take over. He rings for his Driver, whereupon the Man says that his reason for coming was to take them all to the Castle. "If I go," answers Desmond, "I go alone." He won't get in, the Man tells him: "You see, it's not a castle like any other. It is a castle touched by magic."

Once more the door slowly opens. This time it is the Man's turn to be startled. A beautiful, prim, uniformed A.T.S. girl steps in and salutes Desmond, announcing herself as Private Donovan. She may be Desmond's new Driver; but she is also clearly a very old source of irritation to the Man. The Man distrusts her from bitter experience—an experience, according to Donovan, of some four thousand years.

Donovan shows her bag of tricks, too. She asks Desmond about his three dogs, calling them by their proper names. She chides Wesley for having trusted his wife with that psychiatrist: "He's taking advantage of your absence— He took your wife to the Stork Club last night, and then—" "Spoilsport," sneers the Man. Unfeazed by such remarks, she berates Aimé for implying his wife was unfaithful, when he knew full well she was long-suffering and patient.

She further annoys the Man by saying she has brought the car to take them all to the Castle. Ikonenko, coming to, feels he must go to Moscow and confess his failure in his dealings with the Man. Donovan says they will all go to the Castle to visit the Sleeping Beauty, who has lain there for a hundred years.

AIMÉ—The Beauty of the Sleeping Forest. But then, who are you, Miss Donovan?

MAN (*hurt*)—Might as well tell them now. The harm's done. Thanks to you, you silly immortal bitch.

GIRL (*smiling radiantly*)—In the visible world, I have many names. In pre-history, I was the angel charged with the painful duty of chasing Adam and Eve out of the Garden of Eden. . . . In the world of dreams and legends, they call me the Good Fairy.

The Man, piqued that attention has shifted to Donovan, informs the Colonels that he first defeated Donovan in that same garden of Eden. He was the serpent: "The devil was absent. He didn't realize the importance of the occasion. Since then, Donovan and I have been struggling for the driving reins of this ramshackle carriage they call humanity. I can tempt, and so can Donovan, and you, gentlemen, are our battleground. You and Eve and the Sleeping Beauty, and all the peoples and dreams of the world. . . . And you have the wonderful possibility of choosing."

And, in reply to Aimé's questioning him, the Man gives a peal of laughter, followed by an elaborate gesture and answers: "Silly boy, I'm the Wicked Fairy!"

SCENE II

When the party reaches the cobwebbed, dark, eerie palace, the men are allowed to go exploring while the two fairies have a word with each other.

The Wicked Fairy confesses "with the limited sincerity" at his disposal, to being pretty tired of his old routine of tempting mankind to sin. He longs for a change, to do one good deed. Donovan similarly confesses to being fed up with righteousness and would like for once to be bad. As the fairies lean towards each other, a good strong clap of thunder changes their minds for them. "That was a silly game to have played," mutters the Wicked Fairy.

GOOD FAIRY—If the extremes collided they would crush the whole of life between them. How I envy mortals.

WICKED FAIRY—They can choose between us. We have no choice.

He has the idea suddenly, of permitting the Colonels to awaken the Beauty, "each in his own way, without influence." At least he'd try not to interfere. The Good Fairy understands.

On the Colonels' return, they are briefed by the Wicked Fairy: "This will be a temporary awakening for your benefit. She will have to sleep again later— That is—unless you succeed.

IKONENKO—Succeed? Succeed at what?

WICKED FAIRY—In making your ideal a reality, by seducing her.

At this intriguing point, he is deluged with questions. Wesley wants to know if she's got "it." Desmond: "Is she personable?" Aimé: "Est-ce qu'elle a du chien?" And, Ikonenko demands to know: "Is she sexually attractive?"

The Wicked Fairy tells the men where to stand and commands their silence; then, with the Good Fairy at his side, he raises his arms. There is darkness. When the light comes on again, the Fairies and the men are in an early 19th-century Court Theatre. It is all red and gold, and in the stage box at one side, sleep the King and Queen. In the other stage box, the Court Chamberlain lies back in a petrified state. And beyond the proscenium, on the stage itself, is an elaborate bed. In it lies the veiled figure of the Sleeping Beauty.

IKONENKO—It is exactly as I have always imagined it.

The Good Fairy tells them the familiar story of Princess Aurora's christening, the Wicked Fairy's curse, and the eventual pricking of the girl's finger. In this version, the Wicked Fairy had the Chamberlain substitute a real needle for a stage prop. And after years of careful watching on the Good Fairy's part, the Beauty pricked her finger, while acting on this stage, and died. The Good Fairy brought her back to life, but she fell into a deep sleep, and here she lies, still sleeping.

The Colonels are allowed to go up on the stage and look, but not touch her. Wesley gives out the old wolf whistle.

WICKED FAIRY—Look at them up there, prowling round her like wolves round the sheep's pen. To them she is their ideal. They all see her in different ways. Only lust is common to them all.
GOOD FAIRY (*suffering*)—Yes.

But she warns him: "If you try to help men to rape their ideals, to destroy what is sacred and untouchable in their natures, I shall protect the Beauty with all my strength."
The Wicked Fairy promises not to interfere, but the Good Fairy is on guard this time because he wakens his old helper the Chamberlain to stage-manage this show too.
The Wicked Fairy cleverly draws the Colonels downstage away from the Beauty, and an inner curtain drops, hiding her. The Wicked Fairy tells them that to be with her again, and to make love to her, each "must be the character you always hoped to be in your child's heart." . . .

AIMÉ—I have no illusions. The character I always hoped to be is myself.
WICKED FAIRY—Have you no favorite period in history?
AIMÉ—Ah, yes. That is different. The turn of the eighteenth century, when France was inundated with the sun, reflected off her sovereign's pride.

Aimé has quite a turn, however, when he finds he must do all his love-making in front of his colleagues: "I am not prepared to share my ideal with everyone."

WICKED FAIRY—Damned French pride. She is what you see in her, and what you see in her is your own cherished vision.

Aimé hesitates no longer, and rushes off into the wings to dress for his encounter.
The Wicked Fairy starts things moving: he goes to the middle of the little stage and calls down into the orchestra pit to awaken the musicians and instruct them to play eighteenth-century music. The perplexed Colonels are instructed to watch from one stage box, and the Good Fairy from the other.

WICKED FAIRY—Please! You are in the theatre, after all, gentlemen. Now may I crave your silence while we see the naked soul of a certain Col. Aimé Frappot chasing the shadow of the elusive bird which flutters in his heart. And may he catch it.

He sits beside the Good Fairy as the Chamberlain enters with a long taper and starts lighting the footlights.

ACT II

Scene I

The inner curtain again rises—on a playlet full of asides and passionate lunges.

The Beauty, in eighteenth-century dress, is at her dressing table preparing for whatever the day will bring . . . preferably a lover.

BEAUTY—Yes, I have ribboned bonnets, a wardrobe as fine as the richest in Paris, periwigs and toys and baubles, pretty little dogs, black boys to serve chocolate, a Dutch milliner, an Italian dancing master, and all that elegance could wish. (*Melancholy*.) Yet now I lack a lover. But first, a husband, for without a husband to deceive, a lover's an empty pleasure. (*Door bell*.) But hist, one comes. I shall dissemble.

And in comes Aimé, suitably romantic in dress and intention. Says he: "Mademoiselle, methought this to be a coffee house." When that idea has been discarded, the fencing starts.

BEAUTY (*aside*)—I doubt that it is my respect he wants. Yes, alas, he is too good for husband, and too soon for lover. (*To him*.) Are you not afraid to incur my wrath, sir?

AIMÉ—No, Mademoiselle, for it is à la mode to hate in public those you would tumble behind locked doors.

BEAUTY (*aside*)—He speaks like a gentleman indeed. (*To him*.) Then I, sir, am not of the rule, for when I hate, I hate, and there's an end to't.

With each exchange they come nearer the point.

BEAUTY (*aside*)—Now I could love him. Weren't it better to admit I am a maid, or sighing, say, "Alas, sir, what you suppose is true. I have a husband."

AIMÉ (*aside*)—See, she sighs and moans, and each heaving of those twin rotundities doth seem to beckon me.

BEAUTY—Sir, I am indeed cursed with husband, as hideous a vaporous wretch as was ever purg'd by physick, for indeed all he touches, or breathes upon—or fondles—has upon it the cloying stench of Pharmacy.

Thus they play, until he seizes her, and they have a fine, happy tussle. Aimé's about to steal the fatal kiss, when the Beauty shouts: "Help! Help! I am a virgin, sir!"

Aimé is disgusted; the Good Fairy is relieved. But Ikonenko says: "That's not the Beauty! Where are her motherly virtues?"

DESMOND—I certainly can't call this lass innocent. Is that what he sees in her?

WESLEY—She sure knows her way around.

GOOD FAIRY—Yes, that's what he sees in her. But the fatal kiss was avoided, that's all I care about.

The Wicked Fairy appears on the stage, clothed as the gouty old husband of the Beauty's imagination, and livens up the lagging affair.

WICKED FAIRY—Ah. So soon abroad, my love, my chick, my doll? And hast thou drunk thy chocolate yet, and hast thou learned thy minuet and little songs, and hast thou pretty things to tell me? Hm? Eh?

GOOD FAIRY (*heart cry*)—I knew he'd have to interfere!

WICKED FAIRY (*aside to* GOOD FAIRY)—My nature was too strong for me because if he keeps on doing this—he'll never get around to doing that.

The Good Fairy, undefeated, rushes for the wings.

The Beauty is delighted with the Wicked Fairy's pose, and Aimé once more becomes the willing seducer. As she pretends to swoon, the Wicked Fairy all but pushes Aimé into her arms, instructing her to loosen her stays. He then departs, hoping for the worst.

This is avoided by the Good Fairy's sudden appearance as Aimé's mistress, who demands that he choose between the old and the new. Aimé chooses the Good Fairy, saying: "Thou art like an old song, but ill remembered." This brings on a wild Wicked Fairy, completely out of character. He stamps his gouty foot and yowls for the curtain to be rung down.

The audience of Colonels can't make out Aimé or his choice. Desmond states: "The whole thing's very peculiar, if you ask me." It is now Desmond's turn. Choosing an early English period, he goes off into the wings, while the orchestra plays a pavanne, and the Colonels carp at the returned and weary Aimé.

IKONENKO—I fail to understand, Frappot, how you can have chosen as a favorite period the epoch of pre-revolutionary France.

AIMÉ—Why?

IKONENKO—The insincerities which led relentlessly to the revolution were already painfully in evidence.

AIMÉ—Insincerities? Mon Dieu, they said what they thought in those days, and said it wittily.

IKONENKO—Wit is unnecessary.

AIMÉ—So is life.

IKONENKO—No, my friend, you are wrong. Life is necessary, for without life, the world would be unpopulated." . . .

The Good Fairy agrees with him, and he adds: "Without population, there would be no working class." The Good Fairy would like to know where God fits into all this, but she is warned to stop canvassing by the Wicked Fairy.

Now the next show starts. Desmond, bearded and armored, strides up and down before battlement walls. He speaks a harrowing verse, full of raw images, and strong words:

"*Five gray eagles cackeled at my birth*
And the entrails of a wasp lay, by dint of magick
At my moaning mother's feet, who, being brought to bed
Of a two-months child, did presently faint,
And pine, and die, aweary of her sire's black reproaches,
Which, being the first sounds to play upon this Desmond's ear,
Did fill full his thoughts with hatred of all chastity."

As the Beauty appears in trailing medieval dress:

"*There appears before me*
A vision of such galling purity,
That I must defile it quick, or call myself
No more Desmonio.
Twenty years ago by the light of the lately dwindling moon
Did I pit my passions against an Illyrian Nun.
'My vows, my vows,' she cried, but 'twas in vain.
A Maidenhead well lost's a mistress' gain."

And off Desmond goes after the blonde, the desperately Anglo-Saxon, Aurora.

When Desmond seizes her, she fiercely repulses him:

> *"Thou toad-spawn, thine own second worser self,*
> *Thou yellow-painted bauble,*
> *Thou yolkless egg,*
> *I'll none of thee. Go sing thy amorous odes to statues,*
> *Get with child a tree-stump. Marry a broomstick. Away."*

Desmond draws his dagger on her, but it gets stuck in the floor instead of in the lady. Just then the Wicked Fairy provides the needed light touch by entering dressed as a Jester.

BEAUTY—Oh foolish fool.

WICKED FAIRY—How should I not be foolish, being a fool, for were I not a fool, I would be wise, the less like thee, for thou, good lady, art in no wise wise. . . .

The Beauty is cheered up by this sort of thing, and so is Desmond. The Wicked Fairy turns her tears to laughter, her hatred to love, and then transfers that love from himself to Desmond.

BEAUTY—
How I have wronged thee!   Thy eagerness deceived.
O sweet Desmonio, now I am invaded
With a love which knows no satisfaction.
DESMOND—
Let's to't then.

He picks her up in his arms, and starts off. The Good Fairy, dressed as the Illyrian Nun, stops him in his tracks. "For shame," she says. And that's enough to make Desmond drop the Beauty, and fling himself on his knees before the Nun. Once more the Wicked Fairy loses his temper.

Wesley finds this harder to understand than the French version, even though it was in English.

AIMÉ—Perhaps we French know them better than you do. . . . You are such recent friends, while we are such old enemies.

Though it is Ikonenko's turn next, he's none too anxious; this is not a realistic approach to life. But the wicked Fairy tempts him, and he calls for a period of rounded epaulettes with tassels.

The inner curtain goes up, and there, dressed to the nines, is Ikonenko in Czarist uniform, epaulettes and all. He is knitting a mitten while seated on a rope swing. The Beauty dressed in nineteenth-century dress is idly hitting a croquet ball while conversing in a Chekovian monotone.

Ikonenko quotes from Pushkin, and the two of them make a conversational detour around love, life, and the weather, getting nowhere. A shot is heard sporadically, but leaves them undisturbed.

BEAUTY—I was so looking forward to yesterday.

IKONENKO—Sadovsky's dance?

BEAUTY—Yes . . . but now it is over, I cannot look forward to it anymore.

IKONENKO—I did not go. . . .

BEAUTY—Nor did I. . . .

IKONENKO—I stayed here . . . in the drawing room . . . mending the General's watch. . . .

BEAUTY—I was here too . . . in the dining room . . . thinking.

IKONENKO—We were in the house alone.

BEAUTY—Yes.

IKONENKO—And I never knew.

The Wicked Fairy appears in this listless fog, dressed as the long-bearded, eccentric, chirpy uncle of the Beauty. This time he doesn't even come close to staging a seduction scene. Ikonenko simply continues to knit and swing. The Fairy becomes so irritated that he gives the swing a nasty push, tears off his disguise, and cries: "Damn it, you're just not trying!"

IKONENKO—Why should I try? Haven't I seen what happened to the others?

The Good Fairy comes in, padded and costumed. She is amazed: "Do you mean to say I've got dressed for nothing?"

IKONENKO—Aha! You are my wife. I knew you could come if I tried to seduce her. What's the use?

BEAUTY—What's the use?

WICKED FAIRY—What's the use? (*The curtain falls.*)

The next scene reveals the Beauty as an unmistakable street-walker. She is joined in a dive by Wesley dressed as a clergyman.

BEAUTY—If you want me, I'll give you a price. I don't go for opening gambits.
WESLEY (*with a self-righteous smile*)—I don't . . . em . . . want you. I was offering you a cigarette.
BEAUTY (*incredulous*)—For free?
WESLEY—Sure.

The Beauty is pretty sassy until Wesley introduces himself as Father Brietenspiegel: "They call me the Fighting Father."

BEAUTY—Hey, are you Fighting Father Brietenspiegel? *The* Fighting Father Brietenspiegel?
WESLEY—Sure. The guy that started Girls' Town.

Since he is well known in her set, she relaxes and gives him her name. Aurora Mae Duckworth—Rory to the guys.

WESLEY—I want to take you away from here, Rory, but bad.
BEAUTY—Why don't you shut up?
WESLEY—Rory, ever seen the sun rise over the Alleghenies? It comes up like a great big lantern in the sky, and seems to say, "Get up, get up" to all God's creatures. "I'm back again, folks" (*Rises.*), it says. "I've been keeping guys warm right to the other side of the great wide world." And you'd kneel there, Rory, filling your canteen by the brook, and say to it, "Thanks, sun, it's sure good to see you back. You're a pal." And the old sun 'ud say, "Don't thank me, Rory, I'm doing my duty—are you?" And you'd think and smile up at him and say, "Sure, Mr. Sun, I've left the city lights way back of me. (*Is back of juke box.*) It's my turn to build the bonfires for breakfast at Girls' Town." "What's cookin', kids?" he'll call. "Waffles with maple syrup, ham, corn flakes, and real good coffee."
AIMÉ—I have an irresistible desire to brush me teeth.

The Wicked Fairy now makes his inevitable entrance as an escaped convict pal of Rory's—his prison stripes showing brightly under his raincoat. He has a little score to settle with his erstwhile moll.

WICKED FAIRY—I want to settle a little argument we never finished, baby. Remember the time the cops came, and you kept going to the window, saying you felt hot? Sure you felt hot, you dirty double-crossing she-dog. Yeah. (*Pulls out gun and points at girl.*)

Wesley, with gaudy virtue, tries to talk the Wicked Fairy out of shooting. The Fairy backs away, bumping into, and starting up, the juke box. He stops it with a shot, then mellows for a moment. He sits on a table, extends his leg, encircles Rory and pulls her to him. "Listen, Babe, I want a kid."

BEAUTY (*frees herself—pushing his leg away*)—Are you suggesting marriage?

WICKED FAIRY—Don't say it that way, it don't sound so good.

BEAUTY—Listen, louse, I go with guys, but I don't marry them. That's not me. I'm not made that way. That's not the way I tick. I'm one of the little people that like little, simple things. I'm little, and I like little guys, guys that go to the ball game Sundays and stand right there and shout and put their souls into their shouting. I don't want big ideas, Tony Carabosse, on account of they eat you up, like fire, from the inside. It's guys like you try to smash the little things, and the beautiful deep things, and the U. S. Constitution.

IKONENKO—Has she refused?

BEAUTY (*vastly superior*)—And there's something else. Thomas Jefferson once said—

The Wicked Fairy can take no more, is about to shoot her, when Wesley expertly relieves him of his gun. Training the gun on him, he gives the Wicked Fairy a lesson—a scripture lesson. Then to show what a good sport he is, he tosses away the gun and fights the Wicked Fairy man to man, fist to fist. And licks him. Beauty is waiting for him, but he tells her: "I wasn't fighting just for you, Rory, but for the forces of light and freedom all over the world."

Now, by a wonderful stroke of fortune, it turns out that they only call Brietenspiegel "Father"—in truth he is an Episcopalian.

BEAUTY—Whoopee! Hold me tight. Tighter. (*Her eyes shut in ecstasy.*) My holy dreamboat! My Noah's Ark!

The Good Fairy dressed as Wesley's psychiatrist puts a quick end to this. The Wicked Fairy is utterly routed. (*Curtain.*)

But he comes down off the stage, full of another chance for the Colonels. They can stay here asleep at the Beauty's side for a hundred years and then have another go at her. Desmond turns this offer down. He doesn't care much for his wife, but he does love his dogs and wants to go back to them. Ikonenko decides to return too, because he is certain that in a hundred years he would once again fail with the Beauty. "Besides," he says, "I do not wish to forfeit my pension." Aimé surprises them all by deciding to stay. "My dear Fairies, you envy my power to choose, but I am sick of choosing, for at the moment of choice, I always regret what I have not done. Therefore, I long to give myself to the selfless and patient pursuit of a single, elusive woman whom, as a punishment, I shall never possess." And Wesley says: "Well . . . I guess I'm staying too. I sort of like the idea of waking up in a hundred years' time. I go for that. I would like to have another try at the Beauty but even if I don't win her, it will be great to look around in the year 2050 and see what the world is like!—Oh, boy! I told you fellows I was a Romantic at heart— Remember?" So Donovan and the Wicked Fairy split the take: Each has two Colonels.

Beds are provided for Wesley and Aimé at either side of the Beauty's, just beyond touching distance.

The Fairies will trump up an accident to account for the disappearance of the French and American Colonels, while returning the Russian and English ones to civilization.

The Inner Curtain goes up and finds Wesley and Aimé stretched out on their beds, vainly seeking to touch the Beauty.

WESLEY—Were we wrong not to go back?
AIMÉ—What is the use of asking such a question?

At this precise moment, they are asking themselves if they were wrong not to stay. . . . And so to sleep.

THE CRUCIBLE *

A Play in Four Acts

By Arthur Miller

[Arthur Miller *was born in New York in 1915, and brought up in Brooklyn. He is a "much prized" playwright. He won the Avery Hopwood Award while an undergraduate at the University of Michigan and a year later another Hopwood Award. After graduating he walked off with a Theatre Guild prize of $1250. In 1947 he won the Drama Critics Award for "All My Sons"—the play which brought him his first solid fame. In the 1948-49 season he went on with "Death of a Salesman" to win both the Drama Critics Award and the Pulitzer prize. This year's "Crucible" was one of the most discussed plays of the season.*]

IT is Spring of the year 1692, in Salem of the Massachusetts Bay Colony.

The minister of the town, the Reverend Parris, is kneeling at the bedside of his strangely ill daughter, Betty. The sun streams through the leaded panes of the narrow window showing the room's scant furnishing.

As the minister prays over the inert form in the bed, his Barbados slave, Tituba, enters to inquire about the child. The master angrily gets rid of her, and then once more returns to his prayers, this time mixing tears with his entreaties.

His niece, Abigail Williams, finds him thus. A beautiful, untrustworthy girl, an orphan and charge of the minister, she is seemingly concerned over her cousin's illness. She brings into the room her friend, Susanna Walcott, who has been sent to the Doctor's to ask what may be causing the child's strange illness, and for the proper medicine. Susanna reports that the Doctor can find no cure for Betty in all his books, and even bids Parris look to unnatural causes.

PARRIS (*his eyes going wide*)—No—no, there be no unnatural cause here. Tell him I sent for Reverend Hale of Beverly, and Mr. Hale will surely confirm that. Let him look to medicine and put out all thought of unnatural causes here. There be none.

And he tells Susanna to go directly home and speak of none of this.

Abigail reminds her uncle that the parlor is crowded with people, and that there is some talk of witchcraft among them. Parris turns on her, and asks just what is he to tell them: that he saw his children dancing like heathen in the forest? And since they have not been open with him, he does not know what else they may have done.

He pleads with Abigail: "If you know something that may help the doctor, for God's sake tell it to me. (*She is silent.*) I saw Tituba waving her arms over the fire when I came on you. Why was she doing that? And I heard a screeching and gibberish coming from her mouth. She were swaying like a dumb beast over that fire." Abigail pretends innocence to all this, but becomes terrified when her uncle says he saw a naked figure run into the forest on his approach. Because Parris knows he is hated by many of his parishioners, he realizes that knowledge of such goings on would ruin him, and he begs Abigail to be frank with him. She swears there is nothing more to tell. Parris remonstrates with her for endangering his reputation, and asks about her own. He would like to know why Goody Proctor turned her out of her house, and avoided going to church, because "she refused to be close to anything so unclean as Abigail."

ABIGAIL—She hates me, uncle, she must, for I would not be her slave. It's a bitter woman, a lying, cold, sniveling woman, and I will not work for such a woman.

PARRIS—She may be. And yet it has troubled me that you are now seven month out of her house, and in all this time no other family has ever called for your service.

Abigail lashes out that all these women want slaves to work for them, and goes on to denounce Goody Proctor as a gossiping liar.

Mrs. Anne Putnam and her husband come into the room to see Betty. This twisted woman of forty-five is haunted by death. She has buried seven of her own babies, and wants to know all about Betty's illness so as to compare it to her own Ruth's symptoms: "I'd not call it sick; the Devil's touch is heavier than sick. It's death, y'know, it's death drivin' into them, forked and hoofed."

Parris tries to have her drop the theme, but Putnam wants to know if the Reverend Hale of Beverly has been sent for, and Parris must admit that he has done so as a precaution. Mrs. Putnam at once shows her excitement because of Hale's finding a witch in Beverly last year, and to quiet her Parris says: "Now, Goody Anne, they only thought that were a witch, and I am certain there be no element of witchcraft here."

PUTNAM—No witchcraft! Now look you, Mr. Parris—
PARRIS—Thomas, Thomas, I pray you, leap not to witchcraft. I know that you—you least of all, Thomas, would ever wish so disastrous a charge laid upon me. We cannot leap to witchcraft. They will howl me out of Salem for such corruption in my house.

But Putnam is not for leaving the charge alone. He insists that there are vengeful spirits laying hands on the children; and his wife, at Putnam's urging, tells how all her babies died, and how this year she found Ruth becoming strange, too. She then sent Ruth to Tituba, the slave, to speak to her dead children and find out their murderer. Putnam bellows that there is a murdering witch among them; and tells the minister to declare his discovery himself, before he can be charged with it.

A fat, sly eighteen-year-old then comes in. It is the Putnam servant girl, Mercy Lewis, who ostensibly came in to see how Betty was, but is told by the Putnams to go back at once to their Ruth. Thomas finally persuades Parris to meet with the people below, and lead them in prayer. And upstairs, the girls meet and compare notes on how much Parris knows about their dancing and conjuring and Mercy's being seen naked. They are then joined by timid, lonely Mary Warren, who is scared to death that they will be named as witches, and that witchery will hang them. Mercy is quite menacing to Mary but Betty whimpers suddenly, and diverts their attention. Betty comes out of her bewitched state, and neatly accuses Abigail of drinking blood.

ABIGAIL—Betty, you never say that again! You will never—
BETTY—You did, you did! You drank a charm to kill John Proctor's wife! You drank a charm to kill Goody Proctor!

Abigail smashes the child across the face, and Betty collapses on her bed, sobbing. Then Abigail threatens them all: "Now look you. All of you. We danced. And Tituba conjured Ruth Putnam's dead sisters. And that is all. And mark this. Let either of you breathe a word, or the edge of a word, about the other things, and I will come to you in the black of some terrible night and I will bring a pointy reckoning that will shudder you. And you know I can do it—" Abby tries to make Betty sit up, but the girl is once more in her death-like state.

John Proctor then comes in on the girls: seeing his servant Mary Warren, he roughly tells her to go home to his wife, and Mercy Lewis sidles out with Mary.

Abigail admires Proctor as he looks at Betty, then tells him that Betty has just gone silly somehow, that there's no witchcraft here, that the child merely took fright at her father coming upon them dancing in the wood.

PROCTOR (*his smile widening*)—Ah, you're wicked yet, aren't y'! You'll be clapped in the stocks before you're twenty.

ABIGAIL—Give me a word, John. A soft word.

PROCTOR—No, no, Abby. That's done with.

ABIGAIL (*tauntingly*)—You come five mile to see a silly girl fly? I know you better.

PROCTOR (*setting her firmly out of his path*)—I come to see what mischief your uncle's brewin' now. (*With final emphasis.*) Put it out of mind, Abby.

ABIGAIL—John, I am waitin' for you every night.

PROCTOR—Abby, I never give you hope to wait for me.

ABIGAIL—I have something better than hope, I think!

and goes on: "I know how you clutched my back behind your house and sweated like a stallion whenever I come near! Or did I dream that? It's she put me out, you cannot pretend it were you. I saw your face when she put me out, and you loved me then and you do now!"

PROCTOR—Abby, that's a wild thing to say—

but when she goes further, and he pushes her from him, all remnants of softness leave her, and she speaks angrily of his sickly wife, as "a cold sniveling woman, and you bend to her. Let her turn you like a—" Betty screams out as a psalm is heard being sung downstairs. This unnerves Proctor; and Abigail hurries to Betty but cannot quiet her. The singers rush in to see what is wrong. Parris is overwrought, and Mrs. Putnam is sure that Betty couldn't stand to hear the Lord's name.

Rebecca Nurse, greatly respected, aged woman, who leans on her walking stick, and the hearty oldster Giles Corey, eighty-five and still powerful, arrive with the Putnams. Rebecca goes to the child's bedside and immediately has a calming effect. Rebecca, sitting, says: "I think she'll wake in time. Pray calm yourselves. I have eleven children, and I am twenty-six times a grandma, and I have seen them all through their silly seasons, and when it come on them they will run the Devil bowlegged keeping up with their mischief. I think she'll wake when she tires of it. A child's spirit is like a child, you can never catch it by running after it; you must stand still, and, for love, it will soon itself come back." Proctor agrees with her, but Parris states that there's an opinion in the parish that the Devil may be among them.

PROCTOR—Then let you come out and call them wrong. Did you consult the wardens before you called this minister to look for devils?

PARRIS—He is not coming to look for devils!

PROCTOR—Then what's he coming for?

PUTNAM—There be children dyin' in the village, Mister!

PROCTOR—I seen none dyin'. This society will not be a bag to swing around your head, Mr. Putnam.

Rebecca Nurse calms Proctor down, but he insists on answering Putnam, as to why he has not been attending church: "I have trouble enough without I come five mile to hear him preach only hellfire and bloody damnation." And there are many others, he adds, who stay away for the same reason. Parris is thoroughly aroused over this, and takes it out in wrangling with Proctor over some money the parish owes him. He even accuses Proctor of belonging to a faction in the church that is hostile to him; and Putnam takes Parris' side: "Against him and all authority!" Proctor hotly answers that, then, he must find the faction and join it, and he invites Giles Corey to join it with him. It is thus that the Reverend Hale—his arms full of books—finds them when he enters.

As the minister from Beverly meets everyone in friendly fashion, Proctor takes his leave with the warning: "I've heard you're a sensible man, Mr. Hale. I hope you'll leave some of it in Salem."

Parris shows Mr. Hale the sick child, and tells all he knows of what happened in the forest; Mrs. Putnam tells of sending her child to Tituba. Hale then consults one of his large books and speaks of the Devil, saying: "Have no fear now—we shall find him out if he has come among us, and I mean to crush him utterly if he has shown his face!" This is too strong for Rebecca who rises to leave.

The Putnams resent her departure, but Giles stays on for his own reasons: he asks Hale to explain why his own wife reads strange books, and why he cannot say his prayers while his wife is reading them. Hale comments: "Ah! the stoppage of prayer—that is strange" and agrees to discuss this with Corey later. At the moment, however, he wants to get on with Betty's examination. The child completely fails to respond. Hale then turns and asks Abigail about the happenings in the forest, but she denies having a part in them, and blames Tituba. When the slave is brought before Hale, Abigail points at her, and loudly accuses her of making Betty and herself drink blood. All the shocked slave can do is say how much she loves Betty, and: "I don't truck with no Devil!" But Abigail lies on, accusing Tituba of trying to corrupt and tempt her in all manner of ways at night.

Hearing that she may be whipped or hanged as a witch, Tituba chooses now to "confess" and realizing that things will be still easier for her if she distributes the blame a bit, suggests that the Devil has many witches in his company. When Putnam mentions the names of Sarah Good and Osburn as probable witches, Tituba weepingly assents. Then Abigail sees how things are going, joins in the excitement, and cries out a confession too, chanting one further name. This causes Betty to rise suddenly and join in the frenzied name-calling and finger-pointing. The witch hunt has begun.

ACT II

It is eight days later, and at John Proctor's farm there is a growing sense of anxiety. In the dark living room, John and his wife Elizabeth are seated near the fire, discussing Salem, where a new court, headed by the Deputy Governor of the Province, has been set up; they talk, too, of the band of girls, headed by Abigail, that seems able to send anyone to jail merely by screaming out that such a person had bewitched them.

Elizabeth is unable to keep her servant Mary Warren at home. Each day this self-important child attends court as an "official," and joins in the outcry against all kinds of people. Elizabeth urges her husband to go to Salem before it is too late and tell the court what Abigail so lightly told him, that there was no witchcraft at all. But John still hesitates, saying that no one would believe him without a witness. This so angers his wife that she says: "John, if it were not Abigail that you must hurt, would you falter now? I think not." He furiously replies that for months he has done everything in his power to please his wife, and yet she sits coldly in judgment. Elizabeth answers that she does not judge him, he judges himself: "I never thought of you but a good man, John, only somewhat bewildered." John laughs bitterly at this, then sees a shaken Mary Warren entering the door. She has had a full day at court, but has had time to make Elizabeth a doll, which she gives to her. She made it while sending Goody Osburn to the gallows, and while seeing Goody Good save herself by confession. She instructs the Proctors: "They will not hang them if they confess." Proctor is on the verge of whipping the girl, when Mary points to Elizabeth, saying that she saved her life today.

ELIZABETH—I am accused?
MARY WARREN—Somewhat mentioned. But I said I never see no sign you ever sent your spirit out to hurt no one, and seeing I do live so closely with you, they dismissed it.

When asked who was Elizabeth's accuser, Mary pompously declares that as an official of the court, she is sworn to secrecy. Then without a by-your-leave, Mary takes herself off to bed, leaving the Proctors with the awful certainty that Abigail is out to kill Elizabeth.

ELIZABETH—There be a thousand names; why does she call mine? There be a certain danger in calling such a name. I am no Goody Good that sleeps in ditches, nor Osburn, drunk and half-witted. She dare not call out such a farmer's wife but there be monstrous profit in it. She thinks to take my place, John.

Proctor knows that he must now confront Abigail herself, since no official would any longer be of much help, and he picks up his gun preparing to go into Salem.

Mr. Hale quietly entering from the road, interrupts the Proctors' strained leave-taking. There is almost a sense of guilt about him as he explains to the Proctors that he has just come from Rebecca Nurse's house.

ELIZABETH—Rebecca charged!
HALE—God forbid such a one be charged. She is, however, mentioned somewhat.
ELIZABETH (*with an attempt at a laugh*)—You will never believe, I hope, that Rebecca trafficked with the Devil.
HALE—Woman, it is possible.

Proctor protests: "It is hard to think so pious a woman be secretly a Devil's bitch after seventy year of such good prayer." Hale agrees but adds that: "The Devil is a wily one."

Hale's purpose in coming to the farm is to examine the Proctors themselves, and he starts off inquiring about Proctor's absence from church, and why his last child was not baptized. John's given reason is his dislike and contempt for Rev. Parris: "I see no light of God in that man." Hale will not accept that; though when he hears John has helped build the church, he grants that that is in his favor.

Hale asks Elizabeth whether she knows her commandments, and she assents so eagerly that he questions her no further on them. John, when asked the same question, appears less sure, and in consequence is made to recite them. This John does with difficulty, finally managing to remember nine of the commandments, but forgetting the one against adultery. His poor performance so shakes the minister that Elizabeth senses Hale's suspicions about the Proctors and begs John to come right out and tell him about Abigail Williams. Abigail's confession to John that the village children's illness had nothing to do with witchcraft, amazes Hale.

But before the minister takes John into court with his revealing story, there is one more thing that he must find out from the Proctors. Do they believe in witches? Once again, John hesitates, but he will not deny what is spoken of in the Bible. Elizabeth, directly and unequivocally, says she cannot believe in witches: "I cannot believe the Devil may own a woman's soul, Mr. Hale, when she keeps an upright way, as I have. I am a good woman, I know it; and if you believe I may do only good work in the world, and yet be secretly bound to Satan, then I must tell you, sir, I do not believe it."

HALE—You surely do not fly against the Gospel, the Gospel—
PROCTOR—She believes in the Gospel, every word!
ELIZABETH—Question Abigail Williams about the Gospel, not myself!

Hale advises the couple to baptize their child immediately, to attend church regularly, and is about to say that he thinks all will be well with them, when an agitated Giles Corey bursts into the farm room, followed by old Francis Nurse. Both of the old men's wives have been jailed. When one of the husbands appeals in distress to Hale, the minister admits that if such good people are accused, the world has become completely chaotic, but concludes: "Man, remember, until an hour before the Devil fell, God thought him beautiful in heaven."

A wagon rumbles to a stop outside the door. From it come the marshal and clerk of the court with a warrant for Elizabeth's arrest. The Clerk says that he wishes to see the poppets that Mrs. Proctor is reported to have in her possession: told she has none, he discovers the little doll she was given that very evening. Under the doll's skirt, in its body, is found a needle, which is to be Abigail's proof of Elizabeth's intention to harm her. For the girl was similarly stabbed.

Mary Warren is brought before the company to explain how the doll got there. She tells of giving it to Elizabeth, saying that she is doing so of her own free will: "I am entirely myself, I think. Let you ask Susanna Walcott—she saw me sewin' it in court. Or better still, ask Abby, Abby sat beside me when I made it."

When Elizabeth learns that Abigail—with the doll for evidence—accuses her of murder, she cries out: "Why! That girl is murder! She must be ripped out of the world!" But this outburst is taken by the waiting officials as further evidence of her intent to kill Abigail. Then John, in a burst of futile anger, tears up the warrant of arrest, and would be even more violent but for his wife's decision not to resist. Though not unafraid, she manages herself with dignity, and gives the impression that she is constantly thinking of her children's welfare as much as her own salvation. But as Elizabeth is taken away to be chained in the wagon, she pathetically begs her husband to bring her home soon.

Giles and old Mr. Nurse depart shortly after, with Hale's admonition: "Let you counsel among yourselves; think on your village and what may have drawn from heaven such thundering wrath upon you all. I shall pray God open up our eyes."

An angry, desperate Proctor is left with Mary. He is determined that even if he must use force on his frightened servant girl, she shall testify against Abigail. Mary cries: "Abby will charge lechery on you, Mr. Proctor!" "Good," he answers. "Then her saintliness is done with. We will slide together into our pit; you will tell the court what you know."

ACT III

The General Court is in session in the Salem Meeting House proper but its solemn, forbidding, high-beamed anteroom is shortly to become a courtroom, too. It is here that Giles Corey is dragged after causing a disturbance during his wife's trial, and it is here that both he and Francis Nurse must face the censure of hard-bitten Salem Judge Hathorne, and the stern, calculated judgment of the more worldly Deputy Governor Danforth. The latter, a man of sixty, not without humor, isn't one to trifle with, being wholly dedicated to performing his duty. Parris, and the officious clerk Cheever, are here, also, to encourage the court's severity by every means in their power, while the Rev. Hale is present to counsel moderation.

Giles Corey quickly finds out the temper of the court when he tells Danforth: "Your Excellency, we mean no disrespect for—"

DANFORTH—Disrespect, indeed! It is disruption, Mister! This is the highest court of the supreme government of this province.

And when Francis Nurse pleads with Danforth for the chance to show that "the girls are frauds," Danforth asks Nurse: "Do you know who I am?"

FRANCIS—I surely do, sir, and I think you must be a wise judge to be what you are.

DANFORTH—And do you know that near to four hundred are in jails from Marblehead to Lynn, upon my signature . . . and seventy-two condemned by that signature?

FRANCIS—Excellency, I never thought to say it to such a weighty judge, but you are deceived.

Giles and Francis Nurse are then told curtly to submit their evidence in correctly drawn-up affidavits. In the meanwhile, Proctor has arrived before Danforth with his frail witness, Mary Warren. Parris finds their arrival most unpleasant: the girl has avoided court the whole of the past week, feigning illness. Giles, however, explains it: "She has striven with her soul all week, Your Honor; she comes now to tell the truth." Then Parris gets a word in about Proctor: "Beware the man, Your Excellency, this man is mischief!"

Hale urges that Mary be heard, but she is too frightened to speak, so John Proctor tells the Judge for her, that Mary has seen no spirits.

GILES (*eagerly*)—Never.

PROCTOR (*reaching in his jacket*)—She has signed a deposition, sir.

DANFORTH (*instantly*)—No, no. I accept no depositions. (*He is rapidly calculating this.*) Tell me, Mr. Proctor, have you given out this story in the village?

PROCTOR—We have not.

PARRIS—They've come to overthrow the court, sir! This man is—

DANFORTH—I pray you, Mr. Parris— Do you know, Mr. Proctor, that the entire contention of the state in these trials is that the voice of Heaven is speaking through the children!

PROCTOR—I know that, sir—

DANFORTH—And you, Mary Warren, how came you to cry out people for sending their spirits against you?

MARY—It were pretense, sir—

When Danforth inquires about the other girls, she is barely heard to say that all of them were pretending, too. Parris doesn't care for "this lie" to be spread in court. Danforth wants to find out Proctor's true purpose in coming here with Mary. Is it to free his wife, or is it to undermine the court? Proctor says that it is to help Elizabeth. Then, Parris and the ever-officious Cheever make things more difficult for Proctor by sniping away at him. . . . John tore up the warrant for his wife. . . . John plows on Sunday. . . . John is not a proper Christian. And Parris interrupts when John tells Danforth: "Your Excellency, does it not strike upon you that so many of these women have lived so long with such upright reputation, and—"

PARRIS—Do you read the Gospel, Mr. Proctor?

PROCTOR—I read the Gospel—

PARRIS—I think not, or you should surely know that Cain were an upright man, and yet he did kill Abel.

PROCTOR—Aye, God tells us that. (*To* DANFORTH.) But who tells us Rebecca murdered seven babies by sending out her spirit on them? It is the children only, and this one will swear she lied to you.

After Danforth and Hathorne confer, they inform Proctor that Elizabeth has just this morning reported that she was pregnant; all he can reply is that if his wife said so, it must be true; she is incapable of lying.

Danforth then puts this proposition to Proctor: if his wife will be saved for another year, will he now drop his charge? Since John finds it impossible to do this while the lives of his friends are still in jeopardy, Danforth icily orders the three men to present their evidence. First of all they show a list of some ninety-one names of those who have written in behalf of the three wives. This document is immediately construed by Parris as an outright attack on the court, and warrants are ordered issued for every person who signed the petition.

Then Giles' paper is presented to Danforth. This is a very legal bit of work that Corey has drawn up himself; but unfortunately, it contains one unnamed witness. This name he will not divulge to the court fearing to endanger his friend. For this refusal, Giles is accused of contempt. Hale does his best to defend the old man, "We cannot blink it more— There is a prodigious fear of this court in the country." Danforth will not hear such talk, and places Giles under arrest. John is next, and he presents Mary Warren's deposition to Danforth with as much logic and calm reasonableness as he can muster. Hale comes to his aid: "I cannot say he is an honest man; I know him little. But in all justice, sir, a claim so weighty cannot be argued by a farmer. In God's name, sir, stop here; send him home and let him come again with a lawyer—"

DANFORTH (*patiently*)—Now look you, Mr. Hale—

HALE—Excellency, I have signed seventy-two death warrants; I am a minister of the Lord, and I dare not take a life without there be a proof so immaculate no slightest qualm of conscience may doubt it.

DANFORTH—Mr. Hale, you surely do not doubt my justice.

HALE—I have this morning signed away the soul of Rebecca Nurse, Your Honor. I'll not conceal it, my hand shakes yet as with a wound! I pray you, sir, *this* argument let lawyers present to you.

DANFORTH—Mr. Hale, believe me; for a man of such terrible learning you are most bewildered—I hope you will forgive me. I have been thirty-two year at the bar, sir, and I should be confounded were I called upon to defend these people. Let you consider, now— (*To* PROCTOR *and the others.*) And I bid you all do likewise. In an ordinary crime, how does one defend the accused? One calls up witnesses to prove his innocence. But witchcraft is ipso facto, on its face and by its nature, an invisible crime, is it not? Therefore, who may possibly be witness to it? The witch and the victim. None other. Now we cannot hope the witch will accuse herself; granted? Therefore, we must rely upon her victims—and they do testify, the children certainly do testify. As for the witches, none will deny that we are most eager for all their confessions. Therefore, what is left for a lawyer to bring out? I think I have made my point. Have I not?

HALE—But this child claims the girls are not truthful, and if they are not—

DANFORTH—That is precisely what I am about to consider, sir. What more may you ask of me, unless you doubt my probity?

Hale knows he is defeated, and says no more. And Danforth starts his questioning of Mary Warren. She weakly answers him, in almost inaudible tones, as she states that on other occasions she lied, but "I cannot lie no more. I am with God."

The Court then confronts Mary with all her friends: Abigail, Mercy Lewis, Susanna Walcott, and Betty Parris. The timid girl hasn't a chance. Abigail immediately shows what a cool liar she is.

DANFORTH—. . . Now, children, this is a court of law. The law based upon the Bible, and the Bible writ by Almighty God, forbid the practice of witchcraft, and describe death as the penalty thereof. But likewise, children, the law and Bible damn all bearers of false witness. (*Slight pause.*) Now. Then. It does not escape me that this deposition may be devised to blind us; it may well be that Mary Warren has been conquered by Satan, who sends her here to distract our sacred purpose. If so, her neck will break for it. But if she speak true, I bid you now drop guile and confess your pretense, for a quick confession will go easier with you. (*Pause.*) Abigail Williams, rise. Is there any truth in this?
ABIGAIL—No, sir.

And she becomes marvelously indignant as she listens to Mary's confession, and says: "It is a lie," and goes so far as to testify that "Goody Proctor always kept poppets." Abigail, also, has the support of Parris, of officious Cheever, and of Judge Hathorne, all of whom help her with her testimony. This turn of events so upsets John Proctor that he no longer hesitates to accuse Abigail of intent to murder.

DANFORTH—You are charging Abigail Williams with a marvelous cool plot to murder, do you understand that?
PROCTOR—I believe she means to murder.

He tells the court "that this is no child": she was put out of church twice for irreligious behavior, and was seen dancing in the forest. Hale says that "when I first arrived from Beverly, Mr. Parris told me that." Parris unwillingly admits that he saw the girls dance, but won't admit to having seen any of them naked.

Then Judge Hathorne gets permission to cross-question Mary. Why, if she was able to faint and go cold at those other trials, cannot she will herself to faint for them now? "I used to faint because I—I thought I saw spirits . . . But I did not, Your Honor." She tries to explain further: "It were only sport in the beginning, sir, but then the whole world cried spirits, spirits, and I—I promise you, Mr. Danforth, I only thought I saw them but I did not."

Danforth is deeply concerned over this account of Mary's, and asks Abigail if possibly she had been deluded into thinking that she saw spirits. Abigail first becomes haughty, then threatening: "I have been hurt, Mr. Danforth; I have seen my blood runnin' out! I have been near murdered every day because I done my duty pointing out the Devil's people—and this is my reward? To be mistrusted, denied, questioned like a—" Danforth weakens and Abigail openly threatens him: "Let *you* beware, Mr. Danforth. Think you to be so mighty that the power of Hell may not turn *your* wits? Beware of it! There is—" Abigail suddenly goes into a frightened, trance-like act, and whips up her girls against Mary Warren.

Mercy Lewis is the first of the group to join Abigail in her shivering and moaning and calls out: "Mary, do you send this shadow on me?"

MARY WARREN—Lord, save me!

SUSANNA WALCOTT—I freeze, I freeze!

ABIGAIL (*shivering*)—It's a wind, a wind!

MARY WARREN—Abby, don't do that!

DANFORTH—Mary Warren, do you witch her? I say, do you send your spirit out?

Mary can take no more of this, nor can Proctor who leaps wildly at Abigail, and grabs her by the hair until she cries out. John yowls at her: "How do you call Heaven! Whore! Whore!" and ruins himself when he accuses Abigail of lechery. "She thinks to dance with me on my wife's grave!" He tells of this "whore's vengeance" on his wife, because Goody Proctor found out about the two of them, and turned Abigail into the road.

The Court then decides to bring Elizabeth, the wife that never lied, into court. She comes in with Parris, but is allowed only to look at Danforth; she may not consult her husband by word or glance. Thus, the only time in her life that she lies, she does so to save her husband's good name, which he no longer has. Elizabeth refuses to call John a lecher and Abigail a harlot; and so—in the eyes of the court—condemns herself while saving Abigail. Then she is removed from the room. Hale protests it is a natural lie to tell, but Danforth has proved what he wished by his test, and will not listen.

In the clear once more, Abigail puts on a ghastly scene, accusing Mary of bewitching them. The girls with their acting, and mimicking of her every protest, so drive Mary to despair, that she is reduced to whimpering hysteria. Danforth completes her breakdown by threatening her with hanging if she does not confess to witchcraft. This so undoes Mary that she joins in the girls' screaming, until she is heard shrieking accusations at Proctor of being the Devil's man and of conspiring with her to overthrow the court!

Proctor is wild, despairing and defeated as he cries out: "I say— I say—God is dead!" And as he and Corey are taken off to jail, Hale rages: "I denounce these proceedings, I quit this court—" and slams the door behind him.

ACT IV

All Summer long, the Salem jail has been crowded with those condemned by the General Court. Now, before dawn of a Fall morning, a dark cell is being cleared of its filthy prisoners, the confessed Sarah Good and Tituba, to make room for Danforth's final hearing of the unconfessed. When the sun rises, those who will not talk will be summarily hanged.

Danforth and Hathorne are unpleasantly surprised to hear that the Rev. Hale has returned to Salem village and is now with Rebecca and Martha Corey, praying with them. They suspect him of possibly having preached in Andover where the court was overthrown and where there is outright rebellion. But Parris, who joins them, assures the judges that it is fortunate that the Rev. Hale has returned—because he has come to make the women confess. Parris, now, is a very frightened man.

PARRIS—Hear me. Rebecca have not given me a word this three month since she came. Now she sits with him, and her sister and Martha Corey and two or three others, and he pleads with them, confess their crimes and save their lives.

But the women have not weakened, and Parris thinks the hangings should be postponed to give Hale more time. Parris has witnessed unrest in Salem village and is fearful of it: "Now Mr. Hale's returned, there is hope, I think—for if he bring even one of these to God, that confession surely damns the others in the public eye, and none may doubt more that they are linked to Hell. This way, unconfessed and claiming innocence, doubts are multiplied, many honest people will weep for them, and our good purpose is lost in their tears."

An exhausted Hale enters. Sorrow has changed the man. He, too, begs Danforth for more time—no one has yet confessed. Danforth says sternly: "I will not receive a single plea for pardon or postponement. Them that will not confess will hang. Twelve are already executed; the names of these seven are given out, and the village expect to see them die this morning. Postponement now speaks a foundering on my part; reprieve or pardon must cast doubt upon the guilt of them that died till now. . . ." Danforth decides that the court's best chance of obtaining a confession lies with John Proctor; if he is brought from his dungeon, and allowed to see his wife, he might soften in her presence.

Herrick first brings Elizabeth into the cell and removes her chains. The woman now heavy with child, is gaunt and pale, but still shows amazing strength of character. Hale's anxious eloquence: "Live, woman, life is God's most precious gift; no principle, however glorious, may justify the taking of it. I beg you, woman, prevail upon your husband to confess. Let him give his lie. Quail not before God's judgment in this, for it may well be God damns a liar less than he throws his life away for pride. Will you plead with him? I cannot think he will listen to another."

Elizabeth quietly replies: "I think that be the Devil's argument." And she will not shed a tear, or give a promise. She wants only to see her husband.

John Proctor is brought in from his three months' imprisonment in the dungeon. He is no longer himself, he is a prisoner: ragged, filthy and uncertain of movement.

Hale begs the judges that they leave these silent people alone. Danforth warns Proctor that light is coming into the sky, and that he had better make his confession. Then he sweeps out, his retinue following.

The Proctors lightly touch one another, to reassure themselves, then talk of their three sons. They find out about each other, that neither has confessed, that none of their group has. Many others have. But Rebecca would not. And Giles Corey, even under the cruelest torture, would give his torturers no satisfaction, and died at their hands.

John then tells Elizabeth that he, who knows he is no saint, has been thinking of making a confession. "I cannot mount the gibbet like a saint. It is a fraud. I am not that man. . . ." Elizabeth merely says: "And yet you've not confessed till now. That speaks goodness in you." She refuses to judge him, insists that only he can judge himself. But in so doing she tells her husband with much difficulty: "I have sins of my own to count. It needs a cold wife to prompt lechery. . . . I counted myself so plain, so poorly made, no honest love could come to me! Suspicion kissed you when I did; I never knew how I should say my love. It were a cold house I kept!" And then Hathorne comes in on them.

HATHORNE—What say you, Proctor? The sun is soon up.

And John has his answer: "I will have my life."

Then Proctor is able to hear the excitement and exultation in Hathorne's stony voice, as he calls out to the others that Proctor has confessed. And he senses Elizabeth's terror and sorrow; but she tells him to: "Do as you will, do as you will!" John says that he knows what he does is evil; she would do no such thing.

Danforth arrives in a grateful mood, and wishes John to dictate his confession. When John asks why it must be written, Danforth tells him, "Why, for the good instruction of the village, Mister; this we shall post upon the church door!"

Cheever is brought in to write down that John has said he did the Devil's work. And they bring in Rebecca Nurse that she if possible may be influenced by John. But the old lady will have nothing to do with such lies, whereupon Danforth asks John did he ever see Rebecca in the Devil's company. Proctor says "No"; says that he saw none of the condemned with the Devil. When Danforth tells him that a score of other people have already testified to seeing them so, Proctor answers: "Then it is proved. Why must I say it?" As John continues to evade Danforth's questions, the Deputy Governor begins to doubt the man. When John says: "I speak my own sins; I cannot judge another . . . I have no tongue for it," Hale interferes, urges Danforth to let the man sign the confession that they have ready. Under protest, Proctor signs. But before Danforth can take back the paper, to impress the villagers, Proctor grabs it, cries out: "Damn the village! I confess to God, and God has seen my name on this! It is enough!" The court, however, is after more than a spoken confession; it wishes something on paper. But John thinks of his name, of his children, of his friends— Danforth insists that Proctor has not betrayed his friends. Proctor angrily answers: "Beguile me not! I blacken all of them when this is nailed to the church the very day they hang for silence." Proctor now knows that he cannot live without his good name, and with great emotion, tears up the confession. At this Hale calls out:

"Man, you will hang! You cannot!" But Proctor has his answer: "I can. And there's your first marvel, that I can. . . ." He has found enough that he approves of in himself to give him strength. He has the strength to console his weeping wife, to counsel her: "Give them no tear! Tears pleasure them! Show honor now, show a stony heart and sink them with it!" He kisses her passionately; and when Danforth orders the unconfessed to be hanged high over the town, Proctor supports Rebecca Nurse as they go forth from the cell. Elizabeth, left alone with the ministers, Parris and Hale, feels sure "he have his goodness now."

THE EMPEROR'S CLOTHES *

A Play in Three Acts

By George Tabori

[George Tabori *was born in Budapest in 1914 and was educated in Hungary and Germany. Since the early thirties, when he went to England, he has lived in sixteen countries, but he is today a British subject commuting between London, New York and Rome. Besides the two plays recently produced on Broadway—"Flight into Egypt" and "The Emperor's Clothes"—he has written four novels and a number of short stories.*]

ACT I

IT is Christmas time in Budapest in 1930. It has been snowing, and the gallery approach to Elek Odry's apartment is slippery and dangerous. To enter the apartment, one must hold tight to the gallery rail as one first passes the entrance to the Schmitz apartment and then goes down a flight of stone steps to the Odry door.

There is a small entrance hall and then a large, pleasantly cluttered sitting room (running the full length of the gallery) with the grownup's bedroom off one end of it, and the son's and grandmother's rooms, and a kitchen, off the entrance hall.

The sitting room is filled with the possessions of more prosperous days: piano, sideboard, dining-room table and chairs, bookshelves—all arranged near a large-bellied, white-tile stove.

Eleven years ago Elek Odry was a revered and famous professor of classics. Then a military junta took over Hungary, and Elek was dismissed, with many others, from his University post. He has never been able to teach again. Today he earns next to nothing proofreading cheap foreign fiction, and this morning he is asleep at his desk, after a night of correcting proofs.

As the last star disappears in the heavens, and a carol is heard in the distance, Ferike Odry, Elek's charming thirteen-year-old son, comes out of the hall. Carrying his mug of cocoa, he goes for the

---

morning paper, only to find a Man and Child huddled in the entrance. These two are shoeless and coatless, and have had no warm food in days. Ferike pleasantly asks them to come in and warm themselves at the stove, and gives them his cocoa.

The Man discovers Elek sleeping at his desk, and anxiously wishes to leave. Ferike reassures him: "Scholars keep different hours—" and adds, "A great encyclopedia—eagerly awaited by scientific circles. A milestone. You've heard of Professor Odry?" The Man obviously hasn't, but Ferike grandly goes on: "You just saw him. My father." And he shows the ragged couple out.

Bella Odry then comes, in dressing gown, to awaken her husband. She is a very attractive woman, with an old-fashioned, soft kind of looks and masses of red hair. Where her son lives in a world of fantasy, Bella lives with bright memories of her youth.

Elek has difficulty waking after a few hours' sleep. For a moment he is dazed, still remembering a bad dream; and then he becomes lively and playful with Ferike, who climbs into his lap.

FERIKE—Where is the buckaroo?

ELEK—Beyond the blue horizon.

FERIKE—Is he trapped?

ELEK—Trapped, but undaunted. (*They start fencing with imaginary weapons.*)

Elek is loving with his wife. For a moment it seems like a happy little group, at least like a family with pleasant memories. But then the picture changes and other memories crowd back.

ELEK (*goes on laughing to* FERIKE)—It was a great year, my boy. The war had just ended. A good and terrible wind got up—I was going to run for parliament. (*He is downstage now.*) "Friends, countrymen—"

FERIKE (*starts clapping*)—Hear, hear—

BELLA—You two are always playing—

ELEK—"The land is a classroom now!" (*He makes an extravagant gesture, hammering with his left fist against the open palm of his right hand.*) "Let us teach our people liberty, fraternity . . ."

FERIKE—Go on, Papa, go on—

ELEK (*trying to remember*)—I was making a speech. In a village square—

FERIKE—Tremendous crowds . . .

But to Elek who was being cheered by them, they suddenly looked like the enemy, not his friends.

And reality this morning, for Elek, is that: hateful totalitarian crowds; and proofs that haven't been finished; and no money for a Christmas tree.

The rubbed edges, frustrations and grievances of these past years come quickly to the fore now, and Elek becomes louder and more unpleasant with his family, while Bella becomes more and more inadequate. She murmurs French phrases and such things as "Elek —je vous en prie—the servants—"

"What servants?" snaps Elek. "We haven't any servants."

BELLA—The neighbors, then.

ELEK—I shan't be stopped by that bevy of illiterate gossips. This is my house.

BELLA—It happens to be my house, too. These distinguished antiques—

ELEK—If you refer to these funereal chunks of Victorian lumber—

After holding forth on the foolish snobbery of Christmas trees, he finally gets to the point of their quarrel, and admits: "As for the accusation that I can't afford a Christmas tree— Well, I haven't got the money—I haven't got it." More feebly. "The rent's been paid, the fire is warm— After all—this is 1930. When rats go hungry a man may be excused—" He is now distraught. "What am I saying?" He quietly goes off to dress.

His son, all grown-up understanding, says, "His responsibilities are too big—" and "It's this inactivity." For him, his father is a hero.

When Ferike is alone, his dull neighbor, Fat Hugo Schmitz, comes to visit, wanting to play. He calls to a bored Ferike: "Sherlock" so as to be let in. Ferike greets him as "Dr. Watson," without enthusiasm. Hugo lets him know that he is going to the circus. And then he notices the Odrys have no Christmas tree, and comments on that—it's the only house in the block without one.

Ferike, at once on his mettle, invents a fine tale of going to the north woods with his father to choose, and chop, their own magnificent tree. Then, bringing it back by the river and other primitive means, and then finally carting it in style by taxi. At this point, Fat Hugo says they won't have the taxi fare. His family says the Odrys are smart but poor.

FERIKE—Did you ever hear of the Scarlet Pimpernel?
FAT HUGO—No.

FERIKE—English aristocrat. Pretends to be one thing, is another.
FAT HUGO—Maybe, but your father is an ungraced teacher.
FERIKE—Disgraced—to begin with.

But the fat boy persists: "Mother says you don't know where your next meal is coming from," and he so goads Ferike into protecting his family's honor, that he now invents a lulu of a story.

FERIKE (*wildly*)—See this manuscript?
FAT HUGO—Toilet paper.
FERIKE—Pamphlets!
FAT HUGO—Pamphlets? May I read them?
FERIKE—If you want a knife in your back!
FAT HUGO—Very inflammatory?
FERIKE—Very.
FAT HUGO—I won't sneak—
FERIKE—Would you swear by the health of the National Water Polo Team?
FAT HUGO—Never.
FERIKE (*persuasively*)—Why does Hoot Gibson fight the cattle barons?
FAT HUGO—Hoot Gibson? Why?
FERIKE—For the sake of suffering humanity.
FAT HUGO—Suppose I swear?
FERIKE—You'll be one of us.

And that means he'll help occupy the Post Office and remove the Cabinet—the sealed instructions for all of which are in Ferike's little tin box. In return for the honor of being a member of this "dangerous and beautiful" movement, Fat Hugo must give over the milk money intrusted to him by his mother. Then he will be a paying member of the I.P.B., the Illegal Party of Boys. Ferike writes out a receipt for Fat Hugo, and Hugo feeling very elated shouts: "Hooray!" and goes to answer his mother's angry call. Ferike has the money, and Fat Hugo gets slapped and hauled into his apartment, for not giving it to the milkman.

Ferike, putting on his hat and coat, tells his grandmother that he's off to get a tree. Granny, a black-taffeta shadow of an old lady, moves vaguely about the apartment, watching Bella, now dressed for the day, make a telephone call. When Bella rather hastily hangs up and goes to the piano, the old lady replies to Bella's talk about the old days—the charm and gaiety of their past life—with strange sighs and approving little noises.

Elek, cleaned up and calmed down, comes out to announce they'll have their tree as soon as he's finished the proofs. He reads out loud occasionally from the proof sheet of the Western he's working on; he also tells his wife how beautiful she is, how mysterious he used to find her. At the same time, Fat Hugo's father comes out of his door, looks with horror down at the Odrys' flat, crosses himself and goes back in.

Bella plays the piano softly, as her husband recalls the past and his accomplishments as a teacher; his adoring students and their presents to him. He takes a book from the shelf and reads the written dedication from these students. Bella tells him he'll never be happy until he has his old job back once more. This he admits; he even confesses to having gone to the Dean of the school, begging for any teaching position at all, and being shown the door. When Bella suggests other schools, her husband sharply reminds her that he's been blacklisted. Bella shows some impatience with Elek at this point, and dares to tell him about her "chance encounter" with her old beau, Misi—Baron Gonda. "He asked about you very warmly. I told him how you missed teaching. His cousin is at the Ministry—very highly placed."

ELEK—You are nervous.

BELLA—Of course I'm nervous. I can feel your suspicion.

ELEK—I wanted to kill him, once. (*But he is willing to listen to his wife's arguments.*)

BELLA—Elek, when you are free to do what you want, you are a wonderful man—a man one can love and respect. (*Pause.*) He wants you to ring him. He'll give you the details. (*Pause.*) You do want to teach again, don't you?

Elek goes to phone Misi, humbling himself, calling the man "old chap" and "my dear fellow." (While he is talking to the Baron, Mr. Schmitz comes out on the gallery and goes off on some terrifyingly important errand.)

After the amenities, such as they are, are gone through, Elek finds out what the job will be. He asks, disappointedly, "A high school? No—only it'd be funny to start all over again—from the bottom. *Yes,* it *is* better than nothing— It's good of you. Yes. Now?" He looks at Bella. "Certainly. Delighted— Er—see you later, 'old chap.'" He hangs up, irritated. "Old chap!" To Bella, "He's coming over."

Bella is in a state of wild excitement at a visit from Misi, and issues everyone orders. She tells her mother to make canapés and polish the silver, her husband to get out the brandy and glasses, and she herself tries to find a decent jacket for her husband to wear. "Couldn't you wear spats?" she asks him.

ELEK—I lost them in 1921.
BELLA (*kneels down, dusts his shoes*)—I want you to look perfectly divine.
ELEK—Where did you pick up that vile phrase?

Somehow, he finds he doesn't hate Misi any more, and being dressed up by his wife he thinks of his new job, and regains his old self-respect, and he thinks of the subjects he'll be teaching again: "Latin and history," with the same old love.

The handsome Baron arrives with mimosa for Bella, compliments for Bella's mother and pleasant things to say to Elek. Misi, too, notices there is no tree, and when Elek passes it off as something he doesn't believe in, Misi says suavely: "I don't believe in them either, but I like to have friends who do. You used to be a splendid believer in things, Elek. Still anxious to set the world on fire?"

ELEK—Just playing with matches.
MISI—Oh, Elek, don't be disappointing. You used to make me feel so limply agnostic. You were so well informed, too. Elek, what shall I do about my peasants? They still behave as if they wanted to kiss my hand, but they're ready, I fear, to cut my throat. I'd long since have given my lands away, but I'd be blackballed at the Club, and I can't bear the disapproval of my cousins —I have so many cousins. Is this Hitler fellow important? Everyone talks about him. He said the other day he'd defend the West from the East, which sounds absolutely ravishing—except that I'm rather east of the fellow myself. What's the world coming to?

But Misi has absolutely no intention of listening to Elek's views on the economic situation—or to Elek. The Baron makes small talk, as things become rather tense. Elek now realizes his Bella has been seeing Misi, and Misi is getting him a job because of his interest in Bella. But the situation is smoothed over by Misi's easy compliments to Elek. Then he tells him what he has to do for the job. The "formalities are simple. You'll have to write a letter. After all," the Baron adds, "you *were* a naughty boy."

ELEK—Was I?

MISI—Making all those darling, silly speeches— All of man's troubles come from his inability to keep his mouth shut.

BELLA—It's just a formality.

ELEK (*wildly*)—Yes, Bella. Yes, I've read through the lives of the saints: they died grandly, but they never had to worry about the rent. I'll write anything you say, anything. "Give me what I have, or even less; and therewith let me live for what remains of life, if the gods will that anything remain." (*He starts breaking.*) "Let me have a generous supply of books and of food stored a year ahead; nor let me hang and tremble on the uncertain hour."

FERIKE (*bursts in upon them with the scrubby tree he was able to buy. Tells them, boastfully*)—With all the money you gave me— (*Looks at* ELEK.)

BELLA (*embarrassed*)—Father is going to teach again. Uncle Misi is being so kind as to help him.

FERIKE—As if you needed help!

And as Misi wants to get on with the letter, Ferike completes his father's humiliation by painting a scene of wild enthusiasm in the markets when it became known that the tree was for Professor Odry.

Elek writes the letter, word for word, at Misi's dictation, while the child listens with horror. Finally, Ferike can't control himself any longer: "Why do you let him dictate to you—" (Bella hushes him.) "You said the government was—"

ELEK—I said nothing of the sort—

FERIKE—Here in this room—night after night—you patiently explained—

ELEK—The child is raving.

And as he is pushed toward his room, Ferike continues to protest: "Don't write a letter like that."

Driven to fury, Elek starts after his son to give him a thrashing. Ferike runs for the door, and stops dead. Fat Hugo and his father have brought two detectives and a policeman for Ferike. The boy backs away, but his father comes up angrily behind him; and seeing him still angry, Ferike makes a dash for his room. Pushing the bewildered parents aside, the two detectives come into the house. One detective goes after Ferike.

1ST ROTTENBILLER—Got him?

2ND ROTTENBILLER—He's locked himself in the lavatory.

1ST ROTTENBILLER—Will you be good enough to get that child out of the privy? We're from the police.

ELEK (*retreats*)—What?

BELLA (*a tigress now*)—What do you want with my child?

1ST ROTTENBILLER—He's under arrest.

CURTAIN

ACT II

Peter Odry, Elek's younger brother, is trying to keep Bella company while she waits for news of her son. Peter, a badly overworked doctor, stands by the stove, not daring to sit down for fear of going to sleep: "I was up at four-thirty this morning"; he continues absentmindedly, "A man's been dying for six weeks, this morning he begs me to prolong it till after Christmas. He's curious to know what his presents are like. Strange how people are—"

He drinks coffee that Granny brings him, and pleasantly disagrees with Bella's "If you don't wait for Elek he'll never forgive you."

PETER—My brother and I long ago gave up forgiving one another.

BELLA—Nonsense!

PETER—You say so because in your little universe brothers are supposed to love one another, even if they manifestly don't.

Peter in an amiable way proves to her that Elek has hated him from babyhood.

BELLA—That's a fine way to talk about a brother who has gone to the police.

PETER—You'd be surprised at the number of people who are taken to the police.

BELLA (*indignantly*)—My husband has never had anything to do with them!

PETER—I wouldn't be so proud of that. An American, fighting for freedom, was put in jail one day. A friend of his came to see him and asked: "What are you doing in there?" "What are you doing out there?" he replied.

BELLA—Don't start that again.

PETER—That? Bella, don't turn me into a mysterious monster. We live in a militaristic state. Not being one of the generals, I not unnaturally dislike it, because quite apart from terror, it forces you to become either a rat or a saint. A most uncomfortable choice, but I can't escape it. I see too much.

BELLA—You worry too much.

PETER—Oh, Bella, Bella, if only I could sleep for three days—if only nobody wanted to die or be born for three days. Yes, I do worry too much. There's a special kind of insomnia for fools like me— I'm supposed to save lives, but everyone else seems to be in the mortuary business, so I can't sleep.

When the clock strikes three, Bella's nervousness over her son grows uncontrollable. Peter tries to calm her, but then Fat Hugo's mother rings the bell. Bella and Peter both make a dash for the door. After her initial disappointment, Bella courteously asks Mrs. Schmitz in. Mrs. Schmitz is here for two unpleasant purposes: to get back her milk money, and to see that all social relations between the two families are severed. Her resentment at the Odrys' superiority overflows, and she even admits, under Peter's probing, that it was she who had called the police:

MRS. SCHMITZ—Pamphlets! Occupy the Post Office! Illegal parties! Free love, that's what it is! With such talk to poison my sweet child! With such talk to take the milk money! Give me the money, I'll have it disinfected, I will!

PETER—The child didn't know what he was doing.

MRS. SCHMITZ—He didn't, didn't he? Just look at them books. Manuscripts! Look at those pencils, all those pencils, but was there a flag on St. Stephen's Day? And what happened to your husband's job; why did he have to shave off his mustache all of a sudden in 1921? (*She gets her money and departs.*)

When Elek worriedly returns without news of their son, he feels blamed for not bringing Ferike back. He went to police headquarters, he assures Bella: they were nice but could tell him nothing. Peter wants to know about the detective who took the boy away. When he finds out there were two, twin brothers, he knows from experience the Ferike has been taken to the "political" police.

Elek scoffs at the idea of their bothering with a child, but Bella is frantic, and wants to go after Ferike at once. At first Elek won't take Mrs. Schmitz' visit seriously, either. He is, if anything, a bit pleased at his son's description of him, as a leader of plots and intrigue, although frightened of the idea of plots.

ELEK—Why should he say that about me? The police won't believe such fairy tales.

BELLA—He's been gone over two hours.

PETER—The bastards believe anything they want to believe.

ELEK (*wagging his finger*)—You be careful what you're saying—

PETER—They've got to justify their existence. They discover "plots" every day.

ELEK—I won't have such talk in my house!

When the phone rings, no one moves. Bella and Elek are frightened. Bella, told to answer, hears from Misi that "the news is not too good. He couldn't say more on the phone. He is coming over presently."

Elek now treats Bella with great gentleness, gets her some water, helps her to a chair. But when he tries to get to the bottom of his child's fantasies, he bluntly explains matters to himself by saying: "He is a liar, that poor child, a pathological liar."

PETER—Jesus said the Kingdom of God was at hand—it wasn't.

ELEK—Keep your blasphemous tongue out of this—

PETER—He needs a hero. Since you can't oblige, he spins fables. When one is in jail, one dreams of freedom.

Peter tells his brother, under questioning, that Ferike often visits him, and they've even talked politics. Elek is very much agitated at this, feeling his brother is the source of corruption. Peter then tells him he knows nothing about his own son. Elek answers that he is finding out, and starts his own investigation by going through Ferike's treasure box, as if it were the boy's mind.

ELEK (*ruffling the contents*)—What's this?

BELLA—A snail, sweetheart.

ELEK—(*drops it in disgust*)—I was confused, but only for a moment. That child is a liar—he's been made into a liar! (*He takes out a book.*) "Around the World in Eighty Days." Raffles and St. John the Baptist, what next? (*Another book.*) "His Story of the Quakers." Uh-huh, I'm going to call a doctor.

And the idea grows in Elek's mind of calling in a specialist to draw up an official report.

When Misi arrives, he admits to having failed: he has no idea when the child will be coming home. "Cousin Nandor said: 'Wouldn't touch this case with a bargepole. Keep out of it,' he said."

Elek then airs his belief that the child isn't well, that he has a fevered imagination. Misi's only answer is that he can no longer try to get Elek the teaching post.

ELEK (*frightened*)—Misi, he is a child. They won't believe a child's fable.

MISI—It's about his own father, it seems.

Elek asks whether they won't believe what a specialist has to say about Ferike. Peter protests Elek's approach—Ferike is a fine child—"full of poetical fantasies—"

ELEK—One can be a poet without sending one's poor old father to jail.

The Baron thinks there might be something in the specialist idea: "You mean, a mental specialist?" At this clear statement, even Elek hesitates. Peter begs Bella to stop this—"They're trying to have Ferike committed!"

ELEK—I'm trying to do nothing of the sort.

PETER—Finish your thought! What *did* you mean?

ELEK—If a doctor examined Ferike, and testified—

PETER—What, what? That he's a lunatic?

ELEK—I didn't say that—

PETER—To save your goddam neck, you'd send your son to the insane asylum. (ELEK *slaps his face.*)

The Baron takes affront at such uncivilized behavior in front of a lady, and remembers an appointment. But as he leaves, he tells them that his cousin said the Odrys' must now expect a house search. Misi advises them to get rid of any "silly" books that might be lying around. "I sympathize. Bella, you ought to go to the seaside." And he goes off to meet another of his cousins.

Bella is afraid, but she is also ready to fight for her son. She says very quietly: "If anyone dares to suggest my son is a mental case, I'll scratch his eyes out." Elek means to be calm, but panic is slowly welling within him. He asks his brother to leave immediately; he wants the name of a good specialist; he wants Granny

Photo by Zinn Arthur

Ralph Meeker and Janice Rule in "Picnic"

GERALDINE PAGE
as Lily in
"Midsummer"

SHIRLEY BOO
as Leona Samish
"The Time of the C

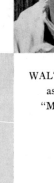

VICTOR MOORE
as Gramps in
"On Borrowed Time"

WALTER SLEZAK
as Joseph in
"My 3 Angels"

TOM EWELL
as Richard Sherman in
"The Seven Year Itch"

IRIS MANN
as Mary Telford
"The Children's H

JOHN WILLIAMS
as Inspector Hubbard in
"Dial 'M' For Murder"

ROSALIND RUSSELL
as Ruth in
"Wonderful Town"

HELEN GALLAGHER
as Hazel in
"Hazel Flagg"

N VERDON
Claudine in
Can-Can"

JOAN McCRACKEN
as Betty in
"Me and Juliet"

EMLYN WILLIAMS
playing 36 characters in
"Bleak House"

DANNY KAYE

ONE POWER
e "reading" of
Brown's Body"

HIRAM SHERMAN
as Master of Ceremonies in
"Two's Company"

Beatrice Straight and Walter Hampden in "The Crucible"

Maurice Evans in "Dial 'M' for Murder"

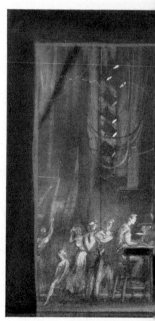

Sketch for Joe Mielziner's set
for "Me and Juliet"

Photograph of Donald Oenslager's set for "Horses in Midstream"

Photo by Vandamm

Sketch for Howard Bay's set
for "The Children's Hour"

Sketch for Lemuel Ayers' set
for "Camino Real"

Costume sketch by Motley
Julia in "Midsummer"

Costume sketch by Irene Sharaff
for "Me and Juliet"

Costume sketch by Miles White for *Sadie Thompson* in "Two's Company"

Costume sketches by Miles White for "Hazel Flagg"

Dino DiLuca, Jose Perez and Shirley Booth in "The Time of the Cuckoo"

John Kerr, Johnny Stewart and Camilla DeWitt in "Bernadine"

and Bella to help him follow Misi's instructions, and burn the books.
"I don't mind going to jail," he says wildly, "provided it's of my
own free will."

ELEK—I won't, however, be pushed into prison by a juvenile
delinquent. When children turn against their fathers, that's the end
of civilization. Help me, all of you. (*He goes to bookcase.*) All
my life I've been a law-abiding citizen. I've paid my taxes, saluted
the flag. (*He holds out a book to* PETER.) Into the fire—
PETER (*horrified*)—Elek—
ELEK—Into the fire! (*When nobody helps him, he does it himself. As he hurls the books one after the other, his family stand by
in horror. He has even thrown away the present from his students.
With fierce self-accusation:*) There'll be no more silly books in this
house! (*He starts pulling out books in a frenzy, letting them fall.*)
No more books, no books, no books at all!

The family's horror is now compounded: the Rottenbillers are
ringing the doorbell. Frantically the family thrust the books back
into the bookcase.
A cheerful Ferike comes into the house: his parents are beside
themselves with joy. The Rottenbillers stand by while the mother
kisses the boy and the father lovingly fusses over him.
Then the Rottenbillers move into the living room, making jokes
about their identical appearance, at which everyone laughs. But
after everyone else has stopped, Elek goes on laughing, uncon-
trollably. The detectives have quietly set up operations at the
dining-room table, pencils ready, dossiers open. Elek is requested
to sit down at the table; the others are requested to remain and
make it a "family party."
The inquisition begins.

2ND ROTTENBILLER—Who is Mr. Hoot Gibson?
ELEK (*relieved smile*)—A movie actor, assuming mostly the role
of an American cowboy.
2ND ROTTENBILLER—When did you see him last?
ELEK—About a month ago—at the Corwin Theatre. The title of
the film was—

He is asked whether he has had any personal contact with Hoot,
any correspondence. The detectives won't accept as an answer that
Ferike is a movie fan—they want to know why Hoot Gibson opposed
the big cattle owners of America. Is he a Secret Service Agent?

Having got nothing interesting from Elek in this direction, they start on another. What is Elek's profession, what university does he teach at, and if not, why not?

1st ROTTENBILLER—Were you ever dismissed from your job?
ELEK—My appointment was allowed to lapse.
2nd ROTTENBILLER—Why?
ELEK (*with growing discomfort*)—Those were turbulent days—
1st ROTTENBILLER—What days?
ELEK—Well, you remember—
2nd ROTTENBILLER—We don't remember, Mr. Odry.
ELEK—At the end of the war—turbulent days—
1st ROTTENBILLER—A good many teachers have never lost their jobs.

They next ask if he ever made any speeches, and when he haltingly replies that everyone was making speeches then, the First Rottenbiller tells him: "*I* wasn't making speeches, Mr. Odry." The Rottenbillers read him chapter and verse of what he had said. All he does is to mumble that it was so long ago he doesn't remember; finally, to his most inflammatory remark—"If the intellectuals and the businessmen can't solve our problems, let the workingman solve them—" he says quickly: "I withdrew that speech." He tells them he wrote a letter. The Rottenbillers have no record of such a letter. Elek insists there must be one. The Rottenbillers merely pass on to the next thrust. Does Elek know Woodrow Wilson, Lloyd George? When did he assume the alias of the Scarlet Pimpernel?

ELEK (*on edge*)—The Scarlet Pimpernel is a fictitious character invented by Baroness Orczy.
1st ROTTENBILLER (*makes a note*)—Orczy?
ELEK (*loses his temper*)—I'm not here to fill in the gaps in your education!

This doesn't help; in fact, he is forced to apologize.

ELEK—But any information based on my son's testimony is a tissue of lies. (FERIKE *moves nearer.*)
1st ROTTENBILLER (*to his brother*)—Listen to that! A father talking about his son—
2nd ROTTENBILLER—Such a nice lad, too.
ELEK (*away from* FERIKE)—It's not his fault, it's pathological.
1st ROTTENBILLER—Oh? May we see the pamphlets?

ELEK (*loudly*)—I don't write pamphlets—I'm only a proof-reader!

2ND ROTTENBILLER—Of what kind of books? Upton Sinclair? Thomas Dreiser?

ELEK—Theodore Dreiser, and I don't—

2ND ROTTENBILLER (*furiously*)—Don't you correct me!

Once again Elek apologizes and says "Thomas Dreiser."

The Rottenbillers note "a grave spiritual crisis" in Elek's not attending Mass. They also note that he is very tolerant toward labor unions.

When they attack his brother Peter, as an agitator and "pacifist swine," Elek makes only a lukewarm defense of him. But the interview ends abruptly when they find that Elek has no prejudice against the Jews. When Elek sees what is happening, he starts to backtrack, to qualify and then to capitulate entirely: "There are too many Jews in this country," he tells the brothers. But then they ask: "Why did you start this illegal movement—? the 'Illegal Party of Boys'?" Elek states he never heard of it.

The Rottenbillers turn to Ferike: "The Leader, isn't he? The Great Hero, isn't he?"

"Yes," replies Ferike, "he is!"

The brothers ignore Elek's violent protest, go to stove and, taking the tongs, haul out a burning book. "In French!" exclaims the First Rottenbiller. "There's no smoke without fire. You'd better come with us, Mr. Odry. The chief would want to compare the child's testimony with yours."

Quietly and coldly, Elek asks for time to speak to his family. The Rottenbillers go outside to wait, and Elek talks to his son. He is now the teacher; his subject is himself and the family. He is determined to strip Ferike of all illusions, of all means of self-deception. He mercilessly starts in: "Now then—am I the hero?" His loyal son answers: "Yes."

Elek tells him all the wrong things he has done since he was six years old, drags out all the skeletons in the family closet. As a child he tried to kill Peter with a pair of scissors; Uncle Julius fled to Brazil, not because he killed someone in a duel, but to abscond with the company funds; Elek deserted during the war, but was not found out. And his magnificent pacifist speeches? Afterwards, he did nothing but apologize for them. "I plagued the authorities for years, begging their pardon—" And who was Ferike's grandfather? The boy proudly answers: "General Schossberg, the Lion of the Carpathians."

BELLA—Elek, don't! (ELEK *looks at her. She steps back.*)

ELEK—Whenever a campaign was approaching a climactic point the dear old boy'd go down with gastric flu. Nor was he a general. He was a colonel, and why was he cashiered? Because of moral turpitude. Granny's strange silence is not due so much to strength of character as to a nervous habit and the shame caused by the revelation that Grandpa was a coward and a drunk—

FERIKE—It's not true!

Elek is not going to stop there. He starts in on his marriage with Bella, and her not wanting Ferike. Peter shouts: "Shut up, you sadist!" "Are you afraid?" Elek asks. The men struggle, but Elek shakes him off and roars: "If I have bred an idiot, let him be cured. Bella, you tell him. What did you say when you found he was on the way? What were your words, Bella? Tell him!"

Bella has to turn away under her son's piercing look, and thus add to the damage. Elek staggers out the door to the Rottenbillers, followed by a hysterical Ferike, who shrieks: "Liar! Liar! Liar!"

ACT III

Bella and Ferike are spending their Christmas night waiting. Ferike, wearing sunglasses, has turned away the beggars from the door and has refused his mother's Christmas offering of his Grandfather's gold watch.

FERIKE—What do I need a watch for?

BELLA—It's pure gold.

FERIKE—I have no appointments to keep.

BELLA—Do me a favor and take it.

He takes it, fiddles with it, winds it, as Bella once more wonders whether she should call Misi. Three hours have passed since they took Elek away for questioning.

Ferike refuses to show anxiety for his father: "They are probably discussing me with a doctor—'He's crazy,' Father will tell them. 'A crazy boy, lock him up.' " Bella reaches for him. "I'd never let them, never—"

Ferike may be somewhat subdued, but his imagination isn't. If only he had left with Peter! What they would do in Africa—Asia. The adventures they would have among the natives and pigmies. ". . . the natives call us Big Paleface and Little Paleface respectively." But they would probably have caught Peter at the frontier, because Elek would have informed on him. And so he brings himself back to the present.

Fat Hugo comes by, to make childish amends. Ferike will have none of him, nor of his apologies. He tells him flatly: "You betrayed me." And he completely disillusions Hugo by saying: "The Hound of the Baskervilles is a fictitious character invented by Conan Doyle." When Hugo leaves and Bella wishes him a Happy Christmas (not wanting him to go off and start more trouble), her son asks: "What are you all afraid of?" and bangs his bedroom door behind him.

Granny now has her innings, waving aloft a letter from the Field Marshal—addressed, she says loudly, to the "Highly respected Widow Schossberg." She recites what the Field Marshal wrote to her on the death of her distinguished husband: "great soldier— brilliant officer—a pillar of the monarchy." She goes back to her room, declaring she will have this letter framed, so all can see it.

Peter now returns, to Ferike's great joy. He says he couldn't make the frontier; but what really happened was he couldn't bear to leave his family and city so defenseless. He advises Bella to "get out of this house, it's rotten through and through," even though he, of his own free will, came back to a city he knew to be "rotten." "Yet I can't leave; I stand here like Lot's wife; I cry out preposterously: 'What's going to happen to you? Who's going to look after you?'—If not I, who? If not now, when?" He goes quickly into the hall, as the Baron walks down the gallery to the Odry door.

Misi is very gay and Christmassy as he enters with parcels tucked under his arm. He makes little jokes with Ferike; but inquires after Elek, too. He knows nothing about him. "They never say much—not even Cousin Tivador," who apparently was the most recent of his cousins on the case.

Having a clear field, Misi, right in front of Ferike, makes very personal remarks to Bella, and then mentions the seaside to the boy. Had he ever been there? He offers a magical description of the Italian Riviera that leaves Ferike completely enthralled.

BELLA—Misi, what are you trying to do?

MISI (*to* FERIKE)—If we leave tomorrow, we'll be in Naples Sunday.

BELLA (*frightened*)—Get out of here!

MISI (*rising quietly*)—What are you waiting for?

BELLA—I'm waiting for my husband.

MISI—"Till shame do us part." (*He goes to table, picks up a spoon and inspects it.*) I'm asking for your life. At my age, I could not put it with more decorum. (*He looks up and about.*) This house has been declared unsafe.

Then Bella learns that Misi made this proposition knowing that Elek has been released and is on his way home.

MISI—I don't want to shake hands with him— I'm what the liberal press so lovingly describes as a reactionary blunderbuss, but if I had a brother, or a friend—(*He puts the knife down.*)—He will have to destroy every mirror in the house, or himself. (*He inspects a plate, turning it around.*) The train leaves the South Station at nine A.M. Ah, Dresden? (*He puts the plate down, touches* BELLA'S *arm lovingly, picks up his hat and coat and leaves.* BELLA *picks up the same plate and inspects it.*)

BELLA (*vaguely*)—Grandpa gave me this. Like all of you he'd have liked it clear and simple. Black or white, love or hatred, honor or shame. Everything was very clear to him until one day he found that nothing was clear. He soused himself in Imperial Tokay. I'm so ashamed.

FERIKE—Oh, Mother.

Even if one must tell the truth, there are so many truths, Bella says. And there are so many kinds of love.

Ferike tells his mother to go to the seaside; he prefers to stay with Peter, to learn to be a doctor: "I'll work and work and work. I'll help *everybody.*" And he urges her to pack, to hurry and pack. He wants to pack his box, too.

When they have gone off for their things, Elek arrives. He mutters complaints about the waste of electricity, and switches off the lights in the hall. Without taking his hat and coat off, he goes into the living room to the stove. He tries to get warm, pressing his body to the tile, all the time continuing his complaints.

Ferike, when he enters the room with a suitcase, finds him next to the stove, and wonders who turned the light out. Elek orders him to put more coals on the fire and to give him a glass of brandy. The boy obeys his father, but gives no sign of being glad to see him.

ELEK (*desperately*)—Want to hear about the fight?
FERIKE—What fight?
ELEK (*laughing like a braggart.* FERIKE *starts to go away*)— You never heard such trigger talk. (FERIKE *stops.*) Son, I gave them hell. Trapped but undaunted— (*Starts fencing,* FERIKE *does*

not play.) The Governor's posse was all over the place. Come on—
(FERIKE *stands, rigid.*) Come on—where is the secret escape hatch?
  FERIKE (*ignores* ELEK, *and coldly calls to* BELLA)—Mother!
He's back.

Elek stands quietly. He starts walking a little blindly, stumbles
against a chair and stops, looking at the suitcase.
  Bella rushes out to Elek, hovers over him anxiously until he says
he's all right; then she too becomes cool to him, even irritated over
keeping his hat and coat on. Then, with the suitcase between them,
Bella asks for further details of his release.

  ELEK—It's all over. I'm back. What difference does it make,
why?
  BELLA (*severely*)—It makes a great difference, indeed.
  ELEK (*with amazed pride*)—Finally—after fifteen years—you demand an answer! Is this my Bella? . . .

Elek tells her what she wanted to know. How they took him to
headquarters, how they saw and were pleased by his fear. (Bella
sits down.) How a brute came in to question him—had his son told
the truth? Then they brought in instruments of torture, though
they had already stripped him of everything: love and honor and a
good night's sleep; but it wasn't enough.

  ELEK—Suddenly he got up and came towards me. Now he was
after the last thing—no longer facts, or information: he wanted
silence; the universal hush of conformity. DID YOUR SON TELL THE
TRUTH? Did he? What did the child say, Bella? I tried to remember and saw his prophets' world of courage and goodness. I
saw myself with his eyes—not a dog begging for a bone, but a man,
Bella, a man enamored of the moon. I heard his small voice: "Liar!
Liar!"—Oh, but it roared in my ears like thunder, "STAND UP!
DON'T BE AFRAID! LOOK AT HIM, LOOK!" and I looked, Bella, and
saw this policeman through a child's eyes too—I saw him naked,
Bella, quite naked, divested of uniform, power and glory, just a
plump little man who thought he was emperor. (*He rises.*) "DID
YOUR SON TELL THE TRUTH?" (*In utter joy and triumph.*) My
son said I was good. I AM good. My son said I was brave. I AM
brave; but what's this, who is this who wants to break me, remake
me, unmake me, who the hell does he think he is, asking me again
and again and again, "Did your son tell the truth? Did he, did he,
did he?" (*Roaring.*) YES! YES! (*Now his left fist, crushed and*

mangled, a bloody handkerchief around it, shoots out of his pocket, banging the table like a hammer.) Yes, yes, yes—

He looks at his hand, amazed at his own agony and turns completely around, leaning against the dining table, holding his left hand with his good one.

Bella runs up to him, but can't look at it and calls for Peter.

Peter comes in, sleepy and crumpled-looking. For a moment he looks angrily at Elek, then sees his hand. He goes over to him, takes his hat off, sees his head wound. Bella goes for Peter's bag, and a bowl. And the two of them tend to Elek, gently removing his coat and jacket and bloody shirt.

Ferike comes in on them as they are washing the body gashes— takes one look, and runs to his father and hugs him.

Elek, proud and strong, gathers his family to him.

CURTAIN

PICNIC *

A Play in Three Acts

By William Inge

[William Inge, *whose "Come Back, Little Sheba," produced in New York in 1950, catapulted him into the ranks of our "most promising" playwrights, has proved the right to this title with his current hit "Picnic," which won both the Pulitzer Prize and the Drama Critics Circle Award.*

Born in Independence, Kansas, in 1913, Inge was educated at the University of Kansas and Peabody College. He taught with Maude Adams at Stephens College, Columbia, Missouri, and once conducted a playwriting class at Washington University in St. Louis. He was drama, film and music editor for the St. Louis Star-Times.]

"THE action of the play is laid on the porches and in the yards of two small houses that sit close beside each other in a small Kansas town." They are run-down, and need paint badly, but somehow the widows who own them have managed to keep them tidy.

Mrs. Flora Owens lives in one house, with her two daughters, Madge and Millie. Her neighbor, Mrs. Helen Potts, takes care of her old invalid mother in the other one.

Behind their houses—beyond the picket fence that separates their yard from the street—appear in the distance the landmarks of a typically Midwestern town: grain elevator, church steeple, railway station. On this very hot Kansas Labor-Day morning—it is the morning before a town-wide picnic—Mrs. Potts is superintending the chores of a handsome young vagrant, Hal Carter. He had arrived on her doorstep to receive a man-sized breakfast, a day's work, and sympathetic treatment from the soft-hearted elderly woman. He now carries away her trash to be burned.

At the Owens' house, sixteen-year-old Millie starts her day by coming out to sneak a cigarette after breakfast. She yowls toughly at the newsboy as he hurls the morning paper against the porch door.

BOMBER (*with a look at the upper window of the house which presumably marks* MADGE's *room*)—Go back to bed and tell your pretty sister to come out. It's no fun lookin' at you. (MILLIE ignores him. BOMBER *doesn't intend to let her.*) I'm talkin' to you, Goonface!

MILLIE (*jumping to her feet and tearing into* BOMBER *with flying fists*)—You take that back, you ornery bastard. You take that back.

The boy jeers at her, and neatly dodges her fists.

Madge, Millie's unusually beautiful sister, gets an entirely different greeting as she steps out on the porch to rub dry her hair. For a brief moment, Bomber is shy with her, then quickly becomes persistent about a late date.

MADGE (*a trifle haughty*)—That wouldn't be fair to Alan. We go steady.

MILLIE—Don't you know what "steady" means, stupid?

BOMBER—I seen you riding around in his Cadillac like you was a duchess. Why do good-looking girls have to be so stuck on themselves?

MADGE—I'm not stuck on myself! You take that back, Bomber Gutzel!

Hal, on his way back from Mrs. Potts' sideyard, sees Bomber annoying Madge and orders him on his way. Bomber realizes he's outclassed and leaves. Hal joins the girls and bums a cigarette off Millie while eyeing Madge. She too is very conscious of him.

But Flora Owens, with some sixth sense, comes out on the porch and asks Hal to leave.

HAL—You the mother?

FLO—Yes. You better run along now.

HAL—Like you say, Lady. It's your house. (*With a shrug of the shoulders he saunters offstage.*)

And Flora Owens boils at the thought of her neighbor befriending any tramp that comes to her door.

A distant train whistle starts Millie thinking of the day when she'll head for New York. Madge, hearing the whistle, dreams of a stranger coming off the train, discovering her in the five and ten cent store, and offering her a glowing life of romance.

Ralph Meeker in "Picnic," Jordan Bentley in "Wonderful Town,"
Alfred Drake in "The King and I" and Jack Cassidy in "Wish You
Were Here"

Flo sends Millie inside, and questions Madge about her relations
with Alan: what they do when they're together?

FLO—Do you like it when he kisses you?
MADGE—Yes.
FLO—You don't sound very enthusiastic.
MADGE—What do you expect me to do—pass out every time **Alan**
puts his arm around me?
FLO—No, you don't have to pass out. (*Gives* MADGE *the dress*
she has been sewing on.) Here. Hold this dress up in front of you.
(*She continues.*) It'd be awfully nice to be married to Alan. You'd
live in comfort the rest of your life, with charge accounts at all **the**
stores, automobiles and trips. You'd be invited by all his friends to
parties in their homes and at the Country Club.

Her daughter doesn't warm to the prospect: she feels uncomfortable and left out of things when she's with Alan's friends. She and they have nothing in common. Flo warns her that a pretty girl's years of power are few; and she must get what she wants right away, or her attractiveness will pass, and so will the years, and it will be too late.

Millie, carrying her sketch book, comes out on the porch again. As she watches her mother holding up the new dress to Madge, she complains that she is always left out of things.

MADGE—If she wants a date, why doesn't she dress up and act decent?

This starts a scrap.

MILLIE—La-de-da! Madge is the pretty one—but she's so dumb they almost had to burn the schoolhouse down to get *her* out of it!

And the reason that she works in a dime store, continues Millie, is that she couldn't even learn shorthand.

Hurt by all this, Madge lashes out and calls Millie a "goon." The fight, now, would really be on, but their mother breaks it up and sends Millie indoors.

FLO—Poor Millie!

MADGE (*raging at the injustice*)—All I ever hear is "poor Millie," and poor Millie won herself a scholarship for four whole years of college.

FLO—A girl like Millie can need confidence in other ways.

Madge wonders, not for the first time, whether her mother doesn't care more for Millie than for her. Her mother denies this, explaining that when Millie was born life with their father was no longer pleasant. Madge's problem is: What use is there in being pretty? She gets tired of always being looked at.

FLO—Don't talk so selfish.

MADGE—I don't care if I am selfish. It's no good just being pretty. It's no good.

Hal interrupts them by coming over for permission to start a fire on such a hot day. The disapproving eyes of the mother, and responsive ones of the daughter, follow him back to work. Flo's roomer, an unmarried schoolteacher of uncertain age, joins Madge and her mother on the porch. Still in kimono, and greased and lotioned with beauty aids, Rosemary Sydney watches Hal working in the yard. She ostensibly disapproves of his working stripped to the waist in full view of everyone; actually she can't keep her eyes off him.

FLO (*looking off at* HAL)—Look at him showing off!
ROSEMARY (*turning prissily away*)—Who does he think is interested? (*She continues to massage her face.*)

A moment later, she can't help taking one more look.

Millie, her usual book in hand, comes out and most uncharacteristically borrows her sister's manicure set.

Then Mrs. Potts comes out of the other house to hang up her wash—trailed from indoors by her old mother's whining: "Helen! Helen!"

The women on the Owens' porch are in agreement over what a rotten life Helen Potts has with her mother, who's so mean that no old ladies' home will take her.

ROSEMARY—She must be mean—if that story's true.
FLO—It is true! Helen and the Potts boy ran off and got married. Helen's mother caught her that very day and had the marriage annulled!
ROSEMARY (*shaking her head*)—She's Mrs. Potts in name only.
FLO—Sometimes I think she keeps the boy's name just to defy the old lady.

Alan Seymour, Madge's beau, drives up and the ladies on the porch have something else to think of. Then Mrs. Potts calls over, wanting to be sure that the Owens girls have noticed her handsome young man. Flo answers for her family: "Helen Potts, I wish you'd stop taking in all sorts of riffraff!"

MRS. POTTS—He isn't riffraff. He's been to several colleges.
FLO—College—and he begs for breakfast!
MRS. POTTS—He's working for his breakfast! Alan, he said he knew you at the university.

Alan doesn't understand who she's talking about and goes inside to see Madge. The women take it easy in the heat; Flo sews, Millie reads, and Rosemary works on her face and gossips.

Alan returns with Madge, who is trying on her new dress. Inadvertently he gets Millie in trouble by asking what she is reading. Carson McCullers proves too strong for schoolteacher Rosemary: the book is full of filthy and degenerate characters, and shouldn't be allowed. Alan comes belatedly to Millie's aid, saying the book is on their required reading list at school. Rosemary is quite sniffy. And now Madge takes a poke at her sister's taste in art. Firmly, Millie tells her unappreciative audience: "Pictures don't have to be pretty."

A sudden explosion in Mrs. Potts' back yard creates momentary excitement. But it was only a bottle of cleaning fluid that Mrs. Potts had carelessly included in the trash.

The ladies go into the house, Mrs. Potts and Millie go to examine the damage, and Hal and his old school-friend Alan have a chance to meet once again. They greet each other with a bit of remembered fraternity horseplay. The last time they saw each other, Alan had lent Hal money to go to Hollywood for a screen test. Hal now gives his ex-roommate an accounting. He got his screen test through a woman's pull, but then balked at a screen career when they wanted to enhance his looks with false teeth, first pulling his own. On the road back from California, he led the healthy life of a ranch hand, and saved his wages. But he lost everything when he was "rolled" by a couple of women.

Hal—Yeah, I was gonna hitchhike to Texas to get in a big oil deal. I got as far as Phoenix when two babes pull up in this big yellow convertible. And one of these dames slams on the brakes and hollers, "Get in, stud!" So I got in. Seymour, it was crazy. They had a shakerful of martinis, right there in the car!

Alan wants to hear every last detail, and hangs on to Hal until Mrs. Potts and Millie have gone back into the house. "So," Hal continues, "when they parked in front of this tourist cabin, I said, 'Okay, girls, if I gotta pay for the ride, this is the easiest way I know.' (*He shrugs.*) But, gee, they musta thought I was Superman."

Apparently they did. "Finally, I passed out! And when I woke up, the dames was gone and so was my two hundred bucks! I went to the police and they wouldn't believe me—they said my whole story was wishful thinking! How d'ya like *that!*"

After this fascinating tale, Alan is surprised to find that Hal envies him. Hal, the campus football hero, admires Alan because he always knows how to think and act. Hal has nothing, not even a father—

the old man died recently while on a bender. But Alan, and Alan's father—perhaps they'd have a job for him?

ALAN—What kind of job did you have in mind?

HAL (*this is his favorite fantasy*)—Oh, something in a nice office where I can wear a tie and have a sweet little secretary and talk over the telephone about enterprises and things. (*As* ALAN *walks away skeptically.*) I've always had the feeling, if I just had the chance, I could set the world on fire.

ALAN—Lots of guys have that feeling, Hal.

HAL (*with some desperation*)—I gotta get some place in this world, Seymour. I got to.

ALAN (*with a hand on* HAL's *shoulder*)—Take it easy.

HAL—This is a free country, and I got just as much rights as the next fellow. Why can't I get along?

Alan promises him a job on the new pipeline, and counsels more patience.

Rosemary, all dolled up in her new Fall finery, comes out hoping coyly for compliments. Her girl friends are going to pick her up and take her to a luncheon and bridge for the new girls on the faculty. Irma Cronkite, and the new Feminine Hygiene teacher, Christine Schoenwalder, come by for Rosemary. They are sprightly and gay, full of daring adventures during Summer vacation. Irma, while at Teachers College in New York, actually landed at the Stork Club.

ROSEMARY—I knew there was a *man* in it.

IRMA—Now, girl! It was nothing serious. He was just a good sport, that's all. We made a bet that the one who made the lowest grade on the final had to take the other to the Stork Club—and I lost—

Full of such prattle, the teachers go off to their luncheon.

Helen Potts suggests that Hal be Millie's date for tonight's picnic; and Alan now invites Hal to go for a swim with him and Millie, while Madge stays home to get the picnic supper ready.

Alan introduces Madge to Hal as the prettiest girl in town. Then Millie and Hal race wildly for the car.

Flo Owens asks Alan, before he leaves, for some reassurance; she finds it hard to believe that Hal was a friend of his at college. Alan promises to see that Hal is kept in line, and Flo goes into the house somewhat less worried. But before Alan can have a moment alone with Madge, Hal is back again. He too wants Alan's help. He has never been on a picnic before.

ALAN—What're you talking about? Everybody's been on a picnic.
HAL—Not me. When I was a kid, I was too busy shooting craps or stealing milk bottles.
ALAN—Well, there's a first time for everything.
HAL—I wasn't brought up proper like *you*. I won't know how to act around all these *women*.
ALAN—Women aren't anything new in *your* life.
HAL—But these are—nice women. What if I say the wrong word or maybe my stomach growls? I feel *funny*.
ALAN—You're a psycho!
HAL—OK, but if I do anything wrong, you gotta try to overlook it. (*He hurries offstage.*)

And now Alan finally gets a promise from Madge that she'll go off alone with him after the picnic.

ACT II

By late afternoon, on this very hot day, Millie has stopped being a tomboy. She has rigged herself up (in her sister's dress) for her picnic date with Hal. She feels strange and happy in her borrowed clothes. Hearing music in the distance, she sways and dances and twirls across the lawn.

The music stops abruptly, just as Madge comes out of the kitchen, feeling put upon and out of sorts. She has fixed the entire picnic supper with no help from her sister. After a moment, however, she compliments Millie on her appearance and even offers to let her keep the dress she is wearing.

MILLIE—Thanks. (*A pause.*) Madge, how do you talk to boys?
MADGE—Why, you just talk, silly.
MILLIE—How d'ya think of things to say?
MADGE—I don't know. You just say whatever comes into your head.
MILLIE—Supposing nothing ever comes into my head?
MADGE—You talked with him all right this morning.
MILLIE—But now I've got a *date* with him, and it's *different!*

And Millie continues, he's such a show-off, such a braggart, and so girl-crazy. Madge, through all of Millie's recital of Hal's behavior, remains uncritical and unimpressed.

Flo is concerned over Millie's date, too. She begs Madge to watch out that Millie doesn't have any of the men's liquor, and then sends Madge in to dress, urging her to be quick and not primp for hours before her mirror.

MADGE—Mom, don't make fun of me.
FLO—You shouldn't object to being kidded if it's well meant.
MADGE—It seems like—when I'm looking in the mirror that's the only way I can prove to myself I'm alive.

The three schoolteachers then trail back, bereft of all their previous gaiety. It had been a Dutch-treat lunch, the bridge was tiresome, and the food was worse.

CHRISTINE—I had a French-fried pork chop and it was mostly fat. What'd you girls have?
ROSEMARY—I had stuffed peppers.
IRMA—I had southern-fried chicken.

Heat, indigestion, and hard reality are upon them. Irma and Christine take leave of Rosemary, who's expecting her evening date. They promise to come by for her on their way to school the following morning.

CHRISTINE (crossing to ROSEMARY)—Girl, I want to tell you, in one afternoon I feel I've known you my whole life.
ROSEMARY (with assurance of devotion)—I look upon you as an old friend already.
CHRISTINE (overjoyed)—Aw . . .

And the two tired women walk to the street.

Rosemary's date drives up shortly after. Howard is a wispish, small-town businessman. As he comes up on the porch, he exudes mild Rotarian good-will. He too compliments Millie on her pretty grown-up appearance.

The boys drive up in Alan's two cars. When Hal joins the group, he has what he imagines is the right remark for each of the assembled picnickers.

To Mrs. Potts, Hal says (expansively, as though making an announcement of public interest): "This little lady, she took pity on me when I was practically starving. I ran into some hard luck when I was travelin'. Some characters robbed me of every cent I had." When introduced by Alan to Rosemary: "I have every respect for schoolteachers, Mam. It's a lotta hard work and not much pay." And to the shopkeeper, Rosemary's boy friend: "Sir, we'll come over as soon as we can fit it into our schedule. . . ."

Unnoticed, Madge watches Hal as he goes on and on about his clothes and background. Mrs. Potts tries to put him at ease with such comforting words as "Clothes don't make the man" and, "Money isn't everything." And he begins to feel more and more expansive. Howard helps this feeling along by telling Hal: "It's a good business town. A young man can go far." By this time Hal's confidence is full-blown. He booms back: "Sir, I intend to go *far.*" Mrs. Potts and Rosemary outline what life would be in this town, and it all dazzles Hal. He plans on settling down here, and "Oh, I'm gonna join clubs and go to church and do all those things."

While Mrs. Potts and Flo pack the baskets, Millie brings out her sketching things and makes Hal pose for her. His ego flourishes.

Then Howard starts passing a bottle around. Rosemary protests. She won't drink. She might lose her job if someone saw her. Anyway, it's against the state law. But after a few of Howard's persuasive "Honeys," she says: "I guess I know why you want me to take a drink—"

HOWARD—Now, Honey, that's not so. Just think you should have a good time like the rest of us. (*To* HAL.) Schoolteachers gotta right to live. Isn't that what you say, young fella?

HAL—Sure, schoolteachers got a right to live.

Rosemary then looks all around, and takes a big swig: "Whew! I want some water!" And she makes a big thing of getting a drink of water where she won't be noticed. She runs around to Mrs. Potts' hydrant. When she calls for Howard, saying she sees a snake, Howard just sends Millie to her. The men are now enjoying their liquor and the sight of Madge dressing before her lighted bedroom window.

HAL (*with some awe of her*)—She's the kind of girl a guy's gotta respect.

HOWARD—Look at her, putting lipstick on that cute kisser. Seems to me, when the good Lord made a girl as pretty as she is, he did it for a reason, and it's about time she found out what that reason is. (*He gets an idea.*) Look, son, if you're agonizin', I know a couple of girls down at the hotel.

HAL—Thanks, but I've given up that sorta thing.
HOWARD—I think that's a very fine attitude.

HAL—Besides, I never had to pay for it.

Millie and Rosemary come back, and catch the men looking up at Madge. Rosemary, after another drink from the bottle, asserts she was just as good-looking when she was Madge's age. Howard soothingly agrees.

ROSEMARY—I had boys callin' me all the time. But if my father had ever caught me showing off in front of the window he'd have tanned me with a razor strap. (*Takes a drink.*) Cause I was brought up strict by a God-fearing man. (*Takes another.*)

Rosemary is becoming aggressive. When the music starts up again, she tries to make Howard dance with her. He protests: "Honey, I'm no good at dancin'." Then she makes Millie dance up and down with her. As they automatically go through the motions, the men hoot at them and burlesque their dancing.

Hal quickly tires of this and takes Millie on. He tries to show her how to follow properly. Rosemary insists that Howard now dance with her. He does, but he certainly doesn't like it.

Mrs. Potts, Flo and Alan come out and watch. They encourage Millie's efforts as Hal teaches her. Then Hal goes into a solo, supposedly still in the role of Millie's teacher, but he offers a very advanced performance.

HAL—Watch close, kid. If you learn this step you'll be the sharpest kid in town.

MILLIE (*observing but baffled*)—Yah—but . . .

HAL—Real loose, see? You give it a little of this—and give it a little of that—

Rosemary, absorbed, dances by herself ignoring the others. Madge, all dressed up in the new dress she was to save for parties in the Fall, comes out in the midst of the dancing. Howard is bowled over by her beauty, and asks her to dance. She accepts.

Mrs. Potts notices them approvingly: "More dancers! We've turned the back yard into a ballroom!" Then Rosemary sees what's going on, and angrily snatches Howard away from Madge. Now Madge can see Hal's performance, and as if she had been doing just those dance steps always, she rhythmically and sensuously dances towards him.

Hal takes her in his arms, and they do a slow primitive body-to-body dance that fascinates their hushed, rapt audience on the porch. Mrs. Potts breaks the spell: "It's like they were *made* to dance together."

Millie now feels out of it all, and begins to drink quietly from the bottle left on the porch. Rosemary feels out of it, too, and begins make an exhibition of herself, dancing and kicking up her legs. Howard notices her legs appreciatively, which makes her briefly happy. But the next minute she's off again, and this time pushes Madge away from Hal. She then grabs at him, and to his embarrassment, and everyone else's, presses herself against him and insists he dance with her. He tries to pull away.

ROSEMARY (*jerking him closer to her*)—Dance with me, young man. Dance with me. I can keep up with you. You know what? You remind me of one of those ancient statues. There was one in the school library until last year. He was a Roman gladiator. All he had on was a shield. (*She gives a bawdy laugh.*) A shield over his arm. That was all he had on. All we girls felt insulted, havin' to walk past that statue every time we went to the library. We got up a petition and made the principal do something about it. (*She laughs hilariously during her narration.*) You know what he did? He got the school janitor to fix things right. He got a chisel and made the statue decent. (*Another bawdy laugh.*) Lord, those ancient people were depraved.

HAL (*he has seldom been made so uncomfortable*)—Mam, I guess I just don't feel like dancin'.

ROSEMARY (*sobering from her story, grabs for* HAL, *catching him by the shirt*)—Where you goin'?

HAL—Mam, I . . .

ROSEMARY (*commanding him imploringly*)—Dance with me, young man. Dance with me.

HAL—I . . . I . . . (*He pulls loose from her grasp but her still clutching hand tears off a strip of his shirt as he gets away.* HOWARD *intervenes.*)

Millie, in the meantime, is having her own kind of problem. She's become sick. In her misery, she screams at her pretty sister as she dashes inside. Kindly Mrs. Potts follows her.

Rosemary now compounds her nastiness by blaming Millie's drinking on poor Hal, and so gets Flo furious at the boy. Howard tries to set things straight, but Rosemary is on a tear by now, and is out for Hal's blood because of her humiliation.

ROSEMARY (*closer to* HAL)—You think just cause you're a man, you can walk in here and make off with whatever you like. You think just 'cause you're young you can push other people aside and not pay them any mind. You think just 'cause you're strong you can show your muscles and nobody'll know what a pitiful specimen you are. But you won't stay young forever, didja ever thinka that? What'll become of you then? You'll end your life in the gutter and it'll serve you right, 'cause the gutter's where you came from and the gutter's where you belong.

HOWARD—Rosemary, shut your damn mouth.

Alan escorts a sober Millie onto the porch, but not knowing what happened, he too blames Hal for the drinking. Mrs. Owens says that Millie will go in the car with them, not with Hal. And she sends Madge upstairs to put on proper clothes for the picnic, telling her to come later with Howard and Rosemary. She then takes her younger daughter and goes to Alan's car. Mrs. Potts follows. Hal is dejected and beaten, as he sits by himself on the edge of the porch.

Rosemary is feeling all washed up too.

ROSEMARY—What made me do it, Howard? What made me act that way?

HOWARD—You gotta remember, men have got feelings, too—same as women. (*To* HAL.) Don't pay any attention to her, young man. She didn't mean a thing.

ROSEMARY (*has gone up to the gate*)—I don't want to go on the picnic, Howard. This is my last night of vacation and I want to have a good time.

HOWARD—We'll go for a ride, Honey.

ROSEMARY—I want to drive into the sunset, Howard! I want to drive into the sunset!

And she runs off followed by Howard, to Howard's car.

Madge quietly comes out and sits on the porch. After a while, she starts quietly and sweetly to perk up Hal, and give him some confidence again.

HAL—What's the use, Baby? I'm a bum. She saw through me like a God-damn X-ray machine. There's just no place in the world for a guy like me.

MADGE—There's got to be.

HAL (*with self-derision*)—Yah?

MADGE—Of course. You're young, and—you're very entertaining. I mean—you say all sorts of witty things, and I just love listening to you talk. And you're strong and—you're very good-looking. I bet Miss Sydney thought so too, or she wouldn't have said those things.

HAL—Look, Baby, lemme level with you. When I was fourteen, I spent a year in reform school. How ya like that?

MADGE—Honest?

He continues that he stole a motorcycle; when he got out of reform school, his mother wasn't even interested in seeing him.

Feeling terribly sorry for him, Madge—at a loss for words—takes his face in her hands and kisses him. She tells him: "I—I'm proud you told me." In her vague way, she understands. "I get so tired of being told I'm pretty."

HAL (*folding her in his arms caressingly*)—Baby, Baby, Baby.

MADGE (*resisting him, jumping to her feet*)—Don't. We have to go. We have all the baskets in our car and they'll be waiting. (HAL *gets up and walks slowly to her, their eyes on each other and* MADGE *quivering with excitement as he draws nearer.*) Really—we have to be going. (HAL *takes her in his arms and kisses her passionately. Then* MADGE *utters his name in a voice of resignation.*) Hal!

HAL—Just be quiet, Baby.

MADGE—Really . . . We have to go. They'll be waiting. . . .

HAL (*picking her up in his arms and starting off. His voice is deep and firm*)—We're not goin' on no God-damn picnic.

Curtain

ACT III

SCENE I

It is past midnight when Rosemary returns to the darkened Owens house. She drags herself to the porch, hardly listening to Howard who follows close behind. She doesn't answer him, except with an occasional grunt, until he announces he must be going home.

ROSEMARY—You can't go off without me.

HOWARD—Honey, talk sense.

ROSEMARY—You can't go off without me— Not after tonight— That's sense.

She pleads from desperation. She no longer cares what people think
or say. Tonight she means what she says.

HOWARD—Now look, Honey, you better go upstairs and get some
sleep. You gotta start school in the morning. We'll talk all this
over Saturday.
ROSEMARY—Maybe you won't be back Saturday. Maybe you
won't be back ever again.

Howard tries to put an end to such talk.

HOWARD—I don't understand. When we first started going together, you were the best sport I ever saw, always good for a laugh.
ROSEMARY (*in a hollow voice*)—I can't laugh any more.

Howard still tries to put this whole conversation aside, preacher,
promises, and all. He wants to wait till next Saturday, or better yet,
just wait. He feels awfully set in his ways. Rosemary says she is
too, and she finds them more unpleasant by the hour.

ROSEMARY—There's too much bad about mine. Each year, I keep
tellin' myself, is the last. Something'll happen. Then nothing ever
does—except I get a little crazier all the time.

After accusing Howard of just leading her on, Rosemary comes right
out with it: "You gotta marry me, Howard."
It is too late tonight, but he must come right over in the morning.
She can get a substitute to fill her job, and he can always pay someone to run his store for a few days.
Howard has been almost co-operative up to this point. Now he
balks. "No."

ROSEMARY (*a muffled cry*)—Howard!
HOWARD—I'm not gonna marry anyone that says, "You gotta
marry me, Howard." I'm not gonna. (*He is silent*. ROSEMARY
weeps pathetic tears. Slowly HOWARD *reconsiders.*) If a woman
wants me to marry her—she can at least say "please."
ROSEMARY (*beaten and humble*)—*Please* marry me, Howard.
HOWARD—Well—you got to give me time to think it over.
ROSEMARY (*desperate*)—Oh, God! Please marry me, Howard.
Please. . . . (*She sinks to her knees.*) Please . . . please. . . .
HOWARD (*embarrassed by her suffering humility*)—Rosemary . . .
I . . . I gotta have some time to think it over. You go to bed now

and get some rest. I'll drive over in the morning and maybe we can talk it over before you go to school. I . . .

With her "please" . . . "please" following him, he leaves, promising to come in the morning. Once more, to no one, Rosemary says, "Please"; she then trails up to bed.

The place is dark and silent again, then Madge—her hands to her teary face—runs to the porch door. Hal, running fast behind her, catches her just before she can enter the house. She tries to push him away. He's all penitence, but still keeps her there. Madge is full of shame.

MADGE—I didn't even know what was happening and then . . . all of a sudden it seems like my whole life was changed.

HAL (*with bitter self-disparagement*)—I oughta be taken out and hung. I'm just a no-good bum. That schoolteacher was right. I oughta be in the gutter.

But he still begs to see her the following night, after work. Madge then remembers she has a date with Alan . . . "If he'll still speak to me."

HAL—Jesus, I'd forgot all about Seymour.
MADGE—So had I.
HAL—I can't go back to his house. What'll I do?
MADGE—Maybe Mrs. Potts could . . .
HAL—I'll take the car back to where we were, stretch out in the front seat and get a little sleep. (*He thinks a moment.*) Baby, how you gonna handle your old lady?
MADGE (*with a slight tremor*)—I . . . I don't know.

Hal is once more full of compunctions, but begs Madge for one more kiss.

MADGE—It . . . It'd just start things all over again. Things I better forget.

But he continues to beg, and promises not to touch her. She weakens, and slowly goes to him, taking his face in her hands to kiss. The kiss is a long one, and Hal is short on will power. He puts his arms around Madge, and all their passion is revived. (MADGE *utters a little shriek, tears herself away from* HAL *and runs into the house,*

sobbing.)   "Don't.   You promised.   I never wanta see you again.
I might as well be dead."

Again, Hal hates himself, and shows it by kicking the earth, and
banging his hands together as he leaves the Owens' yard.

SCENE II

Millie, dressed in a crisp fresh dress, is up early for her first day
of school.   As she perches on the porch, she gets in her secret morning cigarette.

Flo comes out in an unusually sloppy costume.   She's so upset
over Madge's locking herself into her room, that she hasn't thought
to dress, nor has she detected Millie's cigarette.   When Helen Potts
appears on her back step, Flo lets it all out on her: "The next time
you take in tramps, Helen Potts, I'll thank you to keep them on your
own side of the yard."   Pride, however, dictates her answer to
Helen's inquiry: "Of course, she's all right.   She got out of the car
and left that hoodlum alone.   That's what she did."

But her worries are apparent.   Will Alan really come over this
morning?   And will Hal have the nerve to turn up here again?   And
Rosemary Sydney has been acting so peculiar as to be an additional
bother.

Asking Helen Potts to keep an eye out for Alan, Flo goes into the
house to dress, just as Rosemary's teacher friends arrive to pick
her up.

Before they go inside, Christine announces tactlessly: "We missed
seeing Madge on the picnic last night"; and two minutes later, the
newsboy comes by on his bicycle—proclaiming for all to hear that
his brother saw Madge and Hal parked under the bridge last night.
A new note has crept into his voice when he speaks of Madge: he
always knew she could be had.   Only Alan's approach saves Bomber
from Millie's murderous intentions.   He quickly rides off.

As Alan waits for Madge, Millie can't help telling him how much
she likes him.   Alan is touched.   Millie assures him: "I don't expect
you to do anything about it.   I just wanted to tell you."

Howard is the next harried early-morning visitor.   He nervously
tells Millie that he thinks Rosemary's expecting him.   When he
hears that she's surrounded by teachers, he knows he's in for it:
"Golly!"   Howard goes into the house, followed by Millie who
doesn't want to miss anything.   He's ready for the worst.   Alan remains outside waiting to see Madge alone.

Madge comes out and seems quite subdued and unemotional
when Hal is mentioned.

ALAN—At school I spent half of my life getting him out of jams. I knew he'd had a few tough breaks, and I always tried to be sorry for the guy. But this is the thanks I get.

MADGE (*still non-committal*)—Where is he now?

ALAN—Don't worry about Hal! I'll take it on myself now to offer you his official good-by!

Flo joins them, relieved to find Alan, but has no chance to speak with them, for now Millie appears on the porch at the head of an impromptu bridal party. Millie is throwing rice at Rosemary and joining in the excited chorus made up of Christine, Irma, and Mrs. Potts. Howard follows with two suitcases, Rosemary is all dolled up, and there is much chatter—"Here comes the bride. . . . May all your troubles be little ones. . . . You're getting a wonderful girl, Howard Bevans!" Then Howard has to stand by while the women fuss over Rosemary's having something old, something new, something borrowed (Madge provides a handkerchief), something blue (Rosemary turns coy over this concealed item).

Rosemary then gives last-minute instructions to Mrs. Owens, and last-minute compliments to Madge. The "Girls" suggest a new teacher to occupy Rosemary's room. And Howard tells Alan as he helps him with the suitcases: "A man's gotta settle down some time."

ALAN—Of course.

HOWARD—And folks'd rather do business with a married man!

Rosemary is busy with her farewells: "Good-by, Millie. You're going to be a famous author someday and I'll be proud I knew you." Howard asks if she's ready to go.

ROSEMARY—All set and rarin' to go. (*A sudden thought.*) Where we goin'?

HOWARD—Well . . . I got a cousin who runs a tourist camp in the Ozarks. He and his wife could put us up for free.

ROSEMARY—Oh, I love the Ozarks!

And off they go, Rosemary demanding everyone's attention, Mrs. Owens included, when all Flo wants is to get information from Madge about last night. She is thoroughly irritated to have to dance attendance on Rosemary at such a moment, but leaves Madge to see the bridal couple off.

When Madge is left alone, Hal—barefoot, messy and wet—slips out of Mrs. Potts' woodshed. Madge is cool toward him.

HAL—Seymour's old man put the cops on my tail. Accused me of stealin' the car. I had to knock one of the bastards cold and swim the river to get away. If they ever catch up with me, it'll be too bad.

MADGE—You were born to get in trouble.

HAL—Baby, I just *had* to say good-by.

MADGE (*still not giving away to her feelings*)—Where you going?

HAL—The freight train's by pretty soon. I'll hop a ride. I done it lotsa times before.

MADGE—What're you gonna do?

HAL—I got some friends in Tulsa. I can always get a job hoppin' bells at the Hotel Mayo. Jesus, I hate to say good-by.

Madge has still not shown how she feels about him.

When the others return, there is considerable agitation over Hal's presence. Flo is terribly upset and Alan rages. The schoolteachers are fascinated by it all.

Alan tells Hal he'd better get out of town, or else. Hal takes it quietly, but Alan is aching for a fight, and lunges at Hal: "You'll go *now*. What do you take me for?" Hal holds him off: "Look, Kid, I don't wanta fight with *you*. You're the only friend I ever had."

ALAN—We're not friends any more. I'm not scared of you.

And he tackles Hal again, but is quickly pinned to the ground. "Let me go, you God-damn tramp! Let me go!" Flo cries at Hal: "Take your hands off him, this minute." When Hal lets him up, Alan, utterly humiliated, retreats to Helen Potts' steps. And Flo brusquely asks the schoolteachers to leave. This is a private fight.

When Hal hears the train whistle, he begs Madge not to be mad with him. Suddenly, she isn't. Hal beams all over when she tells him she liked him the first moment she saw him. All his confidence rushes back. He tells her: "I'm nuts about you, Baby. I mean it."

MADGE—You make love to lots of girls.

HAL—A few.

MADGE—. . . just like you made love to me last night—

HAL—Not like last night, Baby. Last night was—(*Groping for the word.*)—*inspired*.

As they look into each other's eyes, police-car sirens are heard. Mrs. Potts is confident she can handle the police and goes off to meet them. And still Hal and Madge don't move.

HAL—Do—you love me?

MADGE (*tears forming*)—What good is it if I do?

HAL—I'm a poor bastard, Baby. I've gotta claim the things in this life that're mine. Kiss me good-by. (*He grabs her and kisses her.*) Come with me, Baby. They gimme a room in the basement of the hotel. It's kinda crummy but we could share it till we found something better.

Flo's sense of outrage is overwhelming, but she consoles Madge after Hal rushes for the train. Millie reports that he made it.

MADGE (*a cry of deep regret*)—Now I'll never see him again.

FLO—Madge, believe me, that's for the best.

MADGE—Why? Why?

FLO—At least you didn't marry him.

MADGE (*a wail of anguish*)—Oh, Mom, what can you do with the love you feel? Where is there you can take it?

FLO (*beaten and defeated*)—I . . . I never found out.

Madge goes into the house, crying.

Alan now comes off Helen Potts' steps to say good-by. He tells Flo he won't be back until the Christmas holidays, and refuses to go in the house and say good-by to Madge. Flo is desolate, but the boy has made up his mind and quickly leaves the yard.

What with all the excitement, Millie has forgotten school. Flo now reminds her, and Millie goes after her books. Mrs. Potts confesses to Millie's mother that she liked Hal and his clomping through her neat house. The very fact of his maleness, made her feel good— "And that reminded *me* . . . I'm a woman, and that seemed good too."

Millie, coming out of the house, scornfully comments on Madge's weepiness. Millie's cocky again, but when a boy on his way to school shrieks an insult at her, she controls her usual violent impulses and goes off to school acting the lady.

Flo still nurses a remote idea of Alan's return, and that all will be well between him and Madge. But now Madge comes out on the porch, carrying a small cardboard suitcase, and announcing that she is going to Tulsa. Flo is frantic: "He's no good. He'll never be able to support you. When he does have a job, he'll spend all his money on booze. After a while, there'll be other women."

MADGE—I've thought of all those things.

MRS. POTTS—You don't love someone cause he's perfect, Flo.

FLO—Oh, God.

There is nothing she can do. Madge has made up her mind to go to Hal, even to support herself as a waitress. She has a message for Millie, as she hurries away: "Tell her I've always been proud to have such a smart sister."

Flo is left alone with Mrs. Potts, and Mrs. Potts with her ever-present mother—who now calls: "Helen! Helen!"

MRS. POTTS—Be patient, Mama.

WONDERFUL TOWN *

A Musical Comedy in Two Acts

BOOK BY JOSEPH FIELDS AND JEROME CHODOROV

MUSIC BY LEONARD BERNSTEIN

LYRICS BY BETTY COMDEN AND ADOLPH GREEN

(Based upon the play *My Sister Eileen* by Fields and Chodorov
and the stories by Ruth McKenney)

[JOSEPH FIELDS *and* JEROME CHODOROV. *Joseph Fields is the
eldest son of Lew Fields of Weber and Fields fame. Jerome
Chodorov is the brother of Edward Chodorov, playwright and producer. Both men were born in New York—Fields in 1895, Chodorov
in 1911—and attended schools here. Chodorov went in for newspaper work and Fields, who first thought he wanted to be a lawyer,
turned to writing sketches for many revues, including Ziegfeld's.
They "found each other" in Hollywood and together wrote a play,
"The Schoolhouse on the Lot," which created no great stir. Then
they adapted the Ruth McKenney stories into "My Sister Eileen,"
which proved a tremendous hit, running on Broadway for 865 performances. After this came other successes such as "Junior Miss"
and "The Doughgirls."*

BETTY COMDEN *and* ADOLPH GREEN, *both native New Yorkers,
both born in 1918, both achieved Broadway fame when they wrote
the book and lyrics for "On the Town" and continued their success
with "Two on the Aisle."*

LEONARD BERNSTEIN *is a remarkably talented and versatile musician. ."Wonderful Town" is his second collaboration with Miss
Comden and Mr. Green, for he did the music for "On the Town."
He has conducted many orchestras, notably the New York, Boston
and Philadelphia. Born in Brookline, Massachusetts, in 1918, he
attended Harvard. Upon arriving in New York he gave music les-*

sons and was later appointed assistant conductor of the New York Philharmonic-Symphony Orchestra. From there his rise was rapid.]

The play takes place in Greenwich Village in the thirties.

ACT I

Scene I

IN front of the curtain, which is a semiabstract impression of Greenwich Village, a Guide and a group of gaping Tourists enter to a musical vamp in a style highly characteristic of the 1930's. The Guide gives his customary spiel about Bohemia, and the Villagers freeze into tableaus, while the Tourists chant of quaintness and charm, and . . .

> "Life is calm,
>   Life is sweet,
>   Pleasant and peaceful on Christopher Street . . ."

When the tableaus come to violent life, they show that Life isn't any of those things on Christopher Street.

The Guide points out Appopolous, the modern painter and not-so-modern landlord. Appopolous yells to Lonigan, the policeman on the beat, to "Throw that Violet woman out of my building!"

LONIGAN—What's the beef now, Appopolous?

APPOPOLOUS—I'm very broad-minded, but when a woman gives *rumba* lessons all night, she's gotta have at least a phonograph!

The Guide then points out the Wreck, the out-of-season football professional, and when Lonigan drags forth Violet, the Guide announces:

> "Here is yet another type.
>   Everyone knows the famous Violet,
>   Nicest gal you'd ever meet
>   Steadily working on Christopher Street."

No longer able to say "peaceful and calm" the Tourists now gush:

> "Life is gay,
>   Life is sweet,
>   Interesting people on Christopher Street."

(Everyone dances.)

And the interesting people file by: A man with a sign yells, "Down with Wall Street!" A yogi is for Peace, and two modern dancers work their arms off at their "Rewolt" type of dance.

ALL—
Look! Look!
Poets! Actors! Dancers! Writers!

Here we live,
Here we love,
This is the place for self-expression.
Life is mad,
Life is sweet,
Interesting people on Christopher Street!

The villagers perform a mad dance of self-expression, and the Guide takes his group off to other fascinating parts of the Village.

When a zoot-suited character does his hopped-up strut in front of Appopolous, the landlord-artist tries to rent him a basement "studio."

VALENTI—Down there? (*Pointing to bars of a basement room below street level.*) When I go back to living in caves—I'll see ya, Cornball.

There is a scream offstage and a kid rushes in, carrying a typewriter. Appopolous twists him very expertly. The kid runs off, dropping the typewriter.

Eileen has been running, screaming, after the boy, and Ruth, loaded down with suitcases, has been following her. Now, even after she thanks Appopolous ever so politely, he refuses to give her back her typewriter. He insists on identification. Has she a driver's license?

RUTH—To operate a typewriter? (*But she proves it's hers all right by:*) The letter "W" is missing.

APPOPOLOUS—Now we're getting somewhere. (*Opens case.*)

RUTH—It fell off after I wrote my thesis on Walt Whitman.

APPOPOLOUS (*closes case*)—She's right. Here's your property. The incident is closed. Case dismissed.

RUTH—Who are you? Felix Frankfurter?

APPOPOLOUS (*laughs*)—You can tell they're out-of-towners. They don't know me!

EILEEN—We don't know anybody. We just got in from Columbus today.

RUTH—Please, Eileen, they're not interested.

But they are, particularly Appopolous, who feels these are the right suckers for his basement. Ruth tries to hold back her sister, but Eileen follows Appopolous into the house, and he firmly shuts the door after the girls.

SCENE II

The studio that Appopolous is foisting on the girls is a "basement horror with two day beds, an imitation fireplace and one barred window that looks out on the street above. It's a cross between a cell in solitary confinement and an iron lung."

Appopolous almost slams the door of the bathroom on Ruth's nose as she takes a shocked look. He grandly says he will give them this room for sixty-five dollars a month; Ruth wouldn't take it at any price, but Eileen begs that they stay, just for the one night—she's all tired out. So the girls are hooked. Appopolous literally lifts the money from Ruth's hand, just as a tremendous subterranean BOOM goes off. The girls are paralyzed with fear. Appopolous brazenly says he didn't hear it, he's so accustomed to the blasting of the new subway.

RUTH—You mean they're blasting right underneath us?

APPOPOLOUS—What are you worrying about? Those engineers know how much dynamite to use.

EILEEN—You mean it goes on all the time?

APPOPOLOUS—No— No—they knock off at midnight and they don't start again until six o'clock in the morning! (*He goes out, telling them to "Sleep tight!"*)

EILEEN—Ruth, what are we going to do?

RUTH—We're gonna do thirty days. (EILEEN *exits to bathroom with suitcase.* RUTH *follows, looks in, and steps back in horror.*) Thank God, we took a bath before we left Columbus!

Her next move is to shoo an anxious dog away from their window bars. Eileen, now getting ready for bed, thinks of the Columbus boys she left behind her. Ruth admits that her one advantage over Eileen is just this: she has none to worry over. So saying, she takes her turn at the bathroom. Eileen is getting into bed when she sees a man calmly enter their room and sprawl in a chair. He asks for

Violet, but when told she doesn't live here, he won't budge. Eileen threatens to call the police, and the man laughs at her. Eileen then rushes to the front door and calls for help.

Ruth, coming out of the bathroom, says politely: "How do you do?" But it's the Wreck who makes him go. Their rescuer tells the girls his name is Loomis, but he's "the Wreck." "That's what they called me at Trenton Tech. I would have made all-American, only I turned professional. Well, girls, if anyone busts in on you again, just holler. "I'm a ramblin' Wreck from Trenton Tech—and a helluva engineer. . . ." He goes off singing.

Eileen admits to being scared, as the girls lie down on their boardlike beds, trying to get some sleep. A lamppost right in front of their shadeless window is out to foil that plan. And if this were not enough, a kid runs in front of the window, scraping his stick with a machine-gun effect, against the bars. Then a couple of drunks sing noisily in front of the window, and Eileen nervously tells them to go away. With that the drunks bend down and happily peer in at the helpless girls. Lonigan, the cop, chases them off, but he too bends down to their window: "I don't go for this stuff on my beat. I'm warning you."

By this time, Eileen is miserable and homesick. Ruth goes to her, puts her arm about her and admits that she is homesick, too.

> BOTH (*singing plaintively*)—
> Why, oh why, oh why, oh—
> Why did I ever leave Ohio?
> Why did I wander to find what lies yonder
> When life was so cozy at home?
> Wond'ring while I wander,
> Why did I fly,
> Why did I roam,
> Oh, why oh, why oh
> Did I leave Ohio?
> Maybe I'd better go home.
> Maybe I'd better go home. (*Music continues.*)

After they list all the things they left behind them, they feel cheered up, and go back to their beds, and—a terrific subway blast causes them to dash terrified into each other's arms and sing hysterically:

> "Why, oh why, oh why, oh—
> Why did we ever leave Ohio?"

(They cut off as music continues, and go over to Ruth's bed, huddling together under the covers.)

BOTH (*quietly and sadly*)—
  Wond'ring while we wander,
  Why did we fly,
  Why did we roam,
  Oh why, oh, why oh—
  Did we leave Ohio?
  Maybe we'd better go home
RUTH—
  O—H—I—O
BOTH—
  Maybe we'd better go home.

They sink back exhausted as the lights dim.

There is a bugle fanfare reminiscent of "Reveille," followed by the sound of an alarm clock as the lights come up sharply. It is early morning. Ruth springs up as if shot from a cannon, turns off the alarm and shakes Eileen. Ruth is full of determination. "Come on, Eileen. Up and at 'em! Let's get an early start. We're going to take this town. Get up, Eileen!" She starts briskly toward the bathroom, suddenly winces and clutches her aching back, but limps bravely on. The lights black out.

There is a dance pantomime depicting the girls' struggle to get ahead in the Big City. Everywhere Ruth goes with her manuscripts, publishers are either out to lunch, in conference or just not interested. Everywhere Eileen goes, looking for theatre work, she receives many offers, but never for jobs. At the end the two sisters meet, collapsing glumly on each other's shoulders as the hostile city crowds sing: "Maybe you'd better go home!"

SCENE III

On the street in front of their house Ruth is stranded with a bag of empty milk bottles—and no cash. Eileen joins her with a large bag of sample cereals that the kind manager of a food show pressed upon her. What Ruth longs for is a steak.

Eileen greets Valenti, who "Skeet-skat-skattle-e-o-do" 's past, snapping his fingers: "Hi yah, gate! I got my eye on you! *Solid!* Skeet-skat-skattle-e-o-do—"

Eileen explains that Valenti is the owner of the Village Vortex, a night club, and he's promised her a tryout once she gets herself a name.

Helen and Wreck now have a proposition for the girls. Helen's unsuspecting, strait-laced mother is coming to town, and must know nothing of her daughter's living arrangements. So, while her mother is in town, could Wreck move out of Helen's into the girls' apartment? He could sleep on the kitchen floor.

HELEN—You'd feel a lot safer with the Wreck around. And he's awful handy. He can clean up and he irons swell.

WRECK—But no washing—that's woman's work.

Before Ruth can prevent her, Eileen commits them. All Ruth can now say is: "Something tells me you weren't quite ready to leave Columbus."

EILEEN (*smiles guiltily and goes to the door*)—Coming in?

RUTH—No. I'm taking these stories down to the *Manhatter*— (*Holding up envelope with manuscript.*)—and I'm going to camp beside the water cooler till that editor talks to me. See you later—

But Eileen has found another young man, and has a date with him later. This one is Frank Lippincott, the manager of the Forty-fourth Street Walgreen's. "He hasn't let me pay a single lunch check since I've been going there. . . ."

RUTH—That's right, dear—keep your strength up. You're eating for two now.

Eileen loyally wants Ruth to meet him, so he'll stand her lunch, too.

RUTH—Gee, since I've been in New York, I only met one man, and he said, "Why the hell don't you look where you're going?" (*Shrugs.*) Maybe it's just as well. Every time I meet one I gum it up. I'm the world's leading expert on discouraging men. I ought to write a book about it. "Girls, are you constantly bothered by the cloying attentions of the male sex? Well, here's the solution for you. Get Ruth Sherwood's new best seller—'One Hundred Easy Ways to Lose a Man.'"

EILEEN *laughs and goes into house as* RUTH *sings in a spirit of rueful self-mockery.*)

RUTH—
   He takes you to the baseball game.
   You sit knee to knee—
   He says, "The next man up at bat will bunt, you'll see."
   Don't say, "Oooh, what's a bunt?
   This game's too hard for little me."
(*Spoken.*) Just say, "Bunt? Are you nuts? With one out and two
men on base, and a left-handed batter coming up, you'll walk right
into a triple play, just like it happened in the fifth game of the
World Series in 1923."
   (*Sung.*)
      That's a sure way to lose a man.

      A sure sure way to lose a man,
      A splendid way to lose a man—
      Just throw your knowledge in his face
      He'll never try for second base.

Ruth gives other shattering examples, then the lights dim and she
goes off.

SCENE IV

Ruth has managed to get into the *Manhatter,* and is now in editor
Baker's office. She finds out what she is up against as a pile of
manuscripts is dumped on Baker's desk by an associate editor. The
only advice Baker will give her is:

BAKER—
   Go home!
   Go West!
   Go back where you came from!
   Oh, why did you ever leave Ohio?

When she protests that she has talent, he and his associate editors
tell her of the millions like her, and sing, strumming imaginary
guitars:

EDITORS—
   What a waste,
   What a waste,
   What a waste of money and time!
(RUTH *exits angrily as* BAKER *looks after her sympathetically.*
BAKER *goes back to his desk and starts to read* RUTH'S *manuscripts.*)

BAKER (*reading*)—" 'For Whom the Lion Roars'—by Ruth Sherwood. It was a fine day for a lion hunt. Yes, it was a good clean day for an African lion hunt—a good clean day for a fine clean kill." (*The lights go up on stage left as* BAKER *continues reading. In the ensuing story vignettes, played stage left and musically underscored,* RUTH *portrays all the heroines. These are* RUTH'S *ideas of sophisticated writing, and are acted in exaggerated satiric style.*)

Baker is incredulous at this first piece that is all set to out-Hemingway Hemingway; and disgusted with her next: "Twentieth-Century Blues," a tale of squalor and passion in the problem-drama field. And when he picks up the third, he finds an oh-so-fancy number: "Exit Laughing," that Ruth just possibly might have written after seeing too many movies.

BAKER (*continuing*)—"Exit Laughing"—Everyone agreed that Tracy Farraday was marvelous. Everyone agreed that this was her greatest acting triumph. Everyone agreed that her breath-taking performance in "Kiss Me, Herman," was the climax of a great career.

And so it goes with Tracy at her last party, until Ruth finishes her off:

BAKER (*continuing*)—"Everyone agreed that Tracy was a hypochondriac. Otherwise, why did she always carry a bottle of iodine?" (TRACY, *throughout speech, is rummaging through her purse, pulls out red bottle of iodine and downs the contents.*)
TRACY (*with bitter abandon, giving her greatest performance*)— Everybody! On with the party! (*She executes a wild fandango— then, suddenly clutching her midriff in a paroxysm of agony, she crashes to the floor.*)
MALE GUEST—Tracy!
WOMAN GUEST—Ah—she's just passing out!
TRACY (*pulling herself up on one elbow with difficulty—gallant to the end*)—Yes! Everyone agrees—I'm just passing out—exit laughing! Ha—Ha—Ha—Ha—Ha! (*The guests all toast* TRACY *with:*)
GUESTS—
    What a waste
    What a waste
(BAKER *wearily joins in, throwing this last manuscript down on his desk.*)
    What a waste of money and time!

Scene V

The Street: Helen and her sniffy mother, Mrs. Wade, go into Helen's house, just avoiding Valenti and two bop fans of his—and Frank Lippincott, with a Walgreen's Candy Special.

Valenti snaps himself off, still followed by the kids; and Frank takes the usual look down into the basement window. Eileen comes up the street as he's peering into her place. She accepts his chocolate-covered cherries and reminds him that he's expected to dinner that evening. As he rushes off to Walgreen's "Pandemonium," Eileen, all starry-eyed, sings that maybe she's "A Little Bit in Love." When she has finished and is about to enter the house, she sees someone else peeking in her window, and coldly tells him that Violet doesn't live there any more.

Bob Baker thereupon straightens up and explains that it's Ruth he's looking for. Eileen at once insists that he take potluck with them that evening. Then, as he walks off, that gleam comes into her eye, and she sings:

EILEEN—
  Mm— Mmm—
' I'm a little bit in love
  Never felt this way before
  Mm— Mm— (*Music continues.*)
(LONIGAN *enters slowly.*) Oh, hello, Officer!

LONIGAN (*suspiciously*)—Yeah. (*The* WRECK *enters and goes to house. He is carrying a rolled-up Army mattress.*)

WRECK—I borrowed a mattress, Eileen. That floor in your place is awful hard! (WRECK *goes into the house.* LONIGAN *looks at* EILEEN, *who turns, startled, and puts a hand to her mouth. Blackout.*)

Scene VI

The Back Yard: This is the "garden" that Appopolous boasts about—a dismal place, surrounded by tenements. There are a couple of chairs, a moldy tree and a bench. Across from the girls' kitchen we see the back entrance of Nino's, an Italian restaurant.

Wreck has set up his ironing board outside, and is working on the girls' things, while the Waiter and Chef of Nino's catch a breather in their part of the yard.

Wreck has taken over the running of Ruth and Eileen's household. He has placed the phone on the window sill so he can take their messages, and hands a rejected manuscript to Ruth, when she arrives.

When he blusteringly answers a call for Eileen, Ruth intervenes—
and finds out it's someone new—a Chick Clark.

WRECK—That Eileen does all right for herself. And the funny
part of it is, she's a good girl.
RUTH (*eyeing him*)—When did you find that out?
WRECK—No, you sense those things. I never made a pass at you,
but I could swear *you're* all right.
RUTH—That's the story of my life. (*She goes off with manuscript as* HELEN *enters.*)

Although Helen is lonely without her Wreck, she notices immediately that he irons better for Eileen and Ruth than he ever did
for her. Before she can make something of it, she has to duck under
the ironing board to avoid her mother's disapproving stare. Mrs.
Wade, from the street, does not care for Wreck's appearance. The
Wreck calls her an "old bat" and yells after her, "Didn't you ever
see a man in shorts before?"

HELEN (*wails*)—Wreck! That was Mom!
WRECK—You mean that old wagon was your mother?
HELEN—You've got to get out of here!

There is the slight problem of raising money for Wreck's room at
a "Y," but he swiftly solves that by swiping Appopolous' painting
off the girls' wall and sending Helen off to hock it.
Wreck is now admired by a kid delivering vegetables to the restaurant. Using a cabbage from his basket, the kid calls for signals.

WRECK—45—26—7—hip! (*Catches the ball.*)
CHEF (*enters in front of* NINO's. *To* KID)—E tu che diavolo fai
con quel cavolo?
KID (*to* WRECK)—Pass. (WRECK *passes to* KID—*who passes to*
WAITER, *who catches cabbage in his stomach.*)
CHEF—Che pazzerela! (*Exits.*)
KID—Well, you certainly look in good shape for the football
season.
WRECK—Yeah—for all the good it does me! (*Goes wearily back
to ironing and sings, while a crowd gathers, the saga of his spec-
tacular college career.*)
      Passed without a fuss
      English and Calculus

Never had to cram
Even passed the bar exam
Because I passed that football
Like nothing you ever seen. . . .

After further description of his glorious past, he and the crowd do a football dance, ending with Wreck under a pile of scrimmagers, "hopelessly outclassed." The crowd drifts away and Wreck staggers back to his ironing.

At this point Helen returns with the pawn ticket, all ready to squabble with Eileen over Wreck. Ruth comes in on this "triangle" situation, whereupon Wreck feels the need to protest his innocence and swears, "Why, if I thought about Eileen that way— May God strike me dead on this spot!" He raises his hand solemnly and there is a tremendous BOOM from below. He shrinks guiltily. "He's everywhere, all right," remarks Ruth. Helen then orders Wreck to leave with her, letting the girls receive Violet, the former chatelaine of their basement.

Violet wants to know if there have been any callers for her. When the girls coldly say, "Yes," Violet replies: "I thought so. A lot of my friends don't know I moved yet. In case they come around— would you mind giving out my new cards?" She takes a thick pack of calling cards from her purse and hands them to Eileen. "Thanks loads. So long—" and she leaves.

When Eileen learns that Chick Clark has called, she explains he's a newspaperman she met in an elevator, who was very much interested in Ruth's writing. She now remembers to tell Ruth that Bob Baker dropped by and that she naturally asked him to supper.

RUTH—Naturally. (*Grabs* EILEEN, *kisses her.*) Oh, darling! You are terrific! I'd never have the nerve!

EILEEN—Well, for goodness' sake, why not? He's just a *boy*—

Ruth wonders how to make their place presentable when Eileen tells her that she's asked Frank to dinner, too. Ruth has to worry about mixing these men, and about having no liquor, and nothing but leftovers. And now, as Eileen forgot to mention, Chick Clark arrives.

CHICK (*loosening his collar*)—Wow, it's absolute murder down here, ain't it? (*Staring overhead.*) What is this—an abandoned mine shaft?

RUTH—Are you planning to be with us long, Mr. Clark?
CHICK—Eileen asked me to take potluck with her.

Ruth's worst fears are realized. When Frank comes, Chick ignores his outstretched hand, only notices the bottle Frank has brought. Bob Baker, when he arrives, at least is polite, but this doesn't help much.

CHICK—What the hell is this, a block party?

Ruth, with murder in her heart, says: "You're quite a card, aren't you, Mr. Clark?" Eileen, coming back from a fruitless quest for victuals at Nino's restaurant, thanks Frank for his wine. Then she turns hostessy, and has everyone sit down uncomfortably, facing one another, with nothing to say. They all try to say something, and a "dry discordant note from the orchestra expresses the atmosphere of embarrassed silence" during pauses in the "conversation."

Just as Ruth offers some of the vintage Walgreen wine to the company, Appopolous makes things even more unsociable by discovering the theft of his painting. He starts accusing the girls, or at least someone who came to see them.

APPOPOLOUS—You know everybody who goes into your apartment.
RUTH—We don't know *half* of them.

And she suggests: "Maybe it was the same gang that swiped the Mona Lisa." Threatening to have the law on them, Appopolous leaves.

Another unfestive touch is now added by Helen arriving with Wreck, in his underwear shorts. Frank and Eileen try to smooth things over by passing the wine. But a blast from the subway so startles Frank that he spills his wine all over his white suit. Chick starts people laughing, and Frank takes umbrage and leaves.

Mrs. Wade once more looks down from the street, and this time demands that her daughter leave those "depraved women and their consort." "Not another word. You come right along with me. Don't you dare talk to my Helen again. You're not fit to associate with decent people!"

"You must admit," says Ruth to Bob Baker, "that for a place with a bad location and no neon sign, we're doing a hell of a business."

Eileen goes into the kitchen to heat up the spaghetti, and Chick follows to bother her. Bob now has a chance to tell Ruth that he's read her pieces: she has talent, but she's misused it writing of things she knows nothing about. Ruth is delighted with him for thinking she has talent, and furious with him for dismissing her actual work.

BAKER—I should have known better. You can't take it. You'll never get anywhere until you learn humility—
RUTH—When did you learn yours?

And she runs into the house, leaving a discouraged Baker to sing of his ideal: "A Quiet Girl."
When he goes, Ruth comes out of the kitchen, feeling that she's lost him, and sings:

> "I know a quiet girl,
> Hoping—waiting—
> But he'll never know."

The music continues, but a crash of dishes breaks the mood. Chick's attentions have made Eileen spill the food. He now takes it upon himself to go for beer and sandwiches. Eileen comes out and finds Ruth in an angry, unhappy state—just right for the telephone call that comes for her. It is Chick's city editor, telling her to report to the Brooklyn Navy Yard for a human interest story. She's to interview a shipload of millionaire Brazilian naval cadets. Ruth, full of the "I'll show him" spirit, swaps a runny stocking on her leg for a good one on Eileen's, gathers up the milk bottles to provide carfare, leaps up the stairs and is off to Brooklyn.
Eileen isn't left alone for long. Chick comes back with a bag of bologna sandwiches and ideas of amour. He makes no progress, and when he lets drop that it was he—not his city editor—who sent Ruth to Brooklyn to get her out of the way, he's through. Bob Baker calls to apologize to Ruth, and Eileen gets him to take her out to dinner.

CHICK—That's the worst double cross I ever got! A fine little sneak you turned out to be! (EILEEN *starts to eat a bologna sandwich*. CHICK *grabs it from her hand, as she is taking a bite*. CHICK *goes to bench, picks up empty bag and stuffs* EILEEN's *sandwich in it*.) I ain't fattenin' you up for someone else!" (*Blackout*.)

SCENE VII

At the Brooklyn Navy Yard, Ruth is having a bad time trying to get somewhere without a pass, when one of the cadets she wants to interview catches sight of her. With that, he and seven other white-uniformed cadets crowd around her. Their only answer to all her questions is: "American dance—Conga!" . . . "Conga!" . . . "Conga!"

RUTH—Then will you tell me?

ALL—Si! Si!

RUTH—It's like this— One, two, three, kick— One, two, three, kick. (*She shuffles from side to side in conga step. They follow clumsily. She ad libs:*) That's fine! You've got it! (*Music.*)
What do you think of the USA—NRA—TVA,
What do you think of our Mother's Day,
What do you think of the—

ADMIRALS—Conga!

From then on the going becomes rough; Ruth is tossed from one cadet to the other, but through it all she is determined to get her story and gasps out questions, only to get the one answer: "Conga!" She implores them:

RUTH—
Good neighbors—good neighbors,
Remember our policy—
Good neighbors—I'll help you
If you'll just help me!!

(ADMIRALS *sing serenade, strumming on imaginary guitars.* RUTH *stands totally exhausted.*)

ADMIRALS—Conga! (*They lift her on their backs, careening about.*)

RUTH (*still trying to get her interview*)—Stop!
What do you think of our double malts,
Family vaults,
Epsom salts,
Wouldn't you guys like to learn to waltz?
I know— You just want to—conga!

(*She is whirled about piggy-back in conga rhythm, her hat over her eyes—and finally lifted aloft and carried offstage, as the music builds to a frenetic finish.*)

SCENE VIII

The Back Yard Again: Ruth wasn't able to lose her conga line of cadets; they followed her all the way home.

EILEEN—What did you bring them here for?

RUTH—Bring them! They've been on my tail ever since I left the Brooklyn Navy Yard.

EILEEN—What do they want, anyway?

RUTH—What do you *think* they want?

Ruth suggests that Eileen try her hand at getting rid of them. First of all, Eileen, with her arms outstretched, begs them to go away. They make for the outstretched arms. She shrieks.

EILEEN—Gee, they can't be that dumb.

RUTH—They're not *that* dumb.

Eileen's next idea is to say she's sick, and to act it out by pretending to go to bed. Nothing could be better for the Brazilian navy. This time they really rush her. Eileen cowers behind her sister for protection. When the cadets begin to toss a coin (something like the cadets of St. Cyr) Eileen wants to know what they're doing that for. Ruth isn't sure, "But I've got a hunch it's not me!" The lucky man speaks to the girls in Portuguese. They still aren't sure what he said, but once more they're dragged into a conga line.

There is a terrific subway blast, which the girls think may scare the cadets away. But they quickly recover and close ranks. Eileen then leads the cadet line out the alley into the street, to try to get rid of them. In the meantime, the chef and waiters of Nino's have formed their own line. Baker now drops by and wants to know what's going on.

RUTH (*looks at him and starts to conga by herself*)—Oh, a few friends dropped in.

She leads the Nino force in a wild conga, but is crowded back by the returning Brazilians and a long snake dance of Villagers. Then Mrs. Wade, the one-woman Watch and Ward Society, arrives with Lonigan and another cop. When the cop makes a grab for Eileen, she kicks him. Lonigan drags her away; Baker rushes after them; and Ruth is left to be tossed high in the air by the conga-ing admirals.

CURTAIN

ACT II

Scene I

Eileen has been stashed away in the Christopher Street jail, which by now she appears to own. The officers run her errands, announce her callers and hang up the receiver on anyone she deems undesirable. As Ruth says, on her visit to the jail: "Tell me, Eileen, how many do you keep in help here?"

Eileen—Huh?

Ruth—I just love the way you've done this place. Well, I've got to get to work!

Eileen—Where?

Ruth—The Village Vortex. Your old pal Speedy Valenti gave me a job. (*She doesn't say what kind.*)

Fourth Cop (*enters*)—Eileen, there's a gentleman to see you. (*Hands* Eileen *a business card. She asks him to send* Baker *in.*)

Baker (*enters and naturally greets* Eileen *first, although his real concern is where* Ruth *went after all that excitement last night. To* Ruth.) You do look a little tired.

Ruth—I am. I didn't sleep all night—(*To* Eileen.)—worrying about *you.* So I sat at that typewriter and wrote the story about the Brazilian admirals. It's a darn good story—I know it is! I took your advice—a slice of my own life—and sent it to Chick's city editor—Mr. Bains. (*Sadly.*) But they didn't print it, so I guess it wasn't so good, after all—

Baker—Want *me* to read it?

Ruth—If you feel up to it— (*To* Eileen.) Sorry to eat and run, darling—but I've got to get to work!

Baker—Did you get a job? What are you doing?

Ruth—Oh, it's in the advertising game. (*Looks at wrist watch.*) Cocktail time, already? Well, I've got to fly. 'By, dear—lovely party—such fun. Do ask me again! (*She hurries off.*)

Apparently Eileen's case has become a Pan-American *crise,* so Bob is now going to the Brazilian Consul for help. Traffic being so heavy at the jail, he collides, on leaving, with Frank.

Frank has brought Walgreen's finest, a fan that's given away with each purchase of more than five dollars. After giving it to Eileen for her cell, he proposes that, on her release, the two of them lead the exciting Bohemian existence of Helen and Wreck. Eileen has a cop named Timothy throw Frank out.

All the cops then gather to show Eileen the newspaper stories in which she's featured. Eileen directs Lonigan, for his sins, to take the stories around to Valenti. He meekly sets off.

THIRD COP (*to* EILEEN, *as music begins*)—Oh, Eileen, you brought a breath of the old country into the station house.

FOURTH COP (*in greatly exaggerated Irish brogue*)—Sure and I been feelin' twice as Irish since you came into our lives. (*With that he bursts into a very Irish ballad to his "Darlin' Eileen." The other cops join him and get so wound up they even dance a jig.*)

EILEEN (*trying to cut them off*)—
    Listen, my lads,
    I've something to tell you
    I hope won't impel you to cry and to keen.
    Mother's a Swede and Father's a Scot—
    And Irish I'm not—   And I never have been—

ALL (*they will not hear of this*)—
    Hush you, Eileen!   Hush you, Eileen!
    Fairest colleen that iver I've seen.
    Don't you hand us none of that blarney—
    You come from Killarney,
    You're Irish, Eileen.

(*The dance resumes and ends in a "hats-off" salute to the girl of their dreams,* EILEEN. *Blackout.*)

SCENE II

On the street, in front of the girls' house, a plan is afoot to hood-wink Mrs. Wade into accepting, and even paying for, Wreck as a son-in-law. The Wreck, for once properly dressed, poses as an art connoisseur and compliments Appopolous on the portrait he is paint-ing of Mrs. Wade. Appopolous then introduces the distinguished Mr. Loomis to Mrs. Wade. Mrs. Wade, in turn, introduces Mr. Loomis to her daughter. He in turn asks them all to tea. As Helen sets off on Wreck's arm, Mrs. Wade learns from Appopolous that Wreck comes from a very aristocratic family from Trenton Tech, and they, too, go off arm in arm.

Ruth's job turns out to be advertising the Vortex in bright lights—that are a part of her costume. As Villagers pass by, she and her male companion (both of them wearing evening clothes) light up, with "Vortex" flashing across their chests.

Suddenly Ruth sees Bob approaching and begs the Man not to

light up while she's talking to him.   Bob tells her he was crazy about her piece on the conga line, and is sure his boss will like it, too. Valenti comes along and finds his hired help talking to Baker, and barks:

VALENTI—What's going on here?   Get on the ball!   (MAN *snaps lights on*.   BAKER *stares in wonder*.   RUTH *looks at him unhappily*.)

*Rosalind Russell
and Edith Adams
in "Wonderful
Town"*

Well? What's with you, sister—run out of juice?

RUTH (*lights up and smiles feebly at* BAKER)—Well, it's a healthy job. Keeps me out in the air!

BAKER (*pats her arm reassuringly*)—Good girl! (*He smiles at her and goes off.*)

VALENTI—No socializing on my time. (*Goes to* MAN.) Here's a pitch. You take Sheridan Square. (*Hands flyer to* MAN, *who exits. Then to* RUTH.) Here's your spiel. Come on! Get a mob around you! Make with the pitch! Get hep! (RUTH *is left alone, with a growing crowd of hep cats, who show her how* VALENTI'S *flyer really should be delivered.*)

HEP CATS (*singing and showing her how to get hep*)—
　　Swing! Dig the rhythm!
　　Swing! Dig the message!
　　The jive is jumpin' and the music goes around and around—
　　Whoa—ho—!
RUTH (*getting the idea*)—Oh!
VILLAGERS—
　　Cat, make it solid!
　　Cat, make it groovy!
　　You gotta get your seafood, Mama;
　　Your favorite dish is fish!

(RUTH *catches on how to make it solid and groovy, and delivers the message in a good husky monotone, while the* VILLAGERS *start a wild dance, and* RUTH *leads the works to a "sent" finish. As the mob backs out,* RUTH, *now following in a trance, sings in a hoarse, hypnotic whisper.*)

RUTH—
　　Swing— Swing—
　　Green, no—red, no
　　Me Tarzan— No, no, no
　　That old man Mose
　　He kicked that bucket
　　Down in the well—well, well, well
　　My favorite dish
　　Ahhh—fish!
VILLAGERS—Gesundheit!
RUTH—Thank you.
VILLAGERS—You're welcome.
RUTH (*her hands before her, mesmerized. Walks off in a trance*)—Swing—swing—swing—swing—swing— (*She disappears. Blackout.*)

SCENE III

Back at the studio, Appopolous, his virtue affronted by Eileen's being jailed, is dispossessing the girls. He gives them till six P.M. to move out.

RUTH—Yes, imagine what bad publicity could do to this dump!

That doesn't help matters, and Appopolous stalks out.

Baker comes by to report that his editor cared less for Ruth's story than he did, so he's ready to have it out with him. Ruth doesn't want to get Bob into trouble, but he insists it's a matter of principle—either he knows his business, or he doesn't.

The place begins to fill up: Appopolous pops in and out, announcing how many more minutes till six o'clock; Lonigan arrives with Eileen; and Chick Clark pokes his head in at the window with a message for Ruth from his city editor—he likes her story and wants her to phone him. Eileen sicks Lonigan on Chick, and all he can do before he's nabbed is beg, "Now wait a minute, Eileen. You're gonna louse it up! Tell her to call Mr. Wilson—the city editor!" Lonigan, having chased Chick away, passes Eileen his whistle through the window, and tells her to use it if anything, or anyone, bothers her.

When Baker hears Appopolous is serious about dispossessing the girls, he tells them to hang on till he gets back from giving hell to his editor. But after he leaves, they feel that they'd better light out for Ohio, though Ruth breaks down and admits that she likes Bob, too. Smiling through her tears, she joins Eileen in a chorus of "Ohio."

Valenti now arrives with Appopolous: he is delighted by Eileen's newspaper publicity; offers her a tryout at his club; offers Ruth one —without clothes that light up—too. Appopolous, his virtue less affronted, tells the girls, if they make good, they can stay in his place for life.

Valenti wants to know: "What are you gonna sing, Babe?"

EILEEN—Ruth, remember the song we always used to do at the Kiwanis Club? The "Wrong Note Rag"?

RUTH—Oh, yes—do that one.

VALENTI—It's an oldie, but you'll never know it when I back you up with the licorice stick.

RUTH—The what?

VALENTI—My clarinet. Then for an encore— Tell me, kid— did you ever take 'em off?

EILEEN—What?

VALENTI—You know, *strip?*

RUTH—My sister doesn't strip.

VALENTI—Too bad. We're always looking for new faces. (*Blackout.*)

Scene IV

On the street, in front of the Vortex, Appopolous is selling Wreck to Mrs. Wade, as the foursome—now returning from an elaborate dinner—are on their way to the night club.

Ruth is having trouble with a nervous Eileen, and leaves her to get some black coffee; but Eileen seems to recover quickly enough when Bob Baker returns. Bob is jobless but cheerful, and Eileen tells him he's wonderful to have lost his job over Ruth. When he doesn't register, she tells him, "Don't play dumb!" She then proceeds to prove to him that it wasn't principle that made him fight; "it's love." After Baker tentatively tries the idea out, Eileen, still singing, tells him:

EILEEN—
    Don't try to deny it,
    I know the signs,
    I know it when I see it—
    So just face it,
    Just say it—

And she leaves him to face it—which he does very happily.

Scene V

Everyone is at the Village Vortex, a night club hung with surrealist paintings by every artist who couldn't pay his tab. Valenti leads the band with his clarinet as the crowd dances a slow, writhing jitterbug, packed together like anchovies.

By now the Wreck is toasting his mother-in-law-to-be with Appopolous' champagne, and Eileen, still jittery, is about to go on.

Valenti asks his customers to "Give the little girl a great big hand"; Chick Clark manages to slip Ruth her press card, and Ruth jubilantly saves him from Lonigan. Eileen, no longer queasy, starts to cry over Ruth's landing a newspaper job, and Valenti, hearing her say it's because she's happy, snaps: "Well, *I* ain't. And the customers ain't— Sing or blow!"

Eileen needs Ruth's support, so Ruth, with Valenti's permission, bids the band play the "Wrong Note Rag."

RUTH AND EILEEN (*working in a dead-pan sister-act style*)—
    Oh, there's a new sensation that is goin' aroun'—

Goin' aroun'— Goin' aroun'— Goin' aroun'—
A simple little ditty that is sweepin' the town,
Sweepin' the town— Swee—eepin' the town—
Doo—Doo—Doo—
Doo—Doo—Doo—Doo—Doo—Doo—
They call it the wrong note rag!

The audience eventually joins in and the girls break out into some
fine, high-spirited ragtime. The crowd loves it, and the girls hug
each other for joy.

VALENTI—Well, that's what drove 'em out of Ohio. What are you
gonna do for an encore?

Eileen is overwhelmed, but whispers: "It's Love." While she
sings, Baker finds Ruth and tells her:

"It's love at last,
        I've someone to cheer for."

and Ruth, in his arms, agrees.

MY 3 ANGELS *

A Comedy in Three Acts

By Sam and Bella Spewack

Based on "La Cuisine des Anges" by Albert Husson

[Sam *and* Bella Spewack *have, in twenty-five years as a writing team, produced a total of ten plays and ten films, among them the vastly popular "Boy Meets Girl" which had five companies playing at one time. For "Kiss Me Kate" they collaborated with Shakespeare and Cole Porter and received the Antoinette Perry and Page One Awards. This musical ran for over three years and is still playing in Scandinavia, Australia and England. Mr. Spewack was born in Russia in 1899, and educated at New York public schools and Columbia University. He was a reporter on the* New York World *at eighteen and covered the Genoa Conference in 1922. At about this time he and Bella, who was born in Hungary in 1899, were married. In 1943 he was press attaché for the United States Embassy in Moscow for the Moscow Conference.*

"My 3 Angels" is based on "La Cuisine des Anges," a French play by Albert Husson. *It is Mr. Husson's first play and won the Tristan Bernard Prize when produced by André Certes in Paris in 1952.*]

ACT I

IT is Christmas Eve of 1910. In the steaming hot penal colony of French Guiana's appropriately named Cayenne, the Felix Ducotels live behind his store.

There is a bamboo-curtained door leading from the living room to the general store, but the living-room furniture was imported from France. The door to the family's quarters is opposite an archway leading to a tropical garden. There is a guest room on each side of the living room, one near the garden, the other near the family quarters. A ladder mounts to an open skylight in the thatched roof near the back of the room.

Felix Ducotel, a transplanted, frock-coated Frenchman, runs his

little business in a gentlemanly fashion, neither suspicious of the
many sneak thieves who walk off with his merchandise, nor unpleasant enough to insist that his French compatriots pay their bills.
His wife, Amelie, is the true wife of an easy-going man. She is tartly
aware of her husband's shortcomings, and loves him for his kindness. But after a year of Devil's Island, she still shudders at the
idea of three convicts—murderers—up on her roof, whereas Felix
is delighted with their skill in repairing it.

Amelie has discovered another theft. This time it is a harmonica
—now being played within earshot. Felix will not go out to confront the thief.

FELIX—You don't really expect me—at my age—a man in my
position to run around the streets squabbling with the natives? Be-
sides, it's too hot.
AMELIE—What *are* you going to do?
FELIX—I'll handle the affair.
AMELIE—How?
FELIX—It's a matter of bookkeeping.

As he tries to describe his dreamlike manner of bookkeeping, the
hammering on the roof stops. Amelie can only hope that the little
capital they brought with them from France will cover the unending
thefts. But Felix tells her he invested *that* in a gold mine as a most
practical move for a poor man. Amelie can only pray then that her
daughter marries someone totally impractical.

The Ducotels' charming daughter Isabelle comes in on her way
to the garden. Has their Christmas tree arrived? It has, but her
mother is not at all gay, and chides Isabelle (her other dreamer)
for believing that the Paul she left in France still loves her. He
hasn't written a single letter since they left Cherbourg over ten
months ago.

Isabelle is undisturbed, and patiently repeats to her mother the
agreement that she and Paul had: not to write, in order to impress
Paul's Uncle Henri with their fortitude. The businesslike, rich
Uncle would then realize that their love could withstand anything.
Her mother only comments realistically that Paul is a bright and
ambitious man. "Tell me, my poor darling—why should an ambitious man marry poor—when he can marry rich?"

Felix brings a letter for Isabelle from her former schoolmate Suzanne. She puts it aside to read later, explaining: "It's always the
same letter. 'My dear, I've just had a wonderful holiday at St.
Moritz, while you, poor thing, suffer with the savages in those horrid

jungles. The snow was delicious!' In school she was always the
first with the bad news. Guess who's down with the mumps—
guess who's going to be expelled? Guess who's pregnant!" And
Isabelle goes out to pick flowers, leaving her shocked mother to greet
Mme. Parole, the custom officer's wife.

Madame's in a hurry. Madame demands quick service. She must
have a bottle of Chartreuse for her husband's Christmas surprise.
Felix searches for the Chartreuse which somehow or other isn't where
it should be. Madame Parole, hearing the roofers hammer away,
chatters of the convenience of convict help. Take her jewel of a
cook. . . . "He may be a little effeminate—shall we say peculiar?
But, my dear, it takes all kinds to make a world. He doesn't bother
me. And he adores Ernest. He's so unsophisticated. He thinks
Louis was sent here because he's peculiar. He wasn't, of course.
He strangled a couple of old men. I don't know how many exactly.
I've never asked him. He's so sensitive." She obviously is not.
She wiggles very easily out of settling her large account with Amelie.
When she receives a bottle of brandy from Felix she starts to go.
"Where's my bag? Oh, dear, I left it at home. What a scatter-
brain I am! Oh, well, charge it. I must take a look at my bill one
of these days. . . . Right after the holidays— Must run now—
By— By."

FELIX (*pityingly, smiles*)—What a scatterbrain!
AMELIE—As scatterbrained as a fox—

And as nervy, for she even comes back for Ernest's biscuits. Then
Madame remembers to leave a note her husband had asked her to
deliver. It holds terrible news for Felix. Henri is right here and
demands to be got out of quarantine immediately, so as to waste
no time in checking up on Felix's store.

FELIX—You'd think a man who swindled me out of a first-class
department store—legally, I admit—a cousin—by marriage, I'll admit—still a cousin— We grew up together as boys— (*Reads.*)
"I have two days to give you. I want to make a complete inventory,
and check your books. I shall then make the logical decision. Be
good enough to get me off this damn ship at once."

AMELIE—Logical decision? . . . Felix, is he going to close the
shop?
FELIX—I don't know.
AMELIE—Or get someone else?

Then she guesses that Felix's books are in a terrible mess. He admits they are—"Temporarily—only temporarily."

AMELIE—We can always go home.
FELIX—With what? And to what? At my age? God help us!
(*Loud hammering.*)

Amelie sends her husband off to the Health Authorities to clear Henri, and he in turn reminds her to get both guest rooms ready, because Paul is with Henri. She prepares to do so.

Isabelle, coming in from the garden laden with flowers, is not at all surprised that Paul is here. She is overjoyed, but had expected something of the sort. But she feels apologetic for having been so nasty about Suzanne, and starts to read her letter. As she reads, "Three figures descend the ladder and stop. They look at her. She smiles. They smile. She chuckles, they chuckle silently. She looks solemn. They do too." Suddenly, she gasps and collapses. The three convicts, in their white pajama-like numbered uniforms, go to her. The three are: "Joseph, like Jules, in his forties. He's an ex-forger and ex-promoter. Jules killed a faithless wife—and Alfred, in his twenties, is an ex-playboy who murdered for money—"

Joseph immediately thinks it might have been a poisoned note that knocked out Isabelle. But after picking it up and reading Suzanne's sweet style, he decides against poison. "Darling, Paul and I are engaged. ('Three exclamation points. Engaged in capital letters.') Papa and M. Trochard arranged it just before Paul sailed with his darling uncle. Darling Isabelle, I know how happy you'll be for us. ('Happy capitalized, two exclamation points.') After all, darling, a school-girl crush is not love, as we all know. And let's be frank. That's all there was between you and Paul, and honestly I don't mind. Not a bit. ('Two exclamation points.') But I do want to save Paul embarrassment when he sees you. You know how kind ('capitalized')—how very kind—he is. Don't mistake his kindness for something else. As Paul says, I can't help being kind, and some girls persist in misinterpreting kindness for something else. . . . Want to hear any more?"

JULES—No.

The convicts decide that Suzanne is rich and a "bitch." Young Alfred can't understand how anyone could turn down Isabelle— "She's beautiful." But he's promptly told, "In your position you

don't admire a beautiful woman. Neither party stands to benefit"
—and Joseph orders him off to get some water.

When Amelie comes in to find her daughter prostrated and the
convicts hovering over her, Joseph handles her with great tact and
points out what has happened: "Here's the viperish paragraph—"
He extends sympathy to the family, also, on the arrival of Paul's
Uncle Henri. They have heard everything while repairing the roof.

Isabelle comes to, suddenly, and dramatically wishes only to die.
When she runs to her room Alfred swiftly follows, and then returns
to report that she had no poisons around, and he removed all
weapons—scissors, nail file, etc. And if she wished to jump, she
couldn't fall far, for hers was a ground-floor room. His friends
compliment him on his thoroughness.

JULES—We disapprove of suicide. Especially for young and
charming girls. She'll be all right. Time heals all wounds. We're
authorities on the subject of time. (*The shop bell rings*)

and Joseph, like an old fire horse, is off through the door to the shop.

AMELIE—He's not going to . . . ?
JULES—Wait on the customer? Of course. There's nothing he
likes better. He can sell anything to anyone . . . and has.

Amelie is perplexed: these men aren't her idea of convicts. They
don't talk or look like convicts. "Well," replies Jules, "I wasn't
born in a cell. . . . (ALFRED *quietly disappears towards* ISABELLE'S
room.) And on the other hand, I wasn't sent here for biting my
nails." He had strangled his wife, and it wasn't her fault, either.
He had come home from a trip without forewarning her.

Alfred reports that Isabelle has now reached the weeping stage,
and Joseph returns for some change. He has sold a painting of the
Madonna and Child to the atheistic postmaster.

JOSEPH—He wanted a bedspread.
AMELIE—And you sold him the Madonna and Child? Why,
that's a miracle.
JOSEPH—No, Madame. I appealed to his cupidity. I asked one
simple question. How do you know this isn't a Rembrandt? Besides, I couldn't find a bedspread.

After Joseph gets an additional ten francs out of the postmaster
for the frame, he discovers Felix's account books. He has a passion,
also, for bookkeeping.

But the others, through with their business at the Ducotels', start to leave. Amelie is horrified to see Alfred has a small box containing a snake. This, the men explain, is their deadly poisonous pal Adolphe. He became one of them when he dropped on a guard who was overworking them.

When Alfred darts off again to Isabelle's room, Amelie follows and finds both gone: Her daughter had tried to jump in the river nearby and Alfred had saved her. Jules peers after Isabelle and Alfred. "Alfred has a striking eloquence. Your daughter is no longer thinking of ending it all. In fact, your daughter isn't thinking of anything at the moment."

AMELIE—What?
JULES—Knockout. . . . Only thing to do, Madame.

If she jumped in the river, what would Alfred do? Jump, too. And then—she would struggle. He'd use the approved technique of knocking her out before he could swim back with her. The technique's just as effective ashore, and dryer.

A scratched-up Alfred carries Isabelle back to her mother. Felix comes in to find his daughter once more stretched out, and Joseph riffling through his papers. Amelie goes to the convicts' defense, and Joseph tells Felix: "I hope you'll forgive me for saying I find confusion intolerable." Felix splutters, but his wife takes him away to explain things. The men see no point in waiting for them to return.

JOSEPH (debating)—No, not unless the thanks took a tangible form—money or commodities. But I hate to take from people like that—poor, decent. Give me somebody grasping—greedy—there's your ideal sucker. Who wants to shoot fish in a barrel?

Alfred is still thinking of Isabelle, and his friends become sharp with him.

JULES—Forget her! Remember! We have one advantage—and only one—over other people. We can live without emotion. We can achieve serenity.
JOSEPH—Yes, my young friend, you'd better achieve some serenity pretty damn quick. Of course, we're older, and with our aging glands, serenity comes easier.

Joseph lusts after one thing—the bell rings in the shop, and he gets it: a customer. Jules urges him to enjoy himself, so he beams

and rushes forward to sell a man a white jacket—miles too small.
Felix discovers what he's up to now—"He's out of his mind. The
man'll know it won't fit. He can see—feel it—"

JULES—He won't see or feel anything. He won't get a chance to.
FELIX—But it's not fair . . . it's not ethical. Of course, I sup-
pose you fellows aren't concerned with ethics naturally—I mean—
I don't want to hurt your feelings.
JULES—Not at all— No, some of us are downright crooked.
Our world's just like yours. All kinds. All kinds. The only dif-
ference is we were caught.

Felix passes quickly over this to propose something his wife had
suggested: "I know it's impossible—but she thought if you wanted
to—and could spend the evening here—since it's Christmas Eve and
all that—" Jules and Alfred are touched and pleased and say, "It
can be arranged." "In our world," Alfred spells out, "everything
has its price—just as in yours." "And worth it," Jules adds, "to
spend an evening in a home, a real home. . . ."
Joseph has already started to enjoy his Christmas Eve: he sold
the coat. He tells Felix, "He wouldn't touch that jacket at the
regular price of 27 francs, but at the *reduced* price of 27 francs,
he snapped it up."
Jules dashes off to get a chicken for the dinner. Joseph, though
unwanted, accompanies Felix into the shop. Alfred sets the table
and lectures a revived Isabelle. He finally convinces her that Paul
has come to see her; she agrees to join the family, and Paul and
Uncle Henri, at dinner. Then—as her mother had done with Jules—
she turns sympathetic eyes on Alfred, and asks why he was sent
here. Was it a mistake? "No," he answers, "I was guilty as Hell."
And cheerfully describes his crime, a large one involving robbery
and murder. Isabelle recovers rather quickly from the horror of it
and begins to plan a festive evening. She makes the seating arrangements, and decides that they must ply Uncle Henri with wine.
Felix interrupts the plans: "They won't be here for dinner—"
He hadn't been able to face them tonight, and had left them on the
ship. It will be a Christmas dinner in the bosom of the family—
with just three extra guests.
Alfred uncrates their little tree to Isabelle's sighs: "It's France!
It's home."
Joseph rushes in with another tree.

JOSEPH—Oh, you have a tree!

FELIX—Where on earth did you get *that?*
JOSEPH—I'd better return it.

And he goes out, as Jules enters with an orchid and camellia. Amelie calls from the kitchen: "Felix, I found a chicken in the oven. Where did it come from?" Jules reminds her to praise Him from whom all blessings flow, and presents his flowers, straight from the Governor's gardens, to the ladies.

Joseph now puffs in again with the stolen harmonica, which he had nabbed from a little boy in the garden—but then he returns it to him so he can play carols during dinner.

Felix brings out his wine, and Joseph knowingly inspects it: "Color—bouquet—quite respectable. If I say so myself, I'm something of an expert. I once organized a winery that was the marvel of the trade. Château Joseph. We had no wines, no bottles, not even a cork. But the labels were museum pieces. The Prosecuting Attorney gave me a one-man show."

From the garden comes the sound of the harmonica—Isabelle recognizes the carol *Three Angels*, and calls attention to the three little angels on her tree. "Only my angels are a little shopworn—a little—"

JOSEPH—A little unlucky, Mademoiselle. They were damaged by the long rough journey—bruised by unfeeling hands— (*Angels topple.*) Fallen angels, Mademoiselle.
ISABELLE—I don't care—I'm going to drink to—to my three angels.
JOSEPH—Thank you, Mademoiselle.

ACT II

Later that night, the store bell shatters the rest of the sleeping convicts. They had been making themselves comfortable on the floor and the chairs.

Joseph goes to the shop door and returns with Uncle Henri and Paul. Henri Trochard is a mean, sarcastic and crudely rigid man, and Paul is under his thumb. Uncle Henri lashes out, first at the convicts, then at a sleepy Felix who comes in to greet him. And if these men are not the servants of the house, Felix is entertaining them as friends! Felix admits it.

JOSEPH—The boss means a good servant is always a friend. A bad servant is bound to be an enemy. He'll not only ruin your digestion. He'll even squeal to the police. Believe me, I speak from bitter experience.

HENRI—Have our bags taken to our rooms.

FELIX—Certainly. Amelie has given you these rooms here. I hope you'll forgive the primitive quality of our hospitality. Isabelle fixed your room for you herself, Paul.

Henri orders Paul to his room, and "lock your door when you retire." And he then lets the convicts know: "I intend to sleep with a revolver in my hand." Joseph is at his service: "We clean, oil and polish revolvers." "You," snaps Henri, "won't get your hands on mine."

Henri refuses to be human with Felix, and is less than human with Isabelle when she and her mother come forth to welcome him. "I have no patience with fools, male or female—as I've indicated to your brilliant father. I don't want Paul hounded by a weeping and demanding innocent. Like all young men, he likes a pretty face. Who doesn't? However, he's engaged. Damn good family, and a damn good business. I couldn't buy old Audibert out. Tried hard enough. So I'm marrying him. As simple as that. The girl's a cow, but she'll give milk." The shocked women beat a dignified retreat, after he poohpoohs any feelings of love that Paul may have for Isabelle: "Paul will find no scarcity of women to love in Paris. Experts in their field, too."

Having completed this matter, Henri now proceeds to the financial end of his visit.

"How much business did we do last month? Gross receipts?" Felix hasn't the foggiest notion, and flounders miserably until Joseph enters and, in the role of bookkeeper, rattles off: "Our gross receipts were two thousand eight hundred and fifteen francs and forty-two centimes, sir."

HENRI—What?

JOSEPH—An advance over the preceding month of exactly one thousand, five hundred and eighty-one francs and two centimes. . . . Our figures for October were three hundred and forty-seven, and forty-eight centimes.

HENRI—An advance?

JOSEPH—I am preparing a chart—a graph— You'll forgive the crude quality of cardboard and ink— You will observe here that business declined steadily in the first few months—due to new management—conservative clientele skeptical of anything new—et cetera—then observe that suddenly in August—with the reawakening of confidence—M'sieu's grasp of the affair, et cetera—the line rises, steadily, up, up, up, up—I expect—and I am a cautious observer— a record breaker for December. . . . Right up here. I'll need more cardboard. (*He indicates the line has run off the cardboard.*)

And in answer to Henri's further questions, Joseph describes Felix as a hard-hearted, tough, all-seeing businessman. But Trochard remains unconvinced, and insists that Felix get up at dawn on Christmas morning and be ready to take inventory at seven sharp. He goes to the guest room and leaves behind him a desolate man. Felix knows: "I must produce books tomorrow—and the stock—" It takes more to upset Joseph, who says breezily: "We have all night to straighten those out."

FELIX—It'll take more than one night.
JOSEPH—You don't know my system of inspired accounting. Trouble with most businessmen is they think mathematics is a science. With me, it's an art—

Joseph explains that Felix's books make him look like a thorough cheat, though in fact he is an honest man.

Before Joseph can add any artistic touches to the books, however, Henri comes out to take possession of them for the night. "Don't tell me you want to do a little work on them. I'll keep them in my room tonight. I want them as they are now . . . in all their pristine purity."

FELIX—Your suspicions are—are— (*He stops.*)
JOSEPH—I'm sure the gentleman will apologize in the morning, but if he wants the books, sir, he shall have them.

Joseph gathers up all of them and presents them to Henri, who retires. And Felix, left only with his honor, starts off for bed, afraid of what the morning will bring, but relieved that his conscience is clear.

Paul comes in, impatient for his order of chicken, which Joseph goes off to fill. Isabelle has heard all the talking in the living room, and now comes out and, seeing Paul, rushes into his unwilling arms. She is full of pity for the dreadful year he must have had, letting Uncle keep them apart so long. "How could I have been so blind? As if it matters what he thinks! What can he do? Fire you? Disinherit you? What does that mean?" All that means a great deal to Paul, but he lightly brushes it aside, saying he couldn't bear to have Isabelle condemned to a life of poverty. And of course his uncle has been like a father to him.

ISABELLE—Like a father! Do you know what he said about Suzanne—the girl he picked for you—your fiancée—the Gargoyle?
PAUL—What?
ISABELLE—She's a cow, but she'll give milk!

Then she goes to work on him, and finally forces him to snap his fingers at Uncle Henri—"That for Uncle Henri!"—at the very moment that Henri once more marches from the guest room. When Paul is ordered to his room he offers no resistance; but when Uncle turns on Isabelle, he meets with a good deal. And all at once Uncle Henri becomes thoroughly low, making all kinds of decadent suggestions for her future.

All three convicts overhear Henri's snide remarks, don't like them at all, and close in on him in a menacing fashion. Joseph orders him to bed. Henri blusters: "I'll report this to the authorities in the morning. I'll see to it that you don't get away with this impertinence."

ALFRED—We're naughty!
JOSEPH—Back to bed, sir, I urge you. Before my young friend becomes impatient.
HENRI (*turning to* ISABELLE)—Since they won't take orders from me, would you be good enough to—
ALFRED—The young lady is sleepy. You're tired, Mademoiselle. You must go to bed. The gentleman has nothing more to say to you. Nothing!

As Isabelle goes, Henri reaches in his pocket, but it is Alfred who holds his revolver. He announces that it has been cleaned, and the cartridges were removed at the same time. Henri threatens to have them all arrested in the morning—but he's too late, says Joseph (*indicating* JULES *and* ALFRED). "They've been arrested permanently —I'm only in for a brief twenty years. . . . Sounds long, but when one thinks geologically—historically—a mere flicker of time—" Henri is finally compelled to go to his room, and he angrily does so.

It is a busy night. Isabelle feels she can't sleep before she has a meeting with Paul. Alfred is delegated to get Paul out to the garden bench, even if he has to use force. As Joseph says: "The young man—and mind you, I'm pretty tolerant—strikes me as being quite a stinker."

Jules shortly afterwards receives a worried Amelie in the living room. With a fatherly air, he soothingly tells Amelie there is nothing she can do for her daughter except get some sleep. "You must; you owe it to her. We're here"—and he will take care of anything that has to be done. She acquiesces and goes off meekly to bed.

Alfred and Joseph now join Jules. They feel that Paul, under their coaching, isn't performing badly at all, and if it weren't for Uncle Henri— But in a few hours Henri Trochard will be at work ruining the whole family and reporting the three of them, too.

JOSEPH—One man capable of so much mischief!
ALFRED—He's human.
JOSEPH—I doubt it.
ALFRED—I still say he's human. Know what I mean?

They do, but Joseph at first doesn't go for the idea. He does not care for violence. He concocts, instead, fancy plans involving Uncle's financial downfall that seem impractical even to his friends. Jules, for his part, holds explosive young Alfred back, demanding a fair trial for Henri. This form of justice appeals to all three.

Jules takes the role of the bilious Judge; Alfred is the impatient prosecutor in a huge hurry for a conviction; Joseph is saddled with the defense.

Alfred demands a verdict of guilty. Joseph wants to know what crime his client has committed—and the Judge answers: "He will commit at least three in the morning. In this court, we prevent crime. We don't wait as they do out there till the damage is done, till the victims stare up at us with astonished and unseeing eyes. Our verdicts bring happiness—not further misery—to men who have been punished too late."

ALFRED—Prosecution rests.
JOSEPH—Defense rests. A man can't be expected to win *all* his cases.

Henri is found guilty and sentenced to death—"if it can be arranged conveniently."

Alfred picks up the box containing Adolphe, fixes things so that the snake can get out, and lets it slither through the crack of the guest room door.

Afterwards there is some question whether Adolphe has done his job properly, but the three decide to wait till morning to find out.

In the meantime, after such a full day, they need their sleep, so they settle down to enjoy their last few hours at the Ducotels'.

ACT III

In the early morning sunlight, Joseph sits artistically composing Uncle Henri's last will and testament—as Joseph sees it. Jules comes in with coffee, and is tolerant as always, but unimpressed by the forgery.

JOSEPH—I challenge the experts. There isn't a court in France that won't honor the deathbed request of our poor old Uncle. (*Reads.*) "My conscience has been troubling me grievously of late. I have a curious premonition of death, somehow. I am writing this shortly after midnight and ask that this constitute a codicil to my will. If anything should happen to me I implore my nephew Paul to restore to Felix Ducotel, my cousin, the Galerie Moderne in Cherbourg which I acquired by sharp practice. I could not face the judgment of Providence if this were not done. Paul, you are my heir, and I beg you to help a repentant and tortured sinner by making generous amends to my cousin Felix. I beg of you, Paul, respect my wishes. Be happy, Paul, as I was not. Be honest, Paul, as I was not. Henri Trochard." Be happy! Be honest! Damn good advice to a young man starting out life—with a fortune. And easy to follow—for a young man with a fortune.

Jules has the thought that it would be wise to see if Trochard is really dead. Madame Parole bursts in on them, thus preventing any check-up. She is livid. She accuses Felix of palming off a water-filled display bottle for brandy. Her Christmas Eve was ruined. Joseph takes care of her: "My employer needs his sleep, Madame. He has a big day ahead, a very big day ahead. The turning point of his entire life, you might say. That reminds me— You have a small bill." He knows better than to leave it to Madame to pay up. He grabs her bag and extracts the money. He promises the frightened woman he'll credit it to her account, and ushers her out still carrying her original bottle.

Alfred, in the meantime, has dressed himself in Paul's clothes, and is indulging in the game of "if"—"if" it weren't for his step-father's being so mean, he'd really be in Paul's shoes. Jules humors him. But Joseph, coming back with the codicil to Uncle Henri's will— which he places conspicuously on the sideboard—thinks Alfred had better make sure that Uncle Henri is a corpse.

Alfred goes to Uncle's room as ordered, but returns shortly a very worried man. Henri is "Dead as a mackerel. I'm not worried about him. It's Adolphe!" The snake has disappeared.

JOSEPH—We can't leave Adolphe loose. The poor little thing has no judgment when he bites. How can he differentiate between good and evil without us to guide him?

ALFRED—Maybe the old Uncle was too much for Adolphe and he's crawled off somewhere—sick—maybe he's dying— (*Anxiously.*)

Isabelle finds them all on hands and knees searching every inch of the room. Alfred rises in Paul's finery and receives a left-handed compliment: he looks handsome but lacks Paul's elegance and distinction. Though he's crestfallen, he makes sure of her safety by sending her off to Mass.

They have resumed the hunt when Paul enters in his pajamas. He sees Alfred wearing his clothes: "What the devil are you doing in my suit—my shirt—my shoes—my tie!" Joseph says Alfred was acting as his valet, and tells Alfred to return them to Paul's room: "And while you're there, I suggest you look for the collar button," and gives a wiggle of the hand.

When Amelie comes in with Henri's coffee, Jules takes over and prevents her from going into his room; instead, he seats her on a minutely inspected chair that holds no Adolphe.

Amelie, in a confidential mood, tells Jules that she has come to sympathize with him for having had murderous impulses. She felt that way herself last night about Henri Trochard. But she did nothing. She says she envies his being a man of action, while Jules replies that he only envies her husband. Amelie becomes quite flustered as Jules finishes the little interlude: "Thank you for this Christmas— it'll be a treasured memory. A man in my position doesn't store up many memories— And you—when you get back home to your Brittany—to the kind of home you should have—all this will be an amusing story for a dull dinner party." Amelie doesn't see "a future of dinner parties, dull or otherwise." Jules asks her to have hope: "Things will work out somehow. (PAUL *enters.*) Perhaps he'll work them out."

Paul only complains of Alfred, who is standing on his bed. Jules says: "He's looking for native wild life. He's a great student of nature." Then Paul expresses surprise that his uncle isn't up. If he doesn't go to wake him, "he'll think I overslept. I'd better go in and see." So it is he who finds Henri dead.

PAUL—I don't understand it. His doctors said he would live to be ninety.

JULES—He can sue the doctors for breach of contract.

Felix is summoned by his wife, and in a daze, goes for a doctor to take care of things.

Joseph then thinks it's the time to present sympathy (and his bit of forgery) to Paul. Paul disappoints all three convicts right off by trying to tear it up—after seeing what is in it. Joseph grabs it in time: "All communications! No matter how trivial— (*Pretends to study it.*) And this doesn't seem trivial at all! Not at all! A dying man's last request—his last gasp. A voice from the grave!" Paul protests he meant no harm, that he certainly will follow his uncle's wishes—"I won't contest, I assure you. I repeat: I respect my uncle's wishes. If the document is genuine." Joseph is indignant at this, but Paul says he will consult his lawyers. He is a chip off the old block. He will even carry out his uncle's desires to the extent of marrying Suzanne Audibert! The men are furious. Paul tells them: "I find this conversation distasteful—and impertinent. Once and for all—my relations with Isabelle are my business, not yours. You drove me out there last night at the point of a gun. You told me what to say—how to behave. If she drew certain conclusions, it's your fault—not mine. I'm *not* free to do as I please— Wealth is a responsibility." And, though the men's anger scares him, he threatens to report them to the authorities, then makes a dash for Uncle's room, and locks the door behind him.

JOSEPH—Gentlemen, I'm afraid we've been had.

Jules thinks they might as well hold another trial, but Joseph squashes that idea: "Now, please— Not TWO accidents— We'll never get away with it. And what good would it do? Besides, we haven't got Adolphe."

ALFRED—All our work—down the drain.

Jules adds that at least Amelie can go home again, but that doesn't make Alfred feel any better—he's thinking of Isabelle without the man she wants. He feels like doing all sorts of things to Paul.

JOSEPH—I forbid you. For us Christmas is over. We pack away the tinsel—store the tree—sweep away the debris—and complain vaguely of indigestion.

As he is about to lead the way back to the roof, Paul comes out of Henri's room calling for a doctor. The men aren't too much interested. A snake bit him. The men are fascinated: Was it a little snake—on the ceiling?—on the floor?—on the bed? Paul, between calls for a doctor, lets them know—"In his trousers—in the pocket."

Joseph suggests that he needs air, and over his protests, Jules and Joseph pull him out into the garden protesting: "You're always sending me to that damn bench!"

Alfred quickly goes to pick up Adolphe, and when he comes back with the snake in the box, he meets Isabelle. He stares at her, hides the box, and tries to tell her tactfully that Paul was not a loving kind of man. Joseph comes back in time to contrive for Paul a splendid valedictory, instead: "Gentlemen," he said, "death has made me free to marry my adorable Isabelle, and only death can part us now."

ISABELLE—He said that?

JULES—Even more eloquently.

JOSEPH—If that's conceivable. He said—and these were his very words—"She doesn't realize how shy I am. How can I tell her nothing in this world matters as much to me as her love— Ambition? Wealth? Poof!"

Isabelle is amazed and can't wait to find Paul. "I think he's with your mother," says Jules.

Alfred doesn't approve of the "memorial service they gave that stinker" and is concerned over Isabelle's future. Joseph consoles him: "She's young. Someone'll come along. Someone always does." He adds: "The bell will ring—and there he'll be." It rings, but it is Felix who enters.

FELIX (cheerfully)—Things work out somehow— (Stops.) What am I saying? (Guiltily.) I've got to see my wife. (Exits.)

ALFRED—Well—back to the roof!

JULES—I guess so.

JOSEPH—It's too much to ask destiny to send along the young man we're waiting for at this precise moment. Still, it would have been neater somehow.

Neatly, the bell rings. A very handsome young naval lieutenant bearing a letter of introduction to the Ducotels is received with open arms by the convicts. When they find out he's unmarried, their joy overflows. Even Alfred approves of him. They seat him and insist that he wait.

The lieutenant sees Isabelle on her way to Paul in the garden, and finds her charming. Joseph smilingly tells her: "It's nice to know someone's waiting for you." And though her smile is still inspired by Paul, the lieutenant appreciates it. The convicts march up to the roof, confident that they are no longer needed.

PLAYS PRODUCED IN NEW YORK

June 1, 1952—May 31, 1953

(Plays marked "continued" were still running on June 1, 1953)

WISH YOU WERE HERE

(390 performances)
(Continued)

Musical comedy in two acts by Arthur Kober and Joshua Logan, based on Mr. Kober's play *Having Wonderful Time;* music and lyrics by Harold Rome. Produced by Leland Hayward and Joshua Logan at the Imperial Theatre, June 25, 1952.

Cast of characters—

Teddy Stern	Patricia Marand
Chick Miller	Jack Cassidy
Fay Fromkin	Sheila Bond
Itchy Flexner	Sidney Armus
Pinky Harris	Paul Valentine
Harry "Muscles" Green	John Perkins
Lou Kandel	Sammy Smith
Herman Fabricant	Harry Clark
Marvin	Fred Sadoff
Sonja	Elaine Gordon
Schmutz	Larry Blyden
Eli	Frank Aletter
Barney	Ray Hyson
Sid	Robert Dixon
Lenny	Richard France
Sam	Joe Milan
Monty	Tom Ayre
Henrietta	Mardi Bayne
Gussie	Leila Martin
Irma	Roslynd Lowe
Shirley	Sybil Lamb
Lena	Denise Griffin
Judy	Shirley Ann Prior
Miriam	Nancy Franklin
The New Girl	Florence Henderson
The Girl Diver	Beverly Weston
The Acrobat	Steve Wiland
Eccentric Diver	Joseph Thomas

Waiters: Gus Giordano, Stan Grover, Bill Hogue, Leo Kayeworth, George Lenz, Reid Shelton, Harry Snow, Ray Steele, Tom Tryon, Don Wayne.

Bathing Beauties: Sue Brin, Norma Doggett, Joan Johnston, Phyllis Newman, Gloria Van Deweel, Jan Stuart, Rain Winslow.

Athletes, Guests, Staff Members: Nancy Baker, Joan Berke, Toni Parker, Candi Parsons, Inga Rode, Elliot Feder, Al Lawrence, Don Paterson, Wally Strauss.

Jack Cassidy, Sheila Bond and Paul Valentine in "Wish You Were Here"

The action takes place in Camp Karefree, a Summer camp for adults, "where friendships are formed to last a whole lifetime through," in the heart of Vacationland. The time is the present.

Staged and choreographed by Joshua Logan; settings and lighting by Jo Mielziner; costumes by Robert Mackintosh; musical direction by Jay Blackton; orchestrations by Don Walker; musical continuity by Trude Rittman.

Principal musical numbers—

ACT I

"Camp Karefree" .... Kandel, Waiters, and Ensemble
"Goodbye Love" .... Teddy, Fay, and Girls
"Social Director" .... Itchy and Ensemble
"Shopping Around" .... Fay
"Bright College Days" .... Waiters
"Mix and Mingle" .... Chick and Waiters
"Could Be" .... Girls, Teddy
"Tripping the Light Fantastic" .... Ensemble
"Where Did the Night Go?" .... Chick and Teddy, Ensemble
"Certain Individuals" .... Fay and Ensemble
"They Won't Know Me" .... Chick
"Summer Afternoon" .... Pinky and Ensemble

ACT II

"Don Jose" .... Ichy and Ensemble
"Everybody Love Everybody" .... Fay and Ensemble
"Wish You Were Here" .... Chick and Waiters
"Relax" .... Pinky and Teddy
"Flattery" .... Teddy, Fay, and Itchy
Finale .... Entire Company

SEAGULLS OVER SORRENTO

(12 performances)

Comedy in three acts by Hugh Hastings.   Produced by Charles
Bowden and Philip Langner, in association with Peter Cookson, at
the John Golden Theatre, September 11, 1952.

Cast of characters—

Able Seaman Badger	J. Pat O'Malley
Able Seaman Sims ("Sprog")	Mark Rydell
Able Seaman McIntosh ("Haggis")	Bruce Hall
Able Seaman Turner ("Lofty")	John Randolph
Petty Officer Herbert	Leslie Nielsen
Lt. Comdr. Redmond, D.S.O., D.S.C., R.N.	Guy Spaull
Sub.-Lt. Granger, R.N.	Bill Daniels
Able Seaman Hudson ("Radar")	Walter Brooke
Telegraphist ("Sparks")	Rod Steiger

The action takes place on the mess desk of a disused naval fortress
now converted into a naval experimental base on an island in Scapa
Flow not far from the coast of Scotland. The time is the present.
Act. I.—Scene 1—Early Summer, about 11 A.M.   Scene 2—A week
later, 7:45 A.M.   Act II.—Scene 1—A few hours later.   Scene 2—
A week later, 7:30 A.M.   Act III.—Scene 1—The same evening,
about 8:50 P.M.   Scene 2—The same evening, about midnight.   Scene
3—The following morning, just before 9 A.M.

Staged by Hugh Hastings and Charles Bowden; scenery and lighting by Melvin Bourne; costumes by Mildred Trebor.

A comedy treating—usually at the level of a boy's book—of British navy life. Heroism, hard knocks, humor—with the Enemy, in
this case, a petty officer who tyrannizes over the crew.

(Closed September 20, 1952)

MR. PICKWICK

(61 performances)

Comedy in two acts by Stanley Young, adapted from incidents
in Charles Dickens' *The Pickwick Papers*. Produced by The Playwrights' Company at the Plymouth Theatre, September 17, 1952.

Cast of characters—

Mr. Pickwick	George Howe
Mr. Tupman	Earl Montgomery
Mr. Snodgrass	Anthony Kemble Cooper
Mr. Winkle	Derek Tansley
Mrs. Bardell	Norah Howard
Mrs. Cluppins	Lucie Lancaster
Sam Weller	Clive Revill
Tommy	Richard Case
Mr. Buzfuz	Jacques Aubuchon
Mrs. Weller	Philippa Bevans
Mr. Weller	Louis Hector
Mr. Stiggins	Basil Howes
Mr. Jingle	Nigel Green
Mary	Sarah Marshall

```
Mrs. Leo Hunter ..............................Estelle Winwood
Joe ...................................................C. K. Alexander
Mr. Wardle ........................................Neil Fitzgerald
Miss Emily Wardle ...............................Jane Cooke
Miss Isabella Wardle ..........................Dolores Pigott
Miss Rachel Wardle ...........................Nydia Westman
Mr. Perker .......................................Kurt Richards
Wilberforce .....................................Wallace Acton
Justice ........................................William Podmore
Twinkey ...........................................C. K. Alexander
```

Act I.—Scene 1—Mr. Pickwick's lodgings in Mrs. Bardell's house. Scene 2—The Inn at Chatham. Scene 3—The Garden Party at Mrs. Leo Hunter's. Act. II.—Scene 1—The Inn at Chatham. Scene 2—A courtroom in London. Scene 3—Mr. Pickwick's quarters in Fleet Prison.

Staged by John Burrell; production designed by Kathleen Ankers.

A drastically shortened and slightly sweetened *Pickwick Papers* which, if less inspired than Dickens' book, is also less tedious. Most of the famous incidents and characters are retained, though Mr. Pickwick, rather than Sam Weller, emerges the hero.

(Closed November 8, 1952)

AN EVENING WITH BEATRICE LILLIE

(276 performances)

Series of sketches. Produced by Edward Duryea Dowling at the Booth Theatre, October 2, 1952.

The principals—

Beatrice Lillie	Reginald Gardiner
Eadie and Rack	Xenia Bank
Florence Bray	John Philip

Staged by Edward Duryea Dowling; settings by Rolf Gerard; technical supervisor, Paul C. McGuire.

Sketches and musical numbers—

ACT I

Reginald Gardiner

A STAR'S FIRST NIGHT

```
The Star ...........................................Xenia Bank
The Maid ........................................Florence Bray
The Star's Friend ..............................Beatrice Lillie
```

ONE IN THREE
Reginald Gardiner

WIND
Beatrice Lillie

TRAINS
Reginald Gardiner

FATHER AND SON

```
The Father ...................................Reginald Gardiner
The Son .........................................Beatrice Lillie
```

ANESTHESIA
Reginald Gardiner

Sybil .... Beatrice Lillie
Mrs. Mason .... Florence Bray
Mrs. Barrowdale .... Xenia Bank

THE CONDUCTOR
Reginald Gardiner

ACT II

Eadie and Rack at the pianos
Reginald Gardiner
Beatrice Lillie
Accompanied by Rack
Singer, John Philip
Finale

(Closed May 30, 1953)

THE SACRED FLAME

(24 performances)

Play in three acts by W. Somerset Maugham. Revived by Anthony Parella at the President Theatre, October 6, 1952.

Cast of characters—

Maurice Tabret .... Charles H. McCawley
Dr. Harvester .... John D. Seymour
Mrs. Tabret .... Frances Starr
Nurse Wayland .... Nancy Coleman
Alice .... Joanna Vischer
Major Liconda .... Noel Leslie
Stella Tabret .... Patricia Wheel
Colin Tabret .... Mark Roberts
    The action takes place in the drawing room of Mrs. Tabret's home.
The time is the present. Act I.—An Indian Summer night. Act
II.—Noon of the following day. Act III.—A half-hour later.
    Staged by John Reich; setting and lighting by Leo Kerz.

(Closed October 25, 1952)

IN ANY LANGUAGE

(45 performances)

Comedy in three acts by Edmund Beloin and Henry Garson
(from a story by Henry Garson). Produced by Jule Styne and
George Abbott at the Cort Theatre, October 7, 1952.

Cast of characters—

Valerie McGuire .... Eileen Heckart
Porter .... Fred Porcelli
Second Porter .... Giorgio Spelvino
Signore Rossi .... Dino Terranova
Charlie Hill .... Walter Matthau
Hannah King .... Uta Hagen

```
A Little Waiter ......................................Joe Verdi
Beansy Oliver .......................................Louis Hawkins
Marchesa Del Veccio Sporenza ......................Nita Naldi
Della Fontana ......................................Gloria Marlowe
Aldo Carmenelli ...................................Joe De Santis
A Turkish Gentleman ...........................Maurice Gosfield
Mama Carmenelli ............................Rossana San Marco
Lorenzo .........................................Robert Ottaviano
Grandi ..............................................Lee Papell
Fawzieh ..........................................Francine Bond
Waiter ...........................................Fred Porcelli
Little Girl ......................................Karin Flanagan
Boy ................................................Jove Paone
Signore Mazzi ...................................Alfred Bascetta
Signore Zucco ....................................Philip Barbera
```
   The action takes place in Hannah King's hotel suite in Rome. Act
I.—Late afternoon. Act II.—A week later, about 10 P.M. Scene 2
—Early the next morning. Act III.—Early evening, two days later.
   Staged by George Abbott; scenery and costumes by Raoul Pene du
Bois.

Poorish comedy about a skidding Hollywood star who goes to
Rome to stage a comeback in Italian art films. Alternating saint-
like poses with fishwife outbursts, she gets a Rosselini-like director
to star her in his new film, but proves a flop.

(Closed November 15, 1952)

THE GAMBLER

(24 performances)

Play in two acts by Ugo Betti, adapted by Alfred Drake and Edward Eager. Produced by Thomas Hammond and Wayne Harriss
at the Lyceum Theatre, October 13, 1952.

Cast of characters—

```
David Petri ......................................Alfred Drake
A Station Master ...............................Percy Waram
Ernest Bruni ....................................E. G. Marshall
Commissioner Costa .............................Philip Coolidge
Alma Greich .......................................Anne Burr
Paula Mori ....................................Constance Clausen
Eva Greich Petri .............................Margaret Draper
```
   The action takes place in a town in Italy which had been part of the
No-Man's-Land between Allied-occupied Italy and German-occupied
Italy. The time: After the last World War. Act I.—Scene 1—A
railroad platform. Scene 2—David's room at the hotel. Scene 3—
Costa's room. Scene 4—David's room. Scene 5—Costa's room. Act
II.—Scene 1—David's room. Scene 2—A field. Scene 3—Costa's
room. Scene 4—A railroad platform.
   Staged by Herman Shumlin; settings and lighting by Jo Mielziner;
costumes by Robert Mackintosh; incidental music by David Broek-
man.

A serious, but heavy and lifeless blend of rhetoric and philoso-
phizing. In postwar Italy, an inquiry is conducted concerning the
death of the hero's wife. The hero is accused of her murder: actually—from wishing her dead—he had made it possible for soldiers

to kill her. The wife reappears in spectral form and there are colloquies concerning guilt and marriage, love and hate, good and evil.

(Closed November 1, 1952)

BUTTRIO SQUARE

(7 performances)

Musical play in two acts, based on a play by Hal Cranton from an original story by Gen Genovese; book by Billy Gilbert and Gen Genovese; music by Arthur Jones and Fred Stamer; lyrics by Gen Genovese. Produced by Gen Genovese and Edward Woods at the New Century Theatre, October 14, 1952.

Cast of characters—

Michelino	David Kurlan
Padre	Vincent Barbi
Angela	Rina Falcone
Maria	Joan Morton
Elizabetta	Ann Needham
Dominic	Lionel Ames
Baron D'Alessandro	Ernest Sarracino
Rocco	Ferdinand Hilt
Vittorio	James MacCracken
Cassio	Orville Sherman
Pietro	Ted Thurston
Emelia	Jane Harven
Francesca	Marie Gibson
Pappa Mario	Billy Gilbert
Norina	Charlotte Jones
Carlo	Henry Hamilton
Sergeant McKenzie	Walter Black
Captain Steve Dickson	Lawrence Brooks
Private Poole	James Tarbutton
Tabulator	Leon Daniels
Marisa D'Alessandro	Lois Hunt
Private Burns	Joe Mantell
Corporal Gower	Al Checco
Private Whitfield	George Reeder

The action takes place in a small village in Northeast Italy.
Staged and choreographed by Eugene Loring; settings and lighting by Samuel Leve; costumes supervised by Sal Anthony; choral arrangements and direction by Maurice Levine; dance music composed and arranged by Roger Adams; orchestrations by Don Walker; musical director, Mr. Levine.

A moth-eaten musical about GIs who are forbidden to mix with the girls in an occupied postwar Italian village. There is a good deal of tedious dither by way of a book, some commonplace music, and a large chorus committing much merry-month-of-Mayhem.

(Closed October 18, 1952)

THE TIME OF THE CUCKOO

(263 performances)

Comedy in two acts by Arthur Laurents. Produced by Robert Whitehead and Walter Fried at the Empire Theatre, October 15, 1952.

Cast of characters—

Signora Fioria .... Lydia St. Clair
Eddie Yaeger .... Donald Murphy
June Yaeger .... Geraldine Brooks
Giovanna .... Silva Gaselli
Leona Samish .... Shirley Booth
Mrs. McIlhenny .... Jane Rose
Mr. McIlhenny .... Daniel Reed
Mauro .... Jose Perez
Renato di Rossi .... Dino DiLuca
Vito .... Ruggero Romor

    The action takes place in the garden of the Pensione Fioria, Venice, in the summertime.

    Staged by Harold Clurman; setting and lighting by Ben Edwards; costumes by Helene Pons.

See page 54.

(Closed May 30, 1953)

BERNADINE

(157 performances)

Comedy in two acts by Mary Chase. Produced by Irving L. Jacobs at The Playhouse, October 16, 1952.

Cast of characters—

Arthur Beaumont (Beau .... John Kerr
Leonard Carney (Carney) .... Girard Gillen
Will McElroy (Mac) .... Andy Sanders
Morgan Olson (Dink) .... Billy James
Dave Gibbs (Gibbs) .... Warren Berlinger
Ruth Weldy .... Alney Alba
Selma Cantrick .... Jane Van Duser
Jean Cantrick (Cantrick) .... Camilla De Witt
Buford Weldy (Wormy) .... Johnny Stewart
Marvin Griner (Tub) .... Fred Baker
George Friedelhauser (Fudge) .... Frank Valenza
Helen, a Waitress .... Peggy Cass
Vernon Kinswood (Kinswood) .... Michael Wager
Enid Lacey .... Beverly Lawrence
Last Straw .... Harmon Van Doren
Bellboy .... Richard Camp
A. J. Witnick, Hotel Manager .... Bobby Vail
A Woman .... Katherine Barrett
Ogden Kratke .... Paul Genge

    The action takes place in a city in the Far West between the hours of 2:30 P.M. and 12:30 A.M. Act I.—Scene 1—A street. Scene 2—The back room of the Shamrock, a 3.2 beer parlor. Scene 3—Mrs. Weldy's home. Scene 4—The back room of the Shamrock. Scene 5—Mrs. Weldy's home. Scene 6—The lobby of the Barclay Hotel.

Danny Kaye

Act II.—Scene 1—Enid Lacey's apartment.   Scene 2—A street.
Scene 3—Mrs. Weldy's home.   Scene 4—The back room of the Shamrock.
Staged by Guthrie McClintic; settings and lighting by John Robert
Lloyd; costumes by Noel Taylor.

See page 75.

(Closed February 28, 1953)

THE MILLIONAIRESS

(83 performances)

Comedy in two acts by George Bernard Shaw. Produced by the Theatre Guild, in association with H. M. Tennent, Ltd., at the Shubert Theatre, October 17, 1952.

Cast of characters—

```
Julius Sagamore ...............................Campbell Cotts
The Lady .....................................Katharine Hepburn
Alastair Fitzfassenden ...........................Peter Dyneley
Patricia Smith ..................................Genine Graham
Adrian Blenderbland ...........................Cyril Ritchard
The Doctor ..................................Robert Helpmann
The Man ..................................Bertram Shuttleworth
The Woman ...................................Nora Nicholson
The Manager ...................................Vernon Greeves
```

Act I.—Scene 1—Mr. Julius Sagamore's office in Lincolns Inn Fields, London. A Spring morning. Scene 2—"The Pig and Whistle," a riverside inn. That evening. Act II.—Scene 1—A basement in the Commercial Road. The following morning. Scene 2—"The Pig and Whistle." Five months later.

Staged by Michael Benthall; settings by James Bailey.

Written in 1935, when Shaw was 79, the play tells of the richest woman in England, an aggressive, bullying creature who symbolizes entrenched wealth. Challenged to live on a pittance, she goes to the slums and emerges from them richer than ever. The implication seems to be that unless the rich keep getting richer, they must in time turn poor; that the loss of a farthing is the first step to the loss of a fortune.

(Closed December 28, 1952)

S. M. CHARTOCK'S GILBERT AND SULLIVAN COMPANY

A repertory of four Gilbert and Sullivan operettas was presented by S. M. Chartock's Gilbert and Sullivan Company at the Mark Hellinger Theatre, starting October 20, 1952.

THE MIKADO

(October 20-25, 1952)

Cast of characters—

```
Nanki-Poo ...................................Robert Rounseville
Go-To ...........................................Radley Flynn
Pish-Tush ........................................Frank Rogier
Pooh-Bah ........................................Robert Eckles
Ko-Ko ...........................................Martyn Green
```

Yum-Yum ....Lillian Murphy
Pitti-Sing ....Mary Roche
Peep-Bo ....Dorothy MacNeil
Katisha ....Ella Halman
The Mikado of Japan ....Joseph Macaulay

(8 performances)

THE PIRATES OF PENZANCE

(October 27-November 1, 1952)

Cast of characters—

Samuel ....Frank Rogier
Frederick ....Robert Rounseville
Ruth ....Ella Halman
Richard ....Joseph Macaulay
Kate ....Mary Roche
Edith ....Lillian Murphy
Isabel ....Shirley Pringle
Mabel ....Dorothy MacNeil
Major-General Stanley ....Martyn Green
Edward ....Robert Eckles

(8 performances)

TRIAL BY JURY

(November 3-8, 1952)

Cast of characters—

Foreman of the Jury ....Robert Eckles
Associate ....Roger Franklin
Usher ....Radley Flynn
Defendant ....Earl William
The Learned Judge ....Martyn Green
Counsel for the Plaintiff ....Frank Rogier
The Plaintiff ....Audrey Dearden

Followed by—

H.M.S. PINAFORE

Cast of characters—

Tommy Tucker ....Bonnie Grevatt
Bill Bobstay ....Robert Eckles
Bob Beckett ....Radley Flynn
Little Buttercup ....Ella Halman
Dick Deadeye ....Joseph Macaulay
Ralph Rackstraw ....Robert Rounseville
Captain Corcoran ....Frank Rogier
Josephine ....Lillian Murphy
Sir Joseph Porter ....Martyn Green
Hebe ....Mary Roche

(8 performances)

IOLANTHE

(November 10-15, 1952)

Cast of characters—

Leila .... Mary Roche
Celia .... Audrey Dearden
Fleta .... Eileen Moran
The Fairy Queen .... Ella Halman
Iolanthe .... Glynn Hill
Strephon .... Frank Rogier
Phyllis .... Lillian Murphy
Lord Chancellor .... Martyn Green
Earl of Tolloler .... Earl William
Earl of Mount Ararat .... Joseph Macaulay
Private Willis .... Robert Eckles

(8 performances)

Staged by S. M. Chartock; musical director, Lehman Engel; settings by Ralph Alswang; costumes by Peggy Morrison; assistant conductor, Eugene Kusmiak.

(Closed November 15, 1952)

MY DARLIN' AIDA

(89 performances)

Musical play in two acts by Charles Friedman, based on Verdi's *Aïda;* music by Giuseppe Verdi. Produced by Robert L. Joseph at the Winter Garden, October 27, 1952.

Cast of characters—

Rumford .... William Wilderman
Mayor Brad Sourby .... Stanley Carlson
Aida........ Elaine Malbin (evenings), Eileen Schauler (matinées)
Raymond Demarest............... William Olvis or Howard Jarratt
Jason .... Alonzo Bosan
Morning Star .... Ida Johnson
Zeporah .... Lavinia Williams
Lolly .... Olive Moorefield
Wheat .... George Fisher
Frog .... John Fleming
Liz .... Fredye Marshall
Rebecca .... Billie Allen
Lucy .... Joyce Sellinger
Yancey Hoyt .... William Sutherland
Jessica Farrow .. Dorothy Sarnoff (evenings), Bette Dubro (matinées)
General Farrow .... Kenneth Schon
Choir Soloist .... Theresa Green
Sis .... Ruth Anne Fleming
Dolly .... Ruth McVayne
Bonnie .... Sue Dorris
Maggie .... Muriel Birckhead
Aggie .... Martha Flynn
Laurie .... Lola Fisher
Mary .... Ruth Schumacher
Nellie .... Mary Ann Tomlinson
Bettie .... Jane Copeland
Onnie .... Carol Jones
Maids........... Billie Allen, Jacqueline Hairston, Lavinia Williams

Magician ....Gordon Hamilton
Mrs. Sourby ....Jo Anne Taylor
Howie ....Walter Kelvin
Bull ....Edward Wellman
Steve ....Robert Busch
Hutch ....Thornton Marker
Adam Brown ....William Dillard
Flower ....Jacqueline Hairston
Susie .... Gloria Davy
Lilly ....Charlotte Holloman
Pork ....Ned Wright
Major Stanhope ....William Sutherland

Singers: Muriel Birckhead, Dorothy Candee, Jane Copeland, Gloria Davy, Sue Dorris, Lola Fisher, Ruth Anne Fleming, Martha Flynn, Theresa Green, Charlotte Holloman, Ida Johnson, Carol Jones, Fredye Marshall, Ruth McVayne, Joyce Sellinger, Ruth Schumacher, Jo Anne Taylor, Mary Ann Tomlinson, Robert Baird, Gino Baldi, Robert Busch, Benjamin Cassidy, Jack Dabdoub, Calvin Dash, George Fisher, John Fleming, Arthur Hammond, Walter Kelvin, Thornton Marker, William Noble, Michael O'Carolan, Charles O'Neill, Robert Price, Michael Roberts, William Sutherland, Edgar Thompson, Casper Vecchione, Robert Watts, Edward Wellman, Ned Wright, Robert Yeager.

Dancers: Billie Allen, Betty Buday, Nanci Darken, Bettye Griffin, Dody Goodman, Jacqueline Hairston, Erona Harris, Joan Kruger, Carmelita Lanza, Lavinia Williams, Doris Wright, Paul Gannon, Gordon Hamilton, Eddie Heim, Ed Holleman, Louis Johnson, Joe Nash, Walter Nicks, Paul Olson, Frank Seabolt, Claude Thompson.

Children: Paula Anderson, Denis Bradler, Gail Culberson, Sharyn Kenney, Vincent Yearwood.

The action takes place on and about General Farrow's plantation, near Memphis, Tennessee, during the first year of the Civil War.

Staged by Charles Friedman; supervised and lighted by Hassard Short; production designed and costumed by Lemuel Ayers; choreography by Hanya Holm; music 1 director, Franz Allers; choral director, Robert Shaw; new orchestral arrangements by Hans Spialek; associate producer, Paul Vroom; production associate, Shirley Bernstein.

Principal musical numbers—

ACT I

Scene 1

Prelude and Opening
"My Darlin' Aida" ....Raymond
"Love Is Trouble" ....Jessica, Raymond
"Me and Lee" ....General Farrow, Rumford, Raymond, Aida, Jessica and Company

Scene 2

"March on for Tennessee" ....Aida

Scene 3

"Why Ain't We Free" ....Choir Leader, Women's Choir
"Knights of the White Cross"..Rumford, Raymond, and the Knights

Scene 4

Jamboree ....Jessica and the Girls
Dance ....The Maids
Letter Duet ....Aida, Jessica

Scene 5

Homecoming ....Company
"When You Grow Up" ....Women and Children
Soldiers' March ....Men
Ballet ....Dancers
"King Called Cotton" ....Company
"Gotta Live Free" ....Adam
"Master and Slave"—Sextette.......Adam, Aida, Raymond, Jessica, Rumford, General, and Company
"Sing! South! Sing!" ....Company

ACT II

Scene 1, 2

Spiritual ....The Choir
"I Want to Pray" ....Jessica
"Alone" ....Aida
"Three Stones to Stand On" ....Aida, Adam
"You're False" ....Aida, Adam
"There'll Have to Be Changes Made" ....Aida, Raymond
"Away" ....Aida, Raymond
"Land of Mine" ....Aida, Raymond, Adam

Scene 3

Ballet ....Dancers and Singers

Scene 4

"I Don't Want You" ....Jessica, Raymond

Scene 5

The Trial ....Jessica, Rumford, and the Knights
"You Are My Darlin' Bride" ....Raymond
"Oh, Sky, Goodbye" ....Aida

(Closed January 11, 1953)

DIAL 'M' FOR MURDER

(246 performances)
(Continued)

Play in three acts by Frederick Knott. Produced by James P. Sherwood at the Plymouth Theatre, October 29, 1952.

Cast of characters—

Margot Wendice ....Gusti Huber
Max Halliday...................................Richard Derr
Tony Wendice ....Maurice Evans
Captain Lesgate ....Anthony Dawson
Inspector Hubbard ....John Williams
Thompson ....Porter Van Zandt
    The action takes place in the living room of the Wendices' apartment in London. Act I.—Scene 1—A Friday evening in September. Scene 2—An hour later. Act II.—Scene 1—Saturday evening. Scene 2—Later that night. Scene 3—Sunday morning. Act III.—A few months later, early afternoon.
    Staged by Reginald Denham; setting and lighting by Peter Larkin; costumes by Noel Taylor.

See page 90.

THE DEEP BLUE SEA

(132 performances)

Play in three acts by Terence Rattigan. Produced by Alfred de Liagre, Jr., and John C. Wilson at the Morosco Theatre, November 5, 1952.

Cast of characters—

Hester Collyer ....Margaret Sullavan
Mrs. Elton ....Betty Sinclair

```
Philip Welch ....................................John Merivale
Ann Welch .......................................Stella Andrew
Mr. Miller ......................................Herbert Berghof
William Collyer .................................Alan Webb
Frederick Page ..................................James Hanley
Jackie Jackson ..................................Felix Deebank
```
The action takes place during the course of a day in September, in the sitting room of a furnished flat in the North-West of London. Act I.—Morning. Act II.—Afternoon. Act III.—Evening.

Staged by Frith Banbury; setting and lighting supervised by Charles Elson.

Emotional women's-matinée drama. Hester Collyer gave up husband and social position to run off with a cheap, pleasure-seeking test pilot. Knowing he has tired of her, she unsuccessfully attempts suicide. She again tries, and again fails, to hold her lover; then, unable to face his desertion or to about-face into her husband's arms, she tries suicide a second time. On this occasion a doctor not only saves her life, but restores her courage.

(Closed February 28, 1953)

LES FAUSSES CONFIDENCES

(13 performances)

Comedy in three acts by Marivaux. Produced by S. Hurok, with the co-operation of the Ministry of Foreign Affairs of the French Government, under the auspices of the Association Française d'Action Artistique, at the Ziegfeld Theatre, November 12, 1952.

Cast of characters—

```
Araminte ........................................Madeleine Renaud
Dorante .........................................Jean Desailly
M. Remi .........................................Pierre Bertin
Madame Argante ..................................Marie-Hélène Dasté
Arlequin ........................................Jean-Pierre Granval
Dubois ..........................................Jean-Louis Barrault
Marton ..........................................Simone Valère
Le Comte ........................................Régis Outin
L'Orfèvre .......................................Jean-François Calvé
Le Valet ........................................Jacques Galland
```
Staged by Jean-Louis Barrault; décor and costumes by Maurice Brianchon.

Followed by—

BAPTISTE

Pantomime by Jacques Prevert.

Cast of characters—

```
Baptiste ........................................Jean-Louis Barrault
La Statue .......................................Madeleine Renaud
Le Chanteur .....................................Jean Desailly
La Petite Fille .................................Elina Labourdette
```

Arlequin .... Serge Perrault
Le Gardien de Square .... Jean Juillard
La Lavandière .... Simone Valère
Le Bijoutier .... Jean-Pierre Granval
La Duchesse .... Madeleine Renaud
Les Laquais .... { Jacques Galland
                                                 { Pierre Sonnier
Le Marchand D'Habits .... Beauchamp
                                                 { Simone Valère
Les Invitées .... { Elina Labourdette
                                                 { Anne Carrère
                                                 { Jean-Pierre Granval
Les Invités .... { Jean-François Calvé
                                                 { Jean Juillard

Choreography by Jean-Louis Barrault; music by Kosma; décor by
Mayo; musical director, Pierre Boulez.

(Closed December 20, 1952)

THE CLIMATE OF EDEN

(20 performances)

Play in two acts by Moss Hart, based on Edgar Mittelholzer's
novel *Shadows Move Among Them*. Produced by Joseph M. Hyman
and Bernard Hart at the Martin Beck Theatre, November 13,
1952.

Cast of characters—

Olivia .... Penelope Munday
Berton .... Ken Walken
The Reverend Gerald Harmston .... John Cromwell
Mrs. Harmston .... Isobel Elsom
Mabel .... Rosemary Harris
Garvey .... Ray Stricklyn
Gregory Hawke .... Lee Montague
Logan .... Earle Hyman
Ellen .... Jane White
Howard .... Edward Hall
Robert .... Leon Moore
Mr. Buckingham .... Leslie Barrie
Mrs. Buckingham .... Winnifred Cushing
                                               { Tom Torrisi
                                               { Charles Gordon
Natives .... { Charlotte Wright
                                               { Tamara Thompson
                                               { Millie Daniels
                                               { Sheila Davis
Children .... { Charlynn Wright
                                               { Michael Jackson

The action takes place in the house and church of the Reverend
Gerald Harmston, in the jungle of British Guiana. The time is the
present.

Staged by Moss Hart; scenery by Frederick Fox; lighting by Jean
Rosenthal; costumes by Kenn Barr; incidental music by Trude Rittmann.

See page 117.

(Closed November 22, 1952)

LE PROCES

(4 performances)

Play by André Gide and Jean-Louis Barrault, based on the novel by Franz Kafka. Produced by S. Hurok, with the co-operation of the Ministry of Foreign Affairs of the French Government, under the auspices of the Association Française d'Action Artistique, at the Ziegfeld Theatre, November 17, 1952.

Cast of characters—

Joseph	Jean-Louis Barrault
Franz	Jean Juillard
Wilhelm	Jean-Claude Michel
Madame Grubach	Simone Matil
Le Brigadier	Beauchamp
Mademoiselle Burstner	Anne Carrère
Le Bourreau	Jacques Dacqmine
La Laveuse	Marie-Hélène Dasté
L'Huissier	Jean Desailly
L'Etudiant Berthold	Jean-Pierre Granval
La Jeune Fille	Elina Labourdette
Le Préposé Aux Renseignements	Jean-François Calvé
L'Homme	Jacques Galland
L'Oncle	Pierre Bertin
Leni	Madeleine Renaud
Block	Régis Outin
Le Directeur-Adjoint	Gabriel Cattand
Le Juge D'Instruction	Charles Mahieu

Staged by Jean-Louis Barrault; décor by Félix Labisse.

(Closed November 19, 1952)

ELECTRA

(6 performances)

Tragedy by Sophocles, translated into modern Greek by J. Gryparis. Produced by Guthrie McClintic and the National Theatre of Greece at the Mark Hellinger Theatre, November 19, 1952.

Cast of characters—

Paedagogus	J. Apostolides
Orestes	Thanos Cotsopoulos
Electra	Katina Paxinou
Chrysothemis	Rita Myrat
Clytaemnestra	A. Raftopoulou
Aegisthus	N. Hadziscos
Chorus Leader	H. Zafiriou
Pylades	Al. Deliyannis

Chorus of Women: A. Bellou, A. Capellari, C. Capitsinea, V. Cassavou, I. Cofino, P. Condou, V. Deliyanni, M. Georgala, A. Gregorea, Th. Joannidou, R. Michalopoulou, C. Myrat, J. Vassalou, E. Voziakiadou.

Staged by Dimitry Rondiris; scenery by C. Clonis; music by Dimitri Mitropoulis; costumes designed by Antonios Phocas; orchestra under the direction of George Lykoudis; choreography by Loukia Sakellariou.

(Closed November 23, 1952)

AMPHITRYON

(12 performances)

Comedy by Molière. Produced by S. Hurok, with the co-operation of the Ministry of Foreign Affairs of the French Government, under the auspices of the Association Française d'Action Artistique, at the Ziegfeld Theatre, November 20, 1952.

Cast of characters—

Mercure	Jean-Louis Barrault
Le Char de la Nuit	Pierre Sonnier, Serge Perrault
La Nuit	Elina Labourdette
Sosie	Jean-Pierre Granval
Jupiter	Jean Desailly
Alcmène	Madeleine Renaud
Cleanthis	Anne Carrère
Amphitryon	Jacques Dacqmine
Naucrates	Régis Outin
Posicles	Jean-Claude Michel
Argatiphontidas	Jean-François Calvé

Staged by Jean-Louis Barrault; music by Francis Poulenc; décor and costumes by Christian Berard.

Followed by—

LES FOURBERIES DE SCAPIN

Comedy by Molière.

Cast of characters—

Octave	Gabriel Cattand
Sylvestre	Jean Juillard
Nerine	Marie-Hélène Dasté
Scapin	Jean-Louis Barrault
Hyacinthe	Anne Carrère
Argante	Charles Mahieu
Geronte	Pierre Bertin
Leandre	Jean-François Calvé
Carle	Régis Outin
Zerbinette	Simone Valère

Staged by Louis Jouvet; music by Henri Sauguet; décor and costumes by Christian Berard.

(Closed December 13, 1952)

THE SEVEN YEAR ITCH

(221 performances)
(Continued)

Comedy in three acts by George Axelrod. Produced by Courtney Burr and Elliott Nugent at the Fulton Theatre, November 20, 1952.

Cast of characters—

Richard Sherman	Tom Ewell
Helen Sherman	Neva Patterson
Ricky	Johnny Klein

Miss Morris .... Marilyn Clark
Elaine .... Joan Donovan
Marie What-Ever-Her-Name-Was .... Irene Moore
The Girl .... Vanessa Brown
Dr. Brubaker .... Robert Emhardt
Tom Mackenzie .... George Keane
The Voice of Richard's Conscience .... George Ives
The Voice of the Girl's Conscience .... Pat Fowler
    The action takes place in the apartment of the Richard Shermans,
in the Gramercy Park section of New York City. The time is the
present. Act I.—About eight o'clock on a Summer evening. Act
II.—Scene 1—Evening, the next day. Scene 2—Two hours later.
Act III.—The following morning.
    Staged by John Gerstad; designed and lighted by Frederick Fox;
production supervised by Elliott Nugent; incidental music composed
and arranged by Dana Suesse.

A big, knowing popular success concerning a 39-year-old and
seven-years-married Summer bachelor who has reached the age
when the eye starts to wander and the ego to worry. He gets pleasantly enmeshed with an attractive young girl, but enmeshed even
more with gaudy flights from reality and a galloping conscience.

OCCUPE-TOI D'AMELIE

(4 performances)

Comedy in three acts by Georges Feydeau. Produced by S.
Hurok, with the co-operation of the Ministry of Foreign Affairs of
the French Government, under the auspices of the Association Française d'Action Artistique, at the Ziegfeld Theatre, November 24,
1952.

Cast of characters—

Amélie .... Madeleine Renaud
Yvonne .... Anne Carrère
Palmyre .... Simone Matil
Bibichon .... Jacques Galland
Valcreuse .... Jean-François Calvé
Boas .... Jean-Claude Michel
Adonis .... Jean-Pierre Granval
Pochet .... Beauchamp
Etienne .... Gabriel Cattand
Irène .... Elina Labourdette
Marcel Courbois .... Jean Desailly
Van Putzeboum .... Charles Mahieu
Koschnadieff .... Jean Juillard
Le Prince .... Jacques Dacqmine
Charlotte .... Simone Valère
Mouilletu .... Jean-Louis Barrault
Le Maire .... Régis Outin
Virginie .... Anne Geffe
Cornette .... Pierre Sonnier
    Act I.—Amélie's salon. Act II.—A bedroom in the home of Marcel
Courbois. Act III.—Scene 1—The Town Hall. Scene 2—Amélie's
bedroom. The time: 1900.
    Staged by Jean-Louis Barrault; music by Arthur Honegger; décor
by Félix Labisse; costumes by Jean-Denis Malclés.

(Closed November 26, 1952)

OEDIPUS TYRANNUS

(10 performances)

Tragedy by Sophocles, translated into modern Greek by Photos Politis. Produced by Guthrie McClintic and the National Theatre of Greece at the Mark Hellinger Theatre, November 24, 1952.

Cast of characters—

Oedipus	Alexis Minotis
Priest	Basil Kanakis
Creon	N. Hadziscos
Teiresias	J. Apostolides
Jocasta	Katina Paxinou
Shepherd	P. Zervos
Attendant	Nicos Paraskevas
Messenger	St. Vocovitch
Chorus Leader	Thanos Cotsopoulos

Chorus of Theban Elders: Al. Deliyannis, D. Dimopoulos, N. Papaconstantinou, D. Veakis, Th. Andriacopoulos, B. Andreopoulos, N. Betinis, St. Bogiotopoulos, E. Catsileros, Sp. Lascarides, J. Mavroyenis, G. Moutsios, C. Naos, St. Papadachis.

Staged by Alexis Minotis; music by Katina Paxinou; scenery by C. Clonis; costumes by Antonios Phocas; choreography by Agapi Evangelidou.

(Closed December 7, 1952)

TIME OUT FOR GINGER

(215 performances)
(Continued)

Comedy in three acts by Ronald Alexander. Produced by Shepard Traube and Gordon Pollock, in association with Don Hershey, at the Lyceum Theatre, November 26, 1952.

Cast of characters—

Lizzie	Laura Pierpont
Agnes Carol	Polly Rowles
Howard Carol	Melvyn Douglas
Joan	Mary Hartig
Jeannie	Lois Smith
Ginger	Nancy Malone
Eddie Davis	Conrad Janis
Tommy	Larry Robinson
Mr. Wilson	Roland Wood
Ed Hoffman	Philip Loeb

The action takes place in the living room of the home of Mr. and Mrs. Howard Carol. Act I.—Early Fall, 4:30 one afternoon. Act II.—Scene 1—Four weeks later. Scene 2—A Saturday afternoon, four weeks later. Act III.—The same evening.

Staged by Shepard Traube; scenery and lighting by Eldon Elder.

A very uneven but often amusing farce about family life. It chiefly concerns a teen-age tomboy who tries out for the high-school football team and a father who, when opposition arises, stubbornly backs her up. After much commotion, first at home, and then all over town, Ginger reverts to femininity and conditions to normal.

LA REPETITION OU L'AMOUR PUNI

(4 performances)

Comedy by Jean Anouilh. Produced by S. Hurok, with the co-operation of the Ministry of Foreign Affairs of the French Government, under the auspices of the Association Française d'Action Artistique, at the Ziegfeld Theatre, November 27, 1952.

Cast of characters—

```
La Comtesse ...............................Madeleine Renaud
Monsieur Damiens ............................Pierre Bertin
Le Comte ...............................Jean-Louis Barrault
Hortensia ...................................Elina Labourdette
Hero .........................................Jacques Dacqmine
Villebosse ...............................Jean-François Calvé
Lucile ........................................Simone Valère
```
    Staged by Jean-Louis Barrault; décor and costumes by Jean-Denis Malclès.

(Closed November 29, 1952)

HAMLET

(8 performances)

Play by William Shakespeare, translated into French by André Gide. Produced by S. Hurok, with the co-operation of the Ministry of Foreign Affairs of the French Government, under the auspices of the Association Française d'Action Artistique, at the Ziegfeld Theatre, December 1, 1952.

Cast of characters—

```
Claudius ....................................Jacques Dacqmine
Hamlet ...................................Jean-Louis Barrault
Polonius .......................................Pierre Bertin
Horatio .........................................Jean Desailly
Laertes ....................................Jean-Claude Michel
Rosencrantz ...............................Jean-François Calvé
Guildenstern ...................................Gabriel Cattand
Osric ......................................Jean-Pierre Granval
A Priest ........................................Régis Outin
Francisco .......................................Jacques Galland
Bernardo ........................................Serge Perrault
Marcellus ........................................Régis Outin
Reynaldo ........................................Jacques Galland
Player King .........................................Beauchamp
Lucianus ..........................................Serge Perrault
First Gravedigger ..............................Charles Mahieu
Second Gravedigger ...............................Pierre Sonner
Fortinbras ................................Jean-François Calvé
Gertrude ....................................Marie-Hélène Dasté
Ophelia .........................................Simone Valère
```

Player Queen ....Anne Carrère
Ghost of Hamlet's Father ....Jean Juillard
    Staged by Jean-Louis Barrault; décor and costumes by André
Masson.

(Closed December 6, 1952)

I'VE GOT SIXPENCE

(23 performances)

A play in two acts by John van Druten. Produced by Gertrude
Macy and Walter Starcke at the Ethel Barrymore Theatre, December 2, 1952.

Cast of characters—

Inez Cabral ....Viveca Lindfors
Doreen ....Vicki Cummings
Dr. Ozmunian ....Paul Lipson
Peter Tyndall ....Edmond O'Brien
Mrs. Entwhistle ....Patricia Collinge
Carolyn ....Lois Holmes
Robert Gallagher ....Bert Thorn
    The action takes place in New York over a period of six months.
    Staged by John van Druten; production designed by Boris Aronson;
costumes supervised by Burton J. Miller.

A well-meant but exceedingly inept play preaching man's need
for some kind of faith. It tells of two varieties of modern girl, a
worldly minded one who marries a conventionally pious man for
security and comfort; and an independent-minded one who has an
unhappy love affair with an unhappy writer. On the brink of suicide, she responds to some call from life, and is reunited with a lover
who by now is on the brink of despair.

(Closed December 20, 1952)

SEE THE JAGUAR

(5 performances)

Play in three acts by N. Richard Nash. Produced by Lemuel
Ayers, in association with Helen Jacobson, at the Cort Theatre, December 3, 1952.

Cast of characters—

Hilltop ....Phillip Pine
Yetter ....David Clarke
Janna ....Constance Ford
Gramfa Ricks ....Roy Fant
Mrs. Wilkins ....Margaret Barker
Dave Ricks ....Arthur Kennedy
Brad ....Cameron Prud'homme
Harvey ....George Tyne
Frank ....Arthur Batanides
Meeker ....Ted Jacques

Mrs. Meeker ....Florence Sundstrom
Wally Wilkins ....James Dean
Jee Jee ....Dane Knell
Sam ....Harrison Dowd
Andy ....Harry Bergman
Carson ....Tony Kraber
    Act I.—Brad's store, morning. A day in early Spring. Act II.—
Scene 1—A plateau on Burden Hill, early afternoon. Scene 2—A
clearing on Burden Hill, mid-afternoon. Scene 3—Another clearing
on Burden Hill, later afternoon. Act III.—Scene 1—Brad's store,
dusk. Scene 2—The same, night.
    Staged by Michael Gordon; scenery and costumes designed by Lem-
uel Ayers; incidental music by Alec Wilder.

A portentously symbolic Western in which every little movement
has three meanings of its own. The story—which includes a man-
hunt—concerns a crusading young schoolmaster's struggle against
the local villain who owns the land, bosses the people, coops up the
animals.

(Closed December 6, 1952)

WHISTLER'S GRANDMOTHER

(24 performances)

Comedy in three acts by Robert Finch. Produced by Anthony
Parella at the President Theatre, December 11, 1952.

Cast of characters—

Eddie ....Lonny Chapman
Nick ....Dick Bernie
Lute ....Alan Carney
Sam ....Lou Gilbert
Honest John ....William Nealy
Joy ....Peggy Nelson
Kate (Grandma) ....Josephine Hull
Mr. Carruthers ....William Podmore
    Act I.—An evening in October. A saloon in New York City. Act
II.—Two days later. Eddie's rooms. Act III.—Evening, several days
later. Eddie's rooms. The time is the present.
    Staged by Eugene O'Sullivan; settings and lighting by Leo Kerz.

A feeble comedy about a young saloon-keeper whose hoofer fiancée
craves a wholesome family background she has never known. When
the saloon-keeper hires a lovable old rip to pose as his grandmother,
she converts the back room—and the boys in it—into a Victorian
family parlor.

(Closed January 3, 1953)

TWO'S COMPANY

(90 performances)

Revue in two acts, with music by Vernon Duke, lyrics by Ogden
Nash, and sketches by Charles Sherman and Peter DeVries; addi-

tional lyrics by Sammy Cahn. Produced by James Russo and Michael Ellis at the Alvin Theatre, December 15, 1952.

The principals—

Bette Davis	Hiram Sherman
David Burns	Bill Callahan
Stanley Prager	Ellen Hanley
George Irving	Maria Karnilova
Buzz Miller	Oliver Wakefield
Peter Kelley	Robert Orton's Teen Aces

Nora Kaye

Sketches directed by Jules Dassin; dances and musical numbers staged by Jerome Robbins; entire production under the supervision of John Murray Anderson; settings by Ralph Alswang; costumes by Miles White; musical supervisor and conductor, Milton Rosenstock.

Sketches and musical numbers—

ACT I

"Theatre Is a Lady"

Introduced by Hiram Sherman
Sung and danced by Bill Callahan with the boys and girls

"Turn Me Loose on Broadway"

Sung and danced by Bette Davis
Buzz Miller, Robert Pagent, Job Sanders and Stanley Simmons

"And a Little Child"

Producer .... George Irving
Secretary .... Tina Louise
Dudley Dawson .... David Burns
Rollo .... Michael Mann
Butler .... Franklin Neil
Mrs. Wilkins .... May Muth

"It Just Occurred to Me"

Sung by Peter Kelley, Deborah Remsen and the singing ensemble
Danced by Florence Baum, Barbara Heath, Helen Murielle, Ralph Linn, Robert Pagent, Job Sanders

"Jealousy"

Helen .... Bette Davis
Stanley .... David Burns

"Baby Couldn't Dance"

Girl .... Nora Kaye
Boy .... Bill Callahan
Professor .... Stanley Simmons
Pupils .... Barbara Heath, Florence Baum

"A Man's Home"

Sung by Hiram Sherman

"One's a Crowd"

That One .... Bette Davis
Reggie .... Hiram Sherman
J. C. .... George Irving
Harassed Gentleman .... Stanley Prager
Audience..Teddy Tavenner, Earl Renard, Tina Louise, Basha Regis, Clifford Fearl, Dorothy Hill, May Muth, Eleanor Boleyn, Dorothy Hill, Sue Hight, Robert Neukum

Bette Davis in "Two's Company"

"ROUNDABOUT"

Sung by Ellen Hanley
Danced by Nora Kaye with Ralph Linn, Robert Pagent, William
Inglis, Eleanor Boleyn, Barbara Heath and the dancing ensemble

"THE VOICE OF INEXPERIENCE"

Oliver Wakefield

"ROLL ALONG, SADIE"

Sung and danced by Bette Davis, Hiram Sherman, Buzz Miller,
Ralph Linn and the company

ACT II

"CLEAR BLUE SKY"

Sung by Peter Kelley and Sue Hight
Danced by Maria Karnilova and Robert Pagent
Accompanied by the singers and dancers

"STREET SCENES"

Bette Davis and Hiram Sherman

"ESTHER"

Melvin	David Burns
Esther	Maria Karnilova
Native	Buzz Miller

"WHEN IN ROME"

Strombolini	David Burns
Nina	Helen Murielle
Thomaso	Stanley Prager
Porter	Earl Renard
Jezebela	Bette Davis
Musician	George Irving

"HAUNTED HOT SPOT"

Sung by Ellen Hanley
Danced by

The Stripper	Nora Kaye
The Drummer	Bill Callahan
The Pianist	Buzz Miller

"PURPLE ROSE"

Sybill	Bette Davis
Peter	Hiram Sherman
Horatio	Earl Renard
Terrance	George Irving
Hilary	Clifford Fearl
Hortense	May Muth
Ginger	Deborah Remsen
Camera Man	Maurice Brenner
Butler	Franklin Neil
Maid	Basha Regis
Virgil	Robert Neukum
Cicero	Bill Krach

"JUST LIKE A MAN"

Sung by Bette Davis

FINALE

The Company

(Closed March 8, 1953)

THE GREY-EYED PEOPLE

(5 performances)

Comedy in three acts by John D. Hess. Produced by Albert Selden at the Martin Beck Theatre, December 17, 1952.

Cast of characters—

Delivery Man	John Randolph
Tommy Hart	Edward Brian
Buster Hart	Michael Free
Beatrice Hammond	Sandra Deel
Alice Hart	Virginia Gilmore
Barry Green	Clay Flagg
John Hart	Walter Matthau
Simon Blackwell	Brandon Peters
First Girl Scout	Rosemary Prinz
Second Girl Scout	Sally Jessup
Third Girl Scout	Mary Grace Canfield
Lucille Blackwell	Katherine Anderson
Buff Schneider	Walter Klavun
Richard Jones	Tony Bickley
Policeman	Ted Tiller
A Woman	Jane Lloyd-Jones
Gates	John Martone

The action takes place in the living room of John and Alice Hart in Sweet Hills, a suburb of New York City. The time is the present. Act I.—A Monday in Mid-June. Act II.—Scene 1—Two hours later. Scene 2—Ten-thirty the next morning. Act III.—Five o'clock Friday afternoon.

Staged by Morton Da Costa; setting and lighting by Eldon Elder; costumes by Noel Taylor.

John Hart, an excitable individualist in a conventional suburb, launches a crusade in defense of an ex-Communist who has run afoul of the community. Half the time, the author glibly uses this situation for stage journalism; the other half, he rather callously milks it for laughs.

(Closed December 20, 1952)

THE CHILDREN'S HOUR

(189 performances)
(Continued)

Play in three acts by Lillian Hellman. Revived by Kermit Bloomgarden at the Coronet Theatre, December 18, 1952.

Cast of characters—

Peggy Rogers	Sandra March
Catherine	Nancy Plehn
Lois Fisher	Carolyn King
Mrs. Lily Mortar	Mary Finney
Evelyn Munn	Denise Alexander
Helen Burton	Toni Hallaran
Rosalie Wells	Janet Parker

Janet ....June Connolly
Leslie ....Sandee Preston
Mary Tilford ....Iris Mann
Karen Wright ....Kim Hunter
Martha Dobie ....Patricia Neal
Doctor Joseph Cardin ....Robert Pastene
Agatha ....Leora Thatcher
Mrs. Amelia Tilford ....Katherine Emmet
A Grocery Boy ....Gordon Russell

Act I.—Living room of the Wright-Dobie School, late afternoon in April. Act II.—Scene 1—Living room at Mrs. Tilford's, a few hours later. Scene 2—The same, later that evening. Act III.—Living room of the Wright-Dobie School, November.

Staged by Lillian Hellman; settings by Howard Bay; costumes by Anna Hill Johnstone; associate producer, Peter Glenn.

BE YOUR AGE

(5 performances)

Comedy in three acts by Mary Orr and Reginald Denham. Produced by Alexander H. Cohen and Joseph Kipness, in association with Morris K. Bauer, at the Forty-eighth Street Theatre, January 14, 1953.

Cast of characters—

Lois Holly ....Lee Remick
Grace Tendel ....Nancy Cushman
Bob Foley ....Dean Harens
Potter Erickson ....Bill Story
Archibald K. Holly ....Loring Smith
Gwendolyn Holly ....Hildy Parks
Eliot Spurgeon ....Conrad Nagel
Abigail ....Patricia Ripley
Beatrix Bond ....Martha Randall
Vicki Holly ....Ann Hillary
Binky Butterworth ....Tom Tempest

The action takes place in Archibald K. Holly's residence in Gideon, Ohio. Act I.—Scene 1—A Tuesday morning last June. Scene 2—Two days later, evening. Act II.—Scene 1—The following Monday, early evening. Scene 2—Ten days later, evening. Act III.—Saturday afternoon, ten days later.

Staged by Reginald Denham; setting by Ralph Alswang; costumes by Jocelyn.

Dull, shoddy tale of a college girl who jilts her beau to get engaged to a man who went to school with her father. After much too much ado, the young people are reunited, and the audience lives happier ever after.

(Closed January 17, 1953)

THE LOVE OF FOUR COLONELS

(141 performances)

Comedy in two acts by Peter Ustinov. Produced by the Theatre Guild and Aldrich & Myers at the Shubert Theatre, January 15, 1953.

Cast of characters—

```
Colonel Wesley Breitenspiegel ........................Larry Gates
Colonel Desmond de S. Rinder-Sparrow .............Robert Coote
Colonel Aimé Frappot ..........................George Voskovec
Colonel Alexander Ikonenko ......................Stefan Schnabel
The Mayor of Herzogenberg ....................Reginald Mason
The Man ........................................Rex Harrison
Donovan ....................................Leueen MacGrath
Beauty ..........................................Lilli Palmer
```
Act I.—Allied Military Administration Office, Herzogenberg, Germany. Outside the Castle. Inside the Castle. Act II.—Inside the Castle.

Staged by Rex Harrison; settings and costumes by Rolf Gerard; supervised by Lawrence Langner and Theresa Helburn.

See page 138.

(Closed May 16, 1953)

THE BAT

(23 performances)

Mystery drama in three acts by Mary Roberts Rinehart and Avery Hopwood. Revived by James Withers Elliott at the National Theatre, January 20, 1953.

Cast of characters—

```
Miss Cornelia Van Gorder ........................Lucile Watson
Billy ..........................................Harry Shaw Lowe
Lizzie ..............................................Zasu Pitts
A Stranger ......................................Bert Bertram
Brooks ..........................................Peter Hanson
Miss Dale Ogden ..............................Paula Houston
Doctor Wells ................................Harry Bannister
Anderson ................................Shepperd Strudwick
Richard Fleming ............................Laurence Haddon
Reginald Beresford ............................Charles Proctor
An Unknown Man ..............................Raymond Bailey
```
Act I.—Living room in a country house. Act II.—The same. Act III.—A room on the top floor.

Staged by Jonathan Seymour; settings and lighting by Ralph Alswang; costumes by Alice Gibson.

(Closed February 7, 1953)

MID-SUMMER

(109 performances)

Play in three acts by Viña Delmar. Produced by Paul Crabtree and Frank J. Hale at the Vanderbilt Theatre, January 21, 1953.

Cast of characters—

```
Lily ..........................................Geraldine Page
Mrs. Lenoir ..............................Suzanne Caubaye
Carlo ............................................Jenny Hecht
Rosie ............................................Mary James
Val ..........................................Mark Stevens
```

Mr. Lenoir ....Paul Andor
Julia ....Vicki Cummings
Mr. Strobel ....Howard Smith
Bill Moore ....Robert Emmett
Edouard ....Billy Jeffries
François ....Barry Blake
Dr. Emsley ....Edgar Stehli

The action takes place in a room in the Lenoirs' hotel on 14th Street, New York City, in 1907. Act I.—Scene 1—Early evening. Scene 2— That night. Act II.—Scene 1—The next morning. Scene 2—Early the same evening. Act III.—Morning, the next day.

Staged by Paul Crabtree; setting and lighting by Howard Bay; costumes by Motley.

A sentimental domestic comedy, evoking a splotchy New York in 1907, about a young couple on their uppers. He is a school teacher bitten with the theatre bug, she a loyal, warmhearted, illiterate wife and mother who—in the clash between adventure and security—lets her husband's desire prevail.

(Closed April 25, 1953)

THE CRUCIBLE

(149 performances)
(Continued)

Play in a prologue and two acts by Arthur Miller. Produced by Kermit Bloomgarden at the Martin Beck Theatre, January 22, 1953.

Cast of characters—

Betty Parris ....Janet Alexander
Tituba ....Jacqueline Andre
Reverend Samuel Parris ....Fred Stewart
Abigail Williams ....Madeleine Sherwood
Susanna Walcott ....Barbara Stanton
Mrs. Ann Putnam ....Jane Hoffman
Thomas Putnam ....Raymond Bramley
Mercy Lewis ....Dorothy Jolliffe
Mary Warren ....Jenny Egan
John Proctor ....Arthur Kennedy
Rebecca Nurse ....Jean Adair
Giles Corey ....Joseph Sweeney
Reverend John Hale ....E. G. Marshall
Elizabeth Proctor ....Beatrice Straight
Francis Nurse ....Graham Velsey
Ezekiel Cheever ....Don McHenry
John Willard ....George Mitchell
Judge Hathorne ....Philip Coolidge
Deputy-Governor Danforth ....Walter Hampden
Sarah Good ....Adele Fortin
Hopkins ....Donald Marye

Prologue—A bedroom in Reverend Samuel Parris's house, Salem, Massachusetts, in 1692. Act I.—Proctor's house, eight days later. Act II.—The vestry of the Salem meeting house, two weeks later. Act III.—A cell in Salem jail, three months later.

Staged by Jed Harris; scenery designed by Boris Aronson; costumes designed by Edith Lutyens.

See page 154.

THE FIFTH SEASON

(150 performances)
(Continued)

Comedy in two acts by Sylvia Regan. Produced by George Kondolf at the Cort Theatre, January 23, 1953.

Cast of characters—

Ruby D. Prince	John Kullers
Shelly	Nita Talbot
Lorraine McKay	Phyllis Hill
Ferelli	Norman Rose
Max Pincus	Menasha Skulnik
Johnny Goodwin	Richard Whorf
Frances Goodwin	Augusta Roeland
Marty Goodwin	Dick Kallman
Miriam Oppenheim	Lois Wheeler
Dolores	Dorian Leigh
The Redhead Model	Midge Ware
The Brunette Model	Carolyn Block
Miles Lewis	John Griggs

The action takes place in the office of Goodwin-Pincus, on 7th Avenue, in New York. The time is the present. Act I.—A morning in April. Act II.—Scene 1—An afternoon, the following December. Scene 2—That evening. Act III.—Scene 1—Half an hour later. Scene 2—Early the following morning.

Staged by Gregory Ratoff; scenery by Sam Leve; costume supervision by Edythe Gilfond.

Mechanical farce full of the ups and downs, gags and gimmicks, of Manhattan's garment industry. Along with the shenanigans goes the rather out-of-key tale of a married partner's guilty sinning with a model.

TOUCHSTONE

(7 performances)

Play in two acts by William Stucky. Produced by Elaine Perry at the Music Box, February 3, 1953.

Cast of characters—

Aunt Emma	Evelyn Ellis
Dr. Joseph Clay	Ossie Davis
Cathy Roberts	Patty McCormack
Jimmy Clay	Josh White, Jr.
Major Robert Spaulding	Ian Keith
Dr. Gwendolyn Taliafero	Ann Dere
The Rev. Ronald Thompson	Guy Arbury
Langdon Spaulding	Paul McGrath
Charles Tutwell	Carl Low

The action takes place in the Major's home, somewhere in the horse country of the Upper South. The time is the present, early August.

Staged by Hale McKeen; setting designed and lighted by George Jenkins.

A play concerned with the havoc created in a Southern community by a small Negro boy given to seeing visions. With many

Fred Gwynne, Hurd Hatfield, Philip Bourneuf and Joseph Schild-kraut in "Love's Labour's Lost"

of the townspeople roused to religious hysteria, but the boy's own doctor father convinced that his son needs psychiatric care, the play becomes, in large part, a kind of clash between faith and reason. Though dramatically very faulty, *Touchstone* shows an honest and low-pitched approach to its material.

(Closed February 7, 1953)

LOVE'S LABOUR'S LOST

(15 performances)

Comedy by William Shakespeare. Produced by the New York City Drama Company at the New York City Center of Music and Drama, February 4, 1953.

Cast of characters—

King of Navarre	Jerome Kilty
Longaville	Robert Fletcher
Dumain	Paul Sparer
Berowne	Kevin McCarthy
Dull	Fred Gwynne
Costard	Paul Ballantyne
Don Adriano de Armado	Joseph Schildkraut
Moth	William McIver (Alternate, Oliver Andes)
Jacquenetta	Priscilla Morrill
Boyet	Earl Montgomery
Princess of France	Nancy Marchand
Maria	Cavada Humphrey
Katherine	{ Jan Farrand / Matinées, Amanda Steel
Rosaline	Meg Mundy
Lady-in-Waiting	Amanda Steel
Holofernes	Philip Bourneuf
Sir Nathaniel	Hurd Hatfield
Mercade	Liam Sullivan
Attendants	{ Albert Duclos / Richard Astor

Staged by Albert Marre; setting by Robert O'Hearn; costumes by Robert Fletcher; incidental dances by Todd Bolender; orchestra conducted by William Brooks; assistant director, Richard Baldridge; production supervisor, Lemuel Ayers.

(Closed February 15, 1953)

THE EMPEROR'S CLOTHES

(16 performances)

Play in three acts by George Tabori. Produced by Robert Whitehead, in association with The Playwrights' Company, at the Ethel Barrymore Theatre, February 9, 1953.

Cast of characters—

Elek Odry	Lee J. Cobb
Bella	Maureen Stapleton
Ferike	Brandon de Wilde
Peter	Anthony Ross
Granny	Tamara Daykarhanova
The Baron	Esmond Knight
First Rottenbiller Brother	Michael Strong
Second Rottenbiller Brother	Mike Kellin
The Fat Hugo	Philip Rodd
Mr. Schmitz	Howard H. Fischer
Mrs. Schmitz	Nydia Westman
The Man Without Shoes	David Clarke
A Boy	Richard Case
Milkman	Allan Rich
Policeman } Singer }	John Anderson

The action takes place during one Winter's day in Budapest, 1930. Staged by Harold Clurman; setting and lighting by Lester Polakov; costumes by Ben Edwards.

See page 172.

(Closed February 21, 1953)

ON BORROWED TIME

(78 performances)

Comedy in three acts by Paul Osborn, adapted from Lawrence Edward Watkin's novel of the same name. Revived by Richard W. Krakeur and Randolph Hale, in association with William G. Costin, Jr., at the Forty-eighth Street Theatre, February 10, 1953.

Cast of characters—

Pud .... David John Stollery
Julian Northrup (Gramps) .... Victor Moore
Nellie (Granny) .... Beulah Bondi
Mr. Brink .... Leo G. Carroll
Marcia Giles .... Melinda Markey
Demetria Riffle .... Kay Hammond
A Boy .... Robert Kaline
A Workman .... Gerald Milton
Dr. Evans .... Thayer Roberts
Mr. Pilbeam .... Russell Hicks
Mr. Grimes .... Michael Jeffrey
Sheriff .... Larry Barton

The action takes place in the living room and the backyard of the Northrup home. Act I.—Scene 1—Afternoon. Scene 2—A week later. Scene 3—Dusk; a week later. Act II.—Scene 1—Two hours later. Scene 2—Ten o'clock that night. Act III.—Scene 1—Dawn; the next morning. Scene 2—Dusk; the same day. Scene 3—Later that night.

Staged by Marshall Jamison; scenery, lighting, and costumes by Paul Morrison.

(Closed April 18, 1953)

HAZEL FLAGG

(126 performances)
(Continued)

Musical satire in two acts; book by Ben Hecht, based on a story by James Street and the film *Nothing Sacred;* music by Jule Styne; lyrics by Bob Hilliard. Produced by Jule Styne, in association with Anthony B. Farrell, at the Mark Hellinger Theatre, February 11, 1953.

Cast of characters—

An Editor .... Dean Campbell
Oleander .... Jonathan Harris
Laura Carew .... Benay Venuta
Wallace Cook .... John Howard
Vermont Villagers .... { Carol Hendricks
                                                B. J. Keating
                                                Joan Morton
                                                Dorothy Love
                                                Laurel Shelby
Mr. Billings .... Lawrence Weber

Mr. Jenkins ....Robert Lenn
Hazel Flagg ....Helen Gallagher
Dr. Downer ....Thomas Mitchell
Man on the Street ....George Reeder
Bellboy ....Jerry Craig
Maximilian Lavian ....John Pelletti
Fireman ....Bill Heyer
Miss Winterbottom ....Betsy Holland
Mayor of New York ....Jack Whiting
Whitey ....Sheree North
Willie ....John Brascia
Dr. Egelhofer ....Ross Martin
Chorus Girls .... { Lori Jon
                                      { Virginia Poe

Committeemen .... { Michael Spaeth
                                      { John Bartis
Policeman ....Eric Schepard
   Dancers: Estelle Aza, Chris Carter, Marcella Dodge, Lillian Donau, Anna Friedland, Ruby Herndon, Lori Jon, Sherry McCutcheon, Betty McMillen, Barbara Michaels, Judy Miller, Joan Morton, Margot Myers, Virginia Poe, Eva Ralf, Beryl Towbin, Toni Wheelis, Christopher Brown, Ronald Cecill, Don Crichton, Al Craine, Hugh Lambert, Gerard Leavitt, George Reeder, Eric Schepard, Michael Spaeth.
   Singers: Sara Dillon, Mary Harmon, Carol Hendricks, Betsy Holland, Dorsie Hollongsworth, B. J. Keating, Beverly McFadden, Laurel Shelby, John Bartis, Dean Campbell, David Carter, Jerry Craig, Bob Davis, Bill Heyer, Robert Lenn, David Randall.
   Dances and musical numbers staged by Robert Alton; book directed by David Alexander; scenery designed and lighted by Harry Horner; costumes by Miles White; musical director, Pembroke Davenport; choral arrangements and direction, Hugh Martin; orchestrations, Don Walker.

Synopsis of scenes—

ACT I

Scene 1

Conference Room of Everywhere Magazine; late afternoon
"A Little More Heart" ....Laura, Wallace, Magazine Staff

Scene 2

Dr. Downer's House; the next day
"The World Is Beautiful Today" ....Hazel
"I'm Glad I'm Leaving" ....Hazel

Scene 3

Railroad Depot, Stonyhead; that evening
Dance
"The Rutland Bounce" ....Joan Morton, George Reeder,
                                         Don Crichton, Villagers

Scene 4

A New York Street; the next day
"Hello, Hazel" ....Laura, New Yorkers

Scene 5

Hazel's New York Hotel Suite; later that day
Ballet
"Paris Gown" ....Hazel, Lavian Ronald Cecill,
                                 Gerard Leavitt, George
                               Reeder, Models, Attendants
Reprise: "The World Is Beautiful Today" ....Wallace, Editors

Scene 6

Laura Carew's Office; two weeks later
"Every Street's a Boulevard in Old New York" ....Mayor

Scene 7

Hazel's Hotel Suite; evening; a week later
"How Do You Speak to an Angel?" ....Wallace

Scene 8

A. A Cross Section of New York City; later that evening
"Autograph Chant" ....Autograph Hunters
"I Feel Like I'm Gonna Live Forever" ....Hazel
B. Roseland Ballroom
"You're Gonna Dance with Me, Willie" ....Hazel, Willie, Company

ACT II

Scene 1

A Radio Station in the Hotel; the next morning
"Who Is the Bravest?" ....University Glee Club

Scene 2

Hazel's Hotel Bedroom; the same morning
Ballet
Dream Parade ....Hazel and Company

Scene 3

The Same; several hours later

Scene 4

The Mayor's Luncheon; that afternoon
"Salome" ....Dancing Girls
"Everybody Loves to Take a Bow" ....Laura, Mayor, Men

Scene 5

Under the East River Bridge; later that evening
"Laura De Maupassant" ....Hazel

Scene 6

A Barge on the River's Edge; a little later
Reprise: "Autograph Chant" ....Autograph Hunters

Scene 7

Finale
Reprise: "I Feel Like I'm Gonna Live Forever" ....Company

JOHN BROWN'S BODY

(65 performances)

Adaptation by Charles Laughton of Stephen Vincent Benét's
poem by the same name. Produced by Paul Gregory at the New
Century Theatre, February 14, 1953.

The principals—

Tyrone Power, Judith Anderson, Raymond Massey

Choral group—

Joe Baker, Barbara Ford, Roger Miller, Roy D. Berk, Gillian Gray,
Smith Russell, Jr., Betty Benson, Homer W. Hall, Alexander Ser-
baroli, Paul Bloom, Lester D. Helsdon, Lynda Stevens, Keith Carver,
William Longmire, Robert Vaughan, Stephen Considine, Donna Mc-
Daniel, Gordon B. Wood, Jack B. Dailey, John McMahon.

Soloists—

Stephen Considine, Betty Benson

Dancers—

Donna McDaniel, Alexander Serbaroli

Staged by Charles Laughton; music and effects by Walter Schu-
mann; on-stage choral director, Richard White.

(Closed April 11, 1953)

MAGGIE

(5 performances)

Musical play in two acts, based on Sir James M. Barrie's comedy *What Every Woman Knows;* book by Hugh Thomas; music and lyrics by William Roy. Produced by Franklin Gilbert and John Fearnley at the National Theatre, February 18, 1953.

Cast of characters—

Alick Wylie	Bramwell Fletcher
James Wylie	James Broderick
David Wylie	Frank Maxwell
Maggie Wylie	Betty Paul
John Shand	Keith Andes
Professor Dubois	Henry Hamilton
Mrs. MacLaughlin	Jenny Lou Law
Madame Marstonne	Odette Myrtil
Sybil Tenterdon	Celia Lipton
Williams	Gene Hollmann
Venables	John Hoyt
John Shand (in ballet)	Marc Platt
Maggie Wylie (in ballet)	Alicia Krug
Sybil Tenterdon (in ballet)	Kathryn Lee
Porters	Gene Hollmann, Henry Hamilton, Oran Osburn
Conductor	Paul Ukena

Singers: Marion Lauer, Jan Scott, Joanne Spiller, Gloria Van Dorpe, Robert Busch, John Ford, Henry Hamilton, Gene Hollmann, James E. McCracken, Oran Osburn, Paul Ukena.

Dancers: Adele Aron, Sura Gesben, Jeanne Jones, Patti Karkalits, Nata Lee, Ruby Ann Saber, J. Corky Geil, John George, Alan Howard, David Nillo, Bob St. Clair, Keith Willis.

Staged by Michael Gordon; sets and costumes by Raoul Pene du Bois; choreography by June Graham; lighting by Peggy Clark; musical direction by Maurice Levine; orchestration by Don Walker; dance arrangements by Dean Fuller; production associate, Harry Zevin.

Principal musical numbers—

ACT I

"I Never Laughed in My Life"	John
"Long and Weary Wait"	John and Maggie
"Thimbleful"	Alick, David, James, John, Maggie
"He's the Man"	John, Singers, Dancers
"What Every Woman Knows"	Maggie
"Any Afternoon about Five"	Marstonne
"Smile for Me"	Maggie
"You Become Me"	Maggie and John
"It's Only Thirty Years"	Marstonne and Venables
"The New Me"—Ballet	Maggie, Alick, David, James, Singers and Dancers

ACT II

"The Train with the Cushioned Seats"	David, Alick, James
"People in Love"	John and Sybil
"Practical"	Maggie
"Charm"	Maggie
"Fun in the Country"	Marstonne

(Closed February 21, 1953)

PICNIC

(117 performances)
(Continued)

Play in three acts by William Inge. Produced by the Theatre Guild and Joshua Logan at the Music Box, February 19, 1953.

Cast of characters—

Helen Potts .... Ruth McDevitt
Hal Carter .... Ralph Meeker
Millie Owens .... Kim Stanley
Bomber .... Morris Miller
Madge Owens .... Janice Rule
Flo Owens .... Peggy Conklin
Rosemary Sidney .... Eileen Heckart
Alan Seymour .... Paul Newman
Irma Kronkite .... Reta Shaw
Christine Schoenwalder .... Elizabeth Wilson
Howard Bevans .... Arthur O'Connell

The action takes place in a small Kansas town in the yard shared by Flo Owens and Helen Potts. Act I.—Early morning, Labor Day. Act II.—Late the same afternoon. Act III.—Scene 1—Very early the following morning. Scene 2—A few hours later.

Staged by Joshua Logan; setting and lighting by Jo Mielziner; costumes by Mildred Trebor.

See page 191.

WONDERFUL TOWN

(108 performances)
(Continued)

Musical comedy in two acts, based on the play *My Sister Eileen* by Joseph Fields and Jerome Chodorov and the stories by Ruth McKenney; book by Joseph Fields and Jerome Chodorov; music by Leonard Bernstein; lyrics by Betty Comden and Adolph Green. Produced by Robert Fryer at the Winter Garden, February 25, 1953.

Cast of characters—

Guide .... Warren Galjour
Appopolous .... Henry Lascoe
Lonigan .... Walter Kelvin
Helen .... Michele Burke
Wreck .... Jordan Bentley
Violet .... Dody Goodman
Valenti .... Ted Beniades
Eileen .... Edith Adams
Ruth .... Rosalind Russell
A Strange Man .... Nathaniel Frey
Drunks .... Lee Papell, Delbert Anderson
Robert Baker .... George Gaynes
Associate Editors .... Warren Galjour, Albert Linville
Mrs. Wade .... Isabella Hoopes

Frank Lippencott ....Chris Alexander
Chef ....Nathaniel Frey
Waiter .... Delbert Anderson
Delivery Boy ....Alvin Bean
Chick Clark ....Dort Clark
Shore Patrolman ....Lee Papell
First Cadet ....David Lober
Second Cadet ....Ray Dorian
Policemen ....Lee Papell, Albert Linville, Delbert Anderson,
                         Chris Robinson, Nathaniel Frey,
                         Warren Galjour, Robert Kole
Ruth's Escort ....Chris Robinson
    Greenwich Villagers: Jean Eliot, Carol Cole, Marta Becket, Maxine Berke, Helena Seroy, Geraldine Delaney, Margaret Caddy, Dody Goodman, Ed Balin, Alvin Beam, Ray Dorian, Edward Heim, Joe Layton, David Lober, Victor Moreno, William Weslow, Pat Johnson, Evelyn Page, Libi Staiger, Patty Wilkes, Helen Rice, Delbert Anderson, Warren Galjour, Robert Kole, Lee Papell, Chris Robinson.
    The action takes place in Greenwich Village in the thirties.
    Staged by George Abbott; dances and musical numbers arranged by Donald Saddler; sets and costumes by Raoul Pene du Bois; lighting by Peggy Clark; Miss Russell's clothes designed by Main Bocher; musical direction and vocal arrangements by Lehma Engel; orchestrations by Don Walker.

Principal musical numbers—

ACT I

"Christopher Street" ....Warren Galjour and The Villagers
"Ohio" ....Rosalind Russell, Edith Adams
"Conquering New York" ....Rosalind Russell, Edith Adams,
                         David Lober, Dody Goodman, The Villagers
"One Hundred Easy Ways" ....Rosalind Russell
"What a Waste" ....George Gaynes, Warren Galjour, Albert Linville
Story Vignettes
  Rexford ....Chris Robinson
  Mr. Mallory ....Delbert Anderson
  Danny ....Nathaniel Frey
  Trent ....Lee Papell and Rosalind Russell
"Never Felt This Way Before" ....Edith Adams
"Pass the Football" ....Jordan Bentley and The Villagers
Conversation Piece ....Rosalind Russell, Edith Adams,
                         Chris Alexander, George Gaynes, Dort Clark
"A Quiet Girl" ....George Gaynes
"Conga!" ....Sung by Rosalind Russell
                         Danced by The Cadets

ACT II

"My Darlin' Eileen" .....Edith Adams, Delbert Anderson and Police
"Swing!" ....Rosalind Russell and Villagers
"It's Love" ....George Gaynes and The Villagers
"Wrong Note Rag" ....Rosalind Russell, Edith Adams and
                         The Villagers

See page 212.

THE MERCHANT OF VENICE

(15 performances)

Play in two acts by William Shakespeare. Revived by the New York City Drama Company at the New York City Center of Music and Drama, March 4, 1953.

Cast of characters—

Antonio ....Philip Bourneuf
Salarino ....Earl Montgomery
Salanio ....Paul Sparer
Bassanio ....Paul Stevens
Lorenzo ....Michael Wager
Gratiano ....James Daly
Portia ....Margaret Phillips
Nerissa ....Nancy Marchand
The Neapolitan Prince ....Richard Astor
The English Lord ....Kevin Riley
The German Baron ....Raymond Johnson
Balthazar .... Albert Duclos
The Prince of Morocco ....Earle Hyman
Shylock ....Luther Adler
Tubal ....Richard Venture
Jessica ....Felicia Montealegre
Launcelot Gobbo ....Frank Corsaro
Prince of Aragon ....Robert Fletcher
Duke of Venice ....Robert Fletcher
Court Attendants .....Kevin Riley, Richard Astor, Raymond Johnson
Servants to Portia ....Chris Mahan, Steven Thomas
Dancers ....Beatrice Tompkins, Barbara Walczak, Barbara
           Milberg, Marie Pelus, John Mandia, Stanley Zompakos
    Staged by Albert Marre; scenery and costumes by Lemuel Ayers;
assistant director, Richard Baldridge; choreography, Todd Bolender;
musical direction, William Brooks.

(Closed March 15, 1953)

MISALLIANCE

(114 performances)
(Continued)

Comedy in three acts by George Bernard Shaw. Revived by the
New York City Drama Company at the New York City Center of
Music and Drama, February 18, 1953. After sixteen performances
at the City Center (through March 1) it moved to the Ethel Barrymore Theatre on March 6.

Cast of characters—

Bentley Summerhays ....Roddy McDowall
Johnny Tarleton ....William Redfield
Hypatia Tarleton ....Jan Farrand
Mrs. Tarleton ....Dorothy Sands
Lord Summerhays ....Richard Purdy
Mr. Tarleton ....Barry Jones
Percival ....Richard Kiley
Lina .... Tamara Geva
Gunner ....Jerome Kilty
    The action takes place during the course of one afternoon in Mr.
Tarleton's country home in Surrey on the slope of Hindhead.
    Staged by Cyril Ritchard; setting by John Boyt; costumes by Robert
Fletcher; production supervisor, Lemuel Ayers.

Barry Jones, Tamara Geva and Richard Purdy in "Misalliance"

PORGY AND BESS

(97 performances)
(Continued)

Operetta in three acts, based on the Dorothy and DuBose Heyward play *Porgy;* music by George Gershwin; libretto by DuBose Heyward; lyrics by DuBose Heyward and Ira Gershwin. Revived by Blevins Davis and Robert Breen at the Ziegfeld Theatre, March 10, 1953.

Cast of characters—

Clara	Helen Colbert
Mingo	Jerry Laws
Sportin' Life	Cab Calloway
Serena	Helen Thigpen
Jake	Joseph James
Robbins	Howard Roberts

```
Jim ..........................Hugh Dilworth and Sherman Sneed
Peter (The Honey Man) .......................Joseph Crawford
Lily (The Strawberry Woman) .....................Helen Dowdy
Maria ..........................................Georgia Burke
Porgy .....................................LeVern Hutcherson
                          or Leslie Scott or Irving Barnes
Crown .........................................John McCurry
Annie ........................................Catherine Ayers
Bess ..........................................Leontyne Price
                                     or Urylee Leonardos
Policeman .....................................Sam Kasakoff
Detective .....................................Walter Riemer
Undertaker ...................................William Veasey
Frazier .......................................Moses LaMarr
Ruby .........................................Elizabeth Foster
Crab Man ........................................Ray Yeates
Coroner .......................................Sam Kasakoff
Policeman ........................................Willis Daily
Porgy's Goat ..........................................Jebob
```

Residents of Catfish Row: Joseph Attles, Irving Barnes, Lawson Bates, James Hawthorne Bey, Rhoda Boggs, Walter P. Brown, Miriam Burton, Sibol Cain, Elsie Clark, Charles Colman, Clarice Crawford, Helen Ferguson, Doris Galiber, Ruby Greene, Kenneth Hibbert, George A. Hill, Joy McLean, Pauline Phelps, Edna Ricks, Anabelle Ross, George A. Royston, Dolores Swan, Clyde Turner, Eloise C. Uggams, Barbara Ann Webb. Children: Jacqueline Barnes, George Royston, Jr.

The action takes place in Charleston, South Carolina. The time is the past. Scenes include Catfish Row, Kittiwah Island, and Serena's room.

Staged by Robert Breen; musical director, Alexander Smallens; settings by Wolfgang Roth; costumes by Jed Mace; assistant musical director, Samuel Matlowsky; choral director, Eva Jessye.

Principal musical numbers—

ACT I
Scene 1

```
Lullaby, "Summertime" ..................................Clara
"A Woman Is a Sometime Thing" ........Jim, Jake, Sportin' Life
                                          and Ensemble
Entrance of Porgy: "They Pass by Singing" ...............Porgy
"Crap Game Fugue"
```

Scene 2

```
"Gone, Gone, Gone" ................................Ensemble
"Overflow" .........................................Ensemble
Arioso: "My Man's Gone Now" .............Serena and Ensemble
Train Song: "Leavin' fo' de Promis' Lan' " .....Bess and Ensemble
```

Scene 3

```
Rowing Song: "It Takes a Long Pull" .....Jim, Jake and Ensemble
"I Got Plenty o' Nuttin' " ...............................Porgy
Divorce Scene: "Woman to Lady" .. Porgy, Bess, Frazier, Ensemble
Duet: "Bess, You Is My Woman Now" ...........Porgy and Bess
Picnic Song: "Oh, I Can't Sit Down" ..................Ensemble
```

ACT II
Scene 1

```
"I Ain't Got No Shame" .............Sportin' Life and Ensemble
"It Ain't Necessarily So" .............Sportin' Life and Ensemble
Duet: "What You Want with Bess?" .............Crown and Bess
```

Scene 2

```
"Time and Time Again" ....................Serena and Ensemble
Street Cries ......................Strawberry Woman, Crab Man
Duet: "I Loves You, Porgy" .....................Porgy and Bess
```

Scene 3

"Oh, de Lawd Shake de Heaven" ....Ensemble
"A Redheaded Woman" ....Crown and Ensemble
"Oh, Doctor Jesus" ....Principals and Ensemble

ACT III

Scene 1

"Clara, Don't You Be Downhearted" ....Ensemble

Scene 2

"There's a Boat That's Leavin' Soon for New York" ...Sportin' Life
and Bess

Scene 3

"Buzzard" ....Porgy
"Where's My Bess?" ....Porgy
"I'm on My Way" ....Porgy and Ensemble

MY 3 ANGELS

(95 performances)
(Continued)

Comedy in three acts by Sam and Bella Spewack, based on Albert Husson's French play, *La Cuisine des Anges*. Produced by Saint-Subber, Rita Allen, and Archie Thomson at the Morosco Theatre, March 11, 1953.

Cast of characters—

Felix Ducotel ....Will Kuluva
Amelie Ducotel ....Carmen Mathews
Isabelle Ducotel ....Joan Chandler
Mme. Parole ....Nan McFarland
Joseph ....Walter Slezak
Jules ....Jerome Cowan
Alfred ....Darren McGavin
Henri Trochard ....Henry Daniell
Paul ....Robert Carroll
Lieutenant ....Eric Fleming
Adolphe (a tiny serpent; obviously invisible)
     The action takes place in the family Ducotel's living room back of a general store in Cayenne, French Guiana, December, 1910. Act I.— Christmas Eve. Act II.—Later that night. Act III.—Christmas morning.
     Staged by José Ferrer; setting designed by Boris Aronson; costumes by Lucinda Ballard.

See page 236.

CAMINO REAL

(60 performances)

Play in three acts by Tennessee Williams. Produced by Cheryl Crawford and Ethel Reiner, in association with Walter P. Chrysler, Jr., at the National Theatre, March 19, 1953.

Cast of characters—

Gutman	Frank Silvera
Survivor	Guy Thomajan
Rosita	Aza Bard
1st Officer	Henry Silva
A Gentleman of Fortune	Joseph Anthony
La Madrecita de Los Perdidos	Vivian Nathan
Her Son	Rolando Valdez
Kilroy	Eli Wallach
1st Street Cleaner	Nehemiah Persoff
2nd Street Cleaner	Fred Sadoff
Abdullah	Ernesto Gonzalez
A Bum in a Window	Martin Balsam
A. Ratt	Mike Gazzo
The Loan Shark	Salem Ludwig
The Baron	David J. Stewart
Lobo	Ronne Aul
2nd Officer	William Lennard
A Grotesque Mummer	Gluck Sandor
A Lady of Legend	Jo Van Fleet
Lady Mulligan	Lucille Patton
Waiter	Page Johnson
A Romantic Poet	Hurd Hatfield
Navigator of the Fugitivo	Antony Vorno
Pilot of the Fugitivo	Martin Balsam
Market Woman	Charlotte Jones
2nd Market Woman	Joanna Vischer
Street Vendor	Ruth Volner
Lord Mulligan	Parker Wilson
The Gypsy	Jennie Goldstein
Her Daughter, Esmeralda	Barbara Baxley
Nursie	Salem Ludwig
Eva	Mary Grey
The Instructor	David J. Stewart
Assistant Instructor	Parker Wilson
Medical Student	Page Johnson
An Ancient Knight	Hurd Hatfield

Street Vendors: Aza Bard, Ernesto Gonzalez, Charlotte Jones, Gluck Sandor, Joanna Vischer, Ruth Volner, Antony Vorno.

Guests: Martin Balsam, Mary Grey, Lucille Patton, Joanna Vischer, Parker Wilson.

Passengers: Mike Gazzo, Mary Grey, Page Johnson, Charlotte Jones, William Lennard, Salem Ludwig, Joanna Vischer, Ruth Volner.

At the Fiesta: Ronne Aul, Martin Balsam, Aza Bard, Mike Gazzo, Ernesto Gonzalez, Mary Grey, Charlotte Jones, William Lennard, Nehemiah Persoff, Fred Sadoff, Gluck Sandor, Joanna Vischer, Antony Vorno, Parker Wilson.

The time and place: not specified.

Staged by Elia Kazan; entire production designed by Lemuel Ayers; assistant to the director, Anna Sokolow; incidental music by Bernardo Ségall; production associate, Anderson Lawler.

(See "The Season in New York.")

(Closed May 9, 1953)

HORSES IN MIDSTREAM

(4 performances)

Play in two acts by Andrew Rosenthal. Produced by Gilbert Miller and Donald Oenslager at the Royale Theatre, April 2, 1953.

Cast of characters—

Marie Louise ....Lili Darvas
Ganna ....Ludmilla Toretzka
Charles Pine ....Cedric Hardwicke
Tom Atwood ....Scott Forbes
Trina ....Diana Lynn
A Visitor ....Carol Goodner

The action takes place on the terrace of a small villa on the island of Elba. The time is the present. Act I.—Scene 1—A morning in late May. Scene 2—Three hours later. Act II.—Scene 1—Early evening in late June. Scene 2—That midnight.

Staged by Cedric Hardwicke; production designed and lighted by Donald Oenslager.

An attempt at urbane problem comedy. For thirty years, a now aged New Englander has lived happily in sin with the now elderly French lady novelist for whom he deserted his family. His young granddaughter, on the eve of marrying the family choice, hunts out this family ogre, and is charmed by him and his mistress and the married Englishman she has an affair with. But when she, too, is ready to kick over the traces, grandfather grows moral, implies that one man's destiny may be his granddaughter's downfall—so that the girl, at the end, goes away to think things over. *Horses in Midstream* has all the right dramatic furniture for the kind of play it is, but lacks individual point and luster and sparkle; never, in high-comedy terms, *gets* into midstream.

(Closed April 4, 1953)

ROOM SERVICE

(16 performances)

Comedy in three acts by John Murray and Allen Boretz. Revived by Bernard Hart and Don Hershey, in association with John Murray, at The Playhouse, April 6, 1953.

Cast of characters—

Sasha Smirnoff ....Alexander Asro
Gordon Miller ....John Randolph
Joseph Gribble ....Bartlett Robinson
Harry Binion ....Everett Sloane
Faker Englund ....Stanley Prager
Christine Marlowe ....Georgiann Johnson
Leo Davis ....Jack Lemmon
Hilda Manney ....Jeanne Russell
Gregory Wagner ....Ralph Dunn
Simon Jenkins ....Eric Brotherson
Timothy Hogarth ....Woodrow Parfrey
Dr. Glass ....Horace Cooper
Bank Messenger ....Irving Murray
Senator Blake ....Jack Bittner

The action takes place in Gordon Miller's room in the White Way Hotel. Act I.—A Friday afternoon in Spring. Act II.—The following day. Act III.—Five days later; evening.

Staged by Mortimer Offner; setting and lighting by Frederick Fox.

(Closed April 18, 1953)

Paul Lynde, Ronny Graham, Alice Ghostley, Robert Clary, Eartha

Kitt, June Carroll and Virginia de Luce in "New Faces of 1952"

A DATE WITH APRIL

(13 performances)

Comedy in three acts by George Batson. Produced by Kenneth Banghart and Diana Green at the Royale Theatre, April 15, 1953.

Cast of characters—

Val Corbett	Edmon Ryan
Bella	Louise Larabee
Tony Poole	Herbert Evers
Mrs. Ashley	Evelyn Varden
Elsa Ashley	Constance Bennett
Phyllis Lundgren	Marjorie Peterson

The action takes place in the living room of Elsa Ashley's New York apartment. Act I.—Noon on a bright Spring day. Act II.—Scene 1—Early afternoon, a week later. Scene 2—Later that same night. Act III.—Ten o'clock the next morning.

Staged by Reginald Denham; scenery designed by Robert O'Hearn; special music composed by Jay Chernis.

A very dull trifle about a loving but quick-tempered lady concert pianist and a famous novelist. They live together off and on—often on, but oftener off, in a way that goes on and on and is all too often awful.

(Closed April 25, 1953)

EMLYN WILLIAMS AS CHARLES DICKENS

(24 performances)

Readings from the works of Charles Dickens by Emlyn Williams. Produced by Sol Hurok at the Bijou Theatre, April 20, 1953.

BLEAK HOUSE

Evening performances: April 20, 21, 23, 24, 27, 29; May 2, 4, 5, 7, 8. Matinées: April 22; May 2, 6.

Mr. Williams' dramatization of the Dickens novel, in which he impersonates the following characters:

Miss Flite, a suppliant
Lady Dedlock
Sir Leicester Dedlock
Mr. Tulkinghorn, his lawyer
Esther Summerson
Mr. Guppy, a lawyer's clerk
Mr. Kenge, a solicitor
Mrs. Jellyby, a lady who neglects her home
Caddy, her daughter
Peepy, her small son
Mr. Jellyby
Mr. Krook, an old shop-keeper
Mr. Jarndyce, Esther's guardian

Mr. Harold Skimpole
Mr. Snagsby, a law-stationer
Guster, maidservant to the Snagsbys
Mrs. Perkins
Mrs. Piper
A Coroner
Little Swills, a comic vocalist
Jo, a street-crossing sweeper
Mrs. Pardiggle, a member of many committees
A Brickmaker
Lord Boodle
Miss Volumnia Dedlock

The Hon. Bob Stables
The Rev. Mr. Chadband
Mrs. Chadband
A Police Constable
Inspector Bucket, a detective officer
Mademoiselle Hortense

Mr. Bayham Badger
Mrs. Bayham Badger
Prince Turveydrop
Mr. Turveydrop, his father
Mr. Weevle, Mr. Guppy's friend

MIXED BILL

Evening performances: April 22, 25, 28, 30; May 1, 6, 9.
Matinées: April 25, 29; May 9.

A solo performance of scenes from Dickens' novels and stories.

Program—

"MOVING IN SOCIETY"
  Scenes from *Our Mutual Friend* (1866)
"PAUL"
  Scenes from *Dombey and Son* (1848)
"MR. BOB SAWYER GIVES A BACHELOR PARTY"
  An Episode from *Pickwick Papers* (1837)
"THE SIGNAL MAN"
  A Ghost Story from *Christmas Stories* (1866)
"MR. CHOPS"
  A Story from *Christmas Stories* (1858)
"THE FANCY BALL"
  An Episode from *A Tale of Two Cities* (1859)

(Closed May 9, 1953)

THE PINK ELEPHANT

(5 performances)

Farce in two acts by John G. Fuller. Produced by Eugene Paul, William I. Kaufman, and Blair Walliser at The Playhouse, April 22, 1953.

Cast of characters—

Sonny Bannerman	Bruce Gordon
Priscilla	Joel Wesley
Jerry Elliot	Steve Allen
Bellhop	Lee Krieger
Lee Meredith	Patricia Barry
Peggy Boyd	Jean Casto
Two-Gun Anderson	Arthur Tell
Evans	Martin Tarby
Gilbert Parker	David White
Henry C. Griffin	Howard Smith
Reporter	John O'Hare
Second Bellhop	Jon Richards
Ed Glennon	Heywood Hale Broun
Waiter	Jon Richards
Night Watchman	Charles Pratt
Bubbles LeTroy	Roslyn Valero
A Visitor	Martin Tarby
Maid	Suki Rayner

The action takes place in rooms 718-720-722 of the Hotel Francis Parkman in Kansas City. The time is the present. Act I.—Scene 1— About midnight on a Saturday night before a special meeting of the Republican National Committee. Scene 2—Several hours later. Act

II.—Scene 1—The following evening.   Scene 2—Later that night.
Scene 3—Eight-thirty the following morning.
        Staged by Harry Ellerbe; setting and lighting by Ralph Alswang;
costumes by Guy Kent.

Stock farce about Republican National Committee doings—sexual and political, social and unsocial—in a Kansas City hotel. It tosses gags about as freely as hotel guests toss towels—and often in the same smudged, damp or crumpled shape.

(Closed April 25, 1953)

MEN OF DISTINCTION

(4 performances)

Comedy in three acts by Richard Condon. Produced by Chandler Cowles and Martin Gabel at the Forty-eighth Street Theatre, April 30, 1953.

Cast of characters—

Mayor Thomas Quinlan	Donald Foster
Inspector Dennis Mannion	Rex Williams
Pringle	Vera Fuller Mellish
Peter Hogarth	Robert Preston
Frobisher	Mort Marshall
Claudette Chalfonte	Diana Herbert
Judy Chalfonte	Jean Carson
Carleton Pelter	Chandler Cowles
Edgar Grassthal	Orson Bean
Aunt Florence	Fran Carlon
Edna	Alma Slocum
Barbara Edison	Fran Keegan
Doris Commodore	Hollis Irving
Marvin Flynch	Ralph Bunker
August Volpone	Martin Ritt
Daniel Gaffney	David Burns
Melissa Marguery	K. K. Kensington
Dolores Biltmore	Dulcy Jordan

        The action takes place in the sitting room of Peter Hogarth's mansion in the month of May.
        Staged by Martin Gabel; settings and costumes by David Ffolkes.

A cheating-cheaters comedy centering in New York's vice industry and involving politicians, public-relations big shots, wealthy playboys and others. It followed a classical formula with far less than classical skill.

(Closed May 2, 1953)

CAN-CAN

(28 performances)
(Continued)

Musical comedy in two acts by Cole Porter; book by Abe Burrows. Produced by Cy Feuer and Ernest H. Martin at the Shubert Theatre, May 7, 1953.

Cast of characters—

Bailiff .... David Collyer
Registrar .... Michael Cavallaro
Policemen .... Joe Cusanelli, Jon Silo, Arthur Rubin,
            Ralph Beaumont, Michael DeMarco, Socrates Birsky
Judge Paul Barriere .... C. K. Alexander
Court President, Henri Marceaux .... David Thomas
Judge Aristide Forestier .... Peter Cookson
Claudine .... Gwen Verdon
Gabrielle .... Mary Anne Cohan
Marie .... Beverly Purvin
Celestine .... Jean Kraemer
Hilaire Jussac .... Erik Rhodes
Boris Adzinidzinadze .... Hans Conried
Hercule .... Robert Penn
Theophile .... Phil Leeds
Etienne .... Richard Purdy
Waiter .... Clarence Hoffman
La Mome Pistache .... Lilo
Second Waiter .... Ferdinand Hilt
Café Waiter .... Jon Silo
Café Customer .... Joe Cusanelli
Jailer .... Deedee Wood
Model .... Pat Turner
Mimi .... Dania Krupska
Customers .... Sheila Arnold, David Thomas, Ferdinand Hilt
Doctor .... Michael Cavallaro
Second .... Arthur Rubin
Prosecutor .... Ferdinand Hilt
    Dancers: Meredith Baylis, Shelah Hackett, Ina Hahn, Dania Krupska, Vera Lee, Beverly Tassoni, Pat Turner, Ruth Vernon, Deedee Wood, Ralph Beaumont, Socrates Birsky, Michael DeMarco, Al Lanti, Bert May, Tom Panko, Arthur Partington, Eddie Phillips, Michael Scrittorale.
    The action takes place in Paris, 1893.
    Staged by Abe Burrows; dances and musical numbers staged by Michael Kidd; settings and lighting by Jo Mielziner; costumes by Motley; musical direction by Milton Rosenstock; orchestrations by Philip J. Lang; dance music arranged by Genevieve Pitot.

Principal musical numbers—

ACT I

"Maidens Typical of France" .... The Laundresses
"Never Give Anything Away" .... Pistache
"C'est Magnifique" .... Pistache, Aristide
Quadrille .... Claudine, Laundresses and Friends, with Bert May
"Come Along with Me" .... Jussac and Boris
"Live and Let Live" .... Pistache
"I Am in Love" .... Aristide
"If You Loved Me Truly" .... Boris, Claudine, Theophile, Hercule, Etienne, Gabrielle, Celestine and Marie
    "Montmart'" .... Singing Ensemble

THE GARDEN OF EDEN

Eve ....Claudine
Inchworms ....Ina Hahn, Socrates Birsky
Flamingos ....Shelah Hackett, Arthur Partington
Kangaroos ....Beverly Tassoni, Michael Scrittorale
Penguins ....Eddie Phillips, Deedee Wood
Sea Horses ....Ruth Vernon, Tom Panko
Frogs ....Vera Lee, Al Lanti
Leopards ....Pat Turner, Ralph Beaumont
Snake ....Bert May

"Allez-Vous En" ....Pistache

ACT II

"Never, Never Be an Artist" ..Boris, Theophile, Etienne and Model
"It's All Right with Me" ....Aristide
"Every Man Is a Stupid Man" ....Pistache
The Apaches ....Claudine and Dancers, with Ralph Beaumont
"I Love Paris" ....Pistache
"Can-Can" ....Pistache, Claudine and Laundresses
Finale ....Entire Company

ME AND JULIET

(4 performances)
(Continued)

Musical comedy in two acts; music by Richard Rodgers; book
and lyrics by Oscar Hammerstein II.   Produced by Rodgers and
Hammerstein at the Majestic Theatre, May 28, 1953.

Cast of characters—

EMPLOYMENT IN THE THEATRE

George, 2nd Assistant Stage Manager ....Randy Hall
Sidney, Electrician ....Edwin Philips
Jeanie, Chorus Singer ....Isabel Bigley
Herbie, Candy Counter Boy ....Jackie Kelk
Chris, Rehearsal Piano Player ....Barbara Carroll
Milton, Drummer ....Herb Wasserman
Stu, Bass Fiddle Player ....Joe Shulman
Michael, a Chorus Boy ....Michael King
Bob, Electrician ....Mark Dawson
Larry, Assistant Stage Manager ....Bill Hayes
Mac, Stage Manager ....Ray Walston
Monica, Chorus Dancer ....Patty Ann Jackson
Ruby, Company Manager ....Joe Lautner
Charlie (Me), Featured Lead ....Arthur Maxwell
Dario, Conductor ....George S. Irving
Lily (Juliet), Singing Principal ....Helena Scott
Jim (Don Juan), Principal Dancer ....Bob Fortier
Susie (Carmen), Principal Dancer ....Svetlana McLee
Voice of Mr. Harrison, Producer ....Henry Hamilton
Voice of Miss Davenport, Choreographer ....Deborah Remsen
Hilda, an aspirant for a dancing part ....Norma Thornton
Marcia, another aspirant for a dancing part ....Thelma Tadlock
Betty, successor to Susie as Principal Dancer ......Joan McCracken
Buzz, Principal Dancer ....Buzz Miller
Ralph, Alley Dancer ....Ralph Linn
Miss Oxford, a Bit Player ....Gwen Harmon
Sadie, an Usher ....Francine Bond
Mildred, another Usher ....Lorraine Havercroft
A Theatre Patron ....Barbara Lee Smith
Another Theatre Patron ....Susan Lovell

Ensemble: Company, Stage Crew, Audience.

Dancing Ensemble: Francine Bond, Betty Buday, Penny Ann Green, Lorraine Havercroft, Patty Ann Jackson, Helene Keller, Lucia Lambert, Harriet Leigh, Sonya Lindgren, Elizabeth Logue, Shirley MacLaine, Cheryl Parker, Dorothy Silverherz, Thelma Tadlock, Norma Thornton, Janyce Ann Wagner, Rosemary Williams, Lance Avant, Grant Delaney, John George, Jack Konzal, Ralph Linn, Eddie Pfeiffer, Augustine Rodriguez, Bob St. Clair, Bill Weber.

Singing Ensemble: Adele Castle, Gwen Harmon, Susan Lovell, Theresa Mari, Georgia Reed, Deborah Remsen, Thelma Scott, Barbara Lee Smith, Jack Drummond, John Ford, Henry Hamilton, Richard Hermany, Warren Kemmerling, Michael King, Larry Laurence, Jack Rains.

The action takes place in and around the theatre in which *Me and Juliet* is currently playing.

Staged by George Abbott; scenery and lighting by Jo Mielziner; costumes designed by Irene Sharaff; vocal and orchestral arrangements by Don Walker; musical director, Salvatore Dell'Isola; dances and musical numbers staged by Robert Alton.

Principal musical numbers—

ACT I

"A Very Special Day" ....Jeanie and Trio
"That's the Way It Happens" ....Jeanie and Trio
Dance Impromptu ....Chorus, George and Trio
Overture to *Me and Juliet* ....Dario and Orchestra
Opening of *Me and Juliet* ....Lily, Jim, Susie and Charlie
"Marriage Type Love" ....Charlie, Lily and Singers
"Keep It Gay" ....Bob, Jim and Chorus
"The Big, Black Giant" ....Larry
"No Other Love" ....Jeanie and Larry
Dance ....Ralph, Francine and Elizabeth
"It's Me" ....Betty and Jeanie
First Act Finale of *Me and Juliet* ....Lily, Betty, Charlie Jim, Jeanie and Chorus

ACT II

"Intermission Talk" ....Herbie and Chorus
"It Feels Good" ....Bob
Sequence in Second Act of *Me and Juliet* ......Charlie, Jim, Lily and Dancers
"The Baby You Love" ....Lily and Dancers
"We Deserve Each Other" ....Betty, Jim and Chorus
"I'm Your Girl" ....Jeanie and Larry
Second Act Finale of *Me and Juliet*...........Charlie, Lily, Betty, Jim and Chorus
Finale of Our Play ....Entire Company

OFF BROADWAY

By Garrison P. Sherwood

The Off Broadway theatre continues to serve a very useful purpose. It gives new producers, directors, writers and actors a chance to have their work seen—and they all hope, of course, to attract enough attention to get "On Broadway." Occasionally this Off Broadway theatre brings forth a Geraldine Page and this gives them all a shot in the arm, so to speak, and an added enthusiasm to continue. More times than not, perhaps, they give good productions and in these days of sky-high Broadway production costs they are a real service to the theatre for thus providing so many people a chance to try their wings.

Probably one of the best known of these Off Broadway groups is The Circle in the Square. It is from here that the aforementioned Geraldine Page stepped to a starring role on Broadway as the lead in "Mid-summer." The Circle put on Daniel Polis' "Fortress of Glass" while its highly successful production of "Summer and Smoke" took a vacation. When the latter returned, it remained until mid-April and was followed by Truman Capote's "The Grass Harp."

The Circle has also been presenting a series of Sunday afternoons with well-known authors reading from their own works or commenting on scenes from their plays put on by the group. Among those appearing during the season were: Tennessee Williams, Lillian Hellman, William Inge, Archibald MacLeish, Arthur Miller, Theodore Roethke, Dorothy Parker and Truman Capote. They also did "The Barrier" by Langston Hughes, featuring Muriel Rahn, and Kurt Weill's "Down in the Valley," libretto by Arnold Sundgaard, which, by the way, had striking and authentic costumes by Bobb Nichols—quite an impressive series of Sunday afternoons.

Originals Only, continuing in their new location, presented "Gordon Reilly" by Charles Best, "Love in Our Time" by Anita Granniss and two musicals, "Dakota" and "Surprise Package," the last two by Tom Hill with music by Frances Ziffer, Hortense Belson and Hardy Wieder. All of these proved interesting, especially the first-named.

*Emilie Stevens, Gloria Scott Backé, Bill Goodwin, Stuart Lyons, Lee
Richard and Geraldine Page in "Summer and Smoke"*

Down at the Provincetown Playhouse they did Edward Caulfield's
"First Love" and it was at this theatre that The American Lyric
Theatre presented "Hey, You" with music by Norman Meranus and
lyrics by June Carroll of "New Faces" fame. Also done at this
house was "Noone" by Gil Oriovitz and a production of "The
Rivals."

At the Greenwich Mews Theatre Bernard Shaw's "Widowers'
Houses" had quite a run and this was followed with "Monday's
Heroes" by Les Pine.

William de Lys poured a lot of time and energy AND considerable
money into remodeling the Hudson Theatre down on Christopher
Street. He opened it, October 28th, as the Theatre de Lys with a
musical "Frankie and Johnny" by John Huston, songs by Hilda
Tayor and Eddie Safranski and incidental music by Irwin A.
Bazelon. It closed October 29th.

In the Spring ANTA sponsored the Touring Players Company at this theatre in "Which Way Is Home?", three views of Americans taken from the writings of Stephen Vincent Benét, Gertrude Stein and Mark Lodge. It did not linger long.

Up in Harlem at the New York Elks Community Theatre a Negro group put on a bill of three plays—"Alice in Wonder" by Ossie Davis, "The Other Foot" by Julian Mayfield and "A World Full of Men" also by Mr. Mayfield. They were well received, "Alice in Wonder" getting especially good notices and the acting throughout proved superior. There should certainly be a place in Harlem for a permanent Negro group doing serious production. Ossie Davis also had his "The Big Ideal" produced later in the season at Yugoslav Hall.

At the Barbizon-Plaza The Yiddish Theatre presented "The Devil in Boston" by N. Buckwald, adapted from the play by Lion Feuchtwanger. As directed by Morris Carnovsky it proved to be a strong play on the same subject as "The Crucible."

In January, at the New York Joan of Arc Center, W. S. Gilbert's "Thespis" had a hearing. Arthur Sullivan's music for this play was lost in a fire many years ago and the score for this production was provided by Frank Miller.

The Blackfriars' Guild began their season with "Faith and Prudence" by Lottie Michelson and in February put on "Angelic Doctor" by Brendan Larnen. So successful was this latter play that it remained throughout the balance of the Blackfriars' season, ruling out the possibility of a third production.

Current Stages, a group actually just a stone's throw from Broadway at 1129 Sixth Avenue, started off with a double bill consisting of "No Exit" and "The Marriage Proposal" followed later in the season by "Legend of Lovers" and still later with "You Never Can Tell" by the ever-popular George Bernard Shaw. Then in the Spring they relinquished their stage to a new group, Trio Production, who put on O'Casey's "The Plough and the Stars" which was successful enough to move to the larger Cherry Lane Theatre down in the Village.

And speaking of The Cherry Lane Theatre, The Living Theatre did "Ubu, the King" by Alfred Jarry, translated by Jane Warren and Arnold Devree with John Ashbury's "The Heroes" as a curtain-raiser. These were done early in the season.

Then of course there is The Equity Library Theatre which does fifteen productions every year. This year's list seems to me slightly more impressive than most. The plays, in the order presented, were: "Getting Married," "Hotel Universe," "The Glass Menagerie," "As

You Like It," "The World We Make," "Winterset," "Ah, Wilderness!", "Man and Superman," "Finian's Rainbow," "Mamba's Daughters," "Within the Gates," "The Tragical History of Dr. Faustus," "Deep Are the Roots," "The Sea Gull" and "Hobson's Choice." The restrictions of the Lennox Hill Theatre's stage and the limitations of the ELT budget make the production end of this project such as to discourage all but the most courageous. Yet some of the sets and costumes were the most imaginative and charming seen in New York this year. "The Glass Menagerie" set was startling in its originality, simplicity and effectiveness. I have never seen it better set. Robert Soule should take a deep bow for this as should Mildred Jackson for her splendid lighting. Robert Galster's sets for "Man and Superman" were also exceptional, as were the costumes of Jean Vaughan. Some of the performances were outstanding and the direction uniformly excellent. This all proves, if proving an accepted fact is necessary, that given the plays, the opportunity and a theatre not topheavy with production costs, good, interesting and imaginative productions can be presented to a public longing for just such theatre at a price they can afford.

There were several other ventures—such as The Lighthouse Theatre (productions by the blind). They did "Mrs. Moonlight" for one; a revue called "Merry-Go-Round" at the Amato Opera House; and "Three in One" by Ken Parker at Jan Hus House.

A glance over this entire list shows that there is as much activity off Broadway as there is on. And this list does not include the many fine productions given by the New York colleges. We believe that all of these productions take on an importance far greater than is at first apparent because of the experience and the opportunity afforded the theatre worker. The Off Broadway theatres can be justly proud of their contribution. They may be as proud of showing hundreds that the theatre is *not* for them as well as helping develop those who really have what it takes.

VARIETY'S TABULATION
OF FINANCIAL HITS AND FLOPS

HITS

Deep Blue Sea
Dial "M" for Murder
Dickens Readings (Emlyn Williams)
Evening with Beatrice Lillie
Fifth Season
John Brown's Body
Love of Four Colonels

Millionairess
Picnic
Seven Year Itch
Time of the Cuckoo
Time Out for Ginger
Wish You Were Here
Wonderful Town

STATUS NOT YET DEFINITE

Can-Can
Hazel Flagg

Me and Juliet
My 3 Angels

FAILURES

Bat
Be Your Age
Bernadine
Buttrio Square
Camino Real
Children's Hour
Climate of Eden
Crucible
Date with April
Emperor's Clothes
Gambler
Gilbert & Sullivan (Chartock)
Grey-eyed People
Horses in Midstream
In Any Language
I've Got Sixpence

Maggie
Men of Distinction
Mid-Summer
Misalliance
Mr. Pickwick
My Darlin' Aida
On Borrowed Time
Pink Elephant
Room Service
Sacred Flame
Seagulls over Sorrento
See the Jaguar
Touchstone
Two's Company
Whistler's Grandmother

NON-COMMERCIAL

Barrault-Renaud Co.
Greek National Theatre
Love's Labour's Lost

Merchant of Venice
Porgy and Bess

CLOSED OUT OF TOWN

Anonymous Lover
Certain Joy
Fasten Your Belts
Fig Leaf
Intruder

Josephine
Masquerade
Rise by Sin
Strike a Match
Suspects

Holdovers from 1951–52 Season, Since Clarified

HITS

Male Animal

New Faces

FAILURES

Gigi
Of Thee I Sing
Paint Your Wagon

Sunday Breakfast
Three Wishes for Jamie
Top Banana

STATISTICAL SUMMARY

Plays	Number Performances	
First Lady (Revival)	16	(Closed June 8, 1952)
I Am a Camera	262	(Closed July 12, 1952)
Mrs. McThing	350	(Closed January 10, 1953)
New Faces of 1952	365	(Closed March 28, 1953)
Of Thee I Sing (Revival)	72	(Closed July 5, 1952)
Paint Your Wagon	289	(Closed July 19, 1952)
Pal Joey	540	(Closed April 18, 1953)
Point of No Return	364	(Closed November 22, 1952)
Stalag 17	472	(Closed June 21, 1952)
Sunday Breakfast	16	(Closed June 8, 1952)
The Fourposter	632	(Closed May 2, 1953)
The Male Animal (Revival)	317	(Closed January 31, 1953)
The Moon Is Blue	924	(Closed May 30, 1953)
Three Wishes for Jamie	91	(Closed June 7, 1952)
Top Banana	350	(Closed September 27, 1952)

LONG RUNS ON BROADWAY

To June 1, 1953

(Plays marked with asterisk were still playing June 1, 1953)

Plays	Number Performances	Plays	Number Performances
Life with Father	3,224	Three Men on a Horse	835
Tobacco Road	3,182	Where's Charlie?	792
Abie's Irish Rose	2,327	The Ladder	789
Oklahoma!	2,248	State of the Union	765
Harvey	1,775	The First Year	760
* South Pacific	1,694	Death of a Salesman	742
Born Yesterday	1,642	Sons o' Fun	742
The Voice of the Turtle	1,557	The Man Who Came to Dinner	739
Arsenic and Old Lace	1,444	Call Me Mister	734
Hellzapoppin	1,404	High Button Shoes	727
Angel Street	1,295	Finian's Rainbow	725
Lightnin'	1,291	Claudia	722
Mister Roberts	1,157	The Gold Diggers	720
Annie Get Your Gun	1,147	I Remember Mama	714
Pins and Needles	1,108	Junior Miss	710
Kiss Me, Kate	1,070	Seventh Heaven	704
* Guys and Dolls	1,056	Peg o' My Heart	692
Anna Lucasta	957	The Children's Hour	691
Kiss and Tell	957	Dead End	687
The Moon Is Blue	924	The Lion and the Mouse	686
* The King and I	908	Dear Ruth	683
Carousel	890	East Is West	680
Hats Off to Ice	889	The Doughgirls	671
Follow the Girls	882	Irene	670
The Bat	867	Boy Meets Girl	669
My Sister Eileen	865	Blithe Spirit	657
White Cargo	864	The Women	657
Song of Norway	860	A Trip to Chinatown	657
A Streetcar Named Desire	855	Bloomer Girl	654
You Can't Take It with You	837	Rain	648

313

Plays	*Number Performances*	Plays	*Number Performances*
Call Me Madam	644	Ziegfeld Follies	553
Janie	642	Floradora	553
The Green Pastures	640	Good News	551
The Fourposter	632	Let's Face It	547
Is Zat So?	618	Within the Law	541
The Happy Time	614	The Music Master	540
Separate Rooms	613	Pal Joey	540
Affairs of State	610	What a Life	538
Star and Garter	609	The Red Mill	531
The Student Prince	608	The Boomerang	522
Broadway	603	Rosalinda	521
Adonis	603	Chauve Souris	520
Street Scene	601	Blackbirds	518
Kiki	600	Sunny	517
A Society Circus	596	Victoria Regina	517
Blossom Time	592	The Vagabond King	511
The Two Mrs. Carrolls	585	The New Moon	509
Detective Story	581	Shuffle Along	504
Brigadoon	581	Up in Central Park	504
Brother Rat	577	Carmen Jones	503
Show Boat	572	The Member of the Wedding	501
The Show-Off	571		
Sally	570	Personal Appearance	501
One Touch of Venus	567	Panama Hattie	501
Happy Birthday	564	Bird in Hand	500
The Glass Menagerie	561	Sailor, Beware!	500
Rose Marie	557	Room Service	500
Strictly Dishonorable	557	Tomorrow the World	500

NEW YORK DRAMA CRITICS CIRCLE AWARDS

At their annual Spring meeting, the New York Drama Critics Circle voted William Inge's "Picnic" the best new American play of the season, with Arthur Miller's "The Crucible" as runner-up. As the season's best foreign play the Circle chose Peter Ustinov's "Love of Four Colonels"; as its best musical, "Wonderful Town."
Circle awards have been—

1935-36—Winterset, by Maxwell Anderson
1936-37—High Tor, by Maxwell Anderson
1937-38—Of Mice and Men, by John Steinbeck
1938-39—No award.
1939-40—The Time of Your Life, by William Saroyan
1940-41—Watch on the Rhine, by Lillian Hellman
1941-42—No award.
1942-43—The Patriots, by Sidney Kingsley
1943-44—No award.
1944-45—The Glass Menagerie, by Tennessee Williams
1945-46—No award.
1946-47—All My Sons, by Arthur Miller
1947-48—A Streetcar Named Desire, by Tennessee Williams
1948-49—Death of a Salesman, by Arthur Miller
1949-50—The Member of the Wedding, by Carson McCullers
1950-51—Darkness at Noon, by Sidney Kingsley
1951-52—I Am a Camera, by John van Druten
1952-53—Picnic, by William Inge

PULITZER PRIZE WINNERS

For the fourth time, in the eighteen years that both awards have been made, the Pulitzer Prize went to the same play as the Critics Circle Award. Besides "Picnic," the double award has gone to "The Time of Your Life," "A Streetcar Named Desire" and "Death of a Salesman."

Pulitzer awards have been—

1917-18—Why Marry?, by Jesse Lynch Williams
1918-19—No award.
1919-20—Beyond the Horizon, by Eugene O'Neill
1920-21—Miss Lulu Bett, by Zona Gale
1921-22—Anna Christie, by Eugene O'Neill
1922-23—Icebound, by Owen Davis
1923-24—Hell-bent fer Heaven, by Hatcher Hughes
1924-25—They Knew What They Wanted, by Sidney Howard
1925-26—Craig's Wife, by George Kelly
1926-27—In Abraham's Bosom, by Paul Green
1927-28—Strange Interlude, by Eugene O'Neill
1928-29—Street Scene, by Elmer Rice
1929-30—The Green Pastures, by Marc Connelly
1930-31—Alison's House, by Susan Glaspell
1931-32—Of Thee I Sing, by George S. Kaufman, Morrie Ryskind, Ira and George Gershwin
1932-33—Both Your Houses, by Maxwell Anderson
1933-34—Men in White, by Sidney Kingsley
1934-35—The Old Maid, by Zoë Akins
1935-36—Idiot's Delight, by Robert E. Sherwood
1936-37—You Can't Take It with You, by Moss Hart and George S. Kaufman
1937-38—Our Town, by Thornton Wilder
1938-39—Abe Lincoln in Illinois, by Robert E. Sherwood
1939-40—The Time of Your Life, by William Saroyan
1940-41—There Shall Be No Night, by Robert E. Sherwood
1941-42—No award.
1942-43—The Skin of Our Teeth, by Thornton Wilder
1943-44—No award.

BOOKS ON THE THEATRE

1952-1953

Aeschylus. *Oresteia*. Translated by Richmond Lattimore. University of Chicago Press. $2.50.
A version of Aeschylus' great trilogy by one of the most distinguished of modern translators.

Axelrod, George. *The Seven Year Itch*. Random House. $2.50.

Bentley, Eric. *In Search of Theater*. Knopf. $6.00.
Provocative and wide-ranging essays on plays, playwrights, dramatic theory and theatre technique.

Boas, Frederick. *An Introduction to Eighteenth Century Drama, 1700-1780*. Oxford University Press. $5.00.
Includes estimates of many minor playwrights.

Bowyer, John Wilson. *The Celebrated Mrs. Centlivre*. Duke University Press. $4.50.
The career of the well-known early 18th-century playwright.

Chapman, John (Editor). *Best Plays of 1951-1952*. Dodd, Mead. $4.00.

Chase, Mary. *Harvey*. Oxford University Press. $3.00.

Chekhov, Michael. *To the Actor*. Harper & Bros. $3.00.
On the technique of acting.

Cole, Toby & Chinoy, Helen Krich. *Directing the Play*. Bobbs-Merrill. $4.00.
A source book of stagecraft. First-hand directional comment—both theory and practice—from Antoine, Appia, Gordon Craig and Shaw to Barrault, Logan, Kazan and Clurman.

Corneille. *The Chief Plays*. Translated by Lucy Lockert. Princeton University Press. $5.00.
Blank verse versions of *The Cid, Horace, Cinna, Polyeucte, Rodogune* and *Nicomede*.

Downer, Alan S. *Fifty Years of American Drama*. Henry Regnery. $2.50.

Survey of plays, playwrights, tendencies and techniques between 1900 and 1950.

Duckworth, George E. *The Nature of Roman Comedy.* Princeton University Press. $7.50.
Solid historical and critical survey with a final chapter on the influence of Plautus and Terence on English comedy.

Durland, Frances Caldwell. *Creative Dramatics for Children: A Practical Manual.* The Antioch Press. $1.50 (paper) $2.75 (cloth).

Ervin, St. John. *My Brother Tom: A Play in Three Acts.* Macmillan. $1.50.

Field and Chodorov. *Wonderful Town.* Random House. $2.50.
With music by Leonard Bernstein and lyrics by Betty Comden and Adolph Green.

Fry, Christopher. *An Experience of Critics and The Approach to Dramatic Criticism.* Oxford University Press. $2.25.
Lively exchange between Fry and a number of English drama critics. Prologue by Alec Guinness.

Fujimura, Thomas H. *The Restoration Comedy of Art.* Princeton University Press. $4.00.

Granville, Wilfred. *The Theatre Dictionary.* Philosophical Library. $5.00.
Useful compilation of British and American terms in drama, opera and ballet.

Green, Abel (Editor). *The Spice of Variety.* Holt. $3.50.
Interesting omnibus of material from *Variety*.

Gross, Edwin and Nathalie. *Teen Theater.* Whittlesey House. $3.25.

Hart, Moss. *Climate of Eden.* Random House. $2.50.

Inge, William. *Picnic.* Random House. $2.50.
The Pulitzer and Critics Circle prize play.

Katkov, Norman. *Fabulous Fanny: The Story of Fanny Brice.* Knopf. $3.95.

Kirkland, Jack, and Caldwell, Erskine. *Tobacco Road.* Duell, Sloan & Pierce. $2.50.

Knott, Frederick. *Dial "M" for Murder*. Random House. $2.50.

Kronenberger, Louis. *The Thread of Laughter*. Knopf. $4.50.
English stage comedy from Ben Jonson to Maugham.

Laurents, Arthur. *The Time of the Cuckoo*. Random House.
$2.50.

Le Gallienne, Eva. *With a Quiet Heart: An Autobiography*. Viking
Press. $4.50.
Pleasantly told reminiscences, personal and theatrical, of the last
twenty years. A kind of continuation of *At 33*.

Lynch, James J. *Box, Pit and Gallery*. University of California Press. $5.00.
  A valuable study of "stage and society in Johnson's London."

Mander, Raymond, and Mitchenson, Joe. (Edited by Herbert Marshall.) *Hamlet Through the Ages: A Pictorial Record from 1709*. Macmillan. $7.00.
  Pictorial (largely photographic) miscellany, 9 wing—scene by scene—*Hamlet's* production history.

Mayorga, Margaret (Editor). *Best Short Plays of 1952-1953*. Dodd, Mead. $3.00.

*Nigel Green,
Estelle Winwood,
Clive Revill,
George Howe,
Nydia Westman
and Sarah
Marshall in
"Mr. Pickwick"*

Miller, Arthur. *The Crucible*. Viking Press. $2.75.

Miller, Helen Louise. *Holiday Plays for Teen-Agers*. Plays, Inc. $3.50.

Morehouse, Ward. *Just the Other Day: From Yellow Pines to Broadway*. McGraw-Hill. $3.50.
Engaging reminiscences by the well-known critic and columnist.

Nathan, Robert. *Jezebel's Husband and The Sleeping Beauty: Two Plays*. Knopf. $3.00.

Nicoll, Allardyce. *Shakespeare: An Introduction to His Works*. Oxford University Press. $2.50.
Short survey of Shakespeare's achievements and of some of the theories about them.

Nicoll, Allardyce (Editor). *Shakespeare Survey 5*. Cambridge University Press. $3.00.
Latest volume in this annual series, with articles by Christopher Fry, S. L. Bethell, Peter Alexander and others.

O'Casey, Sean. *Rose and Crown*. Macmillan. $4.75.
Volume V of O'Casey's distinguished autobiography.

Reed, Robert Rentoul, Jr. *Bedlam on the Jacobean Stage*. Harvard University Press. $3.50.
A study of melancholy and madness in Webster, Tourneur, Middleton, Ford and others.

Ruggles, Eleanor. *Prince of Players: Edwin Booth*. Norton. $4.50.
A biography of Edwin Booth.

Shaw, Bernard. *Selected Prose*. (Selected by Diarmuid Russell.) Dodd, Mead. $6.50.
Very valuable 1000 page compilation with over 300 pages that treat of the theatre.

Sprague, Arthur Colby. *Shakespearian Players and Performances*. Harvard University Press. $4.50.
How great performers—Garrick, Mrs. Siddons, Kean, Booth, etc.—played such particular roles as Lear, Lady Macbeth, Othello, Iago.

Stephens, Frances. *Theatre World Annual (London), Volume III*. Macmillan. $3.75.

van Druten, John. *Playwright at Work*. Harper & Bros. $3.00.
   A well-known playwright's engaging and stimulating discussion
of his craft.

Ward, Winifred (Editor). *Stories to Dramatize*. Children's Theatre Press.

Wilde, Oscar. *Five Famous Plays*. Scribner's. $3.50.
   The four famous comedies and *Salome,* in both French and Lord
Alfred Douglas's English translation.

Yeats, W. B. *Collected Plays of W. B. Yeats*. Macmillan. $5.00.
   New Edition.

Young, Stanley. *Mr. Pickwick*. Random House. $2.50.

PREVIOUS VOLUMES OF BEST PLAYS

Plays chosen to represent the theatre seasons from 1899 to 1952 are as follows:

1899-1909

BARBARA FRIETCHIE, by Clyde Fitch. Life Publishing Co.
THE CLIMBERS, by Clyde Fitch. Macmillan.
IF I WERE KING, by Justin Huntly McCarthy. Samuel French.
THE DARLING OF THE GODS, by David Belasco. Little, Brown.
THE COUNTY CHAIRMAN, by George Ade. Samuel French.
LEAH KLESCHNA, by C. M. S. McLellan. Samuel French.
THE SQUAW MAN, by Edwin Milton Royle.
THE GREAT DIVIDE, by William Vaughn Moody. Samuel French.
THE WITCHING HOUR, by Augustus Thomas. Samuel French.
THE MAN FROM HOME, by Booth Tarkington and Harry Leon Wilson. Samuel French.

1909-1919

THE EASIEST WAY, by Eugene Walter. G. W. Dillingham and Houghton Mifflin.
MRS. BUMPSTEAD-LEIGH, by Harry James Smith. Samuel French.
DISRAELI, by Louis N. Parker. Dodd, Mead.
ROMANCE, by Edward Sheldon. Macmillan.
SEVEN KEYS TO BALDPATE, by George M. Cohan. Published by Bobbs-Merrill as a novel by Earl Derr Biggers; as a play by Samuel French.
ON TRIAL, by Elmer Reizenstein. Samuel French.
THE UNCHASTENED WOMAN, by Louis Kaufman Anspacher. Harcourt, Brace and Howe.
GOOD GRACIOUS ANNABELLE, by Clare Kummer. Samuel French.
WHY MARRY?, by Jesse Lynch Williams. Scribner.
JOHN FERGUSON, by St. John Ervine. Macmillan.

1919-1920

ABRAHAM LINCOLN, by John Drinkwater. Houghton Mifflin.
CLARENCE, by Booth Tarkington. Samuel French.
BEYOND THE HORIZON, by Eugene G. O'Neill. Boni & Liveright.

DÉCLASSÉE, by Zoë Akins. Liveright, Inc.
THE FAMOUS MRS. FAIR, by James Forbes. Samuel French.
THE JEST, by Sem Benelli. (American adaptation by Edward Sheldon.)
JANE CLEGG, by St. John Ervine. Henry Holt.
MAMMA'S AFFAIR, by Rachel Barton Butler. Samuel French.
WEDDING BELLS, by Salisbury Field. Samuel French.
ADAM AND EVA, by George Middleton and Guy Bolton. Samuel French.

1920-1921

DEBURAU, adapted from the French of Sacha Guitry by H. Granville Barker. Putnam.
THE FIRST YEAR, by Frank Craven. Samuel French.
ENTER MADAME, by Gilda Varesi and Dolly Byrne. Putnam.
THE GREEN GODDESS, by William Archer. Knopf.
LILIOM, by Ferenc Molnar. Boni & Liveright.
MARY ROSE, by James M. Barrie. Scribner.
NICE PEOPLE, by Rachel Crothers. Scribner.
THE BAD MAN, by Porter Emerson Browne. Putnam.
THE EMPEROR JONES, by Eugene G. O'Neill. Boni & Liveright.
THE SKIN GAME, by John Galsworthy. Scribner.

1921-1922

ANNA CHRISTIE, by Eugene G. O'Neill. Boni & Liveright.
A BILL OF DIVORCEMENT, by Clemence Dane. Macmillan.
DULCY, by George S. Kaufman and Marc Connelly. Putnam.
HE WHO GETS SLAPPED, adapted from the Russian of Leonid Andreyev by Gregory Zilboorg. Brentano's.
SIX CYLINDER LOVE, by William Anthony McGuire.
THE HERO, by Gilbert Emery.
THE DOVER ROAD, by Alan Alexander Milne. Samuel French.
AMBUSH, by Arthur Richman.
THE CIRCLE, by William Somerset Maugham.
THE NEST, by Paul Geraldy and Grace George.

1922-1923

RAIN, by John Colton and Clemence Randolph. Liveright, Inc.
LOYALTIES, by John Galsworthy. Scribner.
ICEBOUND, by Owen Davis. Little, Brown.
YOU AND I, by Philip Barry. Brentano's.
THE FOOL, by Channing Pollock. Brentano's.

MERTON OF THE MOVIES, by George Kaufman and Marc Connelly, based on the novel of the same name by Harry Leon Wilson.
WHY NOT? by Jesse Lynch Williams. Walter H. Baker Co.
THE OLD SOAK, by Don Marquis. Doubleday, Page.
R.U.R., by Karel Capek. Translated by Paul Selver. Doubleday, Page.
MARY THE 3D, by Rachel Crothers. Brentano's.

1923-1924

THE SWAN, translated from the Hungarian of Ferenc Molnar by Melville Baker. Boni & Liveright.
OUTWARD BOUND, by Sutton Vane. Boni & Liveright.
THE SHOW-OFF, by George Kelly. Little, Brown.
THE CHANGELINGS, by Lee Wilson Dodd. Dutton.
CHICKEN FEED, by Guy Bolton. Samuel French.
SUN-UP, by Lula Vollmer. Brentano's.
BEGGAR ON HORSEBACK, by George Kaufman and Marc Connelly. Boni & Liveright.
TARNISH, by Gilbert Emery. Brentano's.
THE GOOSE HANGS HIGH, by Lewis Beach. Little, Brown.
HELL-BENT FER HEAVEN, by Hatcher Hughes. Harper.

1924-1925

WHAT PRICE GLORY? by Laurence Stallings and Maxwell Anderson. Harcourt, Brace.
THEY KNEW WHAT THEY WANTED, by Sidney Howard. Doubleday, Page.
DESIRE UNDER THE ELMS, by Eugene G. O'Neill. Boni & Liveright.
THE FIREBRAND, by Edwin Justus Mayer. Boni & Liveright.
DANCING MOTHERS, by Edgar Selwyn and Edmund Goulding.
MRS. PARTRIDGE PRESENTS, by Mary Kennedy and Ruth Warren. Samuel French.
THE FALL GUY, by James Gleason and George Abbott. Samuel French.
THE YOUNGEST, by Philip Barry. Samuel French.
MINICK, by Edna Ferber and George S. Kaufman. Doubleday, Page.
WILD BIRDS, by Dan Totheroh. Doubleday, Page.

1925-1926

CRAIG'S WIFE, by George Kelly. Little, Brown.
THE GREAT GOD BROWN, by Eugene G. O'Neill. Boni & Liveright.
THE GREEN HAT, by Michael Arlen.
THE DYBBUK, by S. Ansky, Henry G. Alsberg-Winifred Katzin translation. Boni & Liveright.
THE ENEMY, by Channing Pollock. Brentano's.
THE LAST OF MRS. CHEYNEY, by Frederick Lonsdale. Samuel French.
BRIDE OF THE LAMB, by William Hurlbut. Boni & Liveright.
THE WISDOM TOOTH, by Marc Connelly. George H. Doran.
THE BUTTER AND EGG MAN, by George Kaufman. Boni & Liveright.
YOUNG WOODLEY, by John van Druten. Simon & Schuster.

1926-1927

BROADWAY, by Philip Dunning and George Abbott. George H. Doran.
SATURDAY'S CHILDREN, by Maxwell Anderson. Longmans, Green.
CHICAGO, by Maurine Watkins. Knopf.
THE CONSTANT WIFE, by William Somerset Maugham. George H. Doran.
THE PLAY'S THE THING, by Ferenc Molnar and P. G. Wodehouse. Brentano's.
THE ROAD TO ROME, by Robert Emmet Sherwood. Scribner.
THE SILVER CORD, by Sidney Howard. Scribner.
THE CRADLE SONG, translated from the Spanish of G. Martinez Sierra by John Garrett Underhill. Dutton.
DAISY MAYME, by George Kelly. Little, Brown.
IN ABRAHAM'S BOSOM, by Paul Green. McBride.

1927-1928

STRANGE INTERLUDE, by Eugene G. O'Neill. Boni & Liveright.
THE ROYAL FAMILY, by Edna Ferber and George Kaufman. Doubleday, Doran.
BURLESQUE, by George Manker Watters and Arthur Hopkins. Doubleday, Doran.
COQUETTE, by George Abbott and Ann Bridgers. Longmans, Green.
BEHOLD THE BRIDEGROOM, by George Kelly. Little, Brown.
PORGY, by DuBose Heyward. Doubleday, Doran.
PARIS BOUND, by Philip Barry. Samuel French.
ESCAPE, by John Galsworthy. Scribner.

THE RACKET, by Bartlett Cormack. Samuel French.
THE PLOUGH AND THE STARS, by Sean O'Casey. Macmillan.

1928-1929

STREET SCENE, by Elmer Rice. Samuel French.
JOURNEY'S END, by R. C. Sherriff. Brentano's.
WINGS OVER EUROPE, by Robert Nichols and Maurice Browne. Co-
    vici-Friede.
HOLIDAY, by Philip Barry. Samuel French.
THE FRONT PAGE, by Ben Hecht and Charles MacArthur. Covici-
    Friede.
LET US BE GAY, by Rachel Crothers. Samuel French.
MACHINAL, by Sophie Treadwell.
LITTLE ACCIDENT, by Floyd Dell and Thomas Mitchell.
GYPSY, by Maxwell Anderson.
THE KINGDOM OF GOD, by G. Martinez Sierra; English version by
    Helen and Harley Granville-Barker. Dutton.

1929-1930

THE GREEN PASTURES, by Marc Connelly (adapted from "Ol' Man
    Adam and His Chillun," by Roark Bradford). Farrar & Rine-
    hart.
THE CRIMINAL CODE, by Martin Flavin. Horace Liveright.
BERKELEY SQUARE, by John Balderston.
STRICTLY DISHONORABLE, by Preston Sturges. Horace Liveright.
THE FIRST MRS. FRASER, by St. John Ervine. Macmillan.
THE LAST MILE, by John Wexley. Samuel French.
JUNE MOON, by Ring W. Lardner and George S. Kaufman. Scribner.
MICHAEL AND MARY, by A. A. Milne. Chatto & Windus.
DEATH TAKES A HOLIDAY, by Walter Ferris (adapted from the Ital-
    ian of Alberto Casella). Samuel French.
REBOUND, by Donald Ogden Stewart. Samuel French.

1930-1931

ELIZABETH THE QUEEN, by Maxwell Anderson. Longmans, Green.
TOMORROW AND TOMORROW, by Philip Barry. Samuel French.
ONCE IN A LIFETIME, by George S. Kaufman and Moss Hart. Far-
    rar & Rinehart.
GREEN GROW THE LILACS, by Lynn Riggs. Samuel French.
AS HUSBANDS GO, by Rachel Crothers. Samuel French.

ALISON's HOUSE, by Susan Glaspell. Samuel French.
FIVE-STAR FINAL, by Louis Weitzenkorn. Samuel French.
OVERTURE, by William Bolitho. Simon & Schuster.
THE BARRETTS OF WIMPOLE STREET, by Rudolf Besier. Little,
    Brown.
GRAND HOTEL, adapted from the German of Vicki Baum by W. A.
    Drake.

1931-1932

OF THEE I SING, by George S. Kaufman and Morrie Ryskind; music
    and lyrics by George and Ira Gershwin. Knopf.
MOURNING BECOMES ELECTRA, by Eugene G. O'Neill. Horace Live-
    right.
REUNION IN VIENNA, by Robert Emmet Sherwood. Scribner.
THE HOUSE OF CONNELLY, by Paul Green. Samuel French.
THE ANIMAL KINGDOM, by Philip Barry. Samuel French.
THE LEFT BANK, by Elmer Rice. Samuel French.
ANOTHER LANGUAGE, by Rose Franken. Samuel French.
BRIEF MOMENT, by S. N. Behrman. Farrar & Rinehart.
THE DEVIL PASSES, by Benn W. Levy. Martin Secker.
CYNARA, by H. M. Harwood and R. F. Gore-Browne. Samuel
    French.

1932-1933

BOTH YOUR HOUSES, by Maxwell Anderson. Samuel French.
DINNER AT EIGHT, by George S. Kaufman and Edna Ferber. Dou-
    bleday, Doran.
WHEN LADIES MEET, by Rachel Crothers. Samuel French.
DESIGN FOR LIVING, by Noel Coward. Doubleday, Doran.
BIOGRAPHY, by S. N. Behrman. Farrar & Rinehart.
ALIEN CORN, by Sidney Howard. Scribner.
THE LATE CHRISTOPHER BEAN, adapted from the French of René
    Fauchois by Sidney Howard. Samuel French.
WE, THE PEOPLE, by Elmer Rice. Coward-McCann.
PIGEONS AND PEOPLE, by George M. Cohan.
ONE SUNDAY AFTERNOON, by James Hagan. Samuel French.

1933-1934

MARY OF SCOTLAND, by Maxwell Anderson. Doubleday, Doran.
MEN IN WHITE, by Sidney Kingsley. Covici-Friede.
DODSWORTH, by Sinclair Lewis and Sidney Howard. Harcourt,
    Brace.

AH, WILDERNESS, by Eugene O'Neill. Random House.
THEY SHALL NOT DIE, by John Wexley. Knopf.
HER MASTER'S VOICE, by Clare Kummer. Samuel French.
NO MORE LADIES, by A. E. Thomas.
WEDNESDAY'S CHILD, by Leopold Atlas. Samuel French.
THE SHINING HOUR, by Keith Winter. Doubleday, Doran.
THE GREEN BAY TREE, by Mordaunt Shairp. Baker International
    Play Bureau.

1934-1935

THE CHILDREN'S HOUR, by Lillian Hellman. Knopf.
VALLEY FORGE, by Maxwell Anderson. Anderson House.
THE PETRIFIED FOREST, by Robert Sherwood. Scribner.
THE OLD MAID, by Zoë Akins. Appleton-Century.
ACCENT ON YOUTH, by Samson Raphaelson. Samuel French.
MERRILY WE ROLL ALONG, by George S. Kaufman and Moss Hart.
    Random House.
AWAKE AND SING, by Clifford Odets. Random House.
THE FARMER TAKES A WIFE, by Frank B. Elser and Marc Connelly.
LOST HORIZONS, by John Hayden.
THE DISTAFF SIDE, by John van Druten. Knopf.

1935-1936

WINTERSET, by Maxwell Anderson. Anderson House.
IDIOT'S DELIGHT, by Robert Emmet Sherwood. Scribner.
END OF SUMMER, by S. N. Behrman. Random House.
FIRST LADY, by Katharine Dayton and George S. Kaufman. Ran-
    dom House.
VICTORIA REGINA, by Laurence Housman. Samuel French.
BOY MEETS GIRL, by Bella and Samuel Spewack. Random House.
DEAD END, by Sidney Kingsley. Random House.
CALL IT A DAY, by Dodie Smith. Samuel French.
ETHAN FROME, by Owen Davis and Donald Davis. Scribner.
PRIDE AND PREJUDICE, by Helen Jerome. Doubleday, Doran.

1936-1937

HIGH TOR, by Maxwell Anderson. Anderson House.
YOU CAN'T TAKE IT WITH YOU, by Moss Hart and George S. Kauf-
    man. Farrar & Rinehart.
JOHNNY JOHNSON, by Paul Green. Samuel French.
DAUGHTERS OF ATREUS, by Robert Turney. Knopf.

STAGE DOOR, by Edna Ferber and George S. Kaufman. Doubleday, Doran.

THE WOMEN, by Clare Boothe. Random House.

ST. HELENA, by R. C. Sherriff and Jeanne de Casalis. Samuel French.

YES, MY DARLING DAUGHTER, by Mark Reed. Samuel French.

EXCURSION, by Victor Wolfson. Random House.

TOVARICH, by Jacques Deval and Robert E. Sherwood. Random House.

1937-1938

OF MICE AND MEN, by John Steinbeck. Covici-Friede.

OUR TOWN, by Thornton Wilder. Coward-McCann.

SHADOW AND SUBSTANCE, by Paul Vincent Carroll. Random House.

ON BORROWED TIME, by Paul Osborn. Knopf.

THE STAR-WAGON, by Maxwell Anderson. Anderson House.

SUSAN AND GOD, by Rachel Crothers. Random House.

PROLOGUE TO GLORY, by E. P. Conkle. Random House.

AMPHITRYON 38, by S. N. Behrman. Random House.

GOLDEN BOY, by Clifford Odets. Random House.

WHAT A LIFE, by Clifford Goldsmith. Dramatists' Play Service.

1938-1939

ABE LINCOLN IN ILLINOIS, by Robert E. Sherwood. Scribner.

THE LITTLE FOXES, by Lillian Hellman. Random House.

ROCKET TO THE MOON, by Clifford Odets. Random House.

THE AMERICAN WAY, by George S. Kaufman and Moss Hart. Random House.

NO TIME FOR COMEDY, by S. N. Behrman. Random House.

THE PHILADELPHIA STORY, by Philip Barry. Coward-McCann.

THE WHITE STEED, by Paul Vincent Carroll. Random House.

HERE COME THE CLOWNS, by Philip Barry. Coward-McCann.

FAMILY PORTRAIT, by Lenore Coffee and William Joyce Cowen. Random House.

KISS THE BOYS GOOD-BYE, by Clare Boothe. Random House.

1939-1940

THERE SHALL BE NO NIGHT, by Robert E. Sherwood. Scribner.

KEY LARGO, by Maxwell Anderson. Anderson House.

THE WORLD WE MAKE, by Sidney Kingsley.

LIFE WITH FATHER, by Howard Lindsay and Russel Crouse. Knopf.

THE MAN WHO CAME TO DINNER, by George S. Kaufman and Moss
   Hart. Random House.
THE MALE ANIMAL, by James Thurber and Elliott Nugent. Ran-
   dom House, New York, and MacMillan Co., Canada.
THE TIME OF YOUR LIFE, by William Saroyan. Harcourt, Brace
SKYLARK, by Samson Raphaelson. Random House.
MARGIN FOR ERROR, by Clare Boothe. Random House.
MORNING'S AT SEVEN, by Paul Osborn. Samuel French.

1940-1941

NATIVE SON, by Paul Green and Richard Wright. Harper.
WATCH ON THE RHINE, by Lillian Hellman. Random House.
THE CORN IS GREEN, by Emlyn Williams. Random House.
LADY IN THE DARK, by Moss Hart. Random House.
ARSENIC AND OLD LACE, by Joseph Kesselring. Random House.
MY SISTER EILEEN, by Joseph Fields and Jerome Chodorov. Ran-
   dom House.
FLIGHT TO THE WEST, by Elmer Rice. Coward-McCann.
CLAUDIA, by Rose Franken Meloney. Farrar & Rinehart.
MR. AND MRS. NORTH, by Owen Davis. Samuel French.
GEORGE WASHINGTON SLEPT HERE, by George S. Kaufman and
   Moss Hart. Random House.

1941-1942

IN TIME TO COME, by Howard Koch. Dramatists' Play Service.
THE MOON IS DOWN, by John Steinbeck. Viking.
BLITHE SPIRIT, by Noel Coward. Doubleday, Doran.
JUNIOR MISS, by Jerome Chodorov and Joseph Fields. Random
   House.
CANDLE IN THE WIND, by Maxwell Anderson. Anderson House.
LETTERS TO LUCERNE, by Fritz Rotter and Allen Vincent. Samuel
   French.
JASON, by Samson Raphaelson. Random House.
ANGEL STREET, by Patrick Hamilton. Constable & Co., under the
   title "Gaslight."
UNCLE HARRY, by Thomas Job. Samuel French.
HOPE FOR A HARVEST, by Sophie Treadwell. Samuel French.

1942-1943

THE PATRIOTS, by Sidney Kingsley. Random House.
THE EVE OF ST. MARK, by Maxwell Anderson. Anderson House.

THE SKIN OF OUR TEETH, by Thornton Wilder. Harper.
WINTER SOLDIERS, by Dan James.
TOMORROW THE WORLD, by James Gow and Arnaud d'Usseau.
  Scribner.
HARRIET, by Florence Ryerson and Colin Clements. Scribner.
THE DOUGHGIRLS, by Joseph Fields. Random House.
THE DAMASK CHEEK, by John Van Druten and Lloyd Morris. Random House.
KISS AND TELL, by F. Hugh Herbert. Coward-McCann.
OKLAHOMA!, by Oscar Hammerstein 2nd and Richard Rodgers.
  Random House.

1943-1944

WINGED VICTORY, by Moss Hart. Random House.
THE SEARCHING WIND, by Lillian Hellman. Viking.
THE VOICE OF THE TURTLE, by John Van Druten. Random House.
DECISION, by Edward Chodorov.
OVER 21, by Ruth Gordon. Random House.
OUTRAGEOUS FORTUNE, by Rose Franken. Samuel French.
JACOBOWSKY AND THE COLONEL, by S. N. Behrman. Random House.
STORM OPERATION, by Maxwell Anderson. Anderson House.
PICK-UP GIRL, by Elsa Shelley.
THE INNOCENT VOYAGE, by Paul Osborn.

1944-1945

A BELL FOR ADANO, by Paul Osborn. Knopf.
I REMEMBER MAMA, by John Van Druten. Harcourt, Brace.
THE HASTY HEART, by John Patrick. Random House.
THE GLASS MENAGERIE, by Tennessee Williams. Random House.
HARVEY, by Mary Chase.
THE LATE GEORGE APLEY, by John P. Marquand and George S.
  Kaufman.
SOLDIER'S WIFE, by Rose Franken. Samuel French.
ANNA LUCASTA, by Philip Yordan. Random House.
FOOLISH NOTION, by Philip Barry.
DEAR RUTH, by Norman Krasna. Random House.

1945-1946

STATE OF THE UNION, by Howard Lindsay and Russel Crouse.
  Random House.
HOME OF THE BRAVE, by Arthur Laurents. Random House.

DEEP ARE THE ROOTS, by Arnaud d'Usseau and James Gow. Scribner.

THE MAGNIFICENT YANKEE, by Emmet Lavery. Samuel French.

ANTIGONE, by Lewis Galantière (from the French of Jean Anouilh). Random House.

O MISTRESS MINE, by Terence Rattigan. Published and revised by the author.

BORN YESTERDAY, by Garson Kanin. Viking.

DREAM GIRL, by Elmer Rice. Coward-McCann.

THE RUGGED PATH, by Robert E. Sherwood. Scribner.

LUTE SONG, by Will Irwin and Sidney Howard. Published version by Will Irwin and Leopoldine Howard.

1946-1947

ALL MY SONS, by Arthur Miller. Reynal & Hitchcock.

THE ICEMAN COMETH, by Eugene G. O'Neill. Random House.

JOAN OF LORRAINE, by Maxwell Anderson. Published by Maxwell Anderson.

ANOTHER PART OF THE FOREST, by Lillian Hellman. Viking.

YEARS AGO, by Ruth Gordon. Viking.

JOHN LOVES MARY, by Norman Krasna. Copyright by Norman Krasna.

THE FATAL WEAKNESS, by George Kelly. Samuel French.

THE STORY OF MARY SURRATT, by John Patrick. Dramatists' Play Service.

CHRISTOPHER BLAKE, by Moss Hart. Random House.

BRIGADOON, by Alan Jay Lerner and Frederick Loewe. Coward-McCann.

1947-1948

A STREETCAR NAMED DESIRE, by Tennessee Williams. New Directions.

MISTER ROBERTS, by Thomas Heggen and Joshua Logan. Houghton Mifflin.

COMMAND DECISION, by William Wister Haines. Random House.

THE WINSLOW BOY, by Terence Rattigan.

THE HEIRESS, by Ruth and Augustus Goetz.

ALLEGRO, by Richard Rodgers and Oscar Hammerstein 2d. Knopf. Music published by Williamson Music, Inc.

EASTWARD IN EDEN, by Dorothy Gardner. Longmans, Green.

SKIPPER NEXT TO GOD, by Jan de Hartog.

AN INSPECTOR CALLS, by J. B. Priestley.
ME AND MOLLY, by Gertrude Berg.

1948-1949

DEATH OF A SALESMAN, by Arthur Miller. Viking.
ANNE OF THE THOUSAND DAYS, by Maxwell Anderson. Sloane.
THE MADWOMAN OF CHAILLOT, by Maurice Valency, adapted from the French of Jean Giraudoux. Random House.
DETECTIVE STORY, by Sidney Kingsley. Random House.
EDWARD, MY SON, by Robert Morley and Noel Langley. Random House, New York, and Samuel French, London.
LIFE WITH MOTHER, by Howard Lindsay and Russel Crouse. Knopf.
LIGHT UP THE SKY, by Moss Hart. Random House.
THE SILVER WHISTLE, by Robert Edward McEnroe. Dramatists' Play Service.
TWO BLIND MICE, by Samuel Spewack. Dramatists' Play Service.
GOODBYE, MY FANCY, by Fay Kanin. Samuel French.

1949-1950

THE COCKTAIL PARTY, by T. S. Eliot. Harcourt, Brace.
THE MEMBER OF THE WEDDING, by Carson McCullers. Houghton Mifflin.
THE INNOCENTS, by William Archibald. Coward-McCann.
LOST IN THE STARS, by Maxwell Anderson and Kurt Weill. Sloane.
COME BACK, LITTLE SHEBA, by William Inge. Random House.
THE HAPPY TIME, by Samuel Taylor. Random House.
THE WISTERIA TREES, by Joshua Logan. Random House.
I KNOW MY LOVE, by S. N. Behrman. Random House.
THE ENCHANTED, by Maurice Valency, adapted from a play by Jean Giraudoux. Random House.
CLUTTERBUCK, by Benn W. Levy. Dramatists' Play Service.

1950-1951

GUYS AND DOLLS, by Jo Swerling, Abe Burrows and Frank Loesser.
DARKNESS AT NOON, by Sidney Kingsley and Arthur Koestler. Random House.
BILLY BUDD, by Louis O. Coxe and Robert Chapman. Princeton University Press.
THE AUTUMN GARDEN, by Lillian Hellman. Little, Brown & Co.

BELL, BOOK AND CANDLE, by John van Druten.   Random House.
THE COUNTRY GIRL, by Clifford Odets.   Viking Press.
THE ROSE TATTOO, by Tennessee Williams.   New Directions.
SEASON IN THE SUN, by Wolcott Gibbs.   Random House.
AFFAIRS OF STATE, by Louis Verneuil.
SECOND THRESHOLD, by Philip Barry.   Harper & Bros.

1951-1952

MRS. MCTHING, by Mary Coyle Chase.
THE SHRIKE, by Joseph Kramm.   Random House.
I AM A CAMERA, by John van Druten.   Random House.
THE FOURPOSTER, by Jan de Hartog.
POINT OF NO RETURN, by Paul Osborn.   Random House.
BAREFOOT IN ATHENS, by Maxwell Anderson.   Sloane.
VENUS OBSERVED, by Christopher Fry.   Oxford.
JANE, by S. N. Behrman and Somerset Maugham.   Random House.
GIGI, by Anita Loos and Colette.   Random House.
REMAINS TO BE SEEN, by Howard Lindsay and Russel Crouse.   Random House.

WHERE AND WHEN THEY WERE BORN

(Compiled from the most authentic records available)

Abbott, George .... Forestville, N. Y. 1889
Abel, Walter .... St. Paul, Minn. 1898
Adams, Maude .... Salt Lake City, Utah 1872
Addy, Wesley .... Omaha, Neb. 1912
Aherne, Brian .... King's Norton, England 1902
Aldrich, Richard .... Boston 1902
Anders, Glenn .... Los Angeles, Cal. 1890
Anderson, Judith .... Australia 1898
Anderson, Maxwell .... Atlantic City, Pa. 1888
Arthur, Jean .... New York City 1905
Ashcroft, Peggy .... Croydon, England 1907

Bainter, Fay .... Los Angeles, Cal. 1892
Bankhead, Tallulah .... Huntsville, Ala. 1902
Barrymore, Ethel .... Philadelphia, Pa. 1879
Barrymore, Lionel .... Philadelphia, Pa. 1878
Barton, James .... Gloucester, N. J. 1890
Behrman, S. N. .... Worcester, Mass. 1893
Bellamy, Ralph .... Chicago, Ill. 1904
Belmore, Bertha .... Manchester, England 1882
Bergman, Ingrid .... Stockholm 1917
Bergner, Elisabeth .... Vienna 1900
Berlin, Irving .... Russia 1888
Best, Edna .... Hove, England 1900
Blackmer, Sidney .... Salisbury, N. C. 1898
Bolger, Ray .... Dorchester, Mass. 1904
Bondi, Beulah .... Chicago, Ill. 1892
Bourneuf, Philip .... Boston, Mass. 1912
Boyer, Charles .... Figeac, France 1899
Brent, Romney .... Saltillo, Mex. 1902
Brown, Joe E. .... Holgate, Ohio 1892
Burke, Billie .... Washington, D. C. 1885
Byington, Spring .... Colorado Springs, Colo. 1898

Cagney, James .... New York 1904
Cagney, Jeanne .... New York 1920

Reginald Gardiner and Miss Lillie in "An Evening with Beatrice Lillie"

Chatterton, Ruth .... New York 1893
Claire, Ina .... Washington, D. C. 1895
Clark, Bobby .... Springfield, Ohio 1888
Clift, Montgomery .... Omaha, Neb. 1921
Clive, Colin .... St. Malo, France 1900
Cobb, Lee .... New York City 1911
Coburn, Charles .... Macon, Ga. 1877
Collinge, Patricia .... Dublin 1894
Collins, Russell .... New Orleans, La. 1897
Colt, Ethel Barrymore ...... Mamaroneck, N. Y. 1911
Colt, John Drew .... New York 1914
Conroy, Frank .... London, England 1885
Cook, Donald .... Portland, Ore. 1902
Cook, Joe .... Evansville, Ind. 1890
Cooper, Melville .... Birmingham, England 1896
Corbett, Leonora .... London, England 1908
Cornell, Katharine .... Berlin, Germany 1898
Coulouris, George .... Manchester, England 1906
Coward, Noel .... Teddington, England 1899
Cronyn, Hume .... London, Ontario 1912
Crothers, Rachel .... Bloomington, Ill. 1878
Crouse, Russel .... Findlay, Ohio 1893
Cummings, Constance .... Seattle, Wash. 1911

Dale, Margaret .... Philadelphia, Pa. 1880
Dana, Leora .... New York City 1923
Daniell, Henry .... London 1894
Davis, Owen .... Portland, Me. 1874
Derwent, Clarence .... London 1884
Dixon, Jean .... Waterbury, Conn. 1905
Douglas, Melvyn .... Macon, Ga. 1901
Dowling, Eddie .... Woonsocket, R. I. 1894
Drake, Alfred .... New York City 1914
Duncan, Todd .... Danville, Ky. 1900
Dunning, Philip .... Meriden, Conn. 1890
Durante, Jimmy .... New York City 1893

Eldridge, Florence .... Brooklyn, N. Y. 1901
Evans, Edith .... London, England 1888
Evans, Maurice .... Dorchester, England 1901
Evans, Wilbur .... Philadelphia, Pa. 1908
Evelyn, Judith .... Seneca, S. Dak. 1913
Ewell, Tom .... Owensboro, Ky. 1912

Fabray, Nanette .... New Orleans, La. 1921
Fay, Frank .... San Francisco 1897
Ferber, Edna .... Kalamazoo, Mich. 1887
Ferrer, José .... Puerto Rico 1912
Field, Betty .... Boston 1918
Field, Virginia .... London 1917
Fields, Gracie .... Rochdale, England 1898
Fitzgerald, Barry .... Dublin, Ireland 1888
Fitzgerald, Geraldine .... Dublin, Ireland 1914
Flemyng, Robert .... Liverpool 1912
Fletcher, Bramwell .... Bradford, Yorkshire, Eng. ... 1904
Fonda, Henry .... Grand Island, Neb. 1905
Fontanne, Lynn .... London, England 1887
Forbes, Brenda .... London, England 1909
Foy, Eddie, Jr. .... New Rochelle, N. Y. 1907
Francis, Arlene .... Boston, Mass. 1908
Fry, Christopher .... England 1907

Gahagan, Helen .... Boonton, N. J. 1900
Gaxton, William .... San Francisco, Cal. 1893
Geddes, Barbara Bel .... New York 1922
Geddes, Norman Bel .... Adrian, Mich. 1893
George, Grace .... New York City 1879
Gershwin, Ira .... New York 1896
Gielgud, Sir John .... London, England 1904
Gillmore, Margalo .... England 1901
Gilmore, Virginia .... El Monte, Cal. 1919
Gish, Dorothy .... Massillon, Ohio 1898
Gish, Lillian .... Springfield, Ohio 1896
Golden, John .... New York 1874
Goodner, Carol .... New York City 1904
Gordon, Ruth .... Wollaston, Mass. 1896
Greaza, Walter .... St. Paul, Minn. 1900
Greenstreet, Sydney .... England 1880
Guinness, Alec .... London 1914
Gwenn, Edmund .... Glamorgan, Wales 1875

Hagen, Uta .... Göttingen, Germany 1919
Hammerstein, Oscar, II ...... New York City 1895
Hampden, Walter .... Brooklyn, N. Y. 1879
Hardie, Russell .... Griffin Mills, N. Y. 1906
Hardwicke, Sir Cedric .... Lye, Stourbridge, England ... 1893

Harris, Julie .... Grosse Point, Mich. 1925
Hart, Moss .... New York City 1904
Havoc, June .... Seattle, Wash. 1916
Haydon, Julie .... Oak Park, Ill. 1910
Hayes, Helen .... Washington, D. C. 1900
Hayward, Leland .... Nebraska City, Neb. 1902
Heflin, Frances .... Oklahoma City, Okla. 1924
Heineman, Eda .... Japan 1891
Hellman, Lillian .... New Orleans, La. 1905
Helpmann, Robert .... South Australia 1911
Henie, Sonja .... Oslo, Norway 1913
Hepburn, Audrey .... Brussels 1919
Hepburn, Katharine .... Hartford, Conn. 1909
Hiller, Wendy .... Bramhall, England 1912
Holliday, Judy .... New York City 1924
Holm, Celeste .... New York City 1919
Homolka, Oscar .... Vienna 1898
Hull, Josephine .... Newtonville, Mass. 1886
Hull, Henry .... Louisville, Ky. 1890
Hunt, Martita .... Argentine Republic 1900
Hunter, Kim .... Detroit, Mich. 1922
Hussey, Ruth .... Providence, R. I. 1917

Inescort, Frieda .... Hitchin, Scotland 1901
Ives, Burl .... Hunt Township, Ill. 1909

Johnson, Harold J. (Chic) ... Chicago, Ill. 1891
Joy, Nicholas .... Paris, France 1889

Kane, Whitford .... Larne, Ireland 1882
Kanin, Garson .... Rochester, N. Y. 1912
Karloff, Boris .... Dulwich, England 1887
Kaufman, George S. .... Pittsburgh, Pa. 1889
Kaye, Danny .... New York City 1914
Kazan, Elia .... Constantinople 1909
Keith, Robert .... Fowler, Ind. 1898
Kilbride, Percy .... San Francisco, Cal. 1880
King, Dennis .... Coventry, England 1897
Kingsley, Sidney .... New York City 1906
Kirkland, Patricia .... New York 1927
Knox, Alexander .... Ontario 1907
Kruger, Otto .... Toledo, Ohio 1885

Lahr, Bert .... New York City 1895
Landis, Jessie Royce .... Chicago, Ill. 1904
Laughton, Charles .... Scarborough, England 1899
LeGallienne, Eva .... London 1899
Leigh, Vivien .... Darjeeling, India 1913
Leighton, Margaret .... Barnt Green, England 1922
Lillie, Beatrice .... Toronto, Canada 1898
Lindsay, Howard .... Waterford, N. Y. 1899
Linn, Bambi .... Brooklyn, N. Y. 1926
Lockhart, Gene .... Ontario 1892
Loeb, Philip .... Philadelphia, Pa. 1892
Logan, Joshua .... Texarkana, Tex. 1908
Lonergan, Lenore .... Toledo, Ohio 1928
Lukas, Paul .... Budapest, Hungary 1891
Lunt, Alfred .... Milwaukee, Wis. 1893
Lytell, Bert .... New York City 1885

MacMahon, Aline .... McKeesport, Pa. 1899
Mamoulian, Rouben .... Tiflis 1898
March, Fredric .... Racine, Wis. 1897
Martin, Mary .... Weatherford, Texas 1913
Mason, James .... Huddersfield, England 1909
Massey, Raymond .... Toronto, Canada 1896
Matteson, Ruth .... San Jose, Cal. 1905
Maugham, W. Somerset ..... England 1874
McClintic, Guthrie .... Seattle, Wash. 1893
McCormick, Myron .... Albany, Ind. 1907
McCracken, Joan .... Philadelphia, Pa. 1923
McGrath, Paul .... Chicago, Ill. 1900
McGuire, Dorothy .... Omaha, Neb. 1918
Menotti, Gian-Carlo .... Italy 1912
Meredith, Burgess .... Cleveland, Ohio 1908
Merman, Ethel .... Astoria, L. I. 1909
Middleton, Ray .... Chicago, Ill. 1907
Mielziner, Jo .... Paris, France 1901
Miller, Arthur .... New York City 1915
Miller, Gilbert .... New York 1884
Mitchell, Thomas .... Elizabeth, N. J. 1892
Moore, Victor .... Hammonton, N. J. 1876
Moorehead, Agnes .... Clinton, Mass. 1906
Morgan, Claudia .... New York.................1912
Morley, Robert .... Semley, England 1908

Moss, Arnold .... Brooklyn, N. Y. 1910
Muni, Paul .... Lemberg, Austria 1895

Nagel, Conrad .... Keokuk, Iowa 1897
Natwick, Mildred .... Baltimore 1908
Neal, Patricia .... Packard, Ky. 1926
Nesbitt, Cathleen .... Cheshire, England 1889
Nugent, Elliott .... Dover, Ohio 1900

Odets, Clifford .... Philadelphia 1906
Oenslager, Donald .... Harrisburg, Pa. 1902
Olivier, Sir Laurence .... Dorking, Surrey, England 1907
Olsen, John Siguard (Ole) ... Peru, Ind. 1892
O'Malley, Rex .... London, England 1906
O'Neal, Frederick .... Brookville, Miss. 1905
O'Neill, Eugene Gladstone ... New York 1888

Page, Geraldine .... Kirksville, Mo. 1925
Petina, Irra .... Leningrad, Russia 1900
Picon, Molly .... New York City 1898
Pinza, Ezio .... Rome, Italy 1895
Porter, Cole .... Peru, Indiana 1892
Price, Vincent .... St. Louis, Mo. 1914

Rains, Claude .... London, England 1889
Raitt, John .... Santa Ana, Cal. 1917
Rathbone, Basil .... Johannesburg 1892
Redman, Joyce .... Newcastle, Ireland 1918
Reed, Florence .... Philadelphia, Pa. 1883
Rennie, James .... Toronto, Canada 1890
Richardson, Sir Ralph .... Cheltenham, England 1902
Rice, Elmer .... New York City 1892
Roberts, Joan .... New York City 1918
Rodgers, Richard .... New York City 1902
Ross, Anthony .... New York 1906
Ross, Robert .... Port Colburne, Ont. 1901
Royle, Selena .... New York 1905

Sarnoff, Dorothy .... Brooklyn, N. Y. 1919
Saroyan, William .... Fresno, Cal. 1908
Scheff, Fritzi .... Vienna, Austria 1879
Scott, Martha .... Jamesport, Mo. 1914
Segal, Vivienne .... Philadelphia, Pa. 1897

NECROLOGY

Adair, Jean, 80, actress. Played in more than twenty-five Broadway productions in the past thirty years. She made her New York début in "It's a Boy" in 1922. Is well remembered as one of the sweet, murderous old ladies in both the Broadway production and the motion picture of "Arsenic and Old Lace." Her last illness forced her to leave the cast of "The Crucible." Born Canada; died New York, May 11, 1953.

Adler, Sarah, 95, actress. Known as the "mother" and "dowager duchess" of the Yiddish stage, she was the mother of five stage performers including the noted stars, Luther and Stella Adler. Many of her appearances were in companies headed by her husband, the late Jacob P. Adler. She made her stage début at the age of eight in Russia in Schiller's "The Robbers." She came to the United States in the eighties. Born Odessa; died New York, April 28, 1953.

Alda, Frances, 69, opera star. She made her début at twenty-two at the Opéra Comique, Paris. After appearing at Théâtre de la Monnaie (Brussels), Covent Garden (London), and La Scala (Milan), she was brought to the Metropolitan by Gatti-Casazza in 1908. She remained there for the next twenty-one years, singing more than forty roles. Her autobiography "Men, Women and Tenors" was published in 1937. Born Christchurch, New Zealand; died Venice, Italy, September 18, 1952.

Allen, Joseph, 80, actor. Began his stage career in 1896 at the Castle Square Opera Company in Boston. Later in New York he appeared in support of Eddie Foy. Was associated with George M. Cohan in such plays as "Seven Keys to Baldpate" and "The Tavern." It was in this last that he made his line "What's all the shootin' fer?" a national phrase. Born Boston; died Newton, Massachusetts, September 9, 1952.

Armitage, Walter, 46, actor and author. His first New York appearance was in "Melo" in 1931. He toured with Al Jolson in "Wonderbar." He is the author of such vehicles as "The Ruptured Duck," "River Gambler" and "African Vineyard." He also acted in motion pictures, among them "Little Miss

346

Marker" which started Shirley Temple on the road to fame. Born South Africa; died New York, February 22, 1953.

Belmore, Lionel, 86, actor. Served as Sir Henry Irving's stage manager for 17 years. Played many roles in England before coming to the United States where he appeared in many Broadway productions. He was one of a family of ten, all actors and actresses. Born England; died Hollywood, January 30, 1953.

Blayney, May, 79, actress. Made her stage début in 1892 in Islington under Charles Hawtrey's management. She acted for many famous managers, among them Charles Frohman, George Edwardes, Cyril Maude, Charles Wyndham and Herbert Tree. First came to America in 1905 when she appeared with James K. Hackett in "The Walls of Jericho." Other Broadway appearances include "Love Among the Lions" and as Cecily in "The Importance of Being Earnest." She supported Maude Adams in "Chantecler" in 1911. She was once married to A. E. Matthews. Born England; died in the Orange Free State town of Wepener, South Africa, February 10, 1953.

Bordoni, Irene, 59, actress. Made her stage début at 13 in the chorus at the Théâtre des Variétés in Paris. Her first Broadway appearance was in 1912 in "The First Affair." Her first big Broadway hit was in "Hitchy-Koo" in 1917 in support of Raymond Hitchcock. Later she co-starred with H. B. Warner in "Sleeping Partners" and two years later (1920) was the co-star of Sam Bernard in "As You Were." "If You Could Care for Me," one of the songs she sang in this hit, is still popular. In 1922 she starred in "The French Doll," followed by "Little Miss Bluebeard," "Naughty Cinderella," "Paris," "Louisiana Purchase" and others. One of her last appearances was as Bloody Mary in the Chicago company of "South Pacific." Her pretty, charming, saucy and lively appearance coupled with her delightful French accent made her one of the most popular of comediennes. Born Paris; died New York, March 19, 1953.

Brayton, Lily, 76, actress. She first appeared on the stage as a "walk on" in Benson's company in "Richard II." Her most popular role was the lead in the original "Chu Chin Chow" company, which she played over 2000 times. Her last role was as Portia in "Julius Caesar" in 1932. Born Hindley, England; died Dawlish, Devon, England, April 30, 1953.

Burnside, R. H., 82, producer and stage director. Started his career as a call-boy for Gilbert and Sullivan operas at the Savoy Theatre, London. Made stage début in the guise of a dog in "The Bohemian Girl." Came to the United States in 1894 as stage director for Lillian Russell and later turned to playwriting. His plays include "Sergeant Kitty," "The Tourist" and "A Trip to Japan." Was associated with the New York Hippodrome from 1909 to 1923, staging and writing many of the shows there, among them "Hip-Hip Hooray," "Cheer Up," "Happy Days," "Good Times" and "Better Times." It was at the Hippodrome that for years audiences were fascinated by the sight of showgirls walking into a tank of water on the stage and disappearing. He wrote and staged several of the Fred Stone shows such as "Chin-Chin," "Jack o' Lantern," "Tip-Top" and "Stepping Stones." He was Shepherd of the Lambs from 1918 to 1921. Born Glasgow; died Metuchen, New Jersey, September 14, 1952.

Carrington, Katherine, 43, actress. Made her Broadway début in 1927 in the chorus of Winthrop Ames' production of "Iolanthe." Was later in vaudeville and was in "The Little Accident," "The Laugh Parade," "Face the Music," "Music in the Air" and "The Eternal Road." Retired from the stage in 1934. She was married to composer Arthur Schwartz. Born East Orange, New Jersey; died New York, May 2, 1953.

Chambers, Norma, age unrecorded, actress. She graduated from college in 1930 and made her Broadway début in 1935 in "Let Freedom Ring." Other plays in which she appeared include "Bury the Dead," "Prelude," "The Children's Hour," "Richard III," "On Whitman Avenue" and the musical version of "Street Scene." Born Dinwiddie County, Virginia; died New York, December 30, 1952.

Cirker, Mitchell, 70, set designer. He was once electrician for David Belasco. Some forty years ago he formed the firm of Cirker and Robbins with Robert Nelson Robbins. They did sets for "Lightnin'," "Brother Rat," "Room Service" and others. Born New York; died Forest Hills, New York, February 4, 1953.

Coghlan, Gertrude, 73, actress. Niece of Rose Coghlan, daughter of Charles Coghlan and wife of Augustus Pitou. She made her New York début in 1897 in "The Royal Box." She starred in "Becky Sharp" and later appeared in "The Sword of Justice," "The Sorceress" and "The Travelling Salesman." Her last appearance was in Arthur Hopkins' production of "Plumes in the Dust" in 1936. Born Hertfordshire, England; died New York, September 11, 1952.

Conway, Jack, 65, actor and director. Began in show business as an actor in Santa Barbara, California, in 1907. Entered pictures in 1909 and became a star overnight in "Her Indian Hero," reportedly the first feature film shot in Hollywood. His first directorial job was "Old Arm Chair" with Gladys Brockwell in 1914. His most recently directed films include "Saratoga," "Boom Town," "The Tale of Two Cities" and "The Hucksters." Born Graceville, Minnesota; died Pacific Palisades, California, October 11, 1952.

Curran, Homer F., 67, producer. Operated theatres in Los Angeles and San Francisco. In 1922 built the Curran Theatre in San Francisco. Presented the first American production of Noel Coward's "The Queen Was in the Parlour" with Pauline Frederick. In 1939 he established The Civic Light Opera Association of San Francisco. With Edwin Lester he helped produce and write "The Song of Norway." With Russell Lewis and Howard Young he produced "Lady Windermere's Fan" starring Cornelia Otis Skinner. Born Springfield, Missouri; died Beverly Hills, July 18, 1952.

Cushing, Catherine Chisholm, age unrecorded, playwright, songwriter, librettist. She was once editor of *Harper's Bazaar*. Her first produced play was "The Real Thing" in 1911. Two years later May Irwin appeared in her "Widow by Proxy." She also wrote "Jerry" for Billie Burke. Other plays included "Pollyanna" and the musicals "Topsy and Eva" and "Marjolaine." Among the many songs for which she wrote lyrics was "L'Amour Toujours L'Amour." Born in Ohio; died New York, October 19, 1952.

De Rose, Peter, 53, songwriter. While still in school he worked as a stock boy for a music publisher. In 1929 he married May Singhi Breen (The Ukulele Lady) and they formed a team known as "Sweethearts of the Air" which was on the air for sixteen years. He wrote such hits as "Wagon Wheels," "Deep Purple," "Who Do You Know in Heaven" and had just completed scores for Otto Harbach's operetta "Counter Melody" and the Warner motion picture "About Face." He contributed music to many stage productions including "Broadway to Paris," "Yes, Yes, Yvette," "Earl Carroll Vanities" and "Ziegfeld Follies." Born New York; died New York, April 23, 1953.

Devere, Francesca, 61, actress. She was in several Keystone comedies and Mack Sennett pictures. Is best known in New York for her role of Winnie from Washington in "No, No, Nanette." Born in Washington state; died Port Townsend, Washington, September 11, 1952.

Dixon, Lee, 42, actor. Started his career as a chorus boy, then played for several years in vaudeville and was in many musical films. He was in the original Broadway cast of "Oklahoma!" Born Brooklyn; died New York, January 8, 1953.

Duffy, Herbert, age unrecorded, actor. He began his career in Canada and made his Broadway début in 1928 opposite Mae West in "Diamond Lil." Other New York plays included "Another Language," "Boy Meets Girl," "Room Service," "The Land Is Bright" and "Blessed Event." In his thirty-seven years in the theatre he played over four hundred roles. Died Rochester, Minnesota, November 23, 1952.

Dwyer, Ada, 89, actress. Made her stage début in 1890. Some of her plays include "Alone in London," "Don Juan," "Children of the Ghetto." She toured Australia and New Zealand in the title role of "Mrs. Wiggs of the Cabbage Patch"; retired in 1914. Born Salt Lake City; died Washington, D. C., July 4, 1952.

Eames, Emma, 84, opera star. A favorite singer of the late nineteenth and early twentieth centuries. Was at the Metropolitan Opera House from 1891 to 1909. Her last appearances were with the Boston Opera Company in 1911 and 1912, after which she lived in retirement. She was an aunt of the late Clare Eames, actress. Born Shanghai, China; died New York, June 15, 1952.

Edwards, Henry, 69, actor. His first stage appearance was made in 1900 in the English provinces with a small repertory company. He also played with Ben Greet's company. Charles Frohman brought him to New York to appear with Ethel Barrymore in "Tante" in 1913. He appeared in numerous stage and screen plays both here and in England. He was in Maurice Evans' uncut version of "Hamlet." He was Chairman and Manager of the Teddington Film Studios and Director of Paramount British Productions. Born Weston-super-Mare, England; died Chobham, England, November 2, 1952.

Ellis, Edward, 81, actor. Began his 63-year stage career at the age of 9 when he appeared in "Olivia" in Chicago. Among his many plays were "Get Rich Quick Wallingford" and "The Ouija Board." His motion picture credits include "Winterset" and "Remember." Born Coldwater, Michigan; died Los Angeles, July 26, 1952.

Gabriel, Gilbert W., 62, drama critic. His notable career began in 1912 as a reporter on the New York *Sun*. He was a critic for newspapers and magazines from 1917 till his death. Wrote several novels and was with Paramount Pictures as scenarist for two years. Was music critic on the New York *Sun* from 1917 to 1924. Joined the old New York *Telegram-Mail* for his first drama reviewing. Was with the *Sun* as reviewer from 1925 to 1929 when he went to the New York *American* where he remained until 1937. He was a lecturer in drama criticism at New York University. It was he who created the Profile department for *The New Yorker*. At the time of his death he was critic of *Cue* and was president of the New York Drama Critics Circle. Born Brooklyn; died Mt. Kisco, New York, September 3, 1952.

Griffin, Arthur, 75, actor. He had planned a career as a dentist but joined the Paul Scott theatrical company in Fall River, Massachusetts, in 1897. Was active for almost fifty years thereafter on Broadway in numerous plays among which were "Counsellor at Law," "Earl Carroll's Sketch Book," "Sailor Beware," "Elizabeth the Queen," "The Vagabond King" and "Abe Lincoln in Illinois." Born Boston; died Fall River, February 6, 1953.

Hale, Edward Everett, 3d, 46, actor. He was a grandson of Edward Everett Hale, author of "The Man Without a Country," and a descendant of Nathan Hale. He was a graduate of the American Academy of Dramatic Arts and acted on Broadway in "The Father," "The Manhatters," "Cyrano de Bergerac" and "Marching Song." He had been business representative of Actors' Equity and was assistant executive secretary of the New York local of the Radio and Television Directors' Guild, A.F.L. Born Hewlitt, Long Island; died New York, March 19, 1953.

Hall, Dorothy, 47, actress. Started her career as a movie extra in Hollywood and after stock engagements made her New York début in "The Complex" in 1925. Played top roles all through the twenties and thirties in such plays as "The Virgin Man," "Precious" and "The Greeks Had a Word for It." Was with Bert Lahr in "Flying High" and later in "Page Miss Glory," "Behind Red Lights," and others. She also wrote for motion pictures. Born Bradford, Pennsylvania; died New York, February 3, 1953.

Hopkins, Charles, 69, producer, director, actor. Made his first Broadway appearance in 1908 in "Jack Straw" and later joined the Ben Greet Company. In 1911 and 1912 he played with his own stock company in Washington, D. C., and Chicago. Built the Punch and Judy Theatre in West 49th Street, New

York, in 1914. His "Treasure Island" at this theatre was a tremendous success. Later he changed its name to The Charles Hopkins and produced such successes as "Devil in the Cheese," "Mrs. Moonlight," "Michael and Mary" and "The Ivory Door." In 1932 he founded the Charles Hopkins Summer Theatre at Huntington, Long Island. Born Philadelphia; died New York, January 1, 1953.

Harding, Lyn, 85, actor. His full name was David Llewellyn Harding. First stage appearance was at the Theatre Royal, Bristol, 1890, in "The Grip of Iron." Gained his early experience in stock and touring companies. Made an extensive tour through the Far East. Was first seen in London in 1897 in "The Silence of the Night." One of England's most versatile and popular actors, the mere listing of his roles takes up over four columns in "Who's Who in the Theatre." Broadway first saw him in 1912 in "Just to Get Married." Other New York appearances include "Years of Discretion," "The Great Adventure" and "Henry VIII." He established a Broadway record by playing the title role in "Macbeth" for seven and a half months. Born Newport, England; died London, December 26, 1952.

Harrison, Robert, 68, actor. A great-great-grandson of President William Henry Harrison and a great-grandson of Jefferson Davis, he made his first professional appearance at Elitch's Gardens Stock Co. in Denver. He was "discovered" by Nat Goodwin who engaged him for his repertory company. He supported Maude Adams and Otis Skinner in "The Merchant of Venice," he was with Helen Hayes in "Candle in the Wind" and "Harriet." In all he is said to have played over 600 roles. Born Denver; died New York, April 3, 1953.

Hay, Ian, 76, playwright. A popular English author, many of whose works were seen over here. His plays include "The Sport of Kings," "Bachelor Born" and "The Middle Watch." He worked with several collaborators such as Seymour Hicks, P. G. Wodehouse and A. E. W. Mason. Born Scotland; died Petersfield, Hampshire, England, September 22, 1952.

Jackson, Frederic, 67, writer-producer. Among his stage successes were "The Bishop Misbehaves," "School for Husbands," "The Hole in the Wall" and "The King's Messenger." A prolific writer, he hired a Summer theatre in Westchester in 1935 and produced nine of his own plays, one after the other. He began his movie writing in 1912 for the Pearl White series. Some of his more recent pictures include "Stormy Weather" and "Two

Tickets to Heaven." Born Pittsburgh; died Hollywood, May 22, 1953.

James, Rian, 53, novelist, screenwriter and playwright. Started his career on the Brooklyn *Eagle,* where he was columnist for seven years. He was a parachute jumper, stunt man, airmail pilot and vaudeville actor as well as writer. Among his best-known film plays are "Forty-second Street," "Helldorado," "Submarine Patrol" and "The Housekeeper's Daughter." Died Newport Beach, California, April 26, 1953.

Jolson, Harry, 71, vaudeville headliner. He preceded his more famous brother, Al Jolson, on the stage and was a star in vaudeville in his own right. Later the two brothers appeared together, presenting as their first vaudeville venture "The Hebrew and the Cadet." Born Srednik, Poland; died Hollywood, April 26, 1953.

King, Emmett C., 87, actor. As a young actor he supported Alexander Salvini and was a member of Charles Frohman's company. He was with George Arliss in "Alexander Hamilton" and was in "The American Tragedy." Among his many screen roles were appearances in "Barbara Frietchie," "Laugh, Clown, Laugh" and "Woodrow Wilson." Born Griffin, Georgia; died Hollywood, April 21, 1953.

Lawrence, Gertrude, 54, actress. Her first appearance on the stage was at the Brixton Theatre in 1910 as a child dancer in a pantomime "The Babes in the Wood." She toured in sketches in vaudeville and was once understudy for Beatrice Lillie. She first appeared on Broadway in January, 1924, in "Charlot's Revue of 1924." Other New York appearances include "Oh, Kay!", "Candle-Light," "Private Lives," "To-night at 8:30," "Skylark," "Lady in the Dark," "Pygmalion" and "The King and I." She also made several motion pictures, among them "Glass Menagerie." Born London; died New York, September 6, 1952.

Lebedeff, Ivan, 58, actor. He was the son of Basil Lebedeff, a privy councilor to the Russian Empire before the Revolution. Made his screen début in the UFA film "King Frederick" in 1922 and later appeared in French films. He was brought to America by D. W. Griffith to appear in the picture "Sorrows of Satan." His subsequent films include "China Seas," "Foreign Agent," and "Rhapsody in Blue." Wrote novels ("Legion of Dishonor" and "Brothers") as well as several screen plays. Born Russia; died Los Angeles, April 1, 1953.

Lincoln, Elmo, 63, actor. Real name was Otto Elmo Linkenhelt. Was famous as the original Tarzan in motion pictures. Played in the Tarzan series from 1918 to 1923. Came out of retirement in 1949 to play in another Tarzan picture but in a supporting role. Lex Barker was the Tarzan. Died Hollywood, June 27, 1952.

Logan, Stanley, 67, actor, producer and director. First appeared on the stage in the English provinces in 1903. Made London début later in "The Fairy Uncle" and came to New York in 1923 in "Little Miss Bluebeard." Among his stage appearances that followed were "The Dark Angel," "Her Cardboard Lover," "Mrs. Dane's Defense" and "The Sacred Flame." In 1928 he turned to directing and staged such productions as "The Red Robe," "Topaze" and "As Good as New." He also produced, wrote and acted in motion pictures. Born Earlsfield, England; died New York, January 30, 1953.

Love, Mabel, 78, actress. She was only 11 when, in 1886, she made her stage début at the Prince of Wales Theatre, London, as the Rose in "Alice in Wonderland." Two years later she was at London's famous old Gaiety Theatre. A versatile performer as well as a beauty she packed houses wherever she appeared— Paris, London, New York. In 1895 she appeared on Broadway in "His Excellency" and in 1911 in "Man and Superman." After 26 years of retirement she returned to the stage in 1938 in "Profit and Loss." Born England; died Weybridge, England, May 15, 1953.

McDaniel, Hattie, 57, actress. Began her career as a singer in tent shows in small towns. Appeared in more than three hundred films, winning an Academy Award in 1940 for her performance of Mammy in "Gone with the Wind." Created the title role of "Beulah" for screen, radio and television. Was in radio shows with Eddie Cantor and Amos and Andy. Born Wichita, Kansas; died Hollywood, October 26, 1952.

Mack, Nila, 62, actress, writer, producer, director. She first acted in a western repertory company and later was with Alla Nazimova for six years. She appeared on Broadway in many plays, among them "Fair and Warmer" and "A Doll's House." She was producer, director and writer of "Let's Pretend," CBS's oldest continuous radio show. Born Arkansas City, Kansas; died New York, January 20, 1953.

Mankiewicz, Herman J., 56, playwright. He wrote or collaborated on more than forty feature motion pictures beginning with "The Road to Mandalay" starring Lon Chaney. He had been a writer for the New York *Times* and was once drama critic for *The New Yorker*. In 1941 he won the Academy Award with Orson Welles for the best original screen play—"Citizen Kane." For the stage he wrote "The Good Fellow" with George S. Kaufman, "The Wise Man of Borneo" with Marc Connelly and "The Meal Ticket." Born New York; died Hollywood, March 5, 1953.

Mannering, Mary, 76, actress. Made her first appearance on the stage in England in 1892, under her own name of Florence Friend. Played in London and the provinces with great success. Daniel Frohman brought her to this country for his Lyceum Stock Company in 1896 and it was then she changed her name. She made her début here in "The Courtship of Leonie." She became a star in 1900 in "Janice Meredith." Other plays include "Judith," "Glorious Betsy," "A House of Cards" and "The Garden of Allah." She was once married to James K. Hackett. Born in England; died Los Angeles, January 21, 1953.

Maynard, Gertrude, 48, actress. Also known as Mab Maynard. Attended Ohio State University and the American Academy of Dramatic Arts. One of her first stage appearances was in 1932 in "Night over Taos" by Maxwell Anderson, whom she married the following year. She was also seen in "Men in White." Born Montreal; died New York, March 22, 1953.

Pawley, William, 47, actor. Played in stock companies and in motion pictures. Broadway appearances include "Holy Terror," "Bad Girl" and "Gentlemen of the Press." Born Kansas City; died New York, June 15, 1952.

Munsell, Warren P., Jr., 37, playwright and theatre manager. Wrote such plays as "The Jolly Beggar" and "A House Divided." Was general manager last season for "Remains to Be Seen" and "The Grass Harp." Born New York; died Olney, Maryland, July 28, 1952.

O'Neill, Marie, 65, actress. An original member of the Abbey Theatre, she was seen in most of their productions. She was in numerous films and plays in London. New Yorkers saw her in "General John Regan," "The White-Headed Boy," "The Plough and the Stars" and "Mr. Gilhooley." Born Dublin; died London, November 2, 1952.

Parker, John, 77, theatrical journalist. Began writing in 1892. Was London manager, critic and correspondent of the *New York Dramatic Mirror* from 1903 to 1920. Began "Who's Who in the Theatre" in 1912 and edited it (the 11th edition appeared about a year ago) until his death. Born New York; died London, November 18, 1952.

Pemberton, Henry W., 77, actor. Was active in stock and legitimate. At one time he had his own stock company in St. Louis. He is best known for his appearances in "The Gentleman from Mississippi," "Golden Girl" and "Damaged Goods." Died Orlando, Florida, July 26, 1952.

Peters, Susan, 31, actress. Was a popular screen actress in such pictures as "Random Harvest," "Keep Your Powder Dry" and "Dear Barbara." Was paralyzed in a hunting accident, New Year's Day, 1945. Continued her career on the screen in "The Sign of the Ram" and later toured in the stage plays "The Barretts of Wimpole Street" and "Glass Menagerie." Born Spokane, Washington; died Visalia, California, October 23, 1952.

Purdell, Reginald, 56, actor. Starting as a child player he was on the bills of English playhouses constantly throughout his life. New York audiences saw him in 1914 in "The Dear Fool." Among his many motion pictures may be listed "Congress Dances" and "Old Curiosity Shop." Born London; died London, April 22, 1953.

Rosenthal, Harry, 60, pianist, composer, actor. Became known to the theatre world when he appeared in "June Moon" on Broadway in 1930. Subsequently he was seen in several motion pictures, as well as heading his own orchestra. He wrote five operettas including "The Ramboula" and "Sky High Revue" produced in London. Born Belfast, Ireland; died Beverly Hills, California, May 10, 1953.

Shields, Ella, 73, singer. This American-born British vaudeville star was well known for her male impersonations. She was made famous by her popular song "Burlington Bertie of Bow" when she sang it at the London Paladium in 1910. Born Baltimore; died Lancaster, England, August 5, 1952.

Skipworth, Alison, 88, actress. Made her first stage appearance at Daly's Theatre, London, 1894, in "The Gaiety Girl." The following year she made her New York début in "An Artist's Model." Supported Viola Allen in several of Shakespeare's plays. Her many successes include "The Prisoner of Zenda," "39 East," "The Torchbearers," "The Swan" and "Enchanted April." She went to Hollywood in 1930 and made over 100 pictures during the next eight years. In 1940 she was in "When We Were Married" on TV, the first complete play to be televised. Her last Broadway appearance was in "First Step to Heaven" in 1941. Born London; died New York, July 5, 1952.

Smith, Frank L., 67, press agent and theatre manager. For twenty-five years manager of the Shubert theatres, he was President of The Association of Theatrical Press Agents and Managers Union. Born Brooklyn, New York; died New York, February 8, 1953.

Snyder, Gene, 45, dance director. A dancer himself in his young days, he did the choreography for several shows including "Yokel Boy" and "It Happens on Ice." He did the dances for the picture "Top of the Town." Was co-director with Russell Markert of the Rockettes of Radio City Music Hall. Born Fairfax, Minnesota; died New York, April 15, 1953.

Sommers, Harry G., 80, theatre manager. Had his first theatre job in the box office of Hooley's Theatre in Chicago. In 1901 he came to New York to manage the Knickerbocker Theatre and remained there until it was torn down in 1930. He also managed the Avon Theatre and had a hand in the affairs of the New Amsterdam, the Selwyn, the Vanderbilt, the National, the Lyric and the Hudson, as well as operating a Midwestern chain. Born Cairo, Illinois; died New York, May 15, 1953.

Strong, Austin, 71, playwright. He was a grand-stepson of Robert Louis Stevenson. Wrote many popular plays, among them "Bunny," "The Exile," "Three Wise Fools" and "Seventh Heaven." He served on the jury that selected the Pulitzer prize for several years. Born San Francisco; died Nantucket, September 17, 1952.

Thury, Ilona, 77, actress. She attended dramatic school in Hungary and as a girl toured in Serbia and Russia. She came to the United States in 1905 and was active in the German Theatre as a star in "The Merry Widow" and "The Gypsy Baron." She appeared with Hungarian groups in "Sari," "Liliom," "The Devil" and many other plays. Born near Budapest; died New York, April 1, 1953.

Tilley, Vesta, 88, British vaudeville star. Born Matilda Alice Powles, she made her first stage appearance at the age of three-and-a-half at Gloucester in 1867. First appeared in male attire at the age of five and was a male impersonator from then onward. Known in the music halls as the "Great Little Tilley" she made popular many songs, among them "By the Sad Sea Waves," "Burlington Bertie" and "Following in Father's Footsteps." First played in New York at Tony Pastor's in 1894. She retired from the stage in 1920 and in 1934 published her reminiscences. By her marriage to Colonel Sir Walter de Frece,

M.P., she became Lady de Frece.   Born Worcester, England; died London, September 16, 1952.

Verneuil, Louis, 59, playwright.   A former journalist, designer and painter, this French dramatist wrote over sixty plays and frequently played the lead in them.   In this country he is best known for his two-character play "Jealousy" produced some years ago and more recently "Affairs of State."   Born Paris; died Paris, November 3, 1952.

Wallach, Edgar, 68, theatre manager.   He was agent and manager for many well-known stage and screen stars.   Also managed several theatres.   Was one of the founders of the Theatrical Press Representatives.   Recently was manager of a road company of "Brigadoon."   Born Washington, D. C.; died New York, April 10, 1953.

Withee, Mable, age unrecorded, actress.   In 1918 she was with Al Jolson at the Winter Garden in "Sinbad."   Other musicals in which she played include "The Rose of Stamboul," "Dew Drop Inn," "Artists and Models," "Bye, Bye, Bonnie" and "The Cocoanuts" with the Marx Brothers.   Born Detroit; died Bayside, Long Island, November 3, 1952.

THE DECADES' TOLL

(Prominent Theatrical Figures Who Have Died
in Recent Years)

	Born	*Died*
Arliss, George	1869	1946
Baker, George Pierce	1866	1935
Barrymore, John	1882	1942
Bates, Blanche	1873	1941
Belasco, David	1856	1931
Bennett, Richard	1873	1944
Carroll, Earl	1893	1948
Carte, Rupert D'Oyly	1876	1948
Christians, Mady	1900	1951
Cochran, Charles B.	1872	1951
Cohan, George M.	1878	1942
Collier, Willie	1866	1943
Cowl, Jane	1884	1950
Craven, Frank	1890	1945
Crews, Laura Hope	1880	1942
Crosman, Henrietta	1865	1944
Digges, Dudley	1879	1947
Elliott, Maxine	1871	1940
Errol, Leon	1881	1951
Eltinge, Julian	1883	1941
Faversham, William	1868	1940
Fields, Lew	1867	1941
Fields, W. C.	1879	1946
Fiske, Harrison Grey	1861	1942
Frohman, Daniel	1851	1940
Garfield, John	1913	1952
Gaige, Crosby	1883	1949
Gershwin, George	1898	1937
Gest, Morris	1881	1941
Hart, Lorenz	1895	1943
Hart, William S.	1870	1946
Hooker, Brian	1881	1947

359

	Born	Died
Howard, Willie	1883	1949
Jolson, Al.	1886	1950
Jouvet, Louis	1887	1951
Kern, Jerome D.	1885	1945
Lawrence, Gertrude	1898	1952
Lehar, Franz	1870	1948
Leonard, Eddie	1871	1941
Loftus, Cecilia	1876	1943
Lord, Pauline	1890	1950
Mantle, Burns	1873	1948
Marlowe, Julia	1866	1950
Merivale, Philip	1886	1946
Molnar, Ferenc	1878	1952
Moore, Grace	1901	1947
Morgan, Helen	1900	1941
Nazimova, Alla	1879	1945
Nethersole, Olga	1870	1951
Patterson, Joseph Medill	1879	1946
Perry, Antoinette	1888	1946
Powers, James T.	1862	1943
Reinhardt, Max	1873	1943
Romberg, Sigmund	1887	1951
Royle, Edwin Milton	1862	1941
Selwyn, Edgar	1875	1944
Shaw, G. B.	1856	1950
Sheldon, Edward	1886	1946
Skinner, Otis	1858	1942
Tarkington, Booth	1869	1946
Tauber, Richard	1890	1948
Tyler, George C.	1867	1946
Ward, Fannie	1872	1952
Warfield, David	1866	1951
Weber, Joe	1867	1942
Webster, Ben	1864	1947
Whitty, Dame May	1865	1948
Woods, Al H.	1870	1951
Woollcott, Alexander	1887	1943
Youmans, Vincent	1899	1946

INDEX OF AUTHORS

361

INDEX OF PLAYS AND CASTS

Bold face page numbers refer to pages on which
Cast of Characters may be found.

INDEX OF PRODUCERS, DIRECTORS AND DESIGNERS

372